MUIRHEAD LIBRARY OF PHILOSOPHY

An admirable statement of the aims of the Library of Philosophy was provided by the first editor, the late Professor J. H. Muirhead, in his description of the original programme printed in Erdmann's *History of Philosophy* under the date 1890. This was slightly modified in subsequent volumes to take the form of the following statement:

'The Muirhead Library of Philosophy was designed as a contribution to the History of Modern Philosophy under the heads: first of Different Schools of Thought—Sensationalist, Realist, Idealist, Intuitivist; secondly of different Subjects—Psychology, Ethics, Aesthetics, Political Philosophy, Theology. While much had been done in England in tracing the course of evolution in nature, history, economics, morals and religion, little had been done in tracing the development of thought on these subjects. Yet "the evolution of opinion is part of the whole evolution".

'By the co-operation of different writers in carrying out this plan it was hoped that a thoroughness and completeness of treatment, otherwise unattainable, might be secured. It was believed also that from writers mainly British and American fuller consideration of English Philosophy than it had hitherto received might be looked for. In the earlier series of books containing, among others, Bosanquet's *History of Aesthetic*, Pfleiderer's *Rational Theology since Kant*, Albee's *History of English Utilitarianism*, Bonar's *Philosophy and Political Economy*, Brett's *History of Psychology*, Ritchie's *Natural Rights*, these objects were to a large extent effected.

'In the meantime original work of a high order was being produced both in England and America by such writers as Bradley, Stout, Bertrand Russell, Baldwin, Urban, Montague, and others, and a new interest in foreign works, German, French and Italian, which had either become classical or were attracting public attention, had developed. The scope of the Library thus became extended into something more international, and it is entering on the fifth decade of its existence in the hope that it may contribute to that mutual understanding between countries which is so pressing a need of the present time.'

The need which Professor Muirhead stressed is not less pressing today, and few will deny that philosophy has much to do with enabling us to meet it, although no one, least of all Muirhead himself, would regard that as the sole, or even the main, object of philosophy. As

Professor Muirhead continues to lend the distinction of his name to the Library of Philosophy it seemed not inappropriate to allow him to recall us to these aims in his own words. The emphasis on the history of thought also seemed to me very timely; and the number of important works promised for the Library in the very near future augur well for the continued fulfilment, in this and other ways, of the expectations of the original editor.

H. D. LEWIS

MUIRHEAD LIBRARY OF PHILOSOPHY

General Editor: H. D. Lewis

Professor of History and Philosophy of Religion in the University of London

Action by SIR MALCOLM KNOX
The Analysis of Mind by BERTRAND RUSSELL
Belief by H. H. PRICE
Brett's History of Psychology edited by R. S. PETERS
Clarity is Not Enough by H. D. LEWIS
Coleridge as a Philosopher by J. H. MUIRHEAD
The Commonplace Book of G. E. Moore edited by C. LEWY
Contemporary American Philosophy edited by G. P. ADAMS and W. P. MONTAGUE
Contemporary British Philosophy first and second Series edited by J. H. MUIRHEAD
Contemporary British Philosophy third Series edited by H. D. LEWIS
Contemporary Indian Philosophy edited by RADHAKRISHNAN and J. H. MUIRHEAD 2nd edition
The Discipline of the Cave by J. N. FINDLAY
Doctrine and Argument in Indian Philosophy by NINIAN SMART
Essays in Analysis by ALICE AMBROSE
Ethics by NICOLAI HARTMANN translated by STANTON COIT 3 vols
The Foundations of Metaphysics in Science by ERROL E. HARRIS
Freedom and History by H. D. LEWIS
The Good Will: A Study in the Coherence Theory of Goodness by H. J. PATON
Hegel: A Re-examination by J. N. FINDLAY
Hegel's Science of Logic translated by W. H. JOHNSTON and L. G. STRUTHERS 2 vols
History of Aesthetic by B. BOSANQUET 2nd edition
History of English Utilitarianism by E. ALBEE
History of Psychology by G. S. BRETT edited by R. S. PETERS abridged one volume edition 2nd edition
Human Knowledge by BERTRAND RUSSELL
A Hundred Years of British Philosophy by RUDOLF METZ translated by J. H. HARVEY, T. E. JESSOP, HENRY STURT
Ideas: A General Introduction to Pure Phenomenology by EDMUND HUSSERL translated by W. R. BOYCE GIBSON
Identity and Reality by EMILE MEYERSON
Imagination by E. J. FURLONG

Indian Philosophy by RADHAKRISHNAN 2 vols revised 2nd edition
Introduction to Mathematical Philosophy by BERTRAND RUSSELL 2nd edition
Kant's First Critique by H. W. CASSIRER
Kant's Metaphysic of Experience by J. H. PATON
Know Thyself by BERNADINO VARISCO translated by GUGLIELMO SALVADORI
Language and Reality by WILBUR MARSHALL URBAN
Lectures on Philosophy by G. E. MOORE
Lecturers on Philosophy by G. E. MOORE edited by C. LEWY
Matter and Memory by HENRI BERGSON translated by N. M. PAUL and W. S. PALMER
Memory by BRIAN SMITH
The Modern Predicament by H. J. PATON
Natural Rights by D. G. RITCHIE 3rd edition
Nature, Mind and Modern Science by E. HARRIS
The Nature of Thought by BRAND BLANSHARD
On Selfhood and Godhood by C. A. CAMPBELL
Our Experience of God by H. D. LEWIS
Perception by DON LOCKE
The Phenomenology of Mind by G. W. F. HEGEL translated by SIR JAMES BAILLIE revised 2nd edition
Philosophy in America by MAX BLACK
Philosophical Papers by G. E. MOORE
Philosophy and Illusion by MORRIS LAZEROWITZ
Philosophy and Political Economy by JAMES BONAR
Philosophy and Religion by AXEL HÄGERSTROM
Philosophy of Space and Time by MICHAEL WHITEMAN
Philosophy of Whitehead by W. MAYS
The Platonic Tradition in Anglo-Saxon Philosophy by J. H. MUIRHEAD
The Principal Upanisads by RADHAKRISHNAN
The Problems of Perception by R. J. HIRST
Reason and Goodness by BLAND BLANSHARD
The Relevance of Whitehead by IVOR LECLERC
The Science of Logic by G. W. F. HEGEL
Some Main Problems of Philosophy by G. S. MOORE
Studies in the Metaphysics of Bradley by SUSHIL KUMAR SAXENA
The Theological Frontier of Ethics by W. G. MACLAGAN
Time and Free Will by HENRI BERGSON translated by F. G. POGSON
The Transcendence of the Cave by J. N. FINDLAY
Values and Intentions by J. N. FINDLAY
The Ways of Knowing: or the Methods of Philosophy by W. P. MONTAGUE

Muirhead Library of Philosophy

EDITED BY H. D. LEWIS

BELIEF

BELIEF

BY

H. H. PRICE

THE GIFFORD LECTURES DELIVERED AT
THE UNIVERSITY OF ABERDEEN IN 1960

LONDON · GEORGE ALLEN & UNWIN LTD
NEW YORK · HUMANITIES PRESS

FIRST PUBLISHED IN 1969

SBN 04 121009 3

PRINTED IN GREAT BRITAIN
in 11 on 12 point Imprint type
BY UNWIN BROTHERS LIMITED
WOKING AND LONDON

To William Kneale

PREFACE

These lectures were delivered at the University of Aberdeen in 1960. Since then, they have been extensively revised. It soon became obvious that many changes were needed. For example, in Series I far too little had been said about the relation between belief and evidence, and the important and difficult subject of the evidence of testimony had been neglected. Again, in Series II nothing at all had been said about Newman's celebrated distinction between 'notional' and 'real' assent, though his criticisms of Locke's doctrine of Degrees of Assent had been discussed, perhaps at excessive length, in Series I, Lecture 6. The result has been that many of the twenty lectures are now far longer than any orally-delivered lecture could possibly be. Nevertheless, I have thought it proper to preserve the original lecture form as well as I could, and have tried to write throughout as if I were addressing a visible audience.

I wish to express my warm gratitude to the University of Aberdeen for the very great honour it did me in inviting me to deliver the lectures, and for all the kindness I received during my two very happy periods of residence there. I also wish to thank my friend and former pupil, Professor Jonathan Harrison of the University of Nottingham, most warmly for all the help he has given me in preparing the Lectures for publication. I am greatly indebted to him for many valuable comments and suggestions, and for most kindly making arrangements to have the manuscripts typed. Indeed, without his help, and his encouragement too, the Lectures might never have been published at all.

Finally, I hope that I may be allowed to pay my pious tribute to the munificent and far-sighted Founder of these Lectureships, and that my subject, the Epistemology of Belief, has at any rate some connection with the topics which Lord Gifford wished his Lecturers to discuss. Yet anyone who considers the great and good men who have delivered Gifford Lectures in the past—William James, for example, or Samuel Alexander, to name only two—must wonder how he can possibly live up to the standards they have set for their successors. I myself have felt like a humble barn-owl, who is expected to soar in the noon-day sky as if he were an imperial eagle; but all he can do is to flit slowly in the winter twilight just above the hedgerows, searching carefully for very small field-mice which may or may not be there.

CONTENTS

SERIES I

LECTURE 1

INTRODUCTION

THE PLAN OF THESE LECTURES

Belief is a large and complicated subject. It has so many ramifications that one hardly knows where to begin the discussion, and when one has begun one hardly knows where to stop. But a series of lectures should have some sort of plan, as a play (even the most modern one) should have some sort of plot. After all, the lecturer has to communicate his thoughts to you in a one-dimensional order; though if it were only possible, a multi-dimensional mode of presentation, in which an argument or an exposition proceeded in several different directions at the same time, might suit the subject-matter better. It may be that somewhere in the universe there are intelligent beings who can communicate their thoughts in this multi-dimensional way. This might perhaps be one of the advantages of 'the tongue of angels', mentioned by St Paul in a celebrated passage. But it certainly cannot be done in any human tongue. I have to present my thoughts to you one after the other, and they will be less difficult to comprehend if I begin by telling you the plan upon which my one-dimensional series of remarks is to proceed.

The plan I have adopted is this (I admit it is a somewhat arbitrary one). There is to be a central topic, preceded by certain preliminary enquiries, and followed by certain corollaries. The central topic is one which suggests itself very naturally to anyone who reflects on the history of epistemology. He can hardly fail to notice that there are two very different ways of analysing belief. In the traditional way of treating the subject, it is assumed that believing is a special sort of mental occurrence (sometimes described as a 'mental act'). This mental occurrence need not necessarily be introspected by the person in whom it occurs; but it always *could* be introspected by him if he took the trouble to attend to it. On this view, the main task of a philosophy of belief is to examine this introspectible mental occurrence, to analyse it in so far as it admits of analysis, and to distinguish it clearly from other mental occurrences with which it might possibly be confused, for example from the one which occurs when we merely consider a proposition neutrally, without either accepting it or rejecting it. I shall usually refer to this way of treating belief as 'the Occurrence Analysis' and sometimes as 'the Traditional Analysis', though it must be noticed that the tradition prevailed pretty generally until about a generation ago.

The modern way of treating belief is quite different. Believing something is now generally regarded not as an occurrence, introspectible or otherwise, but as a disposition. When we say of someone 'he believes the proposition *p*' it is held that we are making a dispositional statement about him, and that this is equivalent to a series of conditional statements describing what he *would* be likely to say or do or feel if such and such circumstances were to arise. For example, he would assert the proposition (aloud, or privately to himself) if he heard someone else denying it or expressing doubt of it. He would use it, when relevant, as a premiss in his inferences. If circumstances were to arise in which it made a practical difference whether *p* was true or false, he would act as if it were true. If *p* were falsified he would feel surprised, and would feel no surprise if it were verified.

On this view, then, believing a proposition is somewhat like being interested in cricket or having a distaste for gardening. Like these, a belief shows itself or manifests itself in various sorts of occurrences, some mental and some psycho-physical, but it is not itself an occurrence. Acquiring a belief, and losing it, are indeed occurrences, though we are not always able to assign precise dates to them. But the belief itself is not something which happens at a particular moment, but something which we have or possess throughout a period, long or short. And though it is liable to manifest itself by various sorts of occurrences, when and if suitable circumstances arise, none of these occurrences are themselves believings. The occurrent believings or 'acts of believing' which the traditional theorists discussed are on this view mythical entities, much like the 'acts of knowing' which the same traditional theorists also discussed. On this view, therefore, it makes no sense to say of someone at 4.35 p.m. 'he is now believing that it is going to rain', as it does make sense to say of him that he is now looking anxiously at the clouds or wondering whether to ask a passing motorist for a lift.

No doubt most exponents of the traditional analysis would be willing to admit that the sentence 'Jones believes that *p*' *can* be used in a dispositional way. If this were denied, they would be committed to the paradoxical conclusion that when Mr Jones turns his attention to something else, or falls asleep, and ceases for the time being to think of the proposition *p*, he *ipso facto* ceases to believe it. There is obviously a sense in which we can continue to believe a proposition for a long period, for many years perhaps, although we seldom think of that proposition at all. I have believed for a very long time that the earth is approximately spherical in shape, but the occasions on which I actually find myself giving my assent to that proposition are very few and far between.

But those who accept the traditional Occurrence Analysis would insist that this dispositional sense of the word 'believe' is secondary and derivative. We can say of someone, quite correctly, 'he believes that Oxford will win the boat race this year' and that he continues to believe it throughout the months of January and February. But on the traditional view, we mean by this that if at any time during that period he were to consider the proposition 'Oxford is going to win the boat race', an actual belief-occurrence would take place in him—a specific sort of experience which he could notice introspectively if he wished—and this proposition about the boat-race would be its object. Or, in Hume's version of the traditional analysis, if the idea 'Oxford is going to win' were to come into his mind at any time during that period, this idea would actually feel strong or forceful or vivacious to him. This feeling, in turn, might of course affect his actions. If he is an Oxford man he might make arrangements to go to London on Boat-race Day; Hume himself lays some stress on the effects of belief, and so does Cook Wilson, whose version of the traditional Occurrence Analysis is rather different. Nevertheless, it would be insisted that here again the occurrent believing—the actual belief-experience—is primary *in ordine analysandi* and the actions which the man does in circumstances to which the believed proposition is relevant are merely consequential.

With these explanations, I hope it will not be too misleading if the two contrasted ways of treating belief are called 'the Occurrence Analysis' on the one hand and 'the Dispositional Analysis' on the other. Sometimes too I shall call the first 'the Traditional Analysis' and the second 'the Modern Analysis', though this way of speaking is only roughly accurate. I have already pointed out that the Occurrence Analysis was still generally accepted until quite recent times; and it must now be added that the Dispositional Analysis (in a rather over-simplified form) was explicitly formulated by Alexander Bain nearly a century ago, and no doubt hints of it could be found in earlier writers. Indeed, there are some slight hints of it even in Hume himself, as we shall see later.[1]

The exposition and discussion of these two analyses of belief, the occurrence analysis and the dispositional analysis, will be the central topic of these lectures. But before we reach the central topic, we shall have to consider certain questions which arise whichever of the two analyses we accept. These questions concern the relation between belief and knowledge (Lecture 2 'The varieties of knowledge', Lecture 3 'Belief and knowledge'); the relation between belief and evidence (Lecture 4 on the evidence of perception, memory and self-consciousness, Lecture 5 on the evidence of testimony); Locke's doctrine of degrees of assent and Newman's criticism of it (Lecture 6).

I shall then turn to the exposition of the traditional Occurrence Analysis (Lecture 7, 'Hume's analysis of belief'; Lecture 8, 'The entertaining of propositions'; Lecture 9 'Belief and "being under an impression that . . ."'). In the concluding lecture of Series I (Lecture 10) I shall consider an interesting difference of opinion within the traditional 'occurrence' school. We shall find that two of its most illustrious members, Descartes and Hume, take diametrically opposite views concerning the freedom of assent. This difference of opinion, like the one between Newman and Locke, has an important bearing on 'the ethics of belief'. If belief is something wholly involuntary (and Hume maintains, at least in one well known passage, that it is[2]) there could not be such a thing as an 'ethics' of belief at all.

[1] Series I, Lecture 7, pp. 186–8.
[2] *Treatise* (Clarendon Press, ed. Selby-Bigge), p. 624.

The other half of my central topic, the exposition and discussion of the Dispositional Analysis, the comparison of the two analyses, and the attempt to decide which (if either) is correct, will be reserved for Series II, and the first three lectures of that series will be devoted to it. Then, but not till then, we shall be in a position to consider what I called the corollaries. There are a number of important questions about belief which cannot be profitably discussed until we are in possession of the conceptual tools which our examination of the central topic will provide. The first and most obvious of these concerns half-belief (or perhaps 'near-belief' would be a better name for it), a subject which can hardly be discussed at all until we have learned and digested what the dispositional analysis has to teach us. We must also consider the claims that some beliefs have a self-verifying character: Vergil's remark *possunt quia posse videntur*—'they can do it because they think they can'—will serve to illustrate what is meant. If there are self-verifying beliefs, this may be expected to throw some light on the nature of faith. We should all wish to know what kind of an attitude faith is: not religious faith only, though certainly this is the most important sort of faith, but other sorts of faith too, for example the faith which one human being may have in another. This topic may also be approached from another side, by asking what we mean by belief *in* someone or something and how believing 'in' is related to believing 'that'. And here a lecturer under Lord Gifford's foundation will naturally be expected to pay some attention to the belief 'in' a world-outlook or world-view, because this type of belief 'in' is an essential part of the religious attitude. In Series II Lecture 9 I shall have a good deal to say about belief 'in' and about the relation between belief 'in' and belief 'that'.[1] It is a subject on which strange and unplausible views seem to be widely accepted.

It may seem to some of you that these 'corollaries' are far more interesting than the central topic itself, and more interesting too than most of the preliminary ones. In comparison with these great and fundamental questions, our enquiry into the occurrence analysis and the dispositional analysis may seem merely academic or even pedantic. What difference does it really make which of these two analyses of belief—if either—is the correct one? Who

[1] *Aeneid* V, line 231.

cares whether 'Jones believes that *p*' is or is not a purely dispositional statement about Mr Jones?

If anyone takes this view, of course I have some sympathy with him. My reply, however, is that in philosophy the longest way round is often the shortest way home. Let him regard the discussion of my central topic not as an end but as a means. If belief in a religious world-view is what interests us most, we shall be in a better position for considering this subject if we first pay some attention to the nature of belief in general; and one way of doing so is to ask what kind of a statement 'Jones believes that *p*' is, and what is the most adequate way of analysing it.

Nor must it be thought that belief is the exclusive preserve of theologians and philosophers of religion. This is not even true of belief 'in' (for example, one may believe in classical education or in taking daily cold baths.) Still less is it true of belief 'that'. Belief is a state in which we are throughout our waking lives, and often too when we are dreaming. And this applies to the belief which does not amount to knowledge as well as to the belief which does. Belief on evidence which is less than conclusive is a very familiar condition. We are in it all the time about many subjects. We could not live without it. Nor would it be reasonable to try to. We must not suppose that there are only two alternatives, knowledge on the one side and helpless agnosticism on the other. We may still have good reasons for believing when we do not have conclusive ones. A reasonable being, situated as we are, cannot dispense with such beliefs. Very often conclusive evidence is not available to us, or not available as yet, at the time when practical decisions have to be taken, or theoretical inferences drawn, or difficult emotional adjustments made. Then we must make the best use we can of such evidence as we have. Sometimes, too, though less frequently, perhaps, than is supposed, we believe without any evidence at all, or on evidence so flimsy that it hardly deserves the name.

Belief, in fact, is one of the most commonplace and familiar things in the world. It is not something reserved for solemn occasions. And it is just these commonplace and familiar things which raise the most interesting philosophical problems. (Perception is another. What could be more commonplace than seeing or hearing?) As Bertrand Russell has said 'Philosophy, if it cannot *answer* so many questions as we could wish, has at least the power of *asking* questions which increase the interest of the world and show the strangeness and wonder lying just below the surface even in the commonest things of daily life'.[1]

So much for the plan or plot of these lectures. I turn now to some general points which it may be well to mention briefly in this introductory discussion.

THE STUDY OF BELIEF CUTS ACROSS TRADITIONAL BOUNDARIES

There is a traditional boundary between epistemology on the one hand, and moral or practical philosophy on the other. In these lectures we shall sometimes find ourselves crossing that boundary or standing on both sides of it at once. Obviously it will be necessary to say something about moral beliefs. Some difficult problems arise about them, if it be held (as it often is) that the function of moral sentences is to express the speaker's attitude of approval or disapproval.

It is also obvious that there is a connection between belief and will, or, to put it more generally, between belief and the practical side of our nature. We all know too well that there is such a thing as 'wishful thinking', the tendency to believe a proposition because we wish it to be true or fear the consequences which would follow if it were false. On the other hand, our beliefs in their turn affect our actions. They manifest themselves in what we do and in the practical decisions which we take. It must be remembered too that not all 'doing' is public and overt. Directing our thoughts to one subject rather than another is a kind of doing. It alters something, it makes a difference, even if only to what happens subsequently in ourselves. The difference which it makes may be an important one too. What we 'think in our hearts' may sometimes matter more than what we do publicly in the market-place. It may have a powerful effect on our emotions and our wishes. A man's beliefs show themselves in the direction which his thoughts take, and sometimes in his voluntary decision to think about this subject rather than that. The most obvious examples of this are moral and religious beliefs. If a man believes

[1] *The Problems of Philosophy*, pp. 24–5 (Home University Library).

that charity is the greatest of virtues, he will tend to think about the good points in his neighbour's character rather than the bad ones.

Moreover, something rather like the traditional free will problem arises about belief itself, as well as about the actions, overt or not, which we do 'in the light of' or 'under the guidance of' the beliefs which we hold. This is the issue we shall have to discuss when we consider the controversy between Descartes and Hume concerning the freedom of assent (Series I, Lecture 10). In some sense, and within limits, we are free to act as we choose and responsible for our choices. How far, if at all, are we free to assent as we choose? When a proposition comes into our minds, or is propounded to us by others in speech or in writing, are we free to give our assent or to withold it, as we choose? Anyone who speaks about the 'Ethics of Belief'[1] must surely think that in some sense we *are* responsible for holding the beliefs which we do hold, or at least for holding some of them. At first sight it may seem strange to speak of the 'ethics' of belief at all, and I am not sure that the word 'ethics' is the most appropriate. Nevertheless, we all of us do use such quasi-ethical expressions as 'justifiable', 'unjustifiable', 'have a right to', 'have no right to', when we are discussing the beliefs of others, and sometimes when we are discussing our own. What William believes may be true, but he has no justification for believing it on the evidence that he has, though others perhaps have, because they do have good evidence for it. Again, he has no justification for being absolutely convinced that there will be a frost to-night, on the evidence that he has, though he would be justified in holding a mild opinion that there will be. For we commonly think that there are degrees of belief; and when we raise these questions about a man's right to believe something or ask whether he is justified in believing it, we ask not only whether he is justified in believing such and such a proposition at all, on the evidence that he has, but also whether he has a right to believe it to the degree that he does—with the degree of assurance or confidence which he actually shows. We often find that others (and ourselves too) hold firm convictions

[1] The first writer to use this phase, so far as I know, was W. K. Clifford (see the essay with that title in his *Lectures and Essays*). The latest is Professor R. Chisholm in his *Perceiving: a Philosophical Study*, ch. 1.

on subjects about which we are only 'entitled' to have mild opinions. On the other hand, the term 'reasonable', the appropriate term of commendation for beliefs, is applied to actions as well, and here too it is a term of commendation.

Moreover, when we consider the relation between belief and action we come upon another topic which is traditionally supposed to fall within the moral philospher's domain. What are we to say of a man who fails to act upon some belief which he holds, in circumstances to which the proposition believed is obviously relevant? He proposes to catch the 4.45 train from Paddington. He believes, to all appearances sincerely, that the train will leave punctually, and his wish to catch it is also sincere. He has plenty of time to get to the station, there is no lack of transport to take him there, he has plenty of money to pay for a taxicab. Yet he arrives at the station five minutes late and misses the train. This is not unlike the problem of ἀκρασία ('incontinence' 'weakness of will') discussed by Aristotle in Book VII of the *Nicomachean Ethics*.[1] In the example just given, the belief upon which the man fails to act is a belief about a particular event, the departure of a particular train on a particular day. But the same question arises about general beliefs, and this brings us even closer to the problem discussed by Aristotle. For example, no one doubts that all men are mortal. But there are many who die without having made a will.

In these two examples we are, of course, confronted with a special type of 'unreasonable' conduct; and here as elsewhere the term 'unreasonable' conveys some degree of disapproval or censure. The disapproval does not directly concern the student of belief, since the beliefs themselves, in these two examples, were perfectly reasonable ones; what was unreasonable was only the failure to act in accordance with them. But the student of belief does have to ask, as the moral philosopher also does, how that particular type of unreasonableness is possible. And this is an awkward question for anyone who holds, as some philosophers do, that believing a proposition *p* is just a disposition to act as if *p* were true in circumstances to which the proposition is obviously relevant. I shall discuss it in the first lecture of Series II.

There is another traditional boundary-line which we may have

[1] *Nicomachean Ethics*, Book VII, ch. 3.

to cross, though with fear and trembling, in Series II of these lectures. I have already mentioned the curious class of beliefs which I call self-verifying ones,[1] where believing a proposition appears to have a tendency at least to make the proposition true. Are there really cases where 'thinking makes it so'? And if there are, shall we have to revise our ordinary notions about objectivity, and shall we also have to revise our ordinary assumptions about the unreasonableness or even blameworthiness of 'wishful thinking'? These questions are interesting for their own sakes. But when we consider them, we find ourselves confronted with the traditional problem of the relation of mind and body. Some of the beliefs which do at least appear to have a self-verifying tendency are beliefs about the believer's own body. For example, if the patient believes that he is going to recover, this belief of his makes it more likely that he will recover. It may even be that he will not recover unless he believes that he will. Indeed, when Vergil said 'they can do it because they think they can', the 'doing' to which he referred was rowing fast enough to win a boat-race, and this is certainly a bodily activity.

Belief is supposed to be an epistemological subject, whereas the relation of mind and body is a metaphysical one; or at least it was formerly supposed to be, though on some modern views it is not a philosophical subject at all, but a scientific one, and the only philosophically important point about it is the muddle, or series of inter-connected muddles, which have led people to think that it could be settled by purely philosophical methods. But whichever view we take about the status of this ancient problem, it is certainly not an epistemological one. Yet if I am right, the philosophy of belief cannot altogether avoid considering it.

Finally, there is one other traditional border-line which we shall be obliged to cross sometimes, the borderline between epistemology and the philosophy or religion. But neither epistemologists nor philosophers of religion have ever taken that particular line of demarcation very seriously; and even if they had, it would still be the duty of a Gifford Lecturer to disregard it. You are more likely to complain of me for crossing it too rarely than too often.

[1] P. 23, above.

THE 'PERFORMATORY' ASPECT OF FIRST-PERSON BELIEF-SENTENCES

I now turn to a point which may appear to be a purely linguistic one, the difference between first person and third person uses of the verb 'to believe'. There are some philosophers who think that questions concerning language are the only ones which a philosopher should discuss. I do not subscribe to this view. But it seems to me that the difference between first-person and third-person belief-sentences is of considerable philosophical importance. We might easily be led into philosophical mistakes if we neglected it, for instance if all the examples we used in our investigation of belief were of the form '*I* believe that *p*'. First person belief sentences, or more accurately, first person belief sentences in the present tense, have certain peculiarities which other belief-sentences do not share. Nor is this merely a fact about the English language. It is true of some other languages as well, though I would not venture to assert that it is true of all.

The first and most obvious point to notice is this. When someone says in the first person and present tense 'I believe that *p*' (still more if he says 'I believe *in X*') he is not usually giving us a piece of autobiographical information. It is true that just occasionally he might be. He might be announcing to the world a discovery which he has recently made about himself, a surprising discovery which interests him and may be expected to interest others 'Good heavens! I never used to believe it, but now I find that I do' or even 'I thought I did not believe it, but now I find that I do'.

But ordinarily when someone says 'I believe that *p*' he is not giving us a piece of information about himself. He is expressing an attitude, rather than telling us that he has it. And sometimes, in the act of expressing it, he is doing something more as well. Sometimes he is taking a stand in the face of a hostile or sceptical audience. 'This is what I believe. Call me a fool or an idiot if you like.' This presumably is the purpose of the books or essays which are sometimes written with the title *What I believe.* Here the man who says 'I believe that *p*' or 'I believe in *X*' or writes a book called 'What I believe' is making a kind of public declaration, or issuing something like a *pronunciamento.* It is a public act of self-commitment.

I cannot see, however, that the self-commitment is necessarily intended to be irreversible, as theologians who use the phrase often seem to assume. At any rate, a reasonable being should not be expected to commit himself irrevocably to the truth of a proposition, unless he has conclusive evidence that the proposition is indeed true, which he seldom has in cases of this kind. And even imperfectly reasonable beings like outselves do sometimes take a stand in this not-necessarily irrevocable way, without saying or implying or being taken by others to imply that nothing whatsoever could conceivably lead us to change our minds. 'This is what I believe now, on the evidence that I have, however much the rest of you may disagree with me.' When someone says this, he need not be taken to be asserting that his evidence is absolutely conclusive, or that he himself thinks it is, or that he will always continue to believe what he believes now. Indeed, if we interpret his utterance in that way, we may be showing a lack of respect for him and failing to treat him as a reasonable being: for it may be quite obvious that the evidence for what he believes cannot be conclusive. The same is true of a book with the title 'What I believe'. We need not take the title to mean 'What I irrevocably commit myself to'. Such an interpretation might sometimes be justified, but by no means always.

But more often the utterance 'I believe that *p*' has what J. L. Austin calls a performatory character. Or if this taking of a stand is itself a 'performance' in his sense, it is not a very common one. A man who says 'I believe that *p*' is not usually standing up on a soap-box, so to speak. There need be no emphasis on the first personal pronoun. ('What *I* believe is this, whether you believe it or not.') Such declarations are made sometimes, but rather rarely. Much more commonly, we are inviting our hearers to accept what we believe and are assuming that they will. And we are doing more than that. We are conveying to them, giving them to understand, that they will be *justified* in accepting it.

As Austin has shown, the first-person present tense utterance

'I know that *p*' has a guarantee-giving character. When someone says 'I know that *p*', he conveys to us, or gives us to understand, that we may justifiably rely upon the proposition without reserve. It is not of course that he *says* we may thus rely upon it. He has no need to, because this guarantee-giving function is a feature of the conventional usage of the first-person present tense expression 'I know'. It follows that in saying 'I know that *p*' one is claiming to have conclusive evidence for the truth of the proposition *p*; otherwise one would not be in a position to issue this 'hard' or 'cast iron' guarantee.[1]

Something like this applies to the first-person present tense use of the verb 'to believe' and of similar expressions such as 'think that', 'hold the opinion that'. The difference, of course a very important one, is that here the guarantee is weaker. Indeed, it might be said that when the utterance 'I believe' has the taking-a-stand character discussed just now, it also, as it were, *offers* a guarantee, though in this case the speaker has little or no expectation that the guarantee will be accepted, and does not much mind whether it is accepted or not.

'Is Wilkinson in Oxford to-day?' 'Yes, I believe he is.' In giving this answer, one conveys to one's hearer that he may safely rely to a certain degree upon the truth of the proposition 'Wilkinson is in Oxford to-day', but not that he may safely rely upon it without any reservations at all. For example, it will be worth while for him to ring up Wilkinson on the telephone, though not perhaps worth while making a special journey to his house in the suburbs, if time is short and other business is pressing. The guarantee would have been weaker still if our informant had said 'I suspect' (or 'I rather think') that Wilkinson is in Oxford to-day, but I am not at all sure'. Indeed, it might seem too much to say that this utterance gives us anything which deserved to be called a guarantee. All the same, it does gives us something. It is as if he had said 'I do not venture to promise that you will find him if you go to see him, but there is at any rate a chance that you will'. He conveys

[1] Similarly, when I say 'I promise to do *X*' I convey to you (though I do not say) that you may safely rely on my doing *X*. The performatory character of 'I promise to—' was noticed by Hume (*Treatise*, Book III, Part II, Section 5). But so far as I am aware, no one before Austin had noticed that the first person present tense use of cognitive verbs such as 'know' and 'believe' has a performatory character.

to us that we may safely have a small but not entirely negligible degree of confidence with regard to the proposition 'Wilkinson is in Oxford to-day'; and in so doing he claims that he himself has *some* evidence in favour of the proposition, though evidence which is nothing like conclusive.

Now of course any of these guarantees, whether hard ones or soft ones, may turn out to be worthless. If our informant said 'I know that *p*', and we find out afterwards that *p* is false, or even if we find out that it is true but that he had no conclusive evidence for it, we shall be entitled to reproach him for 'letting us down'. It is as if he had offered us a cheque which the bank refuses to cash. If he only said 'I believe that *p*', and it turns out afterwards that *p* is false, we shall not be able to reproach him on that ground. This time the guarantee was not offered to us as a cast iron one, and the claim he tacitly made in offering it was not a claim to have conclusive evidence for the proposition. But even so we *shall* be entitled to reproach him if we find out afterwards that he had no evidence at all for *p* at the time when he said 'I believe that *p*'. Conceivably we might discover this even if the proposition *p* turned out to be true. Wilkinson actually is in Oxford to-day; but our informant, it now turns out, had no evidence whatever for saying that he was, or evidence too weak to justify any degree of belief at all (e.g. the fact that anyone who is a Research Fellow of an Oxford college is in Oxford sometimes). He answered 'Yes, I believe he is' in an irresponsible manner, or just from a wish to please. So he was not entitled to give us any kind of guarantee on this matter, not even the relatively weak one which he did give.

So far we have been concerned with first-person present-tense belief utterances which are made publicly and addressed to others. There can be no doubt that 'I believe that *p*', considered as a piece of social intercourse, does have this performatory aspect. But what happens when one says 'I believe that *p*' privately—to oneself—whether aloud or under one's breath or by means of kinaesthetic or auditory images? If one said it aloud, the remark might of course be overheard by someone else, or recorded by the police by means of a concealed microphone; and similarly if it was written in one's private notebook or diary, someone else might read it afterwards. But this is irrelevant. The remark which was uttered or written down in the notebook was not *addressed* to anyone else. It was not a piece of social intercourse. Can it still have a performatory character?

It seems to me that even here one might conceivably be 'taking a stand'; and a man might conceivably write a book or an essay with the title *What I believe* even though he had no intention whatever of publishing it or showing it to anyone else, or even though he tore it up immediately after he had written it. But if one takes a stand, there must be someone or something against which one takes it. What could this something or someone be? If I say to myself 'I believe that *p*' in the stand-taking way (still more perhaps if I say to myself 'I believe in *X*') I say it in the face of some resistance in myself. It may very well be that I do not want to believe that *p*; for example I do not want to believe that my friend Mr Postlelthwaite has got into trouble. I should much prefer this proposition to be false. I should be much happier if there were not the strong evidence for it which, I have to admit, there actually is. Belief may very well be reluctant. In this case, the reluctance is the result of emotional factors, my liking for Mr Postlethwaite, or the admiration I have hitherto had for him. Sometimes it is the result of habit. Just because one has believed *q* for many years, one is reluctant to give up this belief, and believe *p* instead, where *p* entails the falsity of *q*. There are examples of this even in the history of science. Sometimes, again, one's reluctance to believe has a purely intellectual origin. One is reluctant to believe a proposition because there is much evidence against it. At first it may have been very difficult for Europeans to believe that there is such a creature as the duck-billed platypus. How very unlikely it was that there should be a warmblooded furry animal with webbed feet, which lays eggs and has a beak like a duck! But they were obliged to believe it, however reluctantly, when the testimony of good witnesses became very strong. Hesitations and doubts were no longer justified, and if they persisted it was time to take a stand against them. At such point a sceptical zoologist might well say to himself in his study 'Yes, I do believe there is such a creature after all'.

There is also the rather curious situation in which a man thinks that he believes something, but in a moment of unusual clarity and honesty is obliged to admit that he does not, and even that he ceased to believe it some time ago. He thinks he believes that the coalmines can still earn a profit. Has he not written many letters to the newspapers to say so? But this morning, in his bath, he suddenly realises that he no longer believes this, and has gradually been growing less sure about it ever since he wrote his last letter to *The Times* three weeks ago. Here he is 'taking a stand' when he says to himself 'I no longer believe it', because he would still like to think that he does. He is taking a stand against something in himself, against a lingering wish which he still has. If only he could still go on believing that the coalmines can be made to earn a profit, he could maintain and even enhance the public reputation he has already acquired as a coalmines-advocate, and might even be elected as Member of Parliament for Wigan.

No doubt there is something strange in these examples. How can a man 'tell himself' that he believes such and such a proposition, or again, that he no longer believes it? To some philosophers the whole idea of 'telling oneself' anything may seem absurd, and the idea of 'taking a stand' may seem to make no sense when there is no audience before whom or in the face of whom one takes it. But experience is against them. It is useless to object that something is logically impossible when it does actually happen. Instead, we must just admit that many of us are in some degree divided or dissociated personalities, and perhaps all of us are sometimes. Why indeed should we expect the contrary?

But when someone says 'I believe that *p*' to himself, we cannot easily find anything analogous to the guarantee-giving character which this utterance has in its ordinary social use; or if we ever can, it is only when the degree of dissociation has gone far beyond this, and has reached a stage where we have to speak of two or more distinct personalities connected with a single human organism; and then we have entered either the realm of psychopathology or the realm of psychical research or both at once. Perhaps in the Sally Beauchamp case the personality called Sally *could* be said to be giving a guarantee to Miss Beauchamp when she said 'I believe that *p*'.

So much for the first-person present-tense utterance 'I believe that so-and-so'. The performatory aspects of this are important and should not be neglected, as they were until quite recently; and they are sometimes present even when the sentence is said privately to oneself. We must notice, however, that they are confined to the first person use of the verb 'believe' (and other allied verbs such as 'think that——', 'have the opinion that——'). 'You believe that *p*' or 'he believes that *p*' has no performatory force. And even within the first-person use, the performatory force vanishes when we shift from the present to the past tense. When a man says 'I believed it once' or 'Yes, I thought so myself until yesterday' he is neither taking a stand nor giving a guarantee.

What of the future tense? We can say of someone else 'he will believe it by this time next week' (or 'when he is ten years older') 'though he does not believe it now'. But can one say it of oneself? Just possibly one can. A distinguished philosopher of the last generation is alleged to have said 'I shall die a Behaviourist'. Was not this equivalent to saying 'Before I die, I shall believe certain propositions which I do not yet believe'? An enthusiastic young socialist might say in a cynical moment 'I shall be a Tory by the time I am sixty'; is not this equivalent to saying 'By the time I am sixty I shall believe in the political principles of Edmund Burke, etc., which I now firmly reject'?

If that is the correct interpretation of these rather curious remarks, it would seem that they are on just the same footing as first person belief statements in the past tense, and have neither a stand-taking nor a guarantee-giving character. But we notice that both of them do *express* beliefs which the speakers at present hold—beliefs which they how hold (correctly or not) about their own future beliefs. And in this respect they do have a guarantee-giving character, and probably the philosopher's remark had a stand-taking character as well. We cannot tell just from reading the written words how strong the guarantees offered were. But if we had heard them spoken, we might have been able to notice how confidently they were uttered. If someone says '*p*' in a tone which expresses no doubt, he can be taken as offering us the same 'hard' guarantee which he would have offered if he had said 'I am completely convinced that *p*', though in these particular examples the guarantee might well turn out to be valueless, and the speakers may have been very rash in offering them.

In any case, it should be noticed that first-person belief utterances, in whatever tense, are relatively uncommon; and so far as the present tense is concerned, they are especially uncommon when one is in a state of complete conviction. If one is completely sure that *p*, one normally says just '*p*'. Nor does one normally say it in a particularly emphatic way, but rather in the most matter of fact way possible. One does not say it emphatically, unless or until someone else has contradicted one's statement or expressed doubts of it, or unless one expects that someone will—and sometimes not even then.[1] One just takes it to be a fact that *p*, for example that to-day is early closing day, and does not bother to express one's attitude about it. It is true that we speak of 'saying something in a tone of conviction'. But as Professor Ryle has pointed out, there is no special tone of *complete* conviction. It is rather that a 'doubting' tone is absent.

If someone takes a proposition to be absolutely certain (whether on good grounds or not) he is no longer interested in his own mental attitude with regard to it. He is only interested in the proposition itself, for example the proposition that to-day is early closing day, and in the consequences which can be inferred from it either with certainty or with probability; for instance that it would be useless to call at the oculist's shop this afternoon to collect his new pair of spectacles, even though he did get a postcard this morning to say that they were ready. This is why he does not put his mental attitude into words, unless someone else expresses surprise or incredulity.

He is, however, interested in and concerned about his own mental attitude if it falls short of complete conviction; that is, if it is an attitude of opinion, more firm or less, and still more if it is only an attitude of surmising or suspecting. He is then more likely to say 'I think that *p*' (adding, perhaps, 'but I am not quite sure'), or 'I suspect that *p*' (adding, perhaps, 'but I am not at all sure'). But even then he need not say so, not even to himself. He does rely upon the proposition *p* up to a certain point but no further. But he need not necessarily tell others, or even himself, that he relies upon it to that degree. He will only do so if there is some special point in doing it, for example, if others ask

[1] Newman remarks acutely that 'those who are certain of a fact are indolent disputants' (*Grammar of Assent*, p. 152, Longmans, 1947). This is still true when what they are convinced of is not a fact—provided that they are completely convinced of it.

him 'what do you think about this?' or if he himself thinks they ought to know what his attitude is about it, even though they do not ask.

After all, we have other and more important uses for our beliefs than telling our neighbours that we hold them. We do not go about all the time, or even much of the time, saying to others 'I believe that *p*' 'I am nearly sure, though not quite sure, that *q*' 'I have a suspicion that *r*'. In this respect, beliefs are like emotional attitudes. We do not go about all the time saying 'I rather like Mr X' 'I very much dislike Mr Y'.

Moreoever, beliefs resemble emotional attitudes in another and more disconcerting way. I may dislike Mr Y without knowing ('realizing') that I dislike him, or even when I think that I like him. Similarly, I may believe a proposition *p* without realizing that I believe it. It is possible to be mistaken, and in some sense sincerely mistaken, as to what one's own beliefs are, and also as to the degree of confidence with which one holds them. It is even possible to believe a proposition *p* when one thinks that one disbelieves it or that one has an 'open mind' about it. There are unconscious or repressed beliefs, and there are also subconscious ones (beliefs which we do not know that we have, though we could discover that we have them if we made a not impracticably-great effort of attention.) First-person present-tense belief utterances may therefore fail to convey to others what the speaker's beliefs actually are, because he himself does not always know what they are.

Finally, even if we did formulate all our belief-attitudes in words, and even if the attitudes thus formulated were always the ones we do actually hold, we still could not formulate all of them at once. I should still have my belief that the sun is larger than the earth while I was engaged in saying 'I believe that the earth is larger than the moon'.

I conclude that we should be gravely misled if we supposed that the only, or even the main task of a philosophy of belief is the analysis of first-person present-tense belief statements, though we must not neglect the special and rather peculiar properties which these somewhat uncommon statements have.

BELIEVING A PERSON AND BELIEVING A PROPOSITION

There are two other points about the verb 'to believe' which we should notice. In ordinary English there are several different usages of this word. I have already mentioned the distinction between believing 'in' and believing 'that'. This will be discussed in detail in Series II. But there are two other distinctions about which something may be said now. The first is the distinction between believing a proposition and believing a person.

Most commonly, the verb 'to believe' is followed by a that-clause. I believe that there will be a fog tonight. Here what is believed (the object of the belief) is a proposition, something which is either true or false. This is the usage I have myself adopted so far. Where we say 'Smith believes *p*', 'Jones believed *q* until yesterday', the letters *p* and *q* are what logicians call variables, and the values of these variables are propositions.

But we also speak sometimes of believing a person. He told me that there would be muffins for tea, and I believed him. Alas! there was only buttered toast. It may be that in the history of language this 'personal' usage is the earlier one. Nevertheless, it seems to be logically derivative. We believe a person (or fail to believe him) in so far as he *asserts* something,[1] whether orally or in writing or in some other way, for example by means of signals or gestures. It is not sufficient that he should make some communication to us. The communication must take the special form of an assertion. It would not make sense to say 'He asked me the way to the station and I believed him' or 'He invited me to come to the party, but I did not believe him'. Or if these sentences might conceivably make sense in some special cases, it would only be because we took his request or his invitation to be implying some assertion which he did not actually utter, the assertion that he did actually wish to know the way to the station, or the assertion that he had been authorised to issue invitations to the party.

[1] Of course we may believe a person (or fail to believe him) when he *denies* something. He denied that he was in London last night, and the Dean of his College believed him. But for our present purpose we may assume that denying *p* is equivalent to asserting not-*p*.

In short, we believe a person (or fail to believe him) in so far as he asserts a proposition. Moreover, we only believe *him* in so far as we believe the proposition which he asserts. Similarly, we only fail to believe him in so far as we fail to believe the proposition he asserts. He told me his story and I believed him. In order to believe *him* I must believe *that* the events described in the story did actually happen. Believing a proposition is primary, and believing a person is derivative, because it has to be defined in terms of believing a proposition.

DEGREES OF BELIEF

So much for the distinction between believing a proposition and believing a person. But there is another and more interesting distinction which we must consider. I hardly know whether to call it a difference between two usages of the word 'believe' or a difference of opinion as to what the correct usage is. At any rate, the word is in fact used in two different ways (whether it ought to be or not) and the difference between them is of very considerable philosophical importance.

In the one usage, belief admits of degrees. You may believe something very firmly, or fairly firmly, or mildly. A rough scale of degrees of belief may be constructed, ranging from conviction at the top end to suspecting at the bottom end, with various degrees of opinion somewhere in the middle. According to this usage of the word 'believe', it is possible to believe that it will rain tomorrow morning without being absolutely sure or completely convinced that it will. Moreover, if one's belief does fall short of the highest degree (i.e. does not amount to absolute conviction) one will admit that the proposition believed may be false after all. What one is here admitting is not merely the logical possibility of its being false; for since the proposition believed is an empirical or contingent one, its falsity would not in any case be logically impossible. One is admitting more than this, namely, that the rain may not as a matter of fact occur. One is, of course, claiming (rightly or wrongly) that one has evidence for the proposition believed. But one is not claiming that the evidence is conclusive. The man mentioned in an earlier example who was asked whether Wilkinson was in Oxford and replied 'yes, I believe that he is' was using the word 'believe' in this way; and it is a very familiar use of the word among reasonable men.

Nevertheless there are some (though I hope there are not many now listening to me) to whom this usage of the word 'believe' appears paradoxical or even outrageous. And unfortunately there *is* another usage of it, though not a very common one. We might call it, rather unkindly, the solemn sense of the word 'believe'. According to this second usage of the word, belief does *not* admit of degrees, and we are not allowed to say of someone that he believes a proposition *p* at all unless he is absolutely convinced of it, completely sure about it. If he is not absolutely convinced that *p*, but still accepts the proposition with some degree of confidence, we have to say 'he has the opinion that *p*' or 'he thinks that *p*', but not that he believes it. Archibald has opinions, of course, like everyone else, but he does not *believe* anything. Belief, in this usage of the word, is a matter of all or nothing. Moreover, in this usage of the word 'believe', it would obviously be absurd to say of someone that he believes something firmly or strongly. It would be rather like saying that he slept slumbrously or sat in a sitting posture. For belief in this sense is a firm or strong attitude by definition (or shall I say, a stiff one?).

It cannot be denied that both these uses of the word 'believe' can claim some sanction from common speech, though the second, I think (the solemn or degree-less one), is mostly confined to special contexts, particularly religious and political ones. Some people perhaps would say that it is only applicable to belief *in*. Archibald has opinions, but the trouble with him is that the does not believe *in* anyone or anything. On this view belief *in* is a matter of all or nothing, even if belief *that* admits of degrees. I shall try to argue later[1] that belief 'in' does admit of degrees, or at least that there is a usage of the phrase in which it does. For the present, however, it will be best to confine ourselves to belief 'that'. There are problems enough about belief 'that', and we had better deal with them first, before tackling the still more complicated subject of belief 'in'.

Confining ourselves, then, to belief 'that', let us ask whether belief does or does not admit of degrees. We can now see that this is at least partly a matter of terminological decision. Whatever terminology we adopt, we must agree that there is a more and a

[1] In Series II, Lecture 9.

less about the way one 'holds' or 'accepts' a proposition. There are degrees of *something* here, whether we call them degrees of belief or not. Let us compare (1) suspecting that *p*, (2) holding the opinion that *p*, (3) being almost sure that *p* but not absolutely sure, and (4) being absolutely sure that *p*, completely and unreservedly convinced of it. All these four attitudes have something in common, and they have it in different degrees. I propose to say henceforward that all these four attitudes (and there may of course be others in between) are attitudes of believing. That is, I shall use the word 'believe' throughout these lectures in the sense in which belief does admit of degrees—the weak sense, if one pleases to call it so—and I shall refrain from using it in the 'all or nothing' sense in which it refers exclusively to complete and unreserved conviction. If it is complete conviction that I am talking about, I shall say so. I shall treat complete conviction as the highest degree of belief ('highest' is not equivalent to 'best') and shall avoid the usage in which nothing short of complete conviction is deemed worthy of being called belief at all[1]. If anyone dislikes this terminology and prefers to use the word 'belief' in the degreeless or all-or-nothing sense, he may substitute some phrase like 'accepting a proposition' whenever I speak of believing.

My terminology is not very different from Locke's. Locke speaks of degrees of assent and formulates his 'Ethics of Belief' in terms of degrees of assent.[2] In a reasonable man, he thinks, the degree of his assent varies with the strength of the evidence for the proposition assented to, and one is not entitled to give a high degree of assent to a proposition for which the evidence is weak. But Locke's doctrine of degree of assent (and the 'Ethics of Belief' which goes with it), was vigorously challenged by one of the most celebrated authorities on our subject, Cardinal Newman, in the *Grammar of Assent* ch. VI ('Assent considered as unconditional'). On Newman's view, we do not assent at all unless we assent with complete and unreserved conviction. Newman's criticisms of Locke will be discussed in Lecture 6 of this series.

[1] Cook Wilson (*Statement and Inference*, Part II, ch. 3) appears to regard belief as a state intermediate between opinion and conviction—stronger or firmer than opinion, weaker or less firm conviction. This usage too might perhaps claim some support from common speech.

[2] *Essay concerning Human understanding*, Book IV, chs. 14-16, and ch. 19 ('of Enthusiasm').

LECTURE 2

THE VARIETIES OF KNOWLEDGE

ACTS AND DISPOSITIONS

Before we discuss the relation between belief and knowledge, something must be said about the concept of knowledge itself.

Plato, in the *Theaetetus*, distinguished between possessing a piece of knowledge and using it, and pointed out that we still possess it at times when we are not using it. The possession of a piece of knowledge is an example of what we should now call a disposition. For example, we all possess or 'have' the knowledge that $7 \times 7 = 49$. We acquired this piece of knowledge many years ago and probably we shall retain it for the rest of our lives. But we are not always actually thinking of or attending to this mathematical truth. It actually 'comes into our minds' only occasionally, once a week perhaps, or less often than that. Nevertheless, we have the capacity of recalling this proposition whenever we need to (for example, whenever we are engaged in a calculation to which it is is relevant), and of actually 'realizing' or' acknowledging' that it is true.

This is what is meant by saying that our knowledge that $7 \times 7 = 49$ is a disposition rather than an occurrence. (It is an acquired disposition, of course. There was a time when we learned this mathematical truth.) The disposition shows itself or manifests itself from time to time by actual mental occurrences, for example, when we actually use the proposition $7 \times 7 = 49$ in calculating the size of a carpet. But a disposition is something which we still have or possess at times when it is not actually being manifested at all.

Now in ordinary everyday English the verb 'to know' is generally used in a dispositional sense; not quite invariably perhaps, but certainly the dispositional use of it is by far the most common. To take another example (a piece of empirical knowledge this time) we all know and have long known that there are lions in Africa. We know this even at times when we are not thinking of it at all, and indeed most of us think of it only very seldom. We know it even when we are asleep. You would not say of a sleeping man 'he no longer knows that there are lions in Africa', for that would suggest that he has lost this piece of knowledge and will have to learn it again when he wakes up.

This might indeed be his situation if he were suffering from very severe concussion, or from some very severe emotional shock. Then we might find, when he woke up, that he had lost much of the knowledge which he formerly possessed, and that he did have to learn it again. But we are speaking of normal sleep, and using it as the most striking example to illustrate Plato's distinction between 'possessing' and 'using'; for here a man still possesses all the knowledge he has in his waking hours, but for the time being he is not using any of it, at any rate if his sleep is dreamless. To put it technically, he still has a very large number of acquired dispositions, but for the time being none of them are being actualized.

I have said that in everday speech the verb 'to know' is generally used in the dispositional sense. Philosophers, however, have sometimes talked about *acts* of knowing. They have conceived of knowing as a special sort of mental occurrence, and have asked how it differs from other mental occurrences. This way of speaking is now much less common than it was. It has one rather surprising consequence. If someone knows something, in this act or occurrence sense, it would make sense to ask at what time he knows it. At 1.30 p.m. on Wednesday he was knowing that $7 \times 7 = 49$, and on Sunday morning, just after he woke up, he was knowing that there are lions in Africa. The oddity of such statements as this suggests that there is something odd about the idea of an 'act of knowing'.

We can agree, of course, that acquiring a piece of knowledge—discovering something, finding it out—is a mental occurrence, and there is no harm in calling it a mental act. At such and such a time I suddenly 'saw' or 'grasped' the proof of Pythagoras' theorem. I suddenly 'saw' or 'realized' that given the axioms of Euclid the square on the hypotenuse of a right angled triangle must be equal to the sum of the squares on the other two sides. This seeing or grasping is a dateable mental occurrence; a mental act, if you like.

We can also agree that when once we have acquired a piece of knowledge, e.g. the knowledge that the distance from London to Edinburgh is about 390 miles, this knowledge is liable to be actualized or manifested thereafter by dateable mental occurrences; for instance when someone asks us what the distance from London to Edinburgh is, or when we are trying to work out what a railway ticket from the one place to the other would cost, or how long the journey would take in a train whose average speed is 45 m.p.h. On such occasions we recall or attend to this fact which we know, and this is an actual and dateable occurrence in our mental history: we may call it a 'mental act' if we like. But according to our ordinary usage of the word 'know' it is an act of recalling or using a piece of knowledge we possess, rather than an act of knowing.

It might therefore be thought that the phrase 'act of knowing' is at best a purely technical one, with no sanction at all in ordinary usage. And if so, surely we had better abandon it altogether (as many contemporary philosophers have) since our aim as philosophers is to analyse the concepts we actually have, and not to replace them by different ones? But it is not quite true that the 'act' or 'occurrence' conception of knowing has no basis at all in our ordinary everyday use of language. Sometimes, though not very often, we do find ourselves using the word 'know' in an occurrent sense, to refer to a dateable mental event.

I shall give an autobiographical example. In 1918, when I was learning to fly, aerial navigation hardly existed. We used to find our way by following main roads or railway lines. One day I was lost in a fog over East Anglia. I came down very low and read the name on a small railway station. Then at last I knew where I was. Here the word 'know' is used for a mental occurrence or act, occurring at a particular time (in the late afternoon, as far as I can remember). Something 'dawns on us' at a particular moment. Of course, you can say, if you like, that this is a case of coming to know, or finding something out. But I think it is perfectly intelligible to say 'then I knew'—using the word 'knew' for a dateable occurrence.

Another example can be found in the sentence: 'After that, he knew no more until he woke up in the hospital twenty-four hours later'. Here, knowing does seem to be thought of as a series of mental occurrences, which was interrupted for a certain period of time, and then began again. This example is quite different from the one I gave earlier, when a man is not said to cease to know things when he is asleep. Here, on the contrary, he is said to cease knowing when he becomes unconscious, and for twenty-four hours he does not know anything at all. It seems that the 'occurrent' sense of the word 'know' (in which knowing is conceived as a dateable mental event) does have some foothold in ordinary everyday language, though the dispositional sense of the word is by far the most common one.

It cannot be said, then, that the term 'act of knowing' is a wholly unintelligible one. The mistake made by the philosophers who used it was not that they did talk about mental acts, but that they failed to talk about anything else. They discussed what is called 'the problem of knowledge' as if certain sorts of mental occurrences were the only topic which has to be considered; and, despite what Plato had said, they paid little or no attention to the dispositional sense of the word 'knowledge'—the sense in which our knowledge is something which we possess throughout a period (for many years perhaps) and still possess even when we are not at the moment using it. To ignore this dispositional sense of the word 'know' is a serious error. If the 'act' or occurrence sense of the word were the only one, it would follow that we always lost our knowledge of something the moment we cease to consider it or attend to it. If knowing the distance from London to Edinburgh is just a mental occurrence or mental act, it follows that we cease to know the distance from London to Edinburgh as soon as that act or occurrence comes to an end; we no longer know it, though for a short time we did.

Of course, we do quite often cease to know something. Knowledge may be lost as well as acquired. We may easily lose some piece of knowledge which we previously had. I used to know what my dentist's telephone number is, but I no longer know it. But it would be absurd to say that when we cease to attend to or consider some fact, we *ipso facto* cease to know it. One may add that our knowledge would be of little value to us if the 'mental occurrence' account of it were the whole truth about it. The important thing about a piece of knowledge, once we have got it, is that we are often able to retain it, and recall it to mind again whenever we need it. It is not just a matter of momentary flashes of insight which come and go; it is more like enriching ourselves, acquiring a stock of valuable possessions, which we continue to have at our disposal afterwards.

All this is forgotten or ignored if our philosophical discussion of knowledge is just a discussion of mental acts or mental occurrences. We need not reject the 'act of knowing' terminology altogether, as some contemporary philosophers would wish to do, and certainly the fact that 'act of knowing' is a technical term is not in itself a good reason for abandoning it. But we must not suppose that all the things we need to say about knowledge can be said in a 'mental act' or 'mental occurrence' terminology. Some of the most important of these things cannot. The same applies to belief too, as we shall see later. Here too, as I have already said, we are confronted with a similar contrast between a mental act or occurrence analysis and a dispositional analysis. And here too, as I shall try to show later, the mental act or occurrence analysis is not so completely mistaken as some modern philosophers suppose. But here too some of the most important things we want to say about belief cannot be said in a mental act or mental occurrence terminology.

Professor C. D. Broad has remarked that a mind has two distinctive characteristics, consciousness and retentiveness. A theory of knowledge which takes account only of mental acts or occurrences may perhaps do justice to consciousness, but not to retentiveness. A mind without retentiveness, if such an entity is conceivable—what Leibniz called a *mens momentanea seu carens recordatione*—might have momentary flashes of insight, but it would not have any knowledge in the ordinary sense of the word 'knowledge'. Similarly it might give momentary assent to propositions, but it could not have what we ordinarily call beliefs. The advantage of the dispositional conception of knowledge is that it draws our attention to the memory-dimension which all knowledge has. The point of becoming aware of something is that we are then in a position to remember it afterwards.

KNOWLEDGE OF FACTS AND KNOWLEDGE BY ACQUAINTANCE

In ordinary English the verb 'to know' is sometimes followed by a dependent clause. Most of us know that the Battle of Waterloo was fought in 1815, and as I was writing these words I knew that I was in Oxford and that I was writing them. Such knowledge is sometimes called knowledge of facts. There is some difficulty in this way of speaking. If we adopt it we shall have to say that there are general facts, for example the fact that some cats are black, and even universal facts, such as the fact that all lions are carnivorous, for we know that some cats are black and that all lions are carnivorous. There must also be negative facts, for we can know that there is no tea in the teapot. Furthermore, we shall have to say that there are conditional facts, and even facts expressed in what is called a 'contrary to fact' conditional sentence. For example I know that I am afraid of Alsatian dogs. When I say this, I am not saying that I now have any feeling of fear. What I claim to know is that if I were to see an Alsatian dog near me (which I do not) or that if I believed that there was one near me (which I do not) I should feel fear.

But perhaps these examples are not intolerably odd. Perhaps they only seem so, because we have to use technical terms (the technical terminology of logic) to draw distinctions between one sort of fact and another, distinctions which do not need to be drawn in everyday speech. After all, it surely is a fact that some cats are black and that all lions are carnivorous. There is in fact no tea in the teapot—nothing but hot water—because you forgot to put the tea in. If you claim to have put it in, I shall reply 'the fact is that it is not there'. Conditional facts are more difficult to swallow, especially where the sentences formulating them are *contrary*-to-fact conditional sentences. It is notorious that such sentences are puzzling, and that it is very difficult to find a satisfactory analysis of such a proposition as 'if it were now raining, the streets would be wet'. But what is contrary to fact is not this conditional proposition as a whole, but one (or sometimes both) of its constituent propositions taken separately. It surely *is* a fact—or if you like, it is as a matter of fact the case—that if it were now raining the streets would be wet. We may well be puzzled to say what kind of a fact it is, but can we seriously deny that it is one?

A PRIORI TRUTHS AND EMPIRICAL FACTS

But a more awkward difficulty arises when the sentence which follows the 'that' is an *a priori* sentence. We all know that $7 \times 7 = 49$. Is it a fact that $7 \times 7 = 49$? If it is, there must be *a priori* facts or necessary facts. Sometimes we speak as if there were. For otherwise, what point could there be in calling other facts empirical? We do often speak of empirical facts, from which it would seem to follow that there are also facts which are non-empirical, or at any rate that there might be. If not, what could empirical facts be contrasted with, and what point could there be in applying the word 'empirical' to facts at all?

Why then should it seem odd to speak of necessary facts or *a priori* facts (e.g. mathematical facts or logical facts)? There is no doubt that it does. Of course we might be reluctant to say 'it is *not* a fact that $7 \times 7 = 49$', because this might suggest that the proposition $7 \times 7 = 49$ is false. But we should also be reluctant to say that it *is* a fact that $7 \times 7 = 49$. Why is this? Perhaps it is because 'fact' suggests 'matter of fact'. It is not just a matter of fact that $7 \times 7 = 49$. It is not something we can ascertain by observation or experiment or historical research. A matter of fact is something which just happens to be the case. It is what philosophers call 'contingent'. There happen to be tigers in India, but conceivably there might not have been. But it does not just happen to be the case that $7 \times 7 = 49$ or that 17 is a prime number and 18 is not.

We can avoid these difficulties by speaking of *a priori* truths or necessary truths (rather than *a priori* or necessary facts.) What kind of truths they are, what makes them true, are questions we need not go into at present. It is sufficient to point out that they cannot be denied without contradiction. It is logically impossible that 7×7 should not be equal to 49. But the denial that there are tigers in India involves no contradiction. It is logically possible that there should be no tigers in India, though as a matter of fact there are.

If we return now to 'knowledge that', we can see that there are two course open to us. We can either divide 'knowledge that' into two kinds (1) knowledge of facts (2) knowledge of *a priori* truths; or else we can say that it is just knowledge of truths, and then divide truths into two kinds (1) empirical truths and (2) *a priori* truths. It does not matter much which of these two alternatives we choose, but for my part I prefer the first, because I should like to be allowed to go on using the good old down-to-earth word 'fact'. So I prefer to divide knowledge into (1) knowledge of facts (2) knowledge of *a priori* truths.

KNOWING 'WHO', 'WHAT', 'WHERE', ETC.

We must now notice that when the verb 'to know' governs a dependent clause, it need not be a 'that' clause, though it frequently is. For example one may know *who* did it, or *where* someone is, or *what* he is doing. We may know *when* the Battle of Waterloo occurred, or *how long* this piece of wood is, or *what* the length of it is. We may also know *what* the square root of 144 is, or how many prime numbers there are between 0 and 20. Presumably this way of speaking arose because statements expressing knowledge are often answers to questions. 'I know where he is' in the sense that I have the knowledge needed to answer the question 'Where is he?'. If so, this kind of knowledge is reducible to 'knowledge that'. For example, I know *that* Robert is in the kitchen, and this is what enables me to answer the question 'Where is he?' if anyone asks me. Similarly I know *that* the square root of 144 is 12, and this is what enables me to answer the question 'what is the square root of 144?'. To put the same point more technically: there is some fact of the form 'Robert is now at place *P*' and I claim to know this fact (though I do not state it) when I say I know where he is. Similarly there is some mathematical truth of the form $x^2 = 144$ and I claim to know this truth, though I do not state it, when I say I know what the square root of 144 is.

What has been said will apply to some of the cases in which the dependent clause begins with the word 'how'. If I know how long a piece of wood is, or how many people there are in the room, this is reducible to knowledge 'that' in the way just explained. I know that the piece of wood is $5\frac{1}{2}$ inches long or that there are 15 people in the room, and so I am able to answer the question 'how long is it?' or 'how many people are there in the room?'. But when the dependent clause is of the form 'how to . . .' (e.g. 'Robert knows how to make an omelette') special problems arise, which we must consider later. Sometimes they arise also when other interrogation words are used: e.g. I know *what* to do, he now knows *where* to stop. At any rate we must agree with Professor Ryle that knowing how to . . . is not reducible to knowing that . . .

KNOWLEDGE BY ACQUAINTANCE

We have mentioned various sorts of dependent clauses which may follow the verb 'to know'. But sometimes it is not followed by any dependent clause at all. Instead, it governs an accusative—a noun or a noun-phrase. We speak of knowing Mr Robinson-Smith, or knowing Scotland, or knowing the man who keeps the shop round the corner, or knowing Kensington Gardens in London. What is known in this sense need not always be an individual entity. It might be a group of entities. A traveller may know all the countries of Central America. I myself could claim to know all the counties of England and Wales, though I know some of them much better than others. (As we shall see, knowledge of this kind admits of degrees.) I also know some of the counties of Scotland, but not all. You may know all the members of the Robinson-Smith family, including great-aunts and second cousins, whereas I only know Mr Robinson-Smith himself. This is very different from 'knowledge that'. What is known here is not a fact or a truth but an entity of some kind, or sometimes a group of entities.

Most commonly, the entity is either a thing or a person. I use the word 'thing' with some misgivings. It is a little odd to call Scotland or Kensington Gardens a thing, and if we do call them things, we have to say that both of them are highly complex things. But at any rate they are actual existent entities, and both of them are material entities. A person (or at least all the persons we should ordinarily claim to know) is a material entity too, but that is not all he is; so we ordinarily distinguish between persons and things. Sometimes, too, we distinguish between living organisms, animals and plants, on the one hand, and things on the other. But sometimes we describe organisms as 'living things'.

'Knowledge that' may be called a 'propositional attitude'. But the knowledge we are now discussing is not a propositional attitude at all. It is sometimes called knowledge by acquaintance. One cannot have it unless one has actually encountered the person or thing which is known. To be acquainted with something *A*, you must have been aware of *A* itself. Perhaps we cannot know anything by acquaintance without also coming to know at least some facts or truths about it. But certainly we can know truths or facts about something without being acquainted with it. A student of geography may know many facts about Scotland; but he cannot know Scotland unless he has actually been there and seen at least some parts of it for himself. Students of Roman History may know many facts about Julius Caesar, but they are not in a position to know *him*. One could not know Caesar himself unless one had actually met him, though conceivably a very learned twentieth century historian might know many more facts about Caesar than some of the people who had actually met him.

In some languages these two very different sorts of knowledge are distinguished by the use of two different words: for example *cognoscere* and *scire* in Latin, *connaître* and *savoir* in French, *kennen* and *wissen* in German. And in old English there were the two different verbs *I ken* and *I wiss*. 'Do you ken John Peel?' that is, are you acquainted with him? On the other hand, in the Authorised version of the Bible St Paul says 'I wist not, Brethren, that he was the High Priest'.[1] It is a misfortune, perhaps, that in modern English the distinction between 'kenning' and 'wissing' has been abandoned. In Scotland, the verb 'to ken' still survives in some quarters, but it has to do duty for 'wissing' as well, just as 'know' does in ordinary modern English.[2]

In ordinary everyday speech, what is said to be known in the 'acquaintance' sense is often a perceptible entity of some kind—a person, a town, a country, the large oak tree at the cross-roads.

[1] *Acts of the Apostles*, XXIII, 5.

[2] 'Where is he?' 'I dinna ken' i.e. 'There is no place such that I ken *that* he is in it.

Often, but not always. Someone may know Descartes' version of the Ontological Argument, but not St Anselm's. I never knew the celebrated Oxford philosopher F. H. Bradley, though he was still alive when I was an undergraduate. But I do know some of his philosophical doctrines e.g. his doctrine of Degrees of Truth and Reality. Most of us know Wordsworth's poem about the daffodils. You might ask me whether I know any of Wagner's operas, and be shocked to learn that I do not.

There is some difficulty about these examples, though in all of them it would, I think, be good English to use the word 'know' in its 'acquaintance' sense. For one thing, it is a little odd to call Descartes' version of the Ontological Argument an entity, though it would be true to say that there is such a version of the Ontological Argument, and also that there are certain philosophical doctrines propounded by Bradley; that there are many poems which were written by Wordsworth, the poem about the daffodils among them, and that there are many operas composed by Wagner. Moreover, in the examples mentioned earlier (knowing a person, or a country, or an object such as an oak tree) it was plausible to say that knowledge by acquaintance is not a propositional attitude at all, and that this is the difference between knowledge by acquaintance and 'knowledge that'. But surely Descartes' version of the Ontological Argument is just a set of interconnected propositions; and so is Bradley's doctrine of Degrees of Truth and Reality. What else could it be?

What kind of an entity Wordsworth's poem may be is a more puzzling question still. But certainly there is something propositional about it. 'I wandered lonely as a cloud, which floats on high o'er vales and hills' is surely a proposition (a pretty complex one too). Those two verses describe a possible state of affairs, whatever else they do; whatever other effects they may have on the mind of the reader, they do at any rate enable him to entertain a proposition, though he does not have to believe it. They may even be a description of something which actually happened, a walk which Wordsworth actually took one day in the mountains of Westmorland.

In all these three examples, Descartes' argument, Bradley's doctrine of Truth and Reality, Wordsworth's poem, what we are said to know by acquaintance might perhaps be called 'a propositional structure'. Even Wordsworth's poem is at least a propositional structure, though it is certainly something more. What kind of an entity one of Wagner's operas could be, I do not dare to enquire. The question had better be left to more musically-minded philosophers. I will only venture to say that an opera looks rather like a universal, since the same opera can be performed at many times and places, and is something which 'there is' even at times when it is not actually being performed at all. Some philosophers have held, as we shall see, that universals can be known by acquaintance. If this view is acceptable, perhaps it might do for knowledge of operas as well.

For the moment, however, let us confine our attention to our other examples, in which what is known by acquaintance is apparently a propositional structure of one kind or another. Even so, there is still a very important difference between such knowledge by acquaintance and 'knowledge that'. To know Descartes' version of the Ontological Argument I do not have to *accept* his version of the argument, or indeed anyone else's. All that is required of me is that I should be familiar with the propositions of which the argument consists, including of course those of the form '*p* entails *q*'. To be familiar with this propositional structure, I do have to entertain these propositions and moreover I have to do this for myself (no one else can do it for me). In this sense Descartes' argument is something which I meet with or encounter. But I do not have to accept the argument.

The same applies to Bradley's doctrine of Degrees of Truth and Reality. To know this doctrine, in the acquaintance sense, I have to entertain a set of propositions and familiarize myself with them, but I do not have to accept all of them or even any of them. Similarly, to know Wordsworth's poem about the daffodils, I do have to entertain a series of propositions (I have to do this at least, whatever else I do or have done to me). But obviously I do not have to accept them. It is only necessary that I should consider them. The question whether they are true or false is irrelevant and I neither accept them nor reject them.

But in 'knowledge that' the situation is quite different. If someone knows that Winchester is south of Oxford, he is not only familiar with the proposition 'Winchester is South of Oxford' and capable of entertaining it whenever it is relevant, he also accepts it; moreoever, he accepts it with full conviction, and has sufficient reasons for doing so.

OTHER OBJECTS OF KNOWLEDGE BY ACQUAINTANCE

So far, our examples of knowledge by acquaintance have been taken from ordinary everyday speech. Philosophers, however, have sometimes claimed that there are other objects of acquaintance, very different from those we have been discussing. Russell held at one time that universals are known by acquaintance. He and others have also held that sense-data are objects of acquaintance. Some have thought that there is introspective knowledge by acquaintance—that each of us know by acquaintance at least some of the contents of his own mind.

Do these philosophical doctrines accord with our everyday ways of speaking and thinking? Of course, they might be illuminating, or indeed true, even if they do not. But when a philosopher uses an everyday word or expression (such as 'know' followed by an accusative) it is just as well to be clear whether he is using it in its everyday sense or in a technical sense. We may fall into confusion if we slip from the ordinary usage to the technical one, or back again, without noticing what we are doing. What is intelligible (at least false) when the word is used in the one way might be unintelligible or absurd (not even false) when it is used in the other.

We may notice two features in our ordinary everyday concept of knowledge by acquaintance. On the one hand, knowledge by acquaintance has a first-hand or face-to-face character. Knowledge by acquaintance is contrasted with the second-hand or 'hearsay' knowledge which we get from testimony, spoken or written. It is also contrasted with the knowledge we get by means of inference, for example, when we infer that the postman must have come while we were out because there is now a letter in the letter box, and it was not there when we left. What we learn in either of these two ways is often reliable enough to be counted as knowledge, at least according to our everyday usage of the word. But it is, of course, 'knowledge *that*'. And we ordinarily think of it as being in some way 'indirect'; it lacks the first hand or face-to-face character of knowledge by acquaintance.

But knowledge by acquaintance, in our ordinary way of conceiving it, reflected in everyday language, has another character as well. We should not ordinarily be said to know something by acquaintance unless we had familiarized ourselves with it in some degree, so that we are able to recognize it when we encounter it again. At any rate, we must be able to recognize it in 'easy cases' where there are no special obstacles, such as poor light, defective eyesight, disguises such as false beards etc. We have to ask, therefore, whether the same two features, 'first-handness' and familiarity, are present in these philosophical usages of the term 'knowledge by acquaintance'.

Let us first consider the doctrine that universals are known by acquaintance. If we are willing to use the terminology of universals at all, we do, I think, have to agree that some universals are known by acquaintance in something very like the ordinary everyday usage of the phrase. The word 'universal' itself (used as a substantive) *is* of course a technical term. But when it is maintained that some universals, at any rate, are known by acquaintance the phrase 'known by acquaintance' is *not* being used in a technical way. The two features mentioned just now, first-handness and familiarity, are both present. No one else can tell us what it is like for something to be red, or to be inside something else. Nor can we find this out by inference. We have to see it for ourselves, by actual face-to-face inspection of instances. Moreover, knowing what it is like for something to be red, or inside something else, has the other characteristic which I mentioned. Familiarity is an essential element in it. A man who knows what it is like for something to be red is capable of recognising the colour red when he encounters it again in other instances.

The ordinary everyday speaker, quite innocent of philosophical theories, might ask someone 'Do you know the smell of burnt castor-oil?' And though he does not use the word 'universal' (as a substantive) he does conceive of this smell as something repeatable; this same smell may occur on many different occasions, at many different times and places. Moreoever, he does think of it as something—a repeatable something—which some people are familiar with and capable of recognizing, though others are not; and he thinks of this familiarity as something which can only be acquired by smelling this smell for oneself, in a direct and first hand manner. Once the technical term 'universal' had been explained to him, the ordinary man would have no difficulty at all in understanding the statement that the smell of burnt castor oil is a universal which is known, and can only be known, by acquaintance.

It would, however, be a little odd to say that *all* the universals we conceive of are known by acquaintance. It seems plain that some of them are defined in terms of others, and we learn to conceive of them by understanding the definitions, not by first hand encounter with instances. (These are the universals which Locke called 'complex ideas'.) It might even be that there *are* no instances to be encountered. It is not likely that anyone has ever actually encountered a unicorn. But if we use the terminology of universals, we certainly have to say that 'being a unicorn' is a universal, and that some people know this universal, in the sense that they know what a unicorn would be like if there were one, and would be able to recognize it as a unicorn if by any chance they were to meet it. This knowledge has one of the two features which we noticed in our ordinary everyday concept of knowledge by acquaintance, but it lacks the other. The familiarity is there, but the first-handness is not; or if in a way it is, it is quite a different sort of first-handness, not at all like the 'face to face encounter' which is a feature of our ordinary everyday concept of knowledge by acquaintance. Our familiarity with the concept 'unicorn' did of course have to be acquired, and there was something first hand about the way we acquired it. We had to understand the definition of 'unicorn' ('a horse-like creature with a long horn in the middle of its forehead'). We had to understand it for ourselves, and no one else could do it for us. But this intellectual first-handness, this 'do-it-yourself' character (where the operation done is an intellectual one) is something very unlike a face-to-face encounter.

Nevertheless, if we use the terminology of universals, we still have to say that *some* universals are known by acquaintance and that some *have* to be known in that way if any universals are to be known at all. If universal *A* is defined, in the way just illustrated, in terms of other universals *B*, *C* and *D*, we cannot understand the definition unless we are already familiar with the universals *B*, *C* and *D*. There must then be some 'basic' or 'ground floor' universals (not necessarily the same ones for each person) which we become familiar with by direct first-hand encounter with instances. And these universals are indefinable, or if you prefer, they have only ostensive definitions.

ARE SENSE DATA KNOWN BY ACQUAINTANCE?

The position is rather different with the other philosophical doctrines mentioned on page 54. Let us consider the doctrine that sense data are known by acquaintance. Some philosophers, I think, have regarded sense data as universals. It seems that some of the American Critical Realists did. (Santayana, for instance, seems to have thought of sense data as 'essences'.) I find this view very difficult to understand. But if it is tenable, knowing sense data by acquaintance would just be a special case of knowing universals by acquaintance, and what has already been said about knowing universals by acquaintance would apply.

But certainly most philosophers who have talked about sense data have thought that they were particulars. They thought that every sense datum is an instance of a universal, or rather of several universals, but not that it *is* a universal, nor yet a conjunction of several universals. Now according to our ordinary everyday conception of knowledge by acquaintance, some objects of acquaintance are certainly particulars. Mr Jones is not a mere universal, nor a set of universals. He is an actual existent entity. Or, in the conceptualist terminology, Mr Jones is not just an abstract idea, nor yet a set of many abstract ideas, though many abstract ideas apply to him. Scotland is not just an abstract idea either, nor a set of abstract ideas, but an actual existent entity.

Let us consider Mr Jones, since human beings are perhaps the most typical of all objects of knowledge by acquaintance, according to our ordinary everyday conception of such knowledge. We can certainly say that he is a particular. It is true that we might prefer to call him an individual or a continuant, but certainly he falls on the 'particular' side of the particular/universal antithesis. Nevertheless, he is a very much more complex particular than any sense datum is. He has a vast and perhaps even inexhaustible set of properties, whereas a sense datum has very few. Moreover, some of them are dispositional properties which he still possesses even when they are not being actually manifested (irascibility for instance, or a taste for cross-word puzzles). But it would not make sense to ascribe dispositional properties to sense data at all.

These differences, striking as they are, might of course be irrelevant. There is no reason in principle why quite simple entities should not be known by acquaintance as well as complex ones; nor is there any obvious reason for saying that everything known by acquaintance must have dispositional properties.

But there is another difference which *is* relevant. In a way it is a difference in complexity too, but in this case the complexity is temporal. Such an entity as Mr Jones or Scotland has a vastly greater duration than any sense datum could have. Mr Jones, considered as a physically embodied human being, lasts for seventy years perhaps. (We need not ask whether he continues to exist in a disembodied state thereafter.) Sense data are very fleeting and short lived entities in comparison. We have only to shut our eyes and all the sense data in our visual field cease to exist, to be succeeded by new ones when we open our eyes again. As you walk round the room, you sense a series of different visual fields. Your visual sense data come and go, and are never the same ones in two successive seconds, so long as your walk continues. Occasionally we do have a relatively long-lived sense datum. For example when we hear the sound of a siren or hooter the same auditory sense datum may continue for several minutes. Again, as I sit working in my chair, the 'feel' of the chair beneath me and of the floor beneath my feet (tactual sense data) may continue for quite a long time, and so may a bodily pain (a 'somatic' sense datum) for example a headache, though the degree of attention I give it may vary. But no sense datum lasts for many years, as Mr Jones does, and most of them have a very brief duration indeed.

One consequence of this is that it is very difficult to familiarize oneself with a sense datum. It seldom lasts for long enough. Perhaps if the siren blows for five minutes, by the end of the second minute we are beginning to familiarize ourselves with the disagreeable auditory sense datum we are sensing; and if the headache continues for hours, this somatic sense datum does become familiar to the victim. But if all the sense data we are aware of are known to us by acquaintance, even the very short-lived ones—and this is what some philosophers have maintained—it is clear that the term 'knowledge by acquaintance' is not being used in the way we use it in ordinary speech, but in a technical way. What we find here is rather like what we found in the case of complex universals, but now it is the other way about. In the case of sense data the feature of first-hand encounter is present, and indeed emphasized by the sense datum philosophers themselves. But here it is the feature of familiarization which causes the trouble. If *all* sense data are objects of knowledge by acquaintance in the ordinary everyday sense, it should be possible to familiarize oneself with every sense datum that one experiences, whereas in fact is it possible only in a few exceptional cases.

The particulars which are objects of knowledge by acquaintance, in the ordinary sense of the term, have another important characteristic which sense data lack, and this too is connected with duration. Such existent entities as Mr Jones or Scotland or the oak tree at the cross-roads can not only be encountered, they can be encountered again after an interval, and recognized to be the same entities as they were before. They can be re-visited, even though a long period of non-visiting may intervene between one visit and the next. After twenty years' absence I can go back to the 'dear old place' where I used to spend my holidays, and recognize it to be the same place, despite the changes which have occurred in the interval—the new petrol station which has been put up, the thatched cottage which has been pulled down, the pervasive smell of diesel fumes, the forest of television masts on the roof-tops. Perhaps the intervals between visits have to be shorter when the object of knowledge by acquaintance is a person, because persons are apt to change more rapidly than places do. Someone I used to know well may be unrecognizable (to me) when I meet him again after an interval of thirty years. One's acquaintance with a person has to be 'kept up', as we say, if we are to continue to know him. Still, one does not have to re-encounter him every day, or even once a year. Once in every two or three years is usually enough. Such re-visiting is however impossible with sense data. The visual sense data I am now experiencing cease to exist when I shut my eyes or turn my head.

So much for knowing sense data by acquaintance. It turns out that this use of the term 'knowledge by acquaintance' is a technical one, different from the use it has in ordinary speech, though the two uses do have an important point in common, because knowledge by acquaintance has a first-hand or 'face-to-face' character in both cases alike.

INTROSPECTIVE KNOWLEDGE BY ACQUAINTANCE

We may now turn to the third philosophical doctrine mentioned on page 54 the one concerning introspective knowledge by acquaintance. A person is a self-conscious being, or rather, any normal person who has passed the age of infancy is in some degree a self-conscious being. He is usually aware of some, at any rate, of the events which are going on in his mind at any particular time, though never perhaps of all of them. (At any given time, some of them are beneath the threshold of consciousness or beyond the margin; and probably the position of the threshold varies considerably from one person to another, and for the same person at different times.)

This awareness of the contents of our own minds is often so inattentive that we should be reluctant to call it knowledge; indeed, in some cases we might prefer to say that a person is 'not wholly unaware' of what is going on in his own mind instead of saying that he is aware of it. Sometimes, however, we *notice* what is going on in our own minds, or some part of what is going on. This attentive awareness of some present content of our own minds is what we usually call introspection. Perhaps it is always in some degree retrospection as well, since mental events pass so quickly. Certainly it is in some degree retrospection if we go further, and engage in the much disapproved of practice of introspective study, and try to classify and to analyse these swiftly passing mental events, or to find the most appropriate words for describing them. But it is not necessary to consider this studious sort of introspection. Let us confine ourselves to what one might call ordinary introspection, the attentive awareness of some present content of our own minds. This occurs sometimes in nearly everyone (even, perhaps, in the most behaviouristic psychologist), though more frequently in some persons than in others. Is it a form of knowledge by acquaintance? And if we say it is, shall we be using the term 'knowledge by acquaintance' in a technical sense, or in its ordinary everyday sense?

The factor of 'first-hand encounter' is certainly present. A person just finds or comes upon this thought or image or feeling which is occurring in him at a particular time. And the noticing of it is something he has to do for himself. It *has* to be first-hand; no one else can do it for him. The most that someone else can do is to tell him what to look for. ('Are you sure you are not feeling just a little frightened?')

But though the factor of first-handness is there, the factor of familiarization is absent. The situation, then, is much the same as it is in the doctrine that sense data are known by acquaintance. The contents of our own minds, or at least those contents which are in any sense directly introspectible, are brief events rather than persisting entities. A few of them may last long enough for us to become familiar with them (perhaps we should then be inclined to call them 'mental states' rather than 'mental events'). For instance, I may have a leaden feeling of depression all through the day, quite long enough for me to become only too familiar with it. But certainly this is not true of all the introspectible contents of our own minds; and it would have to be true of all of them if the term 'knowledge by acquaintance' is being used in its ordinary everyday sense in the philosophical doctrine we are discussing, since it is a doctrine about all introspection, or introspection as such.

Of course, we may become introspectively familiar with some of the qualities which introspectible events have (as also with the qualities which sense data have), and may learn to recognize these qualities when they are instantiated again. I have often felt, and noticed, feelings of regret in myself, and next time I have a feeling of regret I shall probably be able to recognize that it is one. But this would just be a special case of what is called knowing a universal by acquaintance. If we use the terminology of universals, we have to say that introspectible events exemplify universals, as everything else does which exists or occurs. Or, to put it in the conceptualist terminology, we are able to acquire concepts or abstract ideas by attending to mental events in ourselves, and noticing their resemblances and differences.

KNOWLEDGE OF OURSELVES

But, it may be said, surely there is a sense in which we do know *ourselves*? No doubt some people have much more self knowledge than others: but surely each of us must know himself in some degree? Such knowledge may or may not be what these philosophers were talking about when they spoke of 'introspective acquaintance'. But we certainly do possess it, and it is an important sort of knowledge. And what is it but knowledge by acquaintance, in the ordinary everyday sense? Here is the verb 'to know' governing an accusative, as it does when we are said 'to know' Mr Jones. What are we to make of the Delphic Oracle's advice *gnōthi seauton* 'Know thyself'? (The verb gignōskein, which the oracle used, is the equivalent of our 'know' in the acquaintance sense.) It was a very good piece of advice too. The Roman poet was not far wrong when he said '"Know thyself" come down from heaven'[1].

Yet despite the verb the Oracle used, a great deal of what we ordinarily call self-knowledge is clearly 'knowledge that', knowledge of facts or truths about ourselves, and especially knowledge about our own dispositions; for example, a person might know that he is resentful and does not easily forgive injuries, or that he is interested in Roman History, or that he likes Mr X much more than he likes Mr Y. Such knowledge about oneself is important, both from a moral and a prudential point of view. It is also difficult to acquire, because there are emotional resistances in all of us which tend to prevent us from acquiring it. Perhaps this is the sort of knowledge which the Oracle had in mind, knowledge about one's own dispositions, or more generally about one's own character (knowing 'what kind of a person one is'). But if so, the knowledge it recommends us to acquire is knowledge 'that', and we must respectfully accuse it of using the wrong verb. Or did it just mean 'Notice what goes on in your own mind as carefully as you can?'

Perhaps the Oracle meant something different from either. Perhaps it was telling us to know the Pure Ego, which according to some philosophers, and some religious teachers too, is the

[1] 'e caelo descendit γνῶθι σεαυτόν

most important element in each man's personality. If there is indeed such an entity, it could conceivably be known by acquaintance in something like the ordinary everyday sense. For according to what we are told about it, it is not an event or happening like a thought or a feeling of anxiety, which comes and then goes. It is either a persistent entity or perhaps a supra-temporal one.

KNOWLEDGE BY DESCRIPTION

Russell distinguished between knowledge by acquaintance and knowledge by description. But it is interesting to notice that the distinction had already been drawn about 100 years before by Jane Austen. In Chapter 21 of *Sense and Sensibility* Lucy says 'I have not known you long, to be sure, personally at least, but I have known you and all your family by description a great while; and as soon as I saw you I felt almost as if you was an old acquaintance'. Perhaps the philosophers of ordinary language, who dislike technical terms, may take some comfort from this passage. The terminology of Miss Austen must surely be good English.

What is it to know someone or something by description? In *Mysticism and Logic*, Essay X ('Knowledge by Acquaintance and Knowledge by Description'),[1] Russell gives the following definition: 'I shall say that an object is known by description when we know that it is "*the* so and so", i.e. when we know that there is one object, and no more, having a certain property.'[1] In the summary at the end of the essay he puts it thus: 'we have *descriptive* knowledge of an object when we know that it is *the* object having some property or properties with which we are acquainted; that is to say, when we know that the property or properties in question belong to one object and no more, we are said to have knowledge of that one object by description, whether or not we are acquainted with the object'.[2]

For our purposes, the most important cases are those in which some object or person is known to us *only* by description, since these are the ones which are most relevant to the distinction

[1] *Mysticism and Logic* (George Allen & Unwin, London), pp. 214-15.
[2] *Ibid*, p. 231.

between knowledge and belief. For example, one cannot know Paris by acquaintance unless one has actually been there, but one may know it by description as the capital of France. The description has to be what Russell calls a definite description ('*The* capital of France'). It is conceivable that France might have two capitals, as the Roman Empire had in the fourth century, Rome and Constantinople. In order to know something by description we have to know that there is something, and only one thing, to which a certain description applies. And of course we do in fact claim to know that there is one city and only one which is a capital of France. Alternatively, a person who has never been there might know Paris by description as the place indicated by this round black spot on a map at which he is looking, since according to the conventions of map-making, such a round spot represents one town and only one.

It will be seen that if we are to know something by description, in Russell's sense, three conditions must be fulfilled, (1) We have to conceive of some characteristic or set of characteristics. The characteristic might be a relational one. (2) We have to know that this characteristic or set of characteristics does in fact characterize something. This is knowledge of the truth of an existential proposition of the form 'There is something which . . .' The existential character of knowledge by description is pointed out by Russell himself.[1] (3) Finally we have to know that the characteristic or set of characteristics in question characterize only one thing.

As has been mentioned already, the first two conditions may be fulfilled when the third is not. Perhaps you have never seen a giraffe. But you may still conceive of a giraffe by means of the description 'a large spotted horse-like creature with two short horns and a very long neck, which enables it to eat the upper foliage of some trees'; and you may know that there are in fact animals to which this description applies. This is an important kind of knowledge, and is obviously quite different from knowledge by acquaintance. Moreoever, it is in a sense knowledge by description, since the understanding of a description is an essential part of it; and the proposition known to be true is an existential one. But this is not what Russell himself calls knowledge by

[1] *Mysticism and Logic*, p. 215.

description, because his third condition is not fulfilled. So far from knowing that there is only one object to which the description applies, you know that there are many, though you do not know how many. Russell's knowledge by description is knowledge by exclusive or identifying descriptions. Perhaps he defined it in this way because he thought of it as a kind of second-best substitute for knowing an individual object or person by acquaintance.

This may also be the explanation of a rather strange linguistic fact. When Russell (or Jane Austen) speaks of knowledge by description, the verb 'to know' takes an accusative. What we are said to know by description is an actual entity of some sort, as opposed to a truth or set of truths. Yet when a piece of knowledge by description is analysed, it turns out to be reducible to knowledge *that*, knowledge of facts or truths. We know *that* a certain description applies to something, and *that* there is only one thing to which it applies. If our knowledge is knowledge that an existential proposition is true, why should we speak as if it was knowledge by acquaintance? Presumably because the second 'that' clause lays a special sort of restriction on the existential proposition formulated in the first one. Whenever we know that an existential proposition is true, we know that a certain description has application, or that a certain concept, or set of concepts, is instantiated. But in this case we also know that the description applies to only one thing, or that the concept or set of concepts has only one instance. And knowledge by acquaintance, at least in the most typical examples of it, has the same 'singular' character. It is knowledge of *this* person or *this* thing, or again of this sense datum or mental image. Even if we hold that universals ('properties') are knowable by acquaintance, as Russell did when he wrote the essay we are discussing, acquaintance with a universal would still be acquaintance with a single, though non-sensible, entity—just *this* universal as opposed to that one.

Nevertheless, the differences between knowledge by acquaintance and knowledge by description are more important than the resemblances. Knowledge by description does not have the character of 'first hand encounter' which knowledge by acquaintance has. There is something indirect or second hand about it. Most frequently we get it from testimony, from reading what others have written, or hearing what they tell us. The testimony may be conveyed to us in a pictorial form, for example by means of photographs or diagrams, or maps, or chronological tables, though we still need the words of other people (written or spoken) to tell us what these visible representations are representations *of*, or how to interpret them, as when we are taught by others how to 'read' a map. But sometimes our knowledge by description is acquired by means of inference. If I see a footprint on the flower-bed, I can infer that some human being and only one has stood there; and by means of very complicated inferences the planet Neptune was known by description before anyone had observed it. There are also mixed cases, where the premisses of our inference are learned from testimony. Some trustworthy witness might tell me that there was a footprint on the flower-bed this morning, though I did not see it myself, and it has since been obliterated by the gardener. And when Neptune was 'calculated into existence by enormous heaps of algebra', it is possible that one (or both) of the astronomers who independently made the calculation was relying on the observations of others, conveyed to him by testimony, as well as observations of his own.

Again, knowledge by description has an abstract character, by its very nature. It is the knowledge that a certain abstract idea, or set of abstract ideas, has one and only one instance. And if we are willing to include knowledge by means of an indefinite description (we have seen that this is in a sense 'descriptive' knowledge too) the abstractness is still more obvious. The knowledge that there are lions in Africa, though perfectly good knowledge as far as it goes, is something very different indeed from actually seeing or touching a lion, or feeling it bite you. However complex an abstract idea is, and even if we do know that it has just one instance and no more, there is still something 'thin' about knowledge by description. It lacks the richness and concrete detail of knowledge by acquaintance. There is something superficial about it, as well as something indirect or second hand. Perhaps it never wholly satisfies us, and never can.

If this is its defect, it does of course have a compensating virtue. The range of knowledge by acquaintance is exceedingly narrow, even if we take the liberal view of it which common sense takes, and allow that such individual entities as persons or horses or trees or dogs can be known by acquaintance. (If it is true, as some philosophers have thought, that the only entities one can know by acquaintance are one's own sense data and some of the contents of one's own mind, the range of knowledge by acquaintance must be narrower still.)

But the range of knowledge by description is vastly wider. By this means, and no other, we can come to know about an enormous multitude of 'existences and objects which we do not see or feel'. Even if we take the most liberal view of knowledge by acquaintance, we still have to say that almost the whole of our historical and geographical knowledge is knowledge by description. One of the most important differences between a civilized person and a savage is that he has far more knowledge by description; and as a result of this, we could say that the civilized person is not quite such a 'stranger in the universe' as the savage is. One of the chief aims of education is to provide us with knowledge by description and the means of getting more.

Finally, it is important to notice that one piece of knowledge by description may depend upon another. If we do not know Mr Harold Wilson by acquaintance, we may still know him by description as the present Prime Minister of Great Britain. But perhaps we are not acquainted with Great Britain either, and it too is only known to us by description, as the largest island to the north-west of the European continent. Again, to take a historical example, the Emperor Tiberius may be known to us by description, e.g. as the successor of Augustus. But Augustus, in his turn, is himself only known to us by description, e.g. as the first Roman Emperor, or as the great-nephew and heir of Julius Caesar; and both the Roman Empire and Julius Caesar are known to us only by description, if known to us at all.

'CIRCULUS IN DESCRIBENDO'

When we consider such examples, knowledge by description seems like a network or chain which hangs unsupported in the air, each link described in terms of another or several others, and that in turn described in terms of another or several others. We seem to be in danger of a fallacy which might be called *circulus in describendo*. Suppose we ask someone what he knows of Paris, and he replies 'All I know of it is that it is the capital of France'. We then ask him what he knows of France, and he says 'All I know of France is that it is the country of which Paris is the capital'. Clearly there is something wrong. *A* is described in terms of *B*, and *B* in terms of *A*.

Sometimes the circle is less obvious because it is larger. France is described as the country which is west of Germany, and Germany as the country which has Belgium on the north-west side of it, and Belgium as the country which is south east of England across the sea, and England as the country which is north of France across the sea. The circle may be so large that it covers the whole of geography, and every single place on the earth's surface is described in terms of others. Or again, it may be so large that it covers the whole history of the Roman Empire.

But if knowledge by description consisted just in 'knowing one's way about' through such a system of interdependent descriptions it would not deserve the name of knowledge, not even of reasonable belief. It would have no relation to reality, to what actually exists or happens, or what has actually existed or happened. This whole conceptual structure of inter-connected descriptions floats in the air until some item in it is related to something which we know by acquaintance. To take a geographical example, if at a certain time I can know England by description as the country containing these objects I see or touch, I can escape from this *circulus in describendo*. And another person can escape from it if he knows France by description as the country containing the objects which he sees or touches at a particular time.

The situation is something like the one we encounter in the Coherence Theory of truth, where there is a system of propositions each one of which is supported in a greater or lesser degree by some or all of the others. The difficulty is that this whole system of mutually supporting propositions need not be true of anything. However complex it is, and however coherent it is, it might still be just a complex and coherent fiction, and no degree of complexity will suffice to save it from being so. To escape from this predicament, there must be a reference to experience somewhere, as some advocates of the Coherence Theory have acknowledged, Bradley for one. With only a little first-hand experience we can sometimes go a very long way. But we must have some empirical facts if such a coherent system is to deserve the honourable title of 'knowledge', or even the less honourable one of 'reasonable belief'.

It comes to this. Knowledge by description is only possible if some of the descriptions mention entities known by acquaintance, for example, this thing here, what I see happening now. We can then describe entities remote in time or space by means of their relations to what is here and now. And this is what we actually do. The network of inter-connected geographical or historical descriptions is 'tied down' at many different points to what we see and touch. For example, if the Emperor Augustus is described as 'the Emperor who began to reign in 31 BC', the year 31 BC can be described as '1993 years before the present year' and 'the present year' as 'the year in which I am *now* writing'. What is here and now for me may be known to you only by description, and what is here and now for you may be known to me only by description. But for each of us there must be something which is here and now, if either of us is to know anything by description. As Russell says 'If we are to obtain a description which we know to be applicable, we shall be compelled, at some point, to bring in a reference to a particular with which we are acquainted'.[1]

'KNOWING HOW TO'

So far, we have been considering only various cognitive senses of the word 'know'. But it also has what may be called a practical sense, when it refers to some kind of expertness or skill or proficiency. This is what Professor Ryle calls 'knowing how to', for example knowing how to ride a bicycle or how to cure someone of influenza. Perhaps the word 'practical' is too narrow. It may suggest that when we know how to do something, the doing has to be some kind of physical activity, such as repairing a puncture. But a man may also know how to solve some purely theoretical problem, for example, how to prove that in a Euclidean rightangled triangle the square on the hypotenuse is equal to the sum of the squares on the other two sides; and on a particular occasion, when he actually does this piece of reasoning,

[1] *Mysticism and Logic*, p. 217.

he might do it entirely 'in his head' without uttering words or drawing a diagram on paper. Still, this *is* knowing how to do something, how to conduct a certain sort of operation, though the operation is an intellectual one. On the other hand, an activity which looks purely physical may be an intellectual one as well, and this may be the most important thing about it, as when someone spends a busy day looking through mediaeval charters or turning the pages of a copy of Domesday Book. The 'knowledge how to', which he manifests in these physical activities, may be a knowledge how to discover the derivation of some puzzling English place-name; and the operation of seeking for its derivation is an intellectual one, a piece of investigation or enquiry designed to discover the truth about something. If the researcher's investigation is successful, the result of it is the acquisition of knowledge *that*, or of reasonable belief *that*.

But sometimes, when the word 'know' appears at first sight to be used in one of its cognitive senses, we discover on further reflection that it is being used at least partly in the 'how to' sense. Knowing the way to the station consists at least partly in knowing how to get there, knowing how to go there from any place within a certain area. But this knowing 'how to' does have a cognitive side too. If I know how to get to the station, I must be able to recognize at least some of the landmarks which I encounter on the way, and to recognize the station itself when I get there. Recognizing is not itself a form of knowing how to.

Similarly, when we say that someone knows a certain piece of country very well, part of what we mean is that he knows how to find his way about it (if he did not, we should say that he did not in fact know it very well). But we also mean that he is familiar with that piece of country or well acquainted with it; and when he finds his way about it, or tells others how to do so, his knowledge 'how to' is a capacity for making practical applications of his familiarity or acquaintance. Again, knowing the meaning of a word consists partly in knowing how to use it in statements, comments, questions, reports, etc., which make sense, or in descriptive phrases which make sense. Knowing the meaning of a syntactical word like 'of' or 'whenever' consists in nothing else but this. One knows how to operate with it, or what to do with it. But with what are called 'object-words', such as 'eat' or 'blue' or 'run', knowing their meaning consists only partly, not wholly, in knowing how to use them in combination with other words. We are also capable of recognising the entities or qualities or occurrences to which they apply.

From the epistemological point of view, the important cases are those in which knowledge in the 'how to' sense is liable to be confused with knowledge in one of its cognitive senses, or those in which one of its cognitive senses is combined with the 'how to' sense, and the verb 'to know' is used to cover both at once without distinguishing them.

Perhaps it is well to add that we are not merely doers. Knowledge by acquaintance and 'knowledge that' (including knowledge by description) are valued for their own sake, and not merely for the sake of the 'know how' which sometimes results from them. Obviously it is useful to know how to do things, but also it is just nice to know how to do them, even though we seldom or never have occasion to do them in fact. Even 'know how' may be valued for its own sake and not mainly for what we can get out of it. Aristotle was surely right when he said 'All men by nature desire to know' and this applies to all the different sorts of knowledge which we have distinguished.

LECTURE 3
BELIEF AND KNOWLEDGE

THE CONTRAST BETWEEN BELIEF AND KNOWLEDGE

So much for various uses of the verb 'to know'. We must bear them in mind when we consider the relations between belief and knowledge. Belief is often contrasted with knowledge, as in 'I do not know where he lives, but I believe he lives in Bradford'. Knowledge is what we aim at in all our enquiries and investigations. But often we cannot get it. Belief is a second best. It is not what we wanted, but it is better than nothing. It may of course be held that knowledge is itself definable in terms of belief, and we shall consider this view later. But anyone who accepts it will still have to distinguish between the sort of belief which amounts to knowledge and the sort which does not. There will still be a contrast between knowledge and 'mere' belief. And some reasonable beliefs, beliefs held on good but not conclusive evidence, will have to be counted as 'mere' beliefs, and contrasted with knowledge, even when the propositions believed are in fact true.

To discuss the contrast between knowledge and belief, let us consider each of the different kinds of knowledge which can be distinguished. Let us first consider the usage in which the verb 'to know' governs an accusative (knowledge by acquaintance). The verb 'to believe' may govern an accusative too. We may believe a person.[1] He told us that the bus would arrive at 10.30, and we believed him, though actually it arrived half an hour earlier and we missed it. But there is no contrast here between believing and knowing. Believing a person is not a second-best substitute for knowing him. It amounts only to believing what he says or writes or otherwise conveys, e.g. by means of a signal or a gesture. Again, I cannot believe, or disbelieve, an inanimate object, though inanimate objects, as well as persons, may be known by acquaintance, at least in the ordinary everyday use of the verb 'to know'

[1] Cf. above Lecture 1, Introduction, pp. 38–9.

with an accusative. One cannot even believe a cat or a dog, though in some circumstances one might trust it or rely on it; (a blind man trusts his guide-dog, and I may trust my cat to miaow if he gets shut up in the attic or the cellar). I think we cannot even believe a parrot or a raven which talks, not even if it utters indicative sentences. One assumes that its utterances have no relation to facts and do not even purport to be true. The most we can do is to draw inferences from these utterances. According to an Indian story, one could infer that a certain house belonged to the philosopher Sankara, because all the parrots in the trees around it were saying 'The Vedas are infallible'. (Someone who wished to visit Sankara asked how to find his house, and this was the advice he received.)

There is no contrast, then, between knowing a person by acquaintance and believing him. What is contrasted with knowing an entity by acquaintance is believing propositions about it or him. The propositions we believe about an entity may be very numerous, and it might be that all of them are true. Still, such belief is a poor substitute for knowledge by acquaintance, though better than nothing. It is indeed a third best. The second best, in this case, is knowledge by description. But sometimes we only believe that there is something to which such and such a description applies; and even when we do know this, we may only believe and not know that there is only one thing to which the description applies. I may believe that there is only one person to whom the description, 'being your brother', applies, when in fact you have two brothers. It may well be that much of the knowledge by description which we ordinarily claim to have is belief rather than knowledge, if only because so much of it depends on testimony[1], spoken or written, and the reliability of the testimony is often taken for granted without much or any investigation.

As we now see, the contrast between belief and knowledge is most obvious when we compare belief 'that' with knowing 'that', knowledge of facts or truths (knowledge by description is a special case of this). We often believe that p, when we do not know that p is true. Such belief 'that' may fairly be called a second-best. Very often, knowledge 'that' is not available, through lack of time or lack of conclusive evidence. I cannot know that William will

[1] See Lecture 5, below

answer my letter by return of post. I cannot even know that he will get it. But I believe that he will. The post office is a fairly efficient organization, though not infallible. I also believe that he will answer by return of post, because I asked him to; he is a kind-hearted person and businesslike rather than otherwise. Of course, he may be ill or incapacitated or away from home; but if he were, the chances are that I should have heard about it. So I can believe with some confidence, though not with complete conviction, that he will answer my letter by return of post, and that his answer will reach me at breakfast time on the day after tomorrow. This belief, though inferior to the knowledge I should like to have, is much better than nothing. It gives me some guidance in my inferences and my actions. I can make plans 'on the assumption that' the answer will come the day after tomorrow. I do not just have to wait and see, although my plans are made with some reservations.

BELIEF AND KNOWING 'HOW TO'

Knowing 'how to', despite its importance in other contexts, does not seem to be contrasted in any obvious way with belief. It is true that in the practical sphere, as in the cognitive, there is a contrast between knowing and making a mistake. Moreoever, in both spheres alike one may forget what one formerly knew, and in both alike the forgetting may be either permanent or temporary. A man may forget how to tie a bow-tie, though he once knew how to do it. Or on a particular occasion, when he is ill or in a great hurry or very tired, he cannot remember how to do it, though ordinarily he can. But there is no contrast here between knowing and believing. There is no such thing as 'believing how to tie a bow-tie' or 'merely believing how to do it', as opposed to knowing how to do it. And though we do speak of thinking how to do something, this is not at all like thinking 'that'. 'Thinking that *p*' is a familiar way of expressing a mild degree of belief (opinion as opposed to conviction). But thinking 'how to' is a state of wondering or questioning.

It is true that if someone is asked whether he knows 'how to' do something, he may reply 'No, but I believe (or think) one does it by taking off the casing and tightening up a nut which one finds inside'. But this is a case of believing that. He believes that the correct way of doing it is so-and-so. Or he might answer, more oddly. 'I believe I know how to do it, but I am not sure.' But this again is believing that. He believes that he has acquired a certain sort of skill or proficiency, but he is not quite sure that he has.

If we wish to find a second-best substitute for knowing how, related to knowing how as 'belief that' is related to 'knowledge that', the most hopeful candidate, perhaps, is 'having an idea (or some idea) how to do it'. Does Watson know how to get an aircraft out of a spin? No, not quite, but he has some idea how to do it. Having an idea how to do something might be described as an imperfect or half-baked skill. It has the same practical character which knowing how has. Like knowing how, it manifests itself in actual performances, but not all of them are successful. If a person has some idea how to get out of a spin, without knowing how to, he will get out of it on three occasions out of five, perhaps, but on the other two he will only be saved from death by the intervention of the instructor. And even on the three more fortunate occasions, he will probably make some bungling movements with the control stick or the rudder-pedal before success is achieved.

Like knowing how, 'having some idea how' may be inarticulate. A man who knows how to do something may be quite unable to tell us, or himself, how he does it. A man who has some idea how to do it is perhaps more likely to be able to tell us how he tries to do it; and this may be why the word 'idea' is used. When a skill is only half-learned, we are more likely to give ourselves verbal instructions. To put it otherwise, a half-learned skill is more likely to be 'conscious' than a fully-learned one. But still, it need not be. The beginner in bicycling has difficulty in learning to mount his bicycle. If all goes well, a time comes when he succeeds more often than not. We then say he has some idea how to do it, and so does he. But he is very unlikely to be able to describe the bodily movements and muscular adjustments that he makes.

Even so, the relation between knowing how to do something and having some idea how to do it is not altogether parallel to the relation between knowing 'that' and believing 'that'. It corresponds rather to the relation between knowing all about something and knowing a little about it. When I believe that *p*, the propositions I believe may be completely false—'nowhere near the truth' as we say. I believe it will be raining by lunchtime to-day, and in fact the weather remains fine for the rest of the week. (If rain had begun to fall at 2.15 p.m. to-day, you might have said that my forecast was 'wrong but not so very far wrong'.) But when a man has some idea how to do something, he is not completely devoid of skill, and his performances are not wholly different from those of the man who knows how to do it. What he does is not wholly wrong; it is only partly wrong, even though he may not succeed in achieving the end he aimed at. But some of our beliefs are wholly wrong.

BELIEF 'IN'

The attempt to pair off the various uses of 'know' with corresponding uses of 'believe' breaks down in the case of knowing how to. There is no 'believing how to'. We meet with a similar difficulty when we consider 'believing in', but this time it is the other way round. There is no 'knowing in' to serve as the optimum for which believing in would be a second-best or inferior substitute.

'Believing in' is an important concept, especially (but not only) in the philosophy of religion. It is also a complex and baffling one. We shall have to discuss it in detail later.[1] Here we are only concerned with its relation to knowledge.

There is a sense of 'believing in' which seems to be reducible quite straightforwardly to 'believing that'. Surely believing in fairies amounts just to believing that there are fairies, and believing in the possibility of interplanetary travel is just believing that interplanetary travel is possible? Yet even in these examples there is perhaps some residue which the 'believing that' analysis leaves out. This residue might be described rather vaguely as 'attaching importance to'. It becomes more obvious if we consider another example, believing in representative government. This does not consist merely in believing that there is such a form of government. It is a valuational attitude as well. The believer in representative government is in favour of that form of government, indeed, strongly in favour of it, and he uses the 'believe in' phraseology

[1] Series II, Lecture 9.

to express this favourable attitude. This valuational aspect of 'believing in' comes still more clearly into view when we consider belief in God.

We must also notice that when the object of 'belief in' is a human being, we may both believe in him and know him by acquaintance—at least in the ordinary everyday sense of 'know'. The belief in Winston Churchill which most Englishmen had during the Second World War existed in those who knew him by acquaintance as well as in those who did not. It may be, however, that many of those who know a person only by description may believe in him firmly, while those who know him by acquaintance have little belief in him or none at all. Probably the Duke of Monmouth was in this unfortunate situation in 1685 and it helped to make his rebellion the tragic failure that it was.

It seems, then, that there is no neat and tidy way of contrasting belief in a person with knowledge of him by acquaintance. It would be an over-simplification to regard such 'belief in' as an inferior substitute for knowledge by acquaintance, and an even worse one to regard it as an inferior substitute for knowledge 'that'.

THE RELATION BETWEEN BELIEF AND KNOWLEDGE

Before we could discuss the relation between belief and knowledge we had to distinguish between different senses of the word 'knowledge', and it turns out that the word 'belief' has several different senses too. Until we have considered these distinctions, we do not clearly understand what question we are trying to answer. Perhaps we can now formulate it a little more clearly.

I may remind you (I ought to have done so before) that the first distinction we considered was between the dispositional and the active or occurrent sense of the verb 'to know'. Now this distinction, if applicable at all, applies both to knowledge and to belief. In both cases alike it is a highly controversial one, and in both the controversy is important. The difference between the traditional occurrence analysis of belief and the modern dispositional analysis is indeed one of the main themes of these lectures. But the distinction between 'dispositional' and 'active' (or 'occurrent') has little relevance to the questions we are now to discuss, if only because it cuts across the distinction between belief and knowledge itself. It cuts across many other distinctions too, for example that between hope and fear, or between love and hate. We might say that its domain is hardly narrower than the whole of the philosophy of mind.

If the disposition-act distinction be omitted, we are left with three senses of the word 'know' (four if you do not count knowledge by description as simply a special case of 'knowledge that') and three of the word 'believe'. They may be tabulated thus:

Knowledge	Belief
1. Knowledge by acquaintance.	1. Believing a person.
2. Knowledge 'that' (knowledge of facts or truths).	2. Belief 'that'.
3. Knowledge 'how to'.	3. Belief 'in'.

As we saw, we are accustomed to contrast belief with knowledge, and to think of it as an inferior substitute for knowledge. Even if we hold that knowledge is itself definable, somehow, in terms of belief (a view we shall consider presently) we still contrast knowledge with 'mere' belief, and the belief which does not amount to knowledge is still regarded as an inferior substitute for the belief which does. But it turns out that this contrast, this relation between an optimum and an inferior substitute, does not apply wholesale, to any sense you like of the word 'know' and any sense you like of the word 'believe'. Knowing how to does not seem to be contrasted with any of the sense of 'believe'. Believing a person is not contrasted with knowing him by acquaintance, as considerations of syntactical symmetry might lead us to expect. Its 'opposite number', on the knowledge side, if it has one, is knowing that the person's statements are true. And believing 'in' is only contrasted with knowledge where the belief in A is reducible without remainder to the belief that *A* exists (believing in fairies, for example).

The contrast between knowledge and belief is most obvious and most direct when we compare 'knowledge that' with 'belief that'. There is also an indirect or two-stage contrast between knowledge by acquaintance and 'belief that'. First, knowledge by acquaintance is contrasted with knowledge by description, which is a second-best substitute for it, and is itself a special case of 'knowledge that'. Then, in its turn, this knowledge that a certain description applies to one and only one entity is contrasted with the belief that it so applies, which is a third best.

The conclusion suggested by our discussion is this. When we enquire into the relation between belief and knowledge, we are mainly concerned with the relation between belief that and knowledge that. In Russell's later terminology we are comparing two 'propositional attitudes'; and they may, of course, be attitudes to the same proposition. If we contrast belief with knowledge and think of it as an inferior substitute for knowledge, the contrast is primarily between 'knowledge that' and 'belief that'. Again, if we define knowledge in terms of belief, we are defining 'knowledge that' in terms of 'belief that'; and the contrast which remains is one between 'knowledge that' and *mere* 'belief that', or between the sort of 'belief that' which amounts to 'knowledge that' and the sort which does not. Let us turn then, to the distinction between 'belief that' and 'knowledge that'. What are we to say about it?

BELIEF 'THAT' AND KNOWLEDGE 'THAT'

We may begin our discussion with a platitude, since one of the chief occupational hazards of a philosopher is neglect of the obvious. If someone knows that *p*, then *p* is true. Of course, he may say he knows this, or claim to know it, or others may say of him that he knows it, and *p* may nevertheless be false. But if he—or anyone else—does know that *p*, this entails that *p* is true. It is a contradiction to say 'John knew that it was raining, but it wasn't'. Moreoever, it is a contradiction to say 'He knew that it is raining, but perhaps it wasn't'. It is even a contradition to say 'He knew that it was raining and perhaps it was'. If he did know that it was raining, it just *was* raining, and there was no 'perhaps' about it.

But believing that *p* does not have these consequences. There is no contradiction whatever in saying 'John believes that *p*, but *p* is false'. And no matter how many people believe that *p*, *p* may still be false.

Might it be that *p* is not even false? Could one believe what is called a 'meaningless proposition'? It is not easy to see how anyone could. For surely there would be nothing to believe? Yet there is a too-familiar state which we describe as 'believing what one does not understand'; a strange feat certainly, but we all seem to be capable of it.

Moreover, there seems to be some sense in which we can sincerely claim to believe a proposition which we do not in fact believe, as we can sincerely claim to know what we do not in fact know. There are some awkward questions here which we shall have to consider later. But we may neglect them now, because they are not very relevant to our present topic. Let us assume that our believer really does believe what he says he believes and that what he believes is at least false (not meaningless). The important point at present is that it need not be true, no matter how firmly he believes it, not even if everyone else believes it too.

It is also important to point out that reasonable beliefs are no exception to this rule. Reasonable beliefs may perfectly well be mistaken. A reasonable belief is one which is in accordance with the evidence. If the relevant facts which are known to me are more favourable to *p* than to not *p*, then it will be reasonable for me to believe *p*. But unless the evidence is conclusive (i.e. is sufficient to make *p* certain), it is still possible that *p* may be false after all. Before Australia was discovered, for example, it was reasonable for Europeans to believe that all adult swans are white. They had a good deal of evidence for believing so. But this proposition eventually turned out to be false.

On the other hand, an unreasonable belief (one held on very weak evidence or no evidence at all) may happen to be correct, though it is no credit to the believer if it is. A man believes that this horse will win the race because he likes the sound of its name, or because the race is on Thursday and Thursday is his lucky day. And perhaps the horse does win; the proposition he believes turns out to be true, though his belief was quite unreasonable.

It follows from this, paradoxically, that there is a sense of the word 'right' in which it may be right (right and proper) for someone to believe a false proposition—viz. when all the evidence he has is in favour of it—and wrong (improper) to believe a true one: viz. when he has no evidence for it, and *a fortiori* when the evidence he does have is against it. Sometimes people are praised for holding correct beliefs and condemned for holding mistaken ones. But if we must indulge in praise or blame about such matters, the relevant point is not the correctness or incorrectness of those beliefs, but their reasonableness or unreasonableness in view of the evidence those people had at the time.

We must, therefore, be careful not to equate the two statements '*X*'s belief is correct' (i.e. what he believes is in fact true) '*X*'s belief is reasonable, given the evidence which he has.' But this is a digression. Let us return to the distinction between belief and knowledge.

It might perhaps be suggested that the difference between them is just a difference of degree. As we have seen already, there are many different degrees of belief, ranging all the way from merely suspecting or surmising at the one end, to complete conviction at the other. And 'knowledge' (it might be said) is the name we give to the highest degree of belief—believing a proposition with complete conviction, being absolutely sure about it.

Now there may be some connection between knowledge and complete conviction. If tomorrow morning after breakfast I have just a mild opinion that it will rain in about an hour's time, no one would say I knew this—even though it does in fact rain fifty-seven minutes later. But it is perfectly obvious that though complete conviction may be a necessary condition of knowledge, we cannot just identify knowledge with complete conviction. No matter how firmly someone believes a proposition—even if he is absolutely sure of it—it still makes sense to say that what he believes is false; and quite often it is in fact false. I may be absolutely convinced that to-day is Tuesday, and yet I may be mistaken. There was a time, presumably, when all mankind were absolutely sure that the earth is flat, but nevertheless this proposition which they were absolutely sure of is false.

It is true, no doubt, that when a man is absolutely convinced of something he may say 'I know it'. He will also act as if he knew it. Being absolutely convinced that today is Tuesday, I take an early bus and go off into the country for the day. I do so without any hesitation or qualm, just as I should if I knew that to-day is Tuesday, and therefore knew that I do not have to lecture this morning. But saying you know (or claiming to know) is one thing, and knowing is another. Again, it is only too obvious that a man may act as if he knew that his spectacles are in his pocket, when in fact he has left them on the dressing table in his bedroom. Lost among a maze of footpaths, he unhesitatingly opens his map, only to find that the cannot read it. It is also true (and perhaps more interesting) that there is something 'linguistically odd' or even absurd in saying, 'I am convinced (absolutely sure) that to-day is Saturday, but I may be mistaken,' just as it is absurd to say 'I know that it is Saturday, but I may be mistaken'. 'Such is my firm and unshakable conviction. But of course I may be wrong.' Those two remarks together amount to something like a contradiction.

We notice, however, that this only applies to conviction statements in the first person singular and the present tense. There is no absurdity at all in saying 'Jones is absolutely convinced that *p*, but he may be mistaken'; and there is no absurdity in saying 'I was absolutely convinced that *p* a week ago, but I may have been mistaken'. Whereas with statements of the form '*X* knows that *p* but he may be mistaken' there is no such distinction. Statements of this form are absurd whatever tense they are made in, and whether they are in the first person or not.

Then what kind of absurdity is there in saying 'I am absolutely convinced that *p*, but I may be mistaken' or 'I am perfectly sure that *p*, but perhaps *p* is false after all'? Only this, that absolute conviction, so long as one has it, prevents one from considering the possibility that one may be mistaken, or at any rate prevents one from taking this possibility seriously (attaching any appreciable probability to it). If someone states that he does attach some probability, even a small one, to the possibility that *p* may be false, this does not exactly contradict his previous statement that he is absolutely convinced of *p*; but it does show that one or other of his two statements cannot be sincere. This oddity which there is in the two statements taken together is moral rather than logical. Nevertheless, it is in fact perfectly possible that *p* may be false, even though the man who is convinced is thereby prevented from considering this possibility seriously so long as his state of absolute conviction remains. On the 'performatory' view, a man who says 'I am absolutely convinced that *p*, but I may be mistaken' is at once giving a guarantee and withdrawing it.[1] (Cf 'I promise to

[1] See Lecture 1, pp. 30–2.

come, but I probably shall not come' 'You must not be at all surprised if I don't'.)

Thus it is quite impossible just to equate knowledge with complete conviction—to say that knowledge just is the highest possible degree of belief.

CAN KNOWLEDGE BE DEFINED IN TERMS OF BELIEF?

Does it follow from this that belief and knowledge differ in kind and not in degree? Shall we say that there are just two quite different states of mind in which we can be: one which is infallible or incapable of being erroneous, namely, a state of knowledge; and another which is fallible or corrigible, namely a state of belief—regardless of the degree of firmness or strength with which the belief is held?

In the past, some philosophers have regarded the distinction between knowledge and belief in this way. But most contemporary philosophers would reject any such view. They would admit that there is a difference, and a very important one, between knowing that something is the case and merely believing that it is the case, without knowing that it is. But they would say the distinction is more like that between success and failure, and is not a distinction between two states of mind at all. So far as their state of mind goes, there need be no difference whatever between the man who knows something and the man who believes something without knowing it. The man who knows something is absolutely sure about it; and the man who merely believes something without knowing it may also be absolutely sure about it. He too may have the highest degree of belief—complete conviction.

As to the contention that knowledge is infallible or incorrigible, this (it would be said) is no more than a matter of definition—a tautology if you like. The verb 'to know' is so used that if someone is sure of something and turns out to be mistaken, we do not call this knowledge. It is as if someone argued that the man who, without a handicap, wins the race cannot fail to run faster than the others. The truth is, that if he had not run faster than the others, we should not call him the winner. On this view, the difference between the man who knows and the man who only believes is like the difference between the winner of the race and the other competitors who ran but do not win.

Let us consider this view further. At first sight, it looks rather like a proposal to identify knowledge with correct belief (what Plato called *orthē doxa*). But of course this would not give us all we want. Even correct belief, we usually think, need not be knowledge. On Saturday I may have believed that Sunday would be a fine day. And perhaps it is a fine day. But if I believed this on Saturday merely because Old Moore's Almanac said so, or merely because I wanted Sunday to be fine, we would hardly say that this belief of mine amounted to knowledge. If we wish to say that knowledge is to be defined, somehow, in terms of correct belief, we shall certainly have to add something about the grounds of the belief. It is not enough that the proposition believed is in fact true; it is also necessary that there should be good reasons for the belief. Plato himself suggests in the *Theaetetus* that knowledge can be defined as *orthē doxa meta logou* ('correct belief with a reason').[1]

Moreover, even though someone's belief is correct, and he does have good reasons for holding it, we should not necessarily be willing to say that we knew. I go down to the station to catch a train. The man in the ticket office tells me that this particular train is always five minutes late. I take his word for it and go off to the refreshment room for a cup of coffee. And sure enough, the train is five minutes late. Here I have a fairly good reason for my belief, and what I believe is in fact true. But we should hardly say I knew that the train would be five minutes late.

Again, I believe that within the next minutes at least one human being will walk past the front door of the Examination Schools. Actually, we will suppose, two people do walk past during that minute, so my belief was correct. Moreover, I had a good reason for holding it, namely my past observations of the degree of crowdedness of this part of the High Street at this hour of the morning on weekdays. But we should hardly be willing to say I knew that at least one human being would walk past during that minute, though certainly I had some evidence (quite good evidence) for believing so, and my belief was in fact correct. My reason for believing was a good reason, but not a conclusive one.

What we require, before we are willing to use the honorific

[1] *Theaetetus*, 201c–d.

word 'knowledge', is that the man's reason for belief should be not merely good but conclusive—sufficient to make the proposition certain. (It need not of course be conclusive in the deductive way.)

So far, we have been trying to work out the conception of knowledge one is committed to, if one starts from the assumption that there need be no difference between the state of mind of the man who knows, and the state of mind of the man who merely believes without knowing. The definition of the term 'knowledge' which this way of looking at the matter leads us to can now be given.

'*A* knows that *p*', we shall have to say, is equivalent to the following:

(1) '*A* believes that *p* with full conviction (is completely sure about it).'
(2) '*p* is in fact true.'
(3) '*A* has conclusive reasons for believing it: not merely good reasons, but reasons sufficient to establish or certify the proposition *p*.'

But now suppose that any of these three conditions fails to be satisfied. If a man believes with less than full conviction, or if what he believes is false, or if he believes with no reason at all, or with reasons which are good but not conclusive, then we shall say that he is 'merely' believing, and does not know—though if he has good though not conclusive reasons, his belief will still be a reasonable one, provided the strength of it is no greater than those reasons justify.

It will be noticed that, according to this definition, the distinction between knowledge and belief which falls short of knowledge is partly one of degree: (1) in the degree of conviction, since if a man believes with something less than complete sureness we refuse to say that he knows; (2) in respect of the strength of the evidence or of the reasons for believing.

On the other hand, it is also required, of course, that the proposition believed should be true. And this is not a matter of degree. Moreover, the distinction between conclusive reasons and reasons which are good but non-conclusive is not wholly a difference of degree, but only partly. Conclusive evidence is not merely stronger than evidence which is good but not conclusive (though it is of course stronger). There is also the difference that conclusive evidence settles the question, while evidence which is less than conclusive does not. And this is not just a difference of degree. Here again, it is more like the difference between success and failure; between winning the prize and failing to win it; between hitting the bull's eye and getting on to some other part of the target.

What shall we say about this account of the difference between knowledge and belief? (Strictly speaking, of course, it is a way of distinguishing between belief which amounts to knowledge and belief which falls short of knowledge: or if you like, it is a way of distinguishing not so much between knowledge and belief, but rather between knowledge and mere belief.)

We must admit that this way of drawing the distinction does fit many of the cases very well. For example, a very great deal of our knowledge, what we all agree to call knowledge, comes from testimony[1]—including written testimony—documents, etc.

Most of our geographical knowledge, and the whole of our historical knowledge, is of this kind, e.g. our knowledge that there is such a country as Australia, or that there are lions in Africa, or that there was an Emperor of the French called Napoleon III. The same applies to the knowledge we get from testimony about quite recent events which are beyond the range of our immediate observation. For instance, by reading to-day's newspaper we 'learn' (come to know) that the Prime Minister made a speech at Bradford yesterday. (If you like, this latter is a kind of short-range historical knowledge.) Again, it could be argued that our inductive knowledge is of the kind this theory requires: that we find out—come to know—what the laws of nature are by a process of accumulating evidence, until the stage comes when the evidence is sufficient to establish such and such a generalisation or make it certain.

SOME DIFFICULTIES IN THE PROPOSED DEFINITION

Nevertheless there is one feature of this definition of knowledge which gets us into difficulty. It does require that if someone knows

[1] On the evidence of testimony, see Lecture 5, below.

that *p*, the question 'How does he know?' always makes sense. According to the definition, he must have reasons (and moreover, sufficient or conclusive reasons) for accepting the proposition *p*, if we are to say he knows that *p*. He need not necessarily be able to put those reasons into words. But he must have them. He must have evidence sufficient to establish or certify the proposition *p*.

But surely there are some cases of knowledge where the question 'How do you know?' has no application? Consider what may be called propositions describing present experiences: e.g. 'There is something brown in my present visual field', 'I am now picturing (imagining) the front of Blackwell's bookshop in Oxford', 'I am wondering what the time is', or 'I have a headache'.

Now when someone makes a statement of this sort the question 'How do you know?' does not apply. How do I know that there is something brown in my present visual field? I do know this. But the word 'how' does not apply, if it is a demand for reasons, as it is when you ask 'How do you know that lunch is at 12.30?'. The only answer I could make to your question is 'I just notice that there is something brown in my present visual field, or that I am wondering what the time is, or that I have a headache'. Or more technically, I could say 'I just know this by inspection' or 'I know it immediately'—that is, without having reasons and without the need of any reasons.

The same applies to some statements describing past experiences. I know that I have often had a headache in the past. How do I know this? I just remember it. And when I say 'I remember it' I am not giving my evidence for the proposition. My knowledge, here again, is immediate; and in so far as I am telling you how I know, the word 'how' refers only to the kind of knowledge which it is, namely memory-knowledge, not to my reasons for the proposition I claim to know.

To put the point in another way, the definition of knowledge we are examining appears to assume that all knowledge is inferential (or 'mediate'). For when we know that *p*, we always have to have reasons for accepting *p*, according to this definition, and moreover, they have to be sufficient or conclusive reasons. But it seems perfectly plain that there is in fact some knowledge which is not inferential at all.

Moreover, it could be argued that there must be some non-inferential (immediate) knowledge, if inferential knowledge itself is to be possible. Unless there were some propositions which we just know to be true, without having and without needing any reasons—some cases where it makes no sense to ask 'What was your reason?' or 'How do you know?'—unless this were so, the other sort of knowledge, when it does make sense to ask for reasons, could not possibly exist.

There is another question which we should consider. If I do have reasons for accepting a proposition *p* (either conclusive ones, or merely reasons which are good but not conclusive) what do these reasons consist of? Sometimes they are other propositions which I likewise accept because I have good reasons for accepting them. How do I know that lunch is at 12.30? 'Well,' I may say 'the College Porter told me, and I saw a notice on the notice board outside the Common Room.' But how do I know that the Porter did tell me this, and that there was this notice outside the Common Room? Well, I just remember having certain visual and auditory experiences. I knew I was having them at the time, and for this knowledge no reason could be given, and none could be demanded. And I know now that I did have them; and I know this, not because of any reasons, but just by remembering it or recalling it.

We get into a rather similar difficulty if we turn to another point in the definition of knowing which I am examining. If we wish to define knowledge in terms of belief (of being sure), we have to use the word 'true' in our definition, because 'John knows that *p*' does entail that *p* is true (or if you like, entails that it is actually the case that *p*). But if we wish to maintain that this definition covers all the sorts of knowledge that there are—that all knowledge consists in being sure for conclusive reasons, of a proposition which is in fact true—we are confronted with a rather awkward difficulty: How do we ever settle the question whether John really does know something which he claims to know? Supposing he does know it, how can we ever find out that he does?

He claims to know that it is raining. We wish to decide whether this claim of his is justified. But in order to settle this question, we must ourselves have means of knowing whether it is raining or not. We must ourselves know whether or not the proposition 'It is raining' is in fact true. Unless this proposition is true, his claim to knowledge is unjustified. And how do we ourselves know whether it is raining or not? Not because of any reasons, but just by looking and seeing, or just by feeling the raindrops—just by having certain experiences. Indeed, how do we know that John makes any claim to knowledge at all? (Unless we do know this, there is no question to settle.) We know this by hearing what he says, or seeing what he writes.

In other words, if it is really possible to test people's claims to knowledge—to settle the question whether they really do know something or merely believe it without knowing—it must also be possible, sometimes, for a proposition to be empirically verified or empirically falsified—verified or falsified directly by experience. This direct empirical verification is a kind of knowledge which cannot be defined in terms of belief. Consider what the situation would be if there were not this possibility of direct empirical verification or falsification. It would follow that there might in fact be many instances of knowledge in the world, many people might be sure of propositions which were as a matter of fact true, and might be sure of them for sufficient reasons; and yet neither we nor they could ever discover that there are all these instances of knowledge. For to discover this, it must be possible for us to find out, for ourselves, what propositions are in fact true. And unless some propositions are directly verifiable or falsifiable nothing can ever be found out at all.

There is a similar difficulty about finding out what reasons John has for believing *p*, or whether he has any. He may in fact have very good ones; but unless we can find out what they are and how good they are, we shall not be able to settle the question whether he does really know what he claims to know. And if we ourselves are sure of something for sufficient reasons and it is in fact true, how do we ourselves know that we are sure of it, that our reasons for believing it are such and such, and that what we are sure of is as a matter of fact true?

We cannot know these things about other people, or about ourselves either, unless at some stage or other there is a possibility of direct empirical verification or falsification. And as I have said already, this direct empirical verification or falsification is a kind of knowledge (a way of finding something out) for which this definition does not provide. For in this case it is pointless to ask for reasons. And moreover, in this case, the knowledge we have is something quite different from belief of any sort. If you like, it does not consist in accepting a proposition, but rather in noticing some actual event or state of affairs.

This difference, between believing on the one hand and just being aware of something on the other, can be seen quite easily by considering a very commonplace example. You and I are sitting opposite each other in the train at night, and I am wondering whether the train will arrive at Basingstoke on time. I can know that I am wondering about this. You, on the other hand, can believe that I am wondering whether the train will arrive on time. You may believe it very firmly; you may be completely sure of it. You may have very good reasons for your belief too. You may see me looking repeatedly at my watch, and putting my face against the window to look at the dark landscape outside. You may even hear me say 'I wonder whether we shall catch the connection at Basingstoke'. But is it not obvious that your 'cognitive situation' is quite different from mine? When I know that I am wondering whether the train will arrive on time, I am just noticing an experience that I have. But this is not at all what you are doing. You are accepting or assenting to a proposition about me and, as it happens, a true one. You may have good reasons for accepting it. But you are certainly not directly aware of the state of affairs which makes the proposition true; whereas that is just what I am directly aware of.

The difference I am trying to point out would still be there, even if you had conclusive reasons for your belief about me (not merely good ones, but conclusive ones). Whether one ever can have conclusive reasons for such a belief about the experiences of another person is, of course, disputable; in ordinary life we do assume that one can, at least sometimes, but philosophers have often denied it. But suppose you did have conclusive reasons for your belief that I am wondering about this, and that you held your belief with complete conviction. Then you would know that I am wondering about it, according to the definition of 'knowledge' which we are examining. But it is still obvious that your knowledge of this mental occurrence in me would be a completely different sort of knowledge from my own. My knowledge is direct and first hand in a way that yours is not. I am noticing an occurrence, whereas you are assenting with conviction to a proposition. In my case it makes no sense to ask for reasons, but in yours it does.

CONCLUSION

So much for the theory that knowledge consists in having a firm belief on sufficient evidence (for sufficient or conclusive reasons) with regard to a proposition which is in fact true. We must admit that there are some sorts of knowledge, or some usages of the word 'know', to which this definition does apply very well: that is, we must admit that there are some sorts of knowledge which can be defined, with suitable precautions, in terms of belief. The precautions are that the following conditions must be satisfied: (*a*) that the proposition believed is true, (*b*) that the believer has conclusive reasons for it, (*c*) that he believes it with full conviction. Moreover, we must admit that with regard to those sorts of knowledge, the distinction between knowing and 'merely believing' is partly a difference of degree. To have knowledge, in these cases, you do have to have more evidence (stronger reasons) than you have when you merely believe without knowing, and mere belief perhaps is possible without any evidence at all.

When we say we know that the sun is larger than the moon, or that the Labour Party won the last election, or that there are kangaroos in Australia, or that this rock was brought here by a glacier, or again that water boils at 212° Fahrenheit at sea level—in all these cases we do mean by the word 'know' just what the definition says we mean. But I have also tried to show that there is another sort of knowledge—immediate or direct knowledge—which is quite different from this, and cannot be defined in terms of belief at all.

LECTURE 4

BELIEF AND EVIDENCE (I)

THE EVIDENCE OF PERCEPTION, MEMORY AND SELF-CONSCIOUSNESS

We should all agree that a person can only believe reasonably when he has evidence for the propositions believed. Moreover, our evidence for a proposition *p* which we believe must be stronger than our evidence (if any) against that proposition, if our belief is to be reasonable. Nor is this all. Belief admits of degrees. And if we are to believe reasonably, the degree of our belief must be no greater than our evidence justifies. For instance, it would be unreasonable to believe a proposition with complete conviction if our evidence, though good as far as it goes, falls short of being conclusive, though it would still be reasonable to believe with a good deal of confidence.

But unfortunately the notion of 'evidence' is full of difficulties. For one thing, the meaning of the word in modern English is quite different from the one its etymology suggests. The Latin word 'evidentia' literally means 'evidentness'. In the French word 'évidence' and the German 'evidenz' the etymological meaning is still retained. But in modern English it only survives in the term 'self-evident'. A self-evident proposition is one which is 'evident of itself'. You have only to consider the proposition itself and then it is evident to you that it is true. We notice however that here, in talking of 'self-evidence', we are concerned with the evidence *of* a proposition and not with the evidence *for* it. It does make sense to speak of the evidentness of a proposition, but it makes none at all to speak of the evidentness for it. And in modern English (apart from this one exceptional case), 'evidence' does always mean 'evidence for . . .'. The evidence for a proposition consists of those considerations which support that proposition or confer some degree of probability upon it, great or little. The evidence for a proposition may be strong or weak, whereas evidentness is a matter of all or nothing. Again, there may be evidence against a proposition, consisting of considerations which decrease the probability of that proposition; whereas the contrast between 'for' and 'against', or between favourable and unfavourable, does not apply to evidentness at all.

Presumably the word 'evidence' came to have this meaning in modern English, because we may acquire information which makes a proposition evident or obvious though it would not have been evident or obvious otherwise. The testimony of the witnesses makes it evident or obvious that the prisoner is guilty. But though this was presumably the first step in the divergence between the modern English sense of the word 'evidence' and its etymological sense of 'evidentness', there was more to come. 'Evidence' eventually came to mean not just considerations which make a proposition evident or obvious, but any considerations which make it in any degree probable.

Another point of terminology may be briefly mentioned. We speak of 'reasons' for believing something, and also of 'evidence' for believing it. What is the relation between the two? The answer is, I think, that the notion of 'reasons for' is wider. We may have reasons for doubting something, or for being surprised at it, or for suspending judgement about it. These three—doubting, being surprised, suspending judgement—are of course, fairly closely related to believing. But we may also have reasons for hoping or fearing, for being anxious, for liking someone or disliking him, or even for being angry with him. Again, we are expected to have reasons for the advice which we offer to someone, or the recommendations we make. Most important of all, we may have reasons for doing something, or for deciding to do it.

In this discussion, however, we are concerned only with reasons for believing. In some of the other cases just mentioned, when we speak of 'reasons for' such and such, it would be quite inappropriate to substitute the word 'evidence' instead. 'What evidence have you for being anxious about John's health?' would be a strange question. And 'what evidence have you for deciding to take the 4.15 train?' would hardly be intelligible. But in the special case of believing, the two questions 'what is your evidence for . . .' and 'what are your reasons for . . .' amount to pretty much the same thing. Perhaps 'reasons' here are primarily concerned with the mental attitude of believing (What reason have you for taking that particular attitude, rather than another, e.g. doubting or disbelieving?) whereas 'evidence' is primarily concerned with the proposition believed (what is the evidence for the proposition that this is the road to Aylesbury?). But when it is belief that we are talking about, there is at any rate a very close relation between the two questions. An answer to either would also serve as a satisfactory answer to the other.[1]

I think, then, that in this discussion we may safely confine ourselves to questions about evidence, though anyone who wishes to may translate what I am going to say into the terminology of 'reasons'.

THE EVIDENCE 'THERE IS' AND THE EVIDENCE X 'HAS'

Now it would often be said that the evidence for a proposition *p* consists of some relevant fact or set of facts which 'support' that proposition, or increase its probability; and that the evidence against *p* consists of some relevant fact or set of facts which 'weaken' that proposition or decrease its probability.

But there are two objections to this formulation. If we are concerned to decide whether a particular person's belief is reasonable (or how reasonable it is, if reasonableness admits of degrees) what we must consider is not just what evidence there is for the proposition he believes, but the evidence which he has for that proposition. He may have evidence for it which others do not have, and equally he may fail to have evidence which others do have. Primitive people, we may suppose, believed pretty firmly that the sun is much smaller than the earth, and about the same size as the moon. Their belief was mistaken. But we must not conclude that it was therefore unreasonable. Neither telescopes nor trigonometry had been invented at that time. The evidence which we have about the size and position of the sun and the moon was not available. They only had the evidence of unaided sense-perception, and this (as far as it goes) really does give some support to the proposition which they believed.

[1] Cf. also the parallel between 'What reasons are there for believing that *p*?', and 'What evidence is there for *p*?': and likewise between 'What reasons have you for believing that *p*?' and 'What evidence have you for *p*?'.

MUST THE EVIDENCE CONSIST OF KNOWN FACTS?

Secondly, there is a difficulty about the word 'fact' ('some relevant fact or set of facts which support the proposition believed'). It follows from what has just been said that if we are asking about the reasonableness of a particular person's belief, we must not just pay attention to the relevant facts which there are. Facts of which a man is completely ignorant, however relevant they may be, can have no bearing at all on the reasonableness of his belief. The only ones which do have a bearing on it are relevant facts which he himself is aware of.

And now we find that the word 'fact' gets us into difficulties. For when we say 'It is a fact that so-and-so', we are making a claim to knowledge. If I speak of the fact that to-day is Friday, I am claiming to know that to-day is Friday. Sometimes, no doubt, when I believe some proposition, my evidence really does consist of some relevant fact which I know. The primitive people I mentioned might fairly claim to know that the sun occupied a much smaller part of their visual field than the terrestial landscape did. But it is by no means obvious that when we believe reasonably our evidence must always consist of some relevant fact or facts which we know in any strict sense of the word 'know'. On the contrary, it seems (at first sight at any rate) that our evidence for a proposition which we believe consists quite often in other propositions which we believe—believe in a sense in which belief is contrasted with or inferior to knowledge. My evidence for believing that the Conservatives will win the next election consists of a lot of propositions which I have read in the newspapers during the last month or two. I believe these propositions more or less firmly: but can I claim to know in any strict sense of the word that all of them are true, or even that most of them are? It does look as if my belief about the next election was supported by nothing better than a set of other beliefs.

At any rate, there is a problem here, and we prevent ourselves from discussing it if we begin by laying down a rule that a belief cannot be reasonable, unless the evidence for it consists of relevant facts known to the believer. Instead of speaking of 'relevant facts' it is better to use some more colourless phrase like 'relevant considerations'; that leaves us free to enquire what kind of considerations they have to be. Might they just consist of other propositions which we already believe, but do not know to be true?

The suggestion that they might is strengthened when we consider the relations between belief and knowledge. As we have seen, we usually draw a distinction between belief and knowledge. It does not make sense to say 'John knows that it is raining, but it isn't': whereas it does make sense to say 'He believes that it is raining, but it isn't'—even though he believes this with complete and unshakable conviction. Here there is a very sharp distinction between belief and knowledge. Any belief, no matter how firmly held, can be mistaken: the proposition believed may still be false, and it still may be false, even when the belief is reasonable. But to speak of 'mistaken knowledge' would be self-contradictory.

We have also seen, however, that some philosophers have suggested that 'knowledge' itself can be defined in terms of 'belief'.[1] But even so, the distinction between knowledge and belief is not abolished. For we still have to distinguish between a belief which amounts to knowledge and a belief which does not; or, if you like, between knowledge on the one hand and 'mere' belief on the other. And thus the question asked just now can still be raised: does the evidence for a reasonable belief have to consist of propositions known to be true, or can it consist (wholly or partly) of propositions which are 'merely' believed?

The suggestion that it can is supported when we consider why we need to have 'mere' beliefs at all. Why not be content with such knowledge as we can get? The answer is that unfortunately we can get so little. If we are to live at all, we must constantly make practical decisions without knowing what the result of our action is going to be. Let us consider an academic person who has to give a lecture in a distant university this evening. When he gets into the train to go there, he certainly does not have conclusive evidence that the train will get him there in time to give his lecture. He has to be content with forming the most reasonable belief that he can on the evidence available. It is inductive evidence: most trains reach their destination not more than half an hour later than the timetable says they will. On the strength of this, he can reasonably believe with some confidence (but not with complete conviction) that he will arrive in time to address his audience.

[1] Lecture 3, pp. 83–91.

But if he had demanded conclusive evidence for this proposition before deciding which train to catch, he would never have got there at all.

Again, when he set out on his journey, he did not know that he would not be stricken by aphasia on the way, or otherwise incapacitated, whether physically or mentally, before he got there. Such things do happen, and he had no conclusive evidence that one of them was not going to happen to him. But on the evidence available to him about the state of his health, he could reasonably believe with considerable confidence (but not with absolute conviction) that he was going to arrive there safe and sound.

One thing, then, which makes us believing beings is that we need beliefs for the guidance our actions and our practical decisions. Belief is a second best, but it is much better than nothing. But we need it in another way too. Knowledge is something which we value for its own sake. (Everyone has some curiosity, and what is curiosity but a desire to know?) But here again, our trouble is that very often knowledge in any strict sense of the term is not available, especially, but not only, when the knowledge we should like to have concerns something rather remote in space or time. If we were to say 'we must have knowledge or nothing' then—very often—we should have to be content with nothing. We should have to remain in a state of suspended judgement, a state of complete 'agnosticism' about many of the questions which interest us (for example what were the motives of the Emperor Constantine when he adopted Christianity?). But though we have not got conclusive evidence which would enable us to know the answer, we may still have evidence which supports one answer rather than another. Thus we may have evidence which makes it probable, though not certain, that Constantine's motives were at least partly political ones, and improbable, though not certainly false, that they were purely religious. And here again reasonable belief is a second best; but still it is very much better than nothing, though knowledge would be better still if only we could have it.

BELIEF AND INFERENCE

Now let us consider what we do with our beliefs when once we have got them. The mathematical philosopher F. P. Ramsey suggested that when we come to believe a proposition, we 'add it to our stock of premisses'. I think he has put his finger on a very important function which our beliefs have. They enable us to draw inferences. Indeed, believing a proposition seems to consist at least partly in a tendency to draw inferences from the proposition believed. If someone claimed to believe that to-day is early closing day and yet set out on a shopping expedition this afternoon, we should doubt whether he did really believe what he claims to believe. For if he really does believe that it is early closing day, he must surely be capable of drawing the very simple inference 'The shops are shut this afternoon'.

As I have said already, we need beliefs for the guidance of our actions and our practical decisions. This is another way of saying that we draw practical inferences from the propositions we believe, or use them (when relevant) as premisses in our practical reasoning. But we draw theoretical inferences from them too. If one likes to put it so, we use them for the guidance of our thoughts as well as our actions. If I believe that the motives for Constantine's conversion were at least partly political, I shall think that this makes it likely that his motives for summoning the Council of Nicaea were partly political also. In other words, when we believe a proposition *p*, we do use that proposition as evidence to support other propositions. The inference we draw from the proposition *p* takes the form '*p*, so probably also *q*'. Indeed, this is one of the most important uses we have for our beliefs, once we have got them. When we come to believe a proposition *p* we consider its implications—what follows from it either certainly or probably. If we are reasonable, the propositions which follow from *p* with certainty are believed as firmly as *p* itself, though not of course more firmly.

Let us take the case of suspecting ('Suspecting is the name traditionally given to the lowest degree of belief). If I suspect that to-day is early closing day, I am entitled to suspect that the shops will be shut this afternoon: indeed I am logically committed to suspecting this, since the second proposition is logically entailed by the first. But I am not entitled to be sure, or even almost sure, that the shops will be closed this afternoon.

If however the inference I make from the proposition believed is what we call a probable inference, '*p*, so probably also *q*', the degree of belief which I give to *q* must be lower than the degree of belief I give to *p*, if I am reasonable. For example, if I am absolutely sure that it is raining now, I am not entitled to be absolutely sure that it will still be raining in five minutes' time (unless I have some other evidence for believing so). But I am entitled to believe this second proposition with considerable confidence.

It will be seen that when we consider the consequences of some proposition which we believe, our belief attitude spreads itself as it were, or extends itself, from that proposition to its consequences. But in a reasonable believer it suffers some degree of diminution on the way, if they are only probable consequences, supported but not logically entailed by the proposition originally believed.

BELIEFS SUPPORTED BY OTHER BELIEFS

We may now return to the relation between belief and evidence. Our conclusion so far is this: on the face of it, it does not seem to be always true that when we believe reasonably our evidence consists of known facts (facts known to the believer). Quite often it seems to consist of other propositions which are themselves 'merely' believed.

But this involves us in an awkward problem. The problem is particularly awkward if we wish to define knowledge itself in terms of belief ('believing a true proposition on conclusive evidence and with full conviction'), and it must be admitted that this definition does fit some sorts of knowledge quite well. If the evidence for a proposition *p* is to be conclusive, surely it must consist of other propositions which are themselves known to be true? So according to this definition of knowledge, these other propositions too must be believed on conclusive evidence. And the evidence for them, in their turn, must consist of still other propositions which are believed on conclusive evidence. Here we seem to have committed ourselves to a regress which has no discernible end—a regress of 'evidence for our evidence for our evidence . . . '.

But the same sort of difficulty arises about beliefs which do not amount to knowledge. For instance, I do not even claim to know that John is away from home to-day; I only claim that it is reasonable for me to believe this with a considerable degree of confidence, the degree of belief which is traditionally called 'opinion'. What evidence do I have for this belief? Well, I am fairly sure (but not quite) that he told me so when I saw him last Tuesday. My opinion is supported by nothing better than another opinion.

To put it metaphorically: we seem to be in a bog or a quagmire with no firm ground anywhere. Or, if one prefers another metaphor, we build up an elaborate structure of beliefs supported by other beliefs, and the whole thing just hangs in the air like a cloud. Is it anything better than a more or less coherent fiction? Some philosophers might be willing to accept this situation. They would say that if a set of propositions is sufficiently coherent, that in itself makes them true. Yet it seems obvious that a highly coherent system of propositions might still be wholly fictitious. (I recently read Professor Tolkien's series of novels called 'The Lord of the Rings'. I was very much impressed by the coherence of this complicated story, and it occurred to me that if the Coherence Theory of Truth were correct the whole story would have to be true!)

Let us try to see whether we can solve the problem in another and more commonsensical way. We shall find, however, that we get into difficulties about two important sorts of evidence which we have for our beliefs, the evidence of memory and the evidence of testimony. In both cases the 'coherence' interpretation has very considerable plausibility.

What I shall try to show is that this regress of 'evidence for our evidence' does have a termination: so that in the long run (though not always immediately) the evidence we have for our beliefs does after all consist of known facts—that is, of facts known to the believer—if we are believing reasonably. But I shall only consider empirical beliefs, what Hume called beliefs concerning matters of fact, and shall not discuss *a priori* or logically necessary propositions. It is not clear to me whether the notion of believing (either reasonably or unreasonably) applies to *a priori* propositions at all, nor whether the notion of evidence applies to them, though the notion of proof certainly does. At any rate, when we speak of the evidence we have for believing something, the type of evidence we have in mind is always or nearly always empirical evidence. It may of course be maintained (and often has been) that some very simple mathematical and logical truths are self-evident. But as we have seen already, in the phrase 'self-evidence', 'evidence' means just evidentness. And in a discussion of belief the word 'evidence' has quite a different sense; it means evidence *for* . . . and that is something which is quite different from evidentness.

There seem to be four different ways in which the series of beliefs supported by other beliefs can be terminated. To put it differently, there are four different sorts of evidence which do not just consist in propositions which are themselves merely believed. They are: (1) the evidence of perception (2) the evidence of self-consciousness (3) the evidence of memory (4) the evidence of testimony. The fourth is the most puzzling, and moreover it is not wholly independent of the first and second. Testimony itself has to be perceived (e.g. heard or read) and it also has to be remembered if it is to be of any use to us. But we do normally think of it as a separate source of evidence for our beliefs, and it raises special difficulties of its own which do not arise about perception, self-consciousness or memory. So in the rest of this lecture I shall only consider the evidence of perception, of self-consciousness and of memory. The evidence of testimony needs a lecture to itself.[1]

THE EVIDENCE OF PERCEPTION

We all think that some questions can be conclusively settled by means of sense-perception; and not only that they can be conclusively settled in that way, but that they very frequently are.

It is true that the epistemology of perception is a complex and highly controversial subject. The analysis of such a simple-looking statement as 'I am now seeing a piece of paper' is very difficult, and many strange opinions have been held about it. The distinction between 'appears' and 'actually is' is puzzling too: for example, on a foggy evening the sun often appears oval, but it is not actually oval. How can something appear to have a quality which it does not actually have, and in what sense exactly can we be said to be 'experiencing' this quality when the thing

[1] See Lecture 5, below.

appears to us to have it? Or should we perhaps say that 'actually is' should itself be defined in terms of 'appears', and hold (as some philosophers have) that such a thing as this chair here is just a class or system of actual and possible appearances?

But in spite of these difficulties, we all do think that some questions can be conclusively settled by the evidence of sense-perception, for example the question 'Are there any matches in this box?' By looking inside, it is possible to know or be certain that there are some matches there, or that there are none. G. E. Moore was surely right in maintaining that we know many propositions of this sort to be true even though we do not know what the correct analysis of them is.

If so, it is perfectly proper to speak of observed facts, as we all do in practice, whatever philosophical theories we may hold. And this is one way (the most familiar way) in which the regress of beliefs supported by other beliefs comes to an end. This regress—the regress of evidence for our evidence, as I called it—is terminated sometimes by an observed fact, that is by a fact ascertained or discovered by means of sense-perception.

For example, suppose I have to go to Cambridge this afternoon, and I decide to take a bus to the railway station. My reason for this decision is that I believe I shall get very wet if I walk all the way. What is my evidence for believing this? It again is something which I believe but do not know. I believe that it will be raining at that time. And what is my evidence for that belief? This again might be something which I believe but do not know. I might have had the misfortune to be blind, or to be shut up all the morning in a room with no window; and then at half past twelve some kind person might have told me that it was raining steadily, and I might just have taken his word for it. But as it happens, I was not in this unfortunate situation. I was able to go out into the garden just before lunch and see for myself that it was raining steadily, to feel the raindrops on my hands and face, to look at quite a large area of the sky and see for myself that there was no break in the clouds there. This was enough to settle the question 'What is the weather like here and now?' It was an observed fact, a fact which I observed for myself at first hand, that at that place and time it was raining steadily and that there was no break in the clouds within my range of vision.

Some philosophers may maintain that this language I have used is too strong. They may tell me that even here I was still only believing, and had no right to use the word 'fact' (which implies a claim to knowledge). But perhaps this dispute is less important than it seems. Suppose we do say that I only believe that it is raining when I have the experience commonly described as 'actually seeing the rain and actually feeling the raindrops'. Nevertheless, we have to admit that my evidence for this believed proposition is as strong as the evidence for any empirical proposition could be, and we cannot well conceive what it would be like to have better evidence for the proposition 'It is raining'. To use an analogy suggested by Professor Ayer, so long as we agree that evidence of this kind gets 'top marks', it does not matter very much where we draw the line between knowledge and belief, or between the beliefs which amount to knowledge and the beliefs which do not. But in actual fact, we should all say that in the circumstances described a person does know that it is raining.

In our reaction against over-sceptical views of perception, we must not of course jump over to the opposite extreme and maintain that all propositions for which we have perceptual evidence are certainly true. There are illusions and hallucinations, and what we perceive is not always as it appears to be. There are perceptual mistakes, and there are several different kinds of them. But we have means of detecting them. Roughly speaking, we do it by finding that the expected consequences of our belief do not occur. For example, in a mirage there appears to be a pool of water some distance away. We go to the place, and instead of seeing the water more clearly and in greater detail (as we should expect to do if it were actually there) we see nothing but an expanse of sand or tarmac, and we cannot get the tactual experiences we expect to have when we put our hands in a liquid.

Again, quite apart from illusions and hallucinations, some perceptual experiences are better from the evidential point of view than others. A single glance is not always enough to settle the question which we wish to ask (for example, the question 'Is that a swan over there?') though it does provide us with some relevant evidence. Often we must move to another point of view. We must come closer, or look at the thing from another direction; or we must switch on the electric light, or put on spectacles. Sometimes we must touch as well as sight. In order to decide whether this is petrol or water, we may have to smell it or even taste it.

So, within the class of propositions for which we have perceptual evidence, we can still distinguish between (1) those which are known or certified and (2) those which are 'only' believed. In this sphere, as in others, there is plenty of room for mere belief which does not amount to knowledge, because our evidence is not conclusive, (although it is good evidence as far as it goes.) The important points for our present argument are these: (1) First, there are some propositions which are perceptually certified, conclusively established by perceptual evidence, and there are many others for which we have strong perceptual evidence although it is not conclusive. (2) Secondly, even when we have only relatively weak perceptual evidence, this is sufficient to bring the regress of 'evidence for our evidence' to an end. The series of beliefs supported by other beliefs is terminated when we get back to a belief supported by perceptual evidence. For this belief, though used to support other beliefs, is not itself supported by another belief. It is supported by something quite different, namely by an experience, for example an experience of seeing or touching or hearing.

THE EVIDENCE OF SELF-CONSCIOUSNESS

This phrase 'an experience' draws our attention to the second source of evidence I wish to consider—the second way in which the series of beliefs supported by other beliefs is brought to an end. This second sort of evidence is the evidence of self-consciousness. In the example I gave before about the rain, the experience of seeing and feeling the raindrops was my own. When someone has an experience of this sort, he need not of course attend to it. But if he does, he can know that he is having it. We can sometimes claim to have knowledge about ourselves, and here again the regress of beliefs supported by other beliefs is brought to an end. For example, I believe that I should make a hopelessly bad soldier or policeman or air-raid warden. What is my evidence? Well, I am a timid person. What is my evidence for believing this? My evidence is not just some other proposition which I believe. It is something I have noticed about myself. I have noticed on a great many occasions that I am easily frightened by persons, objects and situations which do not seem to frighten others at all. I feel fear in the presence of a large dog, or of a man who addresses me in a loud and angry tone of voice, or when I am driving a car on a main road on the day before Bank Holiday, or when I have to go to the dentist, or even sometimes when I have to deliver a lecture. My evidence for believing that I am a timid person is the evidence of self-consciousness, the frequent experiences of fear which I have noticed in myself on many different sorts of occasions.

In the present climate of philosophical opinion it is hardly necessary to point out that a person does need evidence for the statements he makes about himself, especially when they are statements about his own character. In these Behaviouristic days, we are in no danger of claiming that every human being (or every sane adult human being) has a vast store of infallible knowledge about his own mind. The danger nowadays is all the other way. We are more likely to assert that others know or can know far more about us than we know about ourselves, or even that each of us knows almost nothing about himself or his own mind, and that most of the statements he makes about himself express 'mere' beliefs of a highly questionable sort. So if you want to know the truth about yourself you had better ask someone else, and preferably a person who does not like you very much.

No doubt this is a sphere in which we are peculiarly prone to error. That is why the precept *γνῶθι σεαυτόν* ('Know thyself') was needed. Self-knowledge is often a difficult achievement, and it is difficult in several different ways. One difficulty is that many mental states and happenings are so fugitive. They come and go so quickly and do not 'stay put' to be examined. Sometimes, however, the difficulty is just the opposite. A persistent state of mild melancholy or depression which 'colours' all our thoughts and feelings for the whole day, or even for weeks on end, or even throughout the whole of our waking life, is easily overlooked. One may fail to notice it, because there is nothing to contrast it with. More important still, self-knowledge and especially knowledge of one's own character (one's conative and emotional dispositions) is often painful. This is because we are moral beings. Self-knowledge is hardly separable from self-judgement, and only too often the self-judgement has to be of a disapproving kind.

It is not very surprising that self-knowledge is something which we tend to dislike, and that when it comes to us we often do our best to forget about it.

All the same, there is such a thing as self-consciousness. The idea that the only good evidence a person can get for belief about himself is the evidence of testimony is too absurd to be taken seriously, however true it is that external observers may sometimes have more correct beliefs about us than we ourselves have. I can sometimes notice that I am feeling frightened or tired or surprised, that I still feel resentment about an unkind remark made to me yesterday. I do not have to look in a mirror and observe my bodily behaviour in order to ascertain these facts about myself. I can sometimes notice that I am hearing or seeing or thinking, that I am imagining this or wondering about that. I notice these things for myself at first hand and do not need the confirmation of others. Self-consciousness is one source of evidence, and an indispensable source of evidence, for the beliefs which each person has about himself, although the testimony of others who observe his bodily behaviour is also relevant. You may think that this is a platitudinous conclusion. So it is, but platitudes are just the things which Philosophers are liable to forget. What is called 'a firm grasp of the obvious' is less common among learned men than one might suppose.

THE EVIDENCE OF MEMORY

We may now turn to the third way in which the regress of beliefs supported by other beliefs may be brought to an end, namely by means of the evidence of memory. Since sceptical views about memory have been rather prevalent among philosophers, and some have doubted whether there can be memory-knowledge at all, I shall begin by considering the defects of memory.

There are two quite different ways in which a person's memory may be defective. Badness of memory is something like badness of character. There are sins of omission and there are sins of commission. I may fail to do the things I ought to do, or I may do the things I ought not to do; and very likely I have both these kinds of moral defect. There is a similar distinction between omission and commission where defects of memory are concerned. If you ask me where I was on this day of the month ten years ago, I cannot remember at all. Everyone has forgotten very many of his past experiences. And for some of our beliefs about the past—even though it was our own past—we have only the evidence of testimony, for example, what our parents or other relatives have told us about what we did in our childhood. Sometimes the testimony is in a way our own. I might be able to tell you what I was doing on this day of the month ten years ago if I could find my own diary for that year.

In such cases as these the defects of memory are defects of omission. It is important to mention then, but they do not raise any very difficult philosophical problem. The defects of memory which I compared to sins of commission are a different matter. For then it is not just a case of failing to remember but of misremembering, much as sins of commission are misdoings and not just failures to do something. And as reflection on our misdoings gives rise to pessimistic theories of human character, such as the doctrine that human nature is totally depraved, reflection on our mis-rememberings likewise gives rise to sceptical theories of memory. Memory is fallible. It sometimes turns out that what a man sincerely claims to remember did not in fact happen. Then how can we be sure that all our claims to remember are not equally mistaken? Whenever we claim to remember something, it is conceivable that we might be mis-remembering. In that case, how can we know anything about the past at all?

Now there is something wrong with this argument. It cannot even be stated unless we assume that some of our claims to remember are correct, that sometimes when we claim to remember we really are remembering and not mis-remembering. How do we know that memory claims are ever made at all? Because we remember making them ourselves and remember hearing others speak as if they were making them. And how do we know that some of these memory claims were incorrect? Because we are able, somehow, to find out what the facts about the past actually were. And in order to find out what they actually were, we ourselves must rely on memory at some point or other. For example, you claim to remember having lunch with Thomas in London last Thursday, but you must be mistaken. How do we know that you are mistaken? Because we all saw you having lunch in College in Oxford on that day. But we ourselves are relying on our own memories when we say this.

Let us now consider another way in which we might find out that our friend's memory claim is mistaken. Suppose he specifies the time. He claims to remember meeting Thomas in the restaurant in London at 1.5 p.m. Yet he was seen in Oxford at 1.6 p.m. on that day. Surely this is sufficient to show that his memory claim must be mistaken? It is, but only because we assume the validity of certain causal laws. It is not logically impossible that a person should travel from Oxford to London in one minute, but it is causally impossible, the laws of Nature being what they are. We must however ask ourselves what evidence there is for believing that the laws of Nature are of this particular sort. It is empirical evidence, the evidence of observations and experiments. And they are past observations and experiments. But if knowledge of the past is impossible (as the sceptic says it is) past observations and experiments cannot be evidence for anything. Nor will it do to say that we can rely on documentary evidence—books, articles in scientific journals, etc.

We do of course rely on documentary evidence, but here again it is reliance on what we have read, and not just on what we are at this present moment reading. And if it is not strictly correct to speak of the present as momentary, because it has a finite duration and is what is called 'a specious present', still the duration of the specious present is very brief indeed, only a very few seconds. There is another difficulty about documentary evidence which I will just mention. It would be absolutely useless to us, unless we were justified in assuming that ink-marks retain an approximately constant shape and approximately constant spatial relations to one another over long periods of time. But our evidence for this is again empirical (there is no *a priori* reason why they should not change their shapes every other minute or move about all over the page) and it again is the evidence of past experience.

I hope this is enough to show that we can have no ground for thinking that a particular memory claim is mistaken unless we assume that other memory claims are correct.

'SAVING THE APPEARANCES'

The pessimistic way of formulating our conclusion would be this. 'Do what we will, we have to depend on the evidence of memory in the end, however sceptical we try to be. So we must just make the best of it. There is no prospect of getting anything better.' If that is our view, we shall have to proceed in something like the manner recommended in the Coherence Theory of Truth. It will be a case of 'saving the appearances'. We shall try to form a system of mutually supporting memory claims or memory propositions, in which as many of them as possible are retained and as few as possible rejected, though some, no doubt, will have to be rejected. In order to do this, we shall have to suppose that every memory claim has some degree of intrinsic weight or credibility. Unless we put in some proviso of this kind, our system of memory propositions, however coherent we make it, might be no more than a coherent fiction.

But once we have introduced this rather strange property of intrinsic weight or credibility, we can hardly fail to notice that it admits of degrees. Some memory claims have more of it than others. My claim to remember that I had several cups of tea at breakfast this morning has more 'credit-worthiness' than my claim to remember switching off the electric fire before I went to bed last Saturday night. Or again, I claim to remember (or, as we also say, I seem to remember) having seen this man before, when I was in California last winter; but the weight or credit-worthiness of this claim is small, and I could easily be persuaded that it is mistaken.

So if we do proceed in this way, and try to construct a coherent system which will include as many memory claims as possible, we cannot follow the democratic principle of Bentham, that each of them is to count for one and none of them for more than one. Our aim is to 'save the appearances'. But some of the appearances are more worthy of salvation than others, and we must save them first and be prepared to cast out the less worthy candidates, if there is a conflict between a more worthy one and a less.

But once we admit that this property of intrinsic credibility or credit-worthiness varies in degree, we may have to go farther.

Might there not be cases where this property reaches a maximum? Might there not be some memory propositions which present themselves to us with a weight or credibility or credit-worthiness so great that no empirical proposition could possibly have more? On the face of it, there are such memory-propositions and we all of us are sure that there are.

For instance, could any possible adverse evidence induce me to reject the very clear recollection I now have that I have been sitting in a chair and writing for some time? Well, just conceivably it could. Unknown to me, a dose of lysergic acid might have been put into a cup of tea I had at breakfast, and for the past forty-five minutes I might have been in a state of hallucination. But even so, I very clearly recollect that I have for some time been having experiences which were as if I was sitting in a chair and writing, and I cannot conceive of any empirical evidence which would convince me of the contrary.

It seems likely that everyone has such memories pretty frequently, and can recognize them when he has them. Not all of them are memories of the very recent past, though these are the most obvious examples. They may be memories of something which happened many years ago, for example of some episode in a railway journey on one's first visit to the Continent. Such recollections of the distant past tend to be fragmentary and isolated. They usually come to us just as memories of 'long ago', and do not have a determinate date attached to them. To date them, we have to resort to causal inferences or to documentary evidence or oral testimony.

We should also notice that among these 'unshakable' recollections of our past experiences, recollections which no amount of adverse evidence would induce us to withdraw, there are some which have a *general* character. When put into words they take the form of statements which are in one way or another general statements: for example 'I have gone to bed many times', 'I have often been to London', 'I have sometimes played cricket and have very seldom enjoyed it'.

It follows, if I am right, that the task which confronts us in our study of memory is not just one of 'saving the appearances', that is, our apparent or ostensible recollections, with due regard to the fact that some of them are *ab initio* more worthy of salvation than others. For some of them, and not so very few of them either, are improperly described as 'apparent' or 'ostensible'. Mixed in among the appearances which have to be saved there are some realities. They are not just memory-claims but actual memories. Indeed, if this were not so, how could we talk of ostensible or apparent memories at all, or attach any meaning to the phrase 'claim to remember'? What is this which we claim to be doing, or are ostensibly or apparently doing but perhaps not really? It is remembering. There happens to be such a thing. It is logically possible that there might not have been. But if there had been no remembering, there would have been no persons either, and indeed no minds or minded creatures at all. Leibniz' '*mens momentantea seu carens recordatione*' would hardly deserve the name of *mens*.

So much for three sorts of evidence by which the series of beliefs supported by other beliefs is brought to an end: the evidence of perception, of self-consciousness and of memory. The problems we have considered in this chapter are at any rate familiar ones. They have been discussed by philosophers for many centuries. But that cannot be said about the fourth sort of evidence, to which we must now turn, the evidence of testimony. In practice, and in learned enquiries too, we do often rely upon it as a means of terminating the regress of beliefs supported by other beliefs. But to the best of my knowledge, epistemologists have had very little to say about it, and there are no 'standard views' which we might use as starting-points for our discussion. The next lecture, then, is bound to be difficult both for the lecturer and the audience.

LECTURE 5

BELIEF AND EVIDENCE (II)

THE EVIDENCE OF TESTIMONY

Epistemologists do not seem to have paid much attention to the evidence of testimony. But according to our ordinary way of thinking, testimony is one of our most important sources of knowledge. Everyone claims to know a very large number of geographical and historical truths, for which he has only the evidence of testimony. All of us here would claim to know that China is a very large and populous country, though none of us, perhaps, has been within three thousand miles of it. Every English schoolboy knows that Charles II was restored to the throne in 1660, and that Britain was once part of the Roman Empire, though these 'known facts' are facts about the remote past. The same applies to facts about the very recent past as well. If an important debate takes place in Parliament, millions of people claim to know about it next day, just by reading newspapers or listening to the wireless.

To take an even more striking example, each of us would claim to know how old he is, that is, how many years have elapsed since he was born. But he has only the evidence of testimony to assure him that he was born in such and such a year; and equally he has only the evidence of testimony to assure him that this present year is 1967. How do I know, or what grounds have I for believing, that to-day is January 23, 1967? If it is a case of 'being sure and having the right to be sure', I have acquired this right by reading what is written on a calendar, or at the top of the front page of the newspaper which was delivered at my home this morning. I am often uncertain what day of the week it is. Is it Wednesday or Thursday? But in my ordinary unphilosophical moments, I assume that this question can be conclusively settled by consulting the appropriate written sources, such as to-day's newspaper.

Indeed, each of us depends on testimony for almost all that he claims to know about anything which is beyond the range of his own first-hand observation and memory; and one of the most important functions of memory itself is the remembering of what we have learned from other people by means of speech and writing.

This reliance on testimony plays a fundamental part not only in our cognitive lives, but in our practical lives as well. In very many of our practical undertakings we depend in one way or another on the spoken or written information we receive from others. To catch a train, I must rely on the information I receive from the timetable. To catch a bus, I must rely on the written words which I see on the front of it, e.g. the word 'Paddington', which is an abbreviation for 'This object goes to Paddington'. I find my way about the country by relying on the written testimony of sign-posts and milestones, and if I use a map instead, I am relying on testimony too. It could even be said that we are relying on testimony whenever we use a ruler or a tape-measure to measure the length of something, e.g. the testimony of the manufacturer that this stretch on the ruler's edge is $8\frac{1}{2}$ inches long.

But now let us imagine a detached and very reasonable observer of the human scene, brought up on Locke's principle that one must never believe any proposition more firmly than the evidence warrants.[1] Would he not think that our ordinary attitude to testimony is absurdly credulous? Of course, no one believes everything that he is told, nor everything that he reads; still less does he always believe it with complete conviction. But in nine cases out of ten we do give at least some credence to what we are told or what we read. There is of course the tenth case. The answer to some very important question, practical or theoretical, may depend on the correctness of so-and-so's testimony. Then we shall be more cautious. Or the event which he describes to us may be very improbable in the light of all the other relevant evidence which we have, for example, if he tells us that a Flying Saucer landed in the University Parks half an hour ago. Or perhaps it may be very much in the testifier's own interest that we should believe him; for if we do, we shall give him the money for which he asks. Or again, we may have found on many previous occasions that he himself or others like him (beggars for example) made statements which turned out later to be false. Even so, we are

[1] Locke's 'ethics of belief' will be discussed in Lecture 6.

usually prepared to give some weight to the testimony which is offered to us, and it only happens very seldom that we just reject it 'out of hand'. Even habitual liars and romancers tell the truth sometimes. Improbable events do happen. Even when it is to the speaker's own interest that his statement should be true, it does sometimes turn out to be true all the same.

The principle which we follow in the great majority of cases seems to be something like this: What there is said to be (or to have been) there is (or was) more often than not. And that is why our disinterested Lockean observer might think us absurdly credulous. I do not think we extend this principle to the future ('What there is said to be going to be, there will be, more often than not'). We are not quite as credulous as that. We all know how unreliable even our own first-hand predictions can be. But even though we limit our principle to testimony about the present and the past, what justification can we have for accepting it? Must we not admit that our ordinary attitude to testimony is indeed unreasonably credulous?

But suppose we adopted the incredulous or non-credulous attitude which our disinterested Lockean observer would presumably recommend. Let us try to imagine a society in which no one would ever accept another person's testimony about anything, until he had completely satisfied himself about the *bona fides* of that person, his powers of accurate observation and capacity for recalling accurately what he had observed. Such a society would hardly be a society at all. It would be something like the State of Nature described by Hobbes, in which the life of every man is solitary, poor, nasty, brutish and short. What our Lockean observer calls credulity is a necessary condition for social co-operation. What he calls credulity is not only in the long-term interest of each of us. It has a moral aspect too. If some people make a virtue of accepting testimony so readily, they are not wholly mistaken. Am I treating my neighbour as an end in himself, in the way I wish him to treat me, if I very carefully examine his credentials before believing anything he says to me? Surely every person, just because he is a person, has at least a *prima facie* claim to be believed when he makes a statement? This claim is not of course indefeasible. But it might well be argued that we have a duty to trust him unless or until we find pretty convincing reasons for mistrust, and even to give him 'the benefit of the doubt' if we have some reasons for mistrusting him, though not conclusive ones.

A CONFLICT BETWEEN CHARITY AND THE 'ETHICS OF BELIEF'

It is true that there may be something like a conflict of duties here, or at any rate a conflict between two kinds of precepts, those of what is called 'The Ethics of Belief' and precepts of the moral kind, especially the precepts of charity. A charitable person might feel bound to give his neighbours 'the benefit of the doubt' long after Locke's reasonable man had decided that their statements were not worthy of even the lowest degree of belief. Other conflicts within the sphere of charity itself may also arise. For if I believe *A*'s story about *B*'s behaviour yesterday (on the ground that *A* is a person as I am, and must be treated so) I may find that I am being uncharitable to *B* by believing too easily what *A* tells me about him.[1]

Perhaps some religious moralists may think that these conflicts are illusory. Does charity really require that one should shut one's eyes to the facts or the empirically-supported probabilities? If it is an 'unconditional pro-attitude' towards other people, the knowledge or reasonable belief that your neighbour's statements are false will do nothing to weaken it—not even if you think that he is trying his best to deceive you or mislead you. 'He is rather a liar, of course, and I can't believe a word of it, but he is a good fellow all the same.' If you are a charitable person, you are supposed to have a pro-attitude towards him as he is, faults and all ('What he is' of course includes his capacities for becoming better). Surely it is at least logically possible to be at once charitable and clear sighted about the defects, intellectual or moral, of one's neighbours?

This combination of qualities is indeed logically possible, and is even occasionally achieved in some very admirable persons. It may well be true that the conflicts we have mentioned arise

[1] The Christian virtue of humility poses similar problems (concerning a person's beliefs about himself) and perhaps they are more difficult ones.

only for those who are trying to be charitable without yet being so, or are trying to be less uncharitable than they have hitherto been. But unfortunately this is the position in which many of us are most of the time; and then, for us, there can quite well be a conflict between the precepts of charity and the precepts of the Ethics of Belief.

As has been pointed out already, the study of belief is one of the regions where epistemology and moral philosophy overlap. But epistemological questions are our main concern at present.

'ACCEPT WHAT YOU ARE TOLD, UNLESS YOU SEE REASON TO DOUBT IT'

Whatever degree of charity we have, be it great or little, our ordinary practice is to accept what we are told unless or until we see reason to doubt it. We do seem to follow the principle 'What there is said to be (or have been) there is (or was) more often than not'. There are of course certain special occasions when the principle is temporarily switched off as it were, or put into cold storage for a while. When someone says 'I am now going to tell you a story' he is warning us that what he is about to say is not to be taken as testimony. The principle 'What there is said to have been there was, more often than not' is to be ignored for the time being. A similar switching-off occurs when we begin to read a book which we have borrowed from the section marked 'Novels' in the library. The sentences uttered by characters in a play are not to be taken as testimony either, though many of them have the form of statements about empirical matters of fact, for instance, 'The wind bites shrewdly, it is very cold'. We are not to take this as a weather-report. But the important point to notice about these occasions is that they are special and exceptional ones. Special conventions and devices have to be used to convey to us that for the time being the principle we ordinarily follow is not to be applied. And that principle *is* something like 'What there is said to be, or to have have been, there is, or was, more often than not'.

To follow this principle may be socially expedient or even socially indispensable. It may be charitable too. But considered in a cool hour, in the way our detached Lockean observer would consider it, it is a very curious principle indeed. It is not even easy to decide what kind of a principle it is. We are at first inclined to suppose that it is itself a proposition which we believe, something which is itself either true or false. In that case, we cannot dispense ourselves from the task of asking what grounds we have for claiming that it is true, or at any rate more probable than not. Certainly it is neither self-evident nor demonstrable. It looks like an inductive generalisation. If that is what it is, no one of us is entitled to believe it unless he himself, by his own personal observation, has been able to verify at least some of the testimony which he has received from others.

Such first-hand verification is in a way a wasteful procedure. No one would wish to verify all the statements he hears or reads, even if he could. The whole point of testimony is that it is a substitute for first-hand experience, or an extension of first-hand experience, whereby each of us can make use of the experiences which other persons have had. When a piece of testimony is verified by our own first-hand experience, we no longer need it. I want you to tell me what happened on the other side of the hill because I was not able to go there and see for myself. I want Tacitus to tell me what happened in the reign of the Emperor Claudius because I was not alive at the time. The testimony which I cannot verify for myself is the testimony which I need to have. I might as well not have had it, if I can find out for myself that what you tell me is true. On the other hand, unless I can find out for myself that at least some of the things I am told are true, the testimony I receive is equally useless to me, because I have no ground for believing that any of them are true.

The reasonable plan might seem to be that each person should test for himself a not very large part (one tenth perhaps?) of all testimony he receives, thereby rendering that part useless as testimony; and then he would be able to estimate what degree of confidence, great or little, he is entitled to have concerning the remaining nine-tenths. He would sacrifice a little of it in order to be able to use the rest to supplement and extend his own very limited first-hand experience. At least, this would seem to be the reasonable plan if the principle we are discussing ('What there is said to be (or to have been) there is (or was) more often than not') is indeed an inductive generalization.

Now certainly each of us is sometimes able to 'check' the testimony which he receives from others. In a strange town I have often had to ask a passer-by where the nearest post office is, or where the railway station is; and usually (though by no means always) I have found for myself that the information given to me was correct.

But when we consider the enormous number and variety of the beliefs which each of us holds on the evidence of testimony alone, it is obvious that the amount of first-hand confirmation he has is tiny indeed in comparison. It is nothing like large enough to justify the generalisation 'what there is said to be, or have been, there is, or was, more often than not'. In a very simple and primitive society, where no one can read or write or listen to the radio, the situation would be easier. Then, if someone tells me that there was a wolf sitting beside the village well at midnight, I can go to the well myself this morning and see what look like the footmarks of a wolf in the mud beside it. But in a civilised and highly-educated community it is another matter. We have only to consider the vast mass of historical propositions which every educated person believes. I can personally remember a few of the events that happened in the reign of King Edward VII. But I certainly cannot remember anything that happened in the reign of King Edward the Confessor, to say nothing of the reign of Hadrian or Septimius Severus. Yet I do very firmly believe that both these Emperors visited Britain, and that Septimius Severus died at York. I hold this belief on nothing but the evidence of testimony. The best I have managed to do by way of 'checking' the testimony for myself is to read the Latin text of what I am told is a copy of the *Historia Augusta*; and this hardly amounts to first-hand verification.

Suppose however that we re-stated our principle in a much weaker form: 'What there is said to be (or to have been) there is (or was) in at least one case out of every five.' This seems a very modest principle, even a rather sceptical one. But if it is supposed to be an inductive generalisation, the evidence which any one person has for believing it would still be quite insufficient. In a civilized and literate society, the amount of testimony which each of us has been able to test and verify for himself is far too small to justify any inductive estimate of the 'overall' reliability of testimony in general: too small, that is, in relation to the enormous number and variety of all the beliefs he has, which are supported partly or wholly by testimony spoken or written, or conveyed in other ways (for example, by means of maps). Whatever estimate any one person tried to make of its reliability, whether favourable or unfavourable, he would not have nearly enough first-hand evidence to justify it. Indeed, the habit of accepting testimony is so deep-rooted in all of us that we fail to realize how very limited the range of each person's first-hand observation and memory is.

'FIRST-HAND' AND 'SECOND-HAND'

Before we consider whether there is some other way of interpreting our principle, it may be worth while to say something about the contrast between 'first-hand' and 'second-hand'. We contrast the first-hand knowledge which each of us acquires by means of his own observation, introspection and memory with the second-hand knowledge (or beliefs) which he acquires by means of testimony. Yet it is important to notice that there is, after all, something first-hand about the acceptance of testimony itself. Testimony has to be conveyed to us by means of perceptible events or entities—audible or visible words, or sometimes visible signs or gestures; or occasionally by tangible means, as when we converse with a deaf and blind person by 'tapping out' words on his hand. And the person who accepts the testimony must perceive these perceptible events or entities for himself. Unless he has this first hand experience, he cannot accept the testimony, nor even reject it.

It is true of course that I may believe what John said although I did not hear him say it. But then some third person, Bill for instance, must tell me that John said so-and-so; and I must still hear for myself what Bill tells me, or see it for myself if he tells me in writing. How ever many hands or mouths John's story has passed through before it reaches me, it will not reach me at all unless there is some first hand perceptual experience of mine at the end.

The acceptance of testimony is first hand in another way as well. Testimony has to be understood by the person who receives it, and he must understand it for himself. No one else can understand it for him. If it is offered to him in a foreign language which he does not know, or in a technical terminology which he cannot follow, he may ask someone else to translate it or interpret it for him. But he still has to understand for himself what the translator or interpreter tells him.

Sometimes this second condition is fulfilled, but the first—the perceptual one—is not. This happens quite frequently in dreams. In our dream we may have copious and complicated mental imagery, either visual or auditory; quite a complicated story may be presented to our minds, and often we understand it perfectly. We do not just dream that we understand it. Dreaming that one understands what one does not in fact understand can also happen. But I wish to consider the case where we really do understand the words which present themselves to us in our dream—and surely it is not at all an uncommon case. Very often these words are combined into sentences which preport to describe some empirical matter of fact. Sometimes it is as if we just heard them without even seeming to see anyone who utters them.

These sentences, however, do not count as testimony, not even if they turn out subsequently to be true, as they may if the dream is a telepathic of clairvoyant one. They do not count as testimony, because the words composing them are not physical sounds or physical marks which we perceived. The first hand experience we had, when they presented themselves to us, was not an experience of perceiving, but of imaging, though we were not aware of this at the time.

Much the same could be said of waking hallucinations. Suppose you are a motorist trying to find your way to a village in a remote part of Norfolk. You have a visual hallucination of a signpost with the words 'Great Snoring 2½ miles' written on it. What is written on signposts is a form of testimony. But they have to be real physical signposts with real physical letters written on them. Hallucinatory words on an hallucinatory signpost do not count as testimony, though here again it is conceivable that these hallucinatory words do describe what is actually the case. Perhaps you do turn down the little lane which appears to be indicated by the signpost there appears to you to be, and perhaps you do arrive at Great Snoring after 2½ miles. Students of paranormal cognition might then suggest that the visual hallucination was a paranormal experience, the manifestation in consciousness of an unconscious 'extra-sensory perception' of the whereabouts of the village. But whatever we think of this explanation, we can hardly say that you accepted (and acted upon) a piece of testimony, as you would have been doing if the signpost had been a real one, perceived in the normal manner.

The conclusion we must draw is that the testimony received by a particular person can never be more reliable than the first hand experience by means of which he receives it. To be sure, when I am delirious the doctor may tell me that the spoken or written sentences which I claim to hear or to see are not to be taken as testimony, and that I am not to believe them or be at all worried or frightened by them. But then he himself is giving me testimony about the non-testimonious character of these hallucinatory words. Perhaps I believe what he tells me. But I am not entitled to believe it, unless I am first entitled to believe that the sounds he appears to be uttering really are what they appear to be —events in the public and physical world. If I suspect that the words I seem to hear him utter are hallucinatory too, I must also suspect that they are not to be relied on. It comes to this: before I am entitled to believe what someone is saying, I must make sure that it is really being said; and before I am entitled to believe what I read I must make sure that the written words really are there on the page or the signpost or the noticeboard.

Furthermore, one is only entitled to rely on testimony if one understands it correctly. When an English traveller in Italy sees the word 'calda' written on a water-tap he may think it means 'cold' and act accordingly, with unfortunate results. There is nothing wrong with his perceptual capacities. He is not having a visual hallucination or illusion, and he is not dreaming. The word 'calda' is really there on the tap just as it appears to be. But he misunderstands the testimony which is offered to him, and is therefore mistaken when he relies on it. Moreover, the understanding which is required may have to be something more than the mere 'dictionary-knowledge' which would have been quite sufficient in this example. One may need to be able to 'interpret' what is said or written. If the caller is told at the door that Mrs So-and-so is not at home, he may misinterpret what is said to him, and believe mistakenly that the lady is not in the house, though he understands the dictionary-meaning of the words perfectly well. The testimony which we accept can never be more reliable than our own capacity for understanding the words (or signs or gestures) by means of which it is conveyed to us.

If we prefer to put it so, our lack of understanding may prevent us from discovering what the testimony conveyed to us actually is, and what we believe will then be something different from what the speaker or writer was telling us. Viewed in this way, our lack of understanding has the same kind of results as an illusion or hallucination might have. If an Italian were to have an hallucination of the word 'fredda' when he looked at the water-tap, the results for him would be much the same as they were for our English traveller, who thought that 'calda' meant cold.

If we accept a proposition *p* on the evidence of testimony, this evidence can never be stronger than our evidence for believing (1) that certain words have in fact been spoken or written (2) that *p* is in fact the proposition which these words convey. And our evidence for these two beliefs has to be first-hand. Each of us must hear or see for himself, and no-one else can do it for him; and each of us must understand for himself if he understands at all. It is true that someone else may have to explain to me what a particular word or sentence means. But I still have to understand this explanation for myself.

No doubt these considerations are perfectly obvious. It is surely undeniable that there is something first hand about the acquisition of any belief whatever, whether it is based on testimony or not. But we tend to forget this, if we lay great emphasis on the concepts of public verifiability and public knowledge. We speak as though there were some formidable entity called 'the public' (or perhaps we call it 'Science' with a capital S). But there is no such entity, and if there were it could not know anything or verify anything. There are only human beings who co-operate with one another. One very important way in which they do it is by giving each other testimony. I tell other persons that I have verified a proposition *p*, and they tell me that they have verified it too. But each of us has to do his verifying for himself at first hand, however important it is for each of us to learn that others have done it.

What has now been pointed out is that there is also something first hand about this 'learning that others have done it', since each of us must hear or see for himself what others say or write, and each must understand for himself what they are telling him.

ANOTHER INTERPRETATION OF THE PRINCIPLE

We may now return to the principle 'What there is said to be (or to have been) there is (or was) more often than not'. Hitherto we have assumed that this principle is itself something which we believe; and if we interpret it in that way, we shall have to suppose that we believe it very firmly, perhaps even with complete conviction. At any rate, each one of us seems to be guided by it all the time. Of course, we do not believe that what there is said to be or to have been, there *always* is or was; still less do we believe this with complete conviction. The qualification 'more often than not' is an essential part of the principle itself. But even though this qualification is put in and borne in mind, it is difficult to see how such a belief could be reasonable. This is because the degree of our belief (if it is indeed belief) would still be far greater than our evidence justifies.

When we consider the vast amount of testimony which each of us accepts, especially if he is a civilized and educated person, we find that each of us is only able to verify a very small part of it by means of his own first-hand observation and memory. Perhaps there might be enough first-hand verification to justify him in suspecting or surmising that what there is said to be or have been there is, or was, more often than not. ('Suspecting' and 'surmising' are traditional names for the lowest possible degree of belief.) But any higher degree of belief than this would surely be too high, and could not be justified by the amount of first-hand confirmation each of us can get for the vast mass of statements, on all manner of subjects, which he hears or reads. Even if someone were to say 'I think, without being at all sure, that what there is said to be (or to have been) there is (or was) more often than not'—expressing a not very confident opinion—he would still be unreasonably credulous. Credulity may be socially expedient, even socially indispensable, and it may be charitable. But it is credulity still.

There is however another way of interpreting the principle we are discussing. Perhaps it is not itself a proposition which we believe, still less a proposition believed with complete conviction. Instead, it may be more like a maxim or a methodological rule. In that case, it is better formulated in the imperative than the indicative mood. We might put it this way: 'Believe what you are told by others unless or until you have reasons for doubting it.' Or we might say 'Conduct your thoughts and your actions as if what there is said to be (or to have been) there is (or was) more often than not'. If this is what our principle is, we no longer have to ask what evidence there is for believing it, because it is not itself something believed. It does of course concern believing, and could be described as a policy for forming beliefs. But a policy is not itself believable, since it is not itself either true or false. We could perhaps say that we believe 'in' it, in the sense in which some people believe in Classical Education and others believe in taking a cold bath every morning before breakfast. But believing in a policy or procedure is very different from believing that something is the case.

All the same, the adoption of a policy does have to be justified. We cannot ask what evidence there is for it (since it is not something which is either true or false). But we can ask what reasons there are for adopting it; or if it never was consciously adopted, we can ask what reasons there are for retaining it, once we have reflected on it and have noticed what sort of a policy it is. And there are in fact pretty cogent reasons for adopting, or retaining, this particular policy. They are economic reasons (in rather a broad sense of the term) because they are concerned with the intelligent use of scarce resources.

From one point of view, the scarcity from which each of us suffers is a scarcity of first-hand observations, or more generally of first-hand experiences. One of our misfortunes is that no human being is ubiquitous. If I am in Oxford at 10 a.m. this morning, I cannot directly observe what is going on in Newcastle at that time. Indeed, as I sit here looking out of the window, I cannot directly observe what is going on behind the thick screen of thorn-bushes ten yards away. Still less are we 'ubiquitous in time', if such a phrase is allowable. Each of us has some first-hand access to the past by means of his own memories. But the span of time which they cover is very limited. I certainly cannot remember the Norman Conquest, nor even what happened in the year 1890. Moreover, the past which each of us remembers is only his own past, what he himself perceived or felt or did on various past occasions, and what he then came to believe or came to know. He does not even remember the whole of his past, in the sense of being able to recall any part of it he pleases, though it is possible that in some subconscious or unconscious way he 'retains' a good deal more of it than he can now recall. And in the past which he is able to recall, he suffered from the same scarcity of first-hand observations as he does now. He cannot recollect even one occasion when he was able to see through a brick wall, or touch something from a distance of two hundred yards.

But 'scarce' is of course a relative term. After all, each one of us has had a good many first-hand experiences, and goes on having them all the time so long as he is alive and awake. If we call them 'scarce', we must have some good or end in mind, and we are pointing out that no one individual has enough of them to enable him to achieve it. What is this good or end? It is knowledge, which is something we desire for its own sake, and also as a means for achieving other goods which we desire.

To put it in another way, there are many questions which each of us desires to settle or to answer; and no one person has anything like enough first-hand evidence to enable him to settle more than a very few of them. Each of us would like to know what happened before he was born, and what is happening now on the other side of the wall. His own first-hand observations and his own first-hand memories will not enable him to answer these questions. If he cannot *know* the answers to them, he would still like to be able to hold the most reasonable beliefs that he can, on the best evidence he can get. And very often indeed the only evidence he can get is the evidence of testimony. He must either accept what others tell him, for what it may be worth; or else he must remain in a state of suspended judgement, unable to find any answer at all to many of the questions which he desires to answer.

The economic aspect of this situation comes out in another way when we notice that there is an *exchange* of testimony between different individuals. I have some information which you need but do not at present possess, and you have some which I need but do not at present possess. I tell you what I have observed and you have not; and you tell me what you have observed and I have not. This exchange is advantageous to both of us. Though both of us suffer from a deficiency of first-hand knowledge, I can do something to remedy your deficiency and you can do something to remedy mine. But in a way this is something better than an exchange. For I do not lose the information which I give you, as I should if I gave you my hat; and you do not lose the information which you give me in return, as you would if you gave me your umbrella. Both of us gain and neither of us loses.

As has been mentioned already, this exchange of testimony has a moral aspect too. The information you give me will be useless to me, or worse than useless, unless you give it honestly. And if I trust you to give it honestly, you too must be honest in giving your information to me. One way of formulating the policy we are discussing is 'Accept what you are told by others unless or until you have specific reasons for doubting it'; and this is closely related to the moral rule 'Trust your neighbour unless or until you have specific reasons for distrusting him'. Prudence and charity go hand in hand here. Or at least they go hand in hand some of the way, though a seeker after knowledge would probably stop giving his neighbour 'the benefit of the doubt' rather sooner than charity would recommend.

But at present it is the prudential or economic aspect of this exchange of testimony which mainly concerns us. The moral aspect of it is only relevant in so far as the policy we are considering will not in fact succeed, unless there is at least a modicum of honesty and mutual trust among those who practise it. In a community of incorrigible liars or incurable romancers, the exchange of testimony would not help very much to solve the problem which arises from the scarcity of each person's first-hand experiences. And the testimony of incurable theorisers, who cannot report an observed fact without putting their own interpretation on it, would not be much better. Our policy will work best in a community of honest and hard-headed empiricists who have a respect for facts and for one another. It must also be assumed, I think, that the majority of the persons from whom one receives testimony are sane or in their right minds, and are usually capable of distinguishing between hallucinations and normal perceptions. Finally, most testimony (though not all) is given 'after the event', perhaps a long time after. The recipient is then at the mercy of any defects there may be, whether of omission or commission,[1] in the memory of the testifier. So each of us has to assume that the memories of most other persons are not very defective in either of these ways.

We have been discussing a policy for forming beliefs. It is designed to remedy a certain sort of scarcity from which each individual person suffers, a scarcity of first-hand experiences. This policy may be formulated in two ways: (1) 'Accept what you are told, unless or until you have specific reasons for doubting it' (2) 'Conduct your thoughts and actions as if it were true that what there is said to be (or to have been), there is (or was) more often than not'.

Whichever formulation we prefer, we now see that a number of conditions must be fulfilled if this policy is to succeed. It is logically possible that none of them ever are fulfilled, and it is pretty certain that not all of them are always fulfilled in fact. There are incorrigible liars, romancers and theorisers. There are careless observations, defective memories, and hallucinations or dreams mistaken for normal perceptions.

It may well seem that if 'safety first' is one's motto, the wisest course would be not to accept testimony at all. The policy of accepting it, unless or until one has specific reasons for doubting it, is likely to yield a pretty mixed bag of beliefs, in which there will be many incorrect ones. It is likely that there will also be a good many others which will be inaccurate, correct in some respects but incorrect in others. You tell me that an airship is coming over. I believe you, and rush out into the garden to enjoy this unusual spectacle. There is indeed a lighter-than-air aircraft in the sky, but it is only a kite-balloon which has come adrift. Moreover there may in fact be specific reasons for doubting someone's testimony (for example, he has very poor eyesight, or he has a habit of telling others what they want to hear, whether it is true or not). But we may not know that he has these defects, nor have any evidence for believing that he has them. The policy we are considering does not say 'Accept what others say unless

[1] Cf. Lecture 4, pp. 106–7 above.

or until there are specific reasons for doubting it', and would be useless to us if it did. Instead, it says 'unless or until *you have* specific reasons for doubting' or 'unless you and them'. We may very well fail to find them, although they do exist.

But 'safety first' is not a good motto, however tempting it may be to some philosophers. The end we seek to achieve is to acquire as many correct beliefs as possible on as many subjects as possible. No one of us is likely to achieve this end if he resolves to reject the evidence of testimony, and contents himself with what he can know, or have reason to believe, on the evidence of his own first-hand experience alone. It cannot be denied that if someone follows the policy of accepting the testimony of others unless or until he has specific reason for doubting it, the results will not be all that he might wish. Some of the beliefs which he will thereby acquire will be totally incorrect, and others partly incorrect. In this sense, the policy is certainly a risky one. If we prefer the other formulation 'Conduct your thoughts and actions as if it were true that what there is said to be or to have been, there is or was, more often than not' we still have to admit that the policy is a risky one, and it would still be risky if we substituted 'in one case out of every three' for 'more often than not'.

But it is reasonable to take this risk, and unreasonable not to take it. If we refuse to take it, we have no prospect of getting answers, not even the most tentative ones, for many of the questions which interest us (for example 'What is the population of London?' 'Did London exist 300 years ago?' 'If it did, what was its population then?').

It must be admitted, of course, that many of these questions could not even be asked unless some testimony had already been accepted. The stay-at-home inhabitant of Little Puddlecombe has only the evidence of testimony for believing that there is such a place as London at all. And if he is a safety-first philosopher, whose policy it is to reject the evidence of testimony, or to ignore it on the ground that it is so unreliable, he does not even know, or has no ground for thinking, that there *is* the question 'what is the population of London?' and therefore cannot even wish to know the answer to it. Similarly, I could not even wish to know more about the character of the Emperor Severus Alexander unless I already believed that there was such a person; and for this belief I have only the evidence of written testimony. If I were to reject that evidence, I could not even ask what kind of a person he was.

So if anyone refused to follow the policy we are recommending, and preferred the contrary policy of rejecting all testimony unless and until he had conclusive reasons for accepting it, this would certainly save him a great deal of trouble. There would be very many questions about which he would not have to worry himself, because he would not be able to consider them at all. On the other hand, we might be inclined to think that he was rather less than human. He cannot value knowledge very highly, if he does not even attempt to get it when there is a risk that his attempt will fail. He rejects the policy we are recommending because he does not really care very much for the end which it is designed to achieve. He prefers to cultivate his own garden, and a very, very small garden it will be.

In our cognitive enterprises, as in some of our practical ones, 'nothing venture, nothing have' is a better motto than 'safety first'. But it is only better as a means. If you do not want to have, there is no reason why you should venture.

LECTURE 6

DEGREES OF ASSENT: NEWMAN'S CRITICISMS OF LOCKE

In Book IV of the *Essay concerning 'Human Understanding'* Locke maintains that there are degrees of assent. In Section 2 of Book IV, Ch. 15 ('*Of Probability*') he says that as there are degrees of probability 'from the very neighbourhood of certainty and demonstration quite down to improbability and unlikeliness, even to the confines of impossibility', so also there are 'degrees of assent from full confidence and assurance, quite down to conjecture, doubt and distrust'. This epistemological doctrine that assent has degrees is the presupposition of his 'Ethics of Belief', which he formulates later in the same chapter. 'The mind, if it will proceed rationally, ought to examine all the grounds of probability, and see how they make more or less for or against any proposition, before it assents to or dissents from it; and, upon a due balancing of the whole, reject or receive it, with a more or less firm assent, proportionably to the preponderancy of the greater grounds of probability on one side or the other.' (Book IV, ch. 15, Section 5.)

At the beginning of Ch. 16 he puts it thus: 'The grounds of probability . . . as they are the foundation on which our assent is built, so are they also the measure whereby its several degrees are or ought to be regulated.' He returns to the subject in the celebrated chapter *Of Enthusiasm*, where the disposition to regulate the degree of our assent in proportion to the strength of the evidence is connected with the love of truth. One unerring mark of a love of truth for truth's sake, he says, is 'the not entertaining any proposition with a greater assurance than the proofs it is built upon will warrant'. (Book IV, Ch. 19, Section 1.)

The 'grounds of probability' which 'make for or against a proposition' are what we should now call the evidence for or against that proposition. And if we mean by 'the evidence for a proposition' what we often do mean—namely, the evidence which there is for it on the whole when due account has been taken of adverse evidence, if any[1]—we can simplify Locke's rather complicated formulation of his 'Ethics of Belief' as follows: the degree of our assent to a proposition ought to be proportioned to the strength of the evidence for that proposition.

It would follow that there are two questions, and not just one, which we have to ask when we are trying to assess the reasonableness of someone's belief that *p*. First, is he justified in assenting to the proposition *p* at all? Secondly, if he is, is he also justified in assenting to it to the degree that he does? Both questions would have to be settled by considering the evidence for the proposition assented to, making allowance for the evidence against it, if any. We should notice, however, that the evidence we must consider is the evidence which that particular believer himself has for the proposition at the time when his assent is given. This need not necessarily be the same as the evidence which we have. He may happen to be ignorant of relevant facts which are perfectly familiar to ourselves, or familiar with relevant facts of which we happen to be ignorant. I think that Locke himself is making this point when he says—too briefly—in Book IV, Ch. 16, Section 1 'whatever grounds of probability there may be, they yet operate no further on the mind which searches after truth and endeavours to judge right than they appear'.[2]

Both these doctrines of Locke—both the doctrine that assent has degrees, and the 'Ethics of Belief' which he formulates in terms of it—may strike us as just obvious common sense. Do we not have familiar expressions in ordinary language for indicating degrees of assent, for example, 'suspecting that', 'thinking that' (the ordinary phrase for expressing an opinion), 'being almost sure but not quite', 'being absolutely sure'? Another and equally familiar way of indicating the degree of our assent to a proposition is by referring to the degree of surprise we should feel if the proposition turned out to be false. I should be just a little surprised if John did not come to see me this afternoon; or I should be a

[1] This is what Locke himself means by 'the proofs it is built upon' in the passage quoted from Ch. 19, Section 1. Nowadays we should reserve the word 'proofs' for cases where the evidence is conclusive.

[2] The word 'appear' here has its 'present to the mind' sense, not its 'seeming' sense. Cf. 'the moon has just appeared above the horizon', as contrasted with 'it appears larger at the horizon than it does at the zenith'.

good deal surprised if he did not, or I should be greatly surprised if he did not; or I should be astonished if he did not, and should even be willing to eat my hat. Alternatively, we can say that we should not be surprised if the proposition turned out to be true; and perhaps the neatest way of expressing the lowest degree of assent (traditionally called 'suspecting') is to say we should not be altogether surprised if the proposition assented to were true. When one hears the loud alarm-note of the blackbirds in the twilight, as they flit round a large hawthorn bush, one may say 'I should not be altogether surprised if there were an owl roosting in the bush'.

Moreover, do we not all agree with Locke that a lower degree of assent may be justified when a higher degree would not be? Surely we all admit that one may be 'entitled', as we say, to think that *p* (to hold the opinion that *p*) when we are not entitled to be almost sure of it, and still less to be absolutely sure of it? Sometimes too, though only rarely, we think that a man is entitled to assent to a proposition more firmly than he actually does. If an educated Englishman were to say in 1967 'I suspect that Queen Victoria died a good many years ago', we should not deny that he was entitled to suspect so, but we should point out that he was entitled to assent to the proposition a good deal more firmly than he did. And surely we all think that what 'entitles' a person to assent in this degree or in that, or 'justifies' him in doing so, is just what Locke says it is, namely the strength, greater or less, of the evidence which that person has for the proposition assented to?

Of course, we do in fact often give a firmer or stronger assent to a proposition than we are entitled to give, and occasionally a weaker one. Locke's rule that the degree of our assent ought to be proportional to the strength of the evidence is often broken or disregarded. But it is significant that when we are criticized for breaking it, we defend ourselves by claiming (rightly or wrongly) that the evidence for the proposition we assented to—or at least the evidence we ourselves had—was stronger than our critic said it was. It never occurs to us to challenge the authority of the rule itself. We do not say 'No doubt, the evidence is rather weak, but we are entitled to be absolutely convinced all the same'. Or if we do occasionally say, in a moment of exasperation 'Well, that is what I think, evidence or no evidence', we are willing to admit that we are being consciously unreasonable.

Locke's two doctrines, then—that assent has degrees, and that the degree of assent ought to be proportional to the strength of the evidence—may easily seem platitudinous. One would be happy to think that they are. For if they are false, our human condition must be both more miserable and more intellectually disreputable than we commonly suppose. Nevertheless, both these doctrines are vigorously challenged by one of the most celebrated writers on our subject, Cardinal Newman, in his *Grammar of Assent*, Ch. VI, 'Assent considered as unconditional'.[1] In this lecture, I shall discuss Newman's criticisms of Locke; but it will also be necessary to consider the positive doctrine which they are intended to support. This is that assent is unconditional, whereas inference is conditional. It is strange that this interesting but rather difficult chapter has received so little attention from epistemologists, and still less (so far as I know) from expositors of Locke. The issues which it raises are of the greatest importance if we wish to understand what belief is, and what part it plays in human life. I shall try to show that Locke is more nearly right than Newman is on most of the points about which they differ.

Newman begins one of his criticisms of Locke with these words: 'I have so high a respect both for the character and the ability of Locke, for his manly simplicity and outspoken candour, and there is so much in his remarks upon reasoning and proof in which I fully concur, that I feel no pleasure in considering him in the light of an opponent to views, which I myself have ever cherished as true with an obstinate devotion'.[2]

Let us follow this excellent example; for no-one, and certainly no Oxford man, should criticize Newman without praising him. Newman is surely one of the masters of introspective description. No writer on belief has a keener eye for the phenomenological facts than he has, or shows more skill and delicacy of touch in disentangling them from one another; and his argument is illustrated throughout by concrete examples taken straight from life.

[1] *The Grammar of Assent* was first published in 1870. I shall quote from Longmans Edition of 1947. (There is an earlier edition, also published by Longmans, dated 1930. In this the page numbers are different and there is no index.)

[2] *Grammar of Assent* (Longmans, 1947), p. 122.

Moreover, Newman is one of the masters of English prose. The power, and the charm, of his style are so compelling that the reader soon becomes their willing captive; and it seems ungrateful, almost ungracious, to question what has been so felicitously said.

'BORDERING NEAR UPON CERTAINTY'

It must be admitted too that in the first of his criticisms (*Grammar of Assent*, pp. 121-124) Newman has detected an important inconsistency in Locke. In *Essay*, Book IV, Ch. 15, Section 2, Locke says that some propositions 'border so near upon certainty that we make no doubt at all about them, but assent to them as firmly and act according to that assent as resolutely as if they were infallibly demonstrated'. But if such propositions only border near upon certainty, without actually reaching it, how can we be justified (on Locke's own principles) in making no doubt at all about them, and assenting to them as firmly as if they were infallibly demonstrated? Surely we should be violating the precept which Locke himself has laid down? We are here 'entertaining a proposition with a greater assurance than the proofs it is built upon will warrant' and thereby showing ourselves not to be lovers of truth for truth's sake. We are completely sure, when according to Locke's own Ethics of Belief we are only entitled to be very nearly sure. It is true that Locke does not say we are entitled to make no doubt at all about these propositions. He only says that we do not in fact make any doubt about them. But still, he seems to see nothing wrong with this, and to have forgotten all about the cautious precepts of his own Ethics of Belief—precepts which Newman himself emphatically rejects.

Can anything be said in Locke's defence? Something perhaps, but not much. He is surely justified in maintaining that we may (and often should) 'act as resolutely as if the propositions were infallibly demonstrated'. There is nothing in this which is incompatible with a love of truth for truth's sake. Indeed, if we did not act so, we might well be neglecting our love for our neighbour, and also perhaps neglecting our own long-term interest. But if the propositions he has in mind do only border near upon certainty, without actually reaching it, we surely have no right to assent to them as firmly as if they were infallibly demonstrated. Perhaps, however, he was not wholly clear about the difference between propositions which are logically certified (e.g. the conclusion of a mathematical proof) and propositions which are empirically certified. The phrase 'as if they were infallibly demonstrated' suggests that he was not.

'THE TESTIMONY OF PSYCHOLOGICAL FACTS'

As we have seen, Locke maintains two distinct, though connected, theses. One is concerned with what assent is, the other with what it ought to be. At first sight Newman seems not to distinguish clearly between the two. In some of the most brilliantly written pages of the *Grammar of Assent* (pp. 124-130) he offers a number of arguments to show that men do not in fact assent in the way Locke says they ought to. For example, they continue to assent to a proposition, when they have forgotten the evidence (p. 126). Assent, once given, may cease 'while the reasons for it and the inferential act which is the recognition of those reasons, are still present and in force. Our reasons may seem to us as strong as ever, yet they do not secure our assent. Our beliefs, founded on them, were and are not; we cannot perhaps tell when they went' (p. 126). Sometimes, in spite of strong and convincing arguments, assent is never given (p. 127). Sometimes, again, 'good arguments, and really good as far as they go, and confessed by us to be good, nevertheless are not strong enough to incline our minds ever so little to the conclusion at which they point'. Here we do not 'assent a little in proportion to those arguments', which in Locke's view would be the reasonable thing to do. 'On the contrary, we throw the full *onus probandi* on the side of the conclusion, and we refuse to assent to it at all until we can assent to it altogether' (p. 127). Again, what Newman calls moral motives may 'hinder assent to conclusions which are logically unimpeachable'. We all know that 'a man convinced against his will is of the same opinion still' (p. 128). And finally, even in mathematics, 'argument is not always able to command our assent, even though it be demonstrative'—at any rate when the demonstration is long and intricate (p. 128).

We cannot dispute the facts which Newman here points out, and we cannot withhold our admiration for the psychological acumen he shows in describing them. But are they relevant? Can an 'ought' proposition be refuted by factual evidence? Can a doctrine about the way in which it would be reasonable to assent be disproved by pointing out that very often we do not in fact assent in that way? Surely such arguments only show that we often assent, or withhold assent, unreasonably: a conclusion which Locke never intended to dispute and one which he himself emphasises.

But this objection is not altogether fair to Newman. The arguments I have quoted must be taken in their context. What Newman wishes to show is that assent does not admit of degrees at all. And if it does not, it is absurd to lay down rules about the degree which it ought to have. 'Ought' implies 'can'. Such rules would be null and void, because it would not be in our power to follow them, if assent, by its very nature, must be a matter of all or nothing, as Newman holds that it is. This, I take it, is the point of an eloquent passage on p. 124 'He [Locke] takes a view of the human mind, in relation to inference and assent, which to me seems theoretical and unreal . . . he consults his own ideal of how the mind ought to act, instead of interrogating human nature, as an existing thing, as it is found in the world. Instead of going by the testimony of psychological facts,[1] and thereby determining our constitutive faculties and our proper condition, and being content with the mind as God has made it, he would form men as he thinks they ought to be formed, into something better and higher, and calls them irrational and indefensible if (so to speak) they take to the water, instead of remaining under the narrow wings of his own arbitrary theory' (p. 124).

The testimony of psychological facts is, after all, relevant if it shows that Locke's view about the way we ought to assent would only make sense if assent were something quite different from what it actually is. As Newman puts it in the next paragraph 'The first question which this theory leads me to consider is whether there is such an act of the mind as assent at all' (p. 124). 'If there

[1] Cf. also p. 120, 'Abstract argument is always dangerous, . . . I prefer to go by facts.' Newman is after all an Empiricist philosopher, and in this chapter he claims to be more of an Empiricist than Locke is.

is', he goes on 'it is plain it ought to show itself unequivocally as such, as distinct from other acts.' But on Locke's view this is just what it could not do. For if Locke were right, assent would be nothing but inference. 'When I assent, I am supposed, it seems, to do precisely what I do when I infer, or rather not quite so much, but something which is included in inferring; for while the disposition of my mind towards a given proposition is identical in assent and in inference, I merely drop the thought of the premisses when I assent, though not of their influence on the proposition inferred. This, then, and no more after all, is what nature prescribes; and this, and no more than this, is the conscientious use of our faculties, so to assent forsooth as to do nothing but infer' (pp. 124-5). The arguments on pp. 125-9 which I quoted above are intended to show that assent is distinct from inference, on the ground that one can be absent when the other is present, and that the two do not vary concomitantly.

On p. 131 Newman quotes the following passage from Gambier, a writer, he says, 'who claims our respect from the tone and drift of his work'. 'Moral evidence may produce a variety of degrees of assent, from suspicion to moral certainty. . . . For a few of these degrees, though but for a few, names have been invented. Thus when the evidence on one side preponderates a very little, there is ground for suspicion or conjecture. Presumption, persuasion, belief, conclusion, conviction, moral certainty—doubt, wavering, distrust, disbelief—are words which imply an increase or decrease of this preponderancy.'

Admirable remarks, the reader may think, and a very clear expression of what all sensible men have always taken to be obvious. That is not Newman's view. This passage, he says, illustrates what he himself has been insisting upon 'that in teaching degrees of assent, we tend to destroy assent, as an act of the mind, altogether'. Gambier's 'assents' are only inferences, and 'assent' as Gambier uses the word is 'a name without a meaning, the needless repetition of an inference'.[1] The suspicion, conjecture, persuasion, belief, etc., of which Gambier speaks 'are not "assents" at all; they are simply more or less strong inferences of a proposition'. They are 'not variations of assent to

[1] J. E. Gambier (Rector of Langley, Kent) *An Introduction to the Study of Moral Evidence* (Ed, 3, 1824) p. 6.

E*

an inference, but assents to a variation in inferences. When I assent to a doubtfulness or to a probability, my assent, as such, is as complete as if I assented to a truth; it is not a certain degree of assent.[1] And in like manner, I may be certain of an uncertainty' (p. 132). We must conclude, then, that 'if human nature is to be its own witness, there is no medium between assenting and not assenting. Locke's theory of the duty of assenting more or less according to degrees of evidence is invalidated by the testimony of high and low, young and old, ancient and modern, as continually given in their ordinary sayings and doings' (p. 133).

NEWMAN'S CONCEPTION OF INFERENCE

It can now be seen that the notion of inference plays a central part in Newman's criticism of Locke. If he can show that Locke has confused assent with inference, he thinks the doctrine of degrees of assent will lose any plausibility it has; and with the collapse of that doctrine, Locke's Ethics of Belief will collapse too. This is what Newman has in mind in the passage already quoted, where he says that Locke's view of the human mind in relation to inference and assent is 'theoretical and unreal' and accuses him of not being content with the mind as God has made it (p. 124). It would indeed be 'theoretical and unreal' to lay down the rule that the degree of our assent ought to vary with the strength of the evidence, if assent does not admit of degrees at all.

At first sight it appears strange to his modern readers that Newman should think it relevant to devote so much attention to inference when he is discussing the nature of assent. And if the concept of inference is introduced into the discussion, we should expect that his argument would be quite different from the one he actually uses, when he points out, for instance, that our assents may continue 'without the presence of the inferential acts upon which they were originally elicited' (pp. 125-6). Instead, the modern reader would have expected him to point out that when we make an inference we have to assent to the premiss in order to draw the conclusion, and that this is indeed the crucial difference

[1] 'A certain degree' I think means *gradus quidam*, not *gradus certus*. But in the next sentence 'certain' does mean *certus*.

between inferring ('because *p*, therefore *q*') and merely noticing an implication or entailment ('if *p*, then *q*'). Consequently—we might expect him to argue—the notion of assenting is logically prior to the notion of inferring; inferring itself has to be defined in terms of assenting, and therefore it must be wrong to define assenting in terms of inferring, as Locke, on Newman's interpretation of him, is trying to do.

But Newman is so far from using this argument, that he might rather be accused of paying too little attention to the distinction between inferring and noticing an implication. For he insists over and over again that inference is conditional. Indeed, that is why he thinks it so very important to distinguish between inference and assent. Inference is always conditional; assent, on the contrary is always unconditional, and indeed its unconditionality is the most important thing about it. That is what Newman wishes to maintain. If we fail to distinguish assent from inference, or regard it as a mere reduplication or 'echo' of inference (as Newman thinks Locke did) we shall be led to suppose that assent itself is conditional, and this would be tantamount to abolishing assent altogether (pp. 124-5). But once the confusion between inference and assent is removed, once we see that assent is a 'substantive act'[1] in its own right, we are freed from the obsession which prevents us from considering the actual phenomenological facts; and when we do consider them, we shall find that assent, as it actually occurs in human life, is always unconditional.

But why should anyone be even tempted to confuse assent with inference? Presumably because the two do ordinarily go together. Assent, Newman thinks, is normally 'elicited' by an inference. What sort of an inference can it be? It is true, of course, that before assenting to a proposition *p*, we do as a rule pay some attention to evidence relevant to that proposition; and, if we are reasonable, we refrain from assenting unless or until we find that *p* is more probable than not-*p* in relation to this evidence. But it is rather strange to regard this procedure as an inference. It is more naturally described as a procedure of estimation, or, metaphorically, or 'weighing' (we 'weigh' the evidence for and against the proposition). Certainly this is a rational activity

[1] 'If it be only the echo of an inference, do not treat it as a substantive act' (p. 125).

if anything is. Indeed, it is perhaps the one most characteristic of a reasonable man; and certainly it could be described as 'finding reasons for' assenting, or at least as seeking for them. But it is not very natural to think of it as an activity of reasoning or inference.

Nevertheless, when this process of estimation has been successfully completed, its results could be expressed in the form of an inference. 'Because there are the facts *A*, *B* and *C*, the proposition *p* has a greater probability than not-*p*.' 'Because the barometer has fallen, and the temperature has risen a little, and the wind has backed to south west, and the sky is covered with alto-stratus cloud, it is therefore much more probable than not that it will rain within a few hours.' We do not usually put it like that. We usually say 'my reasons for thinking that *p* are these' and then proceed to state them. But still, we could use this 'because . . . therefore' language—'because there are facts *A*, *B* and *C*, *p* is therefore more probable than not-*p*'—and what we express by saying this could no doubt be described as 'an inferential act'.

It must be inferences of this kind that Newman has in mind. For these are the inferences which may be supposed to precede our assents, and if someone is tempted to confuse assent with inference, inferences of this kind must surely be the source of the temptation. This interpretation of Newman's treatment of 'inference' is supported by what Newman himself says on p. 126. As we have seen already, he argues that inference and assent must be distinct acts, because either may be absent when the other is present, and the two do not vary concomitantly. One of his arguments is this: 'Sometimes assent fails, while the reasons for it and the inferential act *which is the recognition of those reasons* are still present and in force.' (p. 126. My italics.)

If that is what the 'inferential act' is, we can now see what Newman means when he distinguishes so carefully between assent and inference. Let us suppose for the present that our reasons for thinking that *p* are less than conclusive, as they frequently are when *p* is a proposition concerning some concrete matter of fact (this is the situation in which Newman is mainly interested). Newman's point is this; it is one thing to recognize reasons for assenting to *p*, and another thing to assent to it. For instance, it is one thing to recognize that there are reasons for believing that it will rain, and another to believe that it will rain. Of course, the proposition that there are such and such reasons for assenting to *p* can itself be assented to. Newman admits this. In his language, we are then assenting to an inference.[1] But the proposition which is assented to in this act of assent is not *p* itself, but the more complex proposition 'There are such and such reasons for assenting to *p*'. Having recognized that there are reasons for assenting to *p*—moderately strong ones, let us suppose—we may then proceed to assent to *p*. But equally we may not. And if we do, it is a different 'mental act'. The reader may dislike the language of 'mental acts'. But still we must admit that assenting is not the same as recognizing reasons for assent. However closely they go together in a reasonable man, even in him they are still different; and we are not always reasonable.

If this is what Newman means when he insists upon the difference between inference and assent, he is clearly right and is drawing our attention to an important distinction. At any rate, he is right where the reasons for assenting to *p* are less than conclusive and recognized by us to be so. It does not follow that he is also right in thinking that Locke overlooked this distinction, nor that he is right in rejecting the doctrine of degrees of assent. If there is something about inference (in Newman's sense of the word) which admits of degrees, it may still be true that there is something about assent which admits of them too; and it may still be true that in a reasonable man the degree of assent varies with the strength of the reasons he recognizes for assenting.

NEWMAN'S USE OF THE WORD 'CONDITIONAL'

But why should such inferences, or indeed any others, be regarded as conditional? In the terminology to which we are now accustomed, a conditional sentence is of the form 'if . . . then . . .'. But these inferences, and indeed all others, are of the form 'because . . . therefore . . .'. And what is called a probable inference is of this

[1] Cf. the phrase he uses in his criticism of Gambier, quoted on p.. 137–138 above. Gambier's 'suspicion, conjecture, persuasion' etc., Newman says, 'are not variations of assent to an inference, but assents to a variation in inferences' (*Grammar of Assent*, p. 132).

form as much as any other inference. When the conclusion is of the form '*p* has such and such a degree of probability', this does not turn the 'because' into 'if'. Again, we sometimes speak of strong and weak inferences, as Newman himself does. We might say 'because there are the facts *A*, *B* and *C*, the proposition *p* is just appreciably more probable than not-*p*'; for example, you still have a quarter of a gallon in the tank, so there is just a chance that we shall get home. This would presumably be called a 'weak' inference. The weakness, however, does not lie in the inference itself, but only in the conclusion inferred. And this weakness, if we call it such, has no tendency to turn the 'because' into an 'if'. What will turn the 'because' into an 'if' is any uncertainty we may have about the premiss. Perhaps it is not certain that you have as much as a quarter of a gallon in the tank; then I shall make a conditional statement 'If you have as much as a quarter of a gallon, there is just a chance that we shall get home'. But in that case I am no longer making an inference. I am only noticing and pointing out an implication. At the most, I am only pointing out that *q would* be inferrible from *p*, if we could be sure that *p* is true. I am certainly not inferring *q* from *p*. How happy I should be if I could!

Can it be that Newman has confused 'if . . . then' with 'because . . . therefore'? Unfortunately he does show some signs of doing so. There is a curious passage on pp. 137 *ad fin*—138 of the *Grammar of Assent*, where he remarks that though we may 'include a condition in the proposition to which our assent is given' this does not make the assent itself conditional; and obviously it does not. When we assent to 'if *p* then *q*' the proposition assented to is conditional, but it does not follow that the assenting is conditional. But he then proceeds to illustrate his point by two examples. In the first, the proposition assented to is '*If* this man is in a consumption, his days are numbered'. In the second it is '*Of this consumptive patient* the days are numbered'. He then says that the two propositions are equivalent, though the second is not stated in the conditional form. But plainly they are not equivalent. The first is of the form 'if *p* then *q*'. The second is of the form 'because *p* therefore *q*'. The second proposition ('Of this consumptive patient . . .') could only be made equivalent to the first by inserting a saving clause into it: 'Of this consumptive patient, assuming that he *is* indeed a consumptive, the days are numbered.' Nevertheless, in the latter part of the same paragraph Newman himself notices the difference I am pointing out. His example is 'There will be a storm soon, for the mercury falls'; and he says that here 'besides assenting to the connexion of the propositions we may assent also to "The mercury falls" and to "There will be a storm" ' (p. 138). The only objection one can make to this concerns the word 'may'. If we say '*for* the mercury falls' we not only may, but do, assent to both the connected propositions, as well as to the connection between them.

It is interesting that in the same paragraph Newman uses the Latin technical term *inferentia* to mean the connection between the antecedent and the consequent in a conditional statement. 'We may give our assent not only to the *inferentia* in a complex conditional proposition but to each of the simple propositions of which it is made up, besides.' An *inferentia* is what we should now call an implication or an entailment, but not what we should now call an inference. An *inferentia* is of the form 'q follows from p'. And of course we may assent to 'q follows from p' without assenting either to p or to q themselves. That is precisely what we do when we say 'if p then q'.

Can this be the reason why Newman holds that inferences are as such conditional? Can he be using the English word 'inference' as the translation of the Latin *inferentia*? There is indeed a rather old-fashioned English usage in which 'p infers q' does mean 'q follows from p'. But in this usage 'infer' is an impersonal verb, like 'entail' or 'have as a consequence'. Its grammatical subject is a proposition, not a person. An *inferentia*, likewise, is a connection between propositions. But Newman repeatedly speaks of an *act* of inference, or an inferential act. The subject of the verb to 'infer' is in his usage a person, as it is in our ordinary usage today. Much as he wishes to insist on the distinction between inference and assent, he clearly holds that they have at least this much in common, that they are both mental acts. Indeed, if they were not, it would hardly be plausible to suggest that anyone could have confused the one with the other, as Newman thinks Locke did. No one is likely to confuse an *inferentia* with an act of assent. The connection between the antecedent and the consequent in a conditional proposition is not an occurrence at all, still less a mental act. We must conclude, then, that though Newman may possibly have been misled by the Latin word *inferentia* in his account of inference, this cannot be the whole explanation of his paradoxical contention that inference is always conditional.

Could we get some further light on this question if we turn to Newman's own chapter on Inference (*Grammar of Assent*, Ch. VIII)? The first sentence of that chapter repeats what he had already said in Ch. VI[1] 'Inference is the conditional acceptance of a proposition' and a few lines later he says 'I proceed to show how inferential exercises, as such, always must be conditional' (p. 197).[2] How does he show it? So far as I can ascertain, he shows it in just two sentences: 'We reason when we hold this by virtue of that; whether we hold it as evident or as approximating or tending to be evident, in either case we so hold it because of holding something else to be evident or tending to be evident' (p. 197). These statements are unexceptionable. But why should they be supposed to show that inference is as such conditional? According to our modern usage of the term 'conditional' they appear to show the exact opposite. For the word 'hold' must surely mean something like 'assert'. And the assertion of both premiss and conclusion (as opposed to the mere entertaining or assuming of them) is just what distinguishes an inference from a conditional statement. '*Holding* this by virtue of that' is something more than just noticing that this would follow provided that were true. When we 'hold this by virtue of that' we express our inferential act or reasoning process by saying 'Because that is so, this is so' and not just by making the conditional statement 'If that be so, this is so'.

It seems, then, that Newman's own chapter on Inference does not help us much, if we wish to understand why he maintained that inference is conditional. But as we read it, and consider what Newman himself was doing when he wrote it, we are reminded of a distinction which may throw some light on this question. It is the distinction between inferring on the one hand, and thinking about inference on the other. The two activities are

[1] On p. 119 (cf. p. 130).

[2] 'An inferential exercise', I think, is any actualization of our capacity for inferring, and is not limited to cases where we are training ourselves to infer correctly or being trained by others to do so.

quite different. Inferring is something that every human being does, and perhaps some of the higher non-human animals do it too. But it is only logicians and philosophers who think *about* inference, as Newman was doing when he wrote this chapter. Thinking about inference is what is called a second-order activity; not just thinking, but thinking about thinking, or rather about one kind of thinking. Now when we think about inference, there is one very important point about it which is most naturally expressed in a conditional statement: the conclusion can only be drawn if (provided that) we assert the premisses, or on condition that we do assert them. This does not mean, of course, that the conclusion can only be true if the premisses are true, nor yet that the conclusion can only be asserted if the premisses are asserted. But it can only be inferred from these premisses if these premisses are asserted. Newman makes the point himself when he says that in an inference 'we hold this by virtue of that'. But though we do find it natural to make use of this conditional statement when we are thinking about inference, or trying to say what inference is, it does not follow that a person who is himself inferring does or should express his thought in a conditional statement. What he says, if he puts his inference into words, is not 'If *p* then *q*' but 'Because *p*, therefore *q*'.

It is not, I think, incredible that Newman should have failed to distinguish between inferring and thinking about inference. The distinction between first-order statements and second-order statements is easily overlooked even now, and could be still more easily overlooked, even by a man of genius, at a time when the terms 'first-order' and 'second-order' had not yet been invented. But when we do draw the distinction, we see that the second-order conditional statement, which we naturally use in thinking about inference, is only another way of expressing the obvious fact that to acquire knowledge by means of inference we must have some uninferred knowledge already. We could, of course, say, if we pleased, that inference is 'conditioned' by the possession of previous information, using the word 'conditioned' in a pre-Pavlovian sense. But then we must distinguish between 'conditional' and 'conditioned'. From the fact that inference is in this sense 'conditioned' it does not follow that inference is conditional, though just possibly Newman may have thought that it did.

But though Newman may perhaps have failed to distinguish between statements expressing inferences and second-order statements about inference, and may also have failed to draw the distinction between 'conditional' and 'conditioned', neither of these suggestions, nor both together, will explain everything that he says about the conditional character of inference. For when he says that inference is conditional, he must mean by 'conditionality' some character which admits of degrees. Otherwise, someone who mixed up inference with assent, as Newman thinks Locke did, would not have been led thereby to hold that assent has degrees, and Newman's whole criticism of Locke's doctrine of degrees of assent would fall to the ground. The whole point of that criticism is to try to convince us that the doctrine of degrees of assent loses all its plausibility as soon as the distinction between inference and assent is clearly drawn. But if we use the word 'conditional' in its ordinary modern sense (the sense in which we speak of conditional sentences or conditional statements) what could possibly be meant by saying that there are degrees of conditionality? Can one conditional sentence be more, or less, conditional than another? 'If he comes I shall slip out by the back door, if you will give me the key now, and if I can find my umbrella.' Is this a more conditional sentence than 'If he comes, I shall slip out by the back door'? It is a more complex conditional sentence, certainly, because there are three 'if' clauses in it instead of one. But what could we mean by saying that it is more conditional? How strange it would be to say 'John has made a very conditional statement, much more conditional than yours!' It is still more strange to say that one inference can be more conditional than another, as Newman is bound to say that it can; for otherwise he could not maintain that Locke's doctrine of degrees of assent results from confusing assent with inference.

THE 'CONDITIONAL' CHARACTER OF INFERENCE

It certainly cannot be denied that when Newman describes inference as conditional he speaks in a way which is bound to puzzle his modern readers; and the more they reflect on this contention of his, and on the importance he obviously attaches to it, the more puzzled they are likely to be. We must try, if we can, to go behind the unfortunate terminology he uses. Perhaps we may be able to do so, if we reflect upon the argument of his chapter as a whole. The aim of *Grammar of Assent*, Ch. VI, is to show that assent itself is *un*conditional. If it can be shown that assent is unconditional, Newman thinks it will also have been shown that there are no degrees of assent; and then Locke's theory of assent, and consequently his 'Ethics of Belief', can be consigned to the oblivion they deserve. Perhaps we shall see the point of this puzzling contention that inference is conditional if we remember that 'conditionality', in Newman's view, is not only a character which inference has, but also a character which assent lacks. Whatever 'conditional' may mean, it must at any rate be equivalent to 'not unconditional'. To put it in another way, we should fix our attention on the *contrast* between the conditional character which he attributes to inference, and the unconditional character which he attributes to assent.

Just where does the contrast lie? It appears to have something to do with doubt or with the presence of mental reservations. Newman's view is that assent, if given at all, has to be given without any doubt or any mental reservations. He is perfectly explicit about this. 'Assent is an adhesion without reserve or doubt to the proposition to which it is given' (p. 130). Again, on p. 139 he speaks of 'the absolute absence of all doubt or misgiving in an act of assent'; and on the very first page of the chapter, using the word 'absolute' in another sense, he has said that 'assent is in its nature absolute and unconditional' (p. 119)—absolute, presumably, because it resembles a decree of an absolute monarch.

To put it vulgarly, his view is that assent always has a 'whole hog' character or a 'neck or nothing' character. You put all your money on the proposition assented to, you commit yourself to it unreservedly, though fortunately (I think we must say fortunately) your assent may fail later or be withdrawn. To use another vulgar metaphor, if you assent you have to 'take the plunge' or 'go off the deep end', because there is no shallow one; you must assent in this all-or-nothing way if you assent at all. This or something like this is what Newman seems to mean by 'unconditional' when he maintains that assent is unconditional.

If this is the correct interpretation of his words, we must all hope that assent is *not* in his sense 'unconditional', or at any rate not always. There may be many cases where such an unconditional assent is perfectly justified, but surely there are many more where it is not. If assent has to have this all-or-nothing character, a reasonable person will often have to choose the alternative 'nothing': that is, he will have to suspend judgement and withhold assent, unless and until conclusive evidence is forthcoming, which perhaps it never will be. But however dismaying his doctrine is, Newman himself certainly does hold that assent, if given at all, his to be given undoubtingly and without any mental reservations.

If this is what the 'unconditional' character of assent amounts to, it is natural to suppose that the 'conditional' character of inference amounts to just the opposite, and that when Newman describes inference as conditional, he means by 'conditional' something like 'attended with doubt' or 'not free from mental reservations'.

That this, or something like this, is what he means emerges fairly clearly from a passage near the beginning of Ch. VI, where he is stating the view of Locke and Locke's followers which he proposes to criticize, and sums it up in these words: 'Thus assent becomes a sort of necessary shadow, following upon inference, which is the substance; and is never without some alloy of doubt because inference in the concrete never reaches more than probability. . . . Assent cannot rise higher than its source: inference in such matters is at best conditional, therefore assent is conditional also' (p. 120).

Here Newman seems to say that if assent did have some alloy of doubt it would *ipso facto* be conditional, and moreover would have acquired its alloy of doubt by being the shadow of inference. Inference, or at least inference in the concrete, is intrinsically dubious in some degree; and so assent, if it were indeed the shadow of inference, would be dubious derivatively. He is still more explicit in the section on Opinion in Ch. IV, where he contrasts opinion with inference: 'We are even obstinate in them [our opinions]—whereas inference is in its nature and by its profession conditional and uncertain' (pp. 45 *fin*-46). It may be noticed that in this statement the qualifying words 'in the concrete' are omitted.

We are justified, I think, in concluding that the character which inference has and assent lacks is something like doubtfulness or dubiety. According to Newman, inference is always in some way doubtful or hesitant, and assent never. This is what he appears to mean by calling inference conditional and assent unconditional. But why should anyone choose to use the word 'conditional' when what he means is 'doubtful' or 'attended with doubt'? This may well puzzle the modern reader. But it would have appeared less puzzling two generations ago, when it was not uncommon for philosophers to maintain that the function of a conditional clause was to express doubt or questioning. Cook Wilson, for instance, thought that a conditional statement states a connection between two questions. Nowadays, however, we usually think that the function of the word 'if', or of the 'if . . . then' form of statement, is to convey an implication or an entailment.

It has been suggested already that 'inference' in Newman's usage (at least when he is contrasting inference with assent) means 'recognizing reasons for thinking that *p*'. Indeed, in one passage he himself speaks of 'the inferential act which is the recognition of those reasons' i.e. reasons for assent (p. 126). If so, the doctrine that inference is always conditional comes to this: when we recognize reasons for thinking that *p*, without as yet assenting to it, we have some degree of doubt about the proposition *p*. However strong our evidence may be, it still leaves room for doubt, at any rate where it is empirical evidence.

Perhaps Newman would even wish to define degrees of probability in terms of degrees of dubitability, and to say that '*p* is more probable than *q* on evidence *E*' means '*p* is less doubtful than *q* on evidence *E*'. At any rate, what impresses him most about probable propositions is their dubitability, and not the guidance which they give us (imperfect but better than nothing) in our expectations and our conduct. I shall suggest later that this somewhat depressing way of looking at probability prevented him from seeing what Locke had in mind in his doctrine of degrees of assent. But Newman does of course try to console himself, and us, by maintaining that when we not only recognize reasons for thinking that *p* but do actually assent to it, all our doubts are flung to the winds.

'CONDITIONALITY', CONFIDENCE AND DOUBT

As we have seen, Newman thinks that if assent can be shown to be unconditional, Locke's doctrine of degrees of assent will collapse at once, and his Ethics of Belief with it. Why is this consequence supposed to follow? What is the connection between 'being conditional' on the one hand, and 'having degrees' on the other? The modern reader is somewhat puzzled by the way in which Newman switches back and forth between these two concepts without any explanation. The title of his chapter is 'Assent considered as unconditional'. On the second page (p. 120) he states the doctrine which he is going to criticize, and it is the doctrine of degrees of assent. But when he actually makes his criticisms, what he criticizes is the doctrine that assent is always conditional, or rather, the doctrine that it is always conditional when the proposition assented to is neither self-evident nor demonstratively proved. There are occasional references to degrees of assent later, notably in the passage where he discusses and rejects the views of Gambier (pp. 131-2). But the main target of his criticisms throughout is the contention that assent 'in concrete matters' is conditional, which Locke had never said it was.

But perhaps we can now see why Newman should think that there is a very close connection between the two statements 'assent admits of degrees' and 'assent in concrete matters is conditional', or even that they are two ways of saying the same thing. It is because 'conditional' in his sense of the term means something like 'attended with doubt'. Doubt does admit of degrees, even though conditionality in our sense of the term does not. If in assenting to a proposition concerning matters of fact we do often have doubts, great or small, about that proposition, and if we always ought to have some unless the reasons for assenting are conclusive and recognized by ourselves to be so, it will follow that assent admits of degrees.

It is true that Locke and his followers usually think of assent as having degrees of confidence, rather than degrees of doubtfulness. Locke's usual word is 'assurance'. For example, in the passage about loving truth for truth's sake which Newman finds so disagreeable, Locke speaks of 'not entertaining a proposition with greater assurance than the proofs it is built upon will warrant'.[1] But elsewhere, in the passage which Newman commends for its inconsistency with this one, the word 'assurance' is used to mean the highest degree of assent.[2] To avoid this ambiguity it is better to use the word 'confidence' in stating Locke's view. (He himself speaks once of 'full assurance and confidence'.[3])

CONFIDENCE AND DOUBT

What is the relation between Locke's degrees of confidence and Newman's degrees of doubt? I now wish to suggest that what Locke thinks of as confidence and Newman as doubt are not two different states of mind, but the same one looked at in different ways and measured, as it were, on different scales. When someone entertains a proposition with just a little confidence ('suspecting' in the terminology of Locke and his followers) we can equally well say that he has a good deal of doubt about it. When he entertains a proposition with a good deal of confidence but less than the maximum (opinion, but not conviction) we can equally well say that he has some doubt about the proposition, though not very much. When he is completely sure, we can equally well say that he entertains the proposition with no doubt at all.

Here, as in his treatment of probability, Newman prefers to look at the dark side of the picture, whereas Locke prefers to look at the bright side. Let us imagine a conversation between them. Locke says, 'I have considerable confidence that it will be a fine day to-morrow' and considers this a satisfactory state of affairs as far as it goes. In the same circumstances, and on the same evidence, Newman says, 'I have some doubt whether it will be a fine day to-morrow', and considers this an unsatisfactory state of affairs, because it does not go far enough. But Locke has to admit that he has some doubt about the proposition, and Newman has to admit that he has less doubt about it than he has about the proposition 'It will rain continuously to-morrow all

[1] *Essay*, Book IV, Ch. 19, section 1.

[2] *Essay*, Book IV, Ch. 16, section 6. 'Our belief thus grounded rises to assurance.' Newman remarks that 'assurance' is here equivalent to 'certitude' (*Grammar of Assent*, p. 122).

[3] *Essay*, Book IV, Ch. 15, section 2.

day, from dawn to dusk'. And as for satisfactoriness or unsatisfactoriness, they do not altogether disagree about this either. At any rate both agree that certainty would be better if they could get it, and both agree that they have got something which does at least take them beyond sheer suspense of judgement.

We may draw two conclusions from this. The first is that if Newman can show that assent is always 'unconditional' (undoubting), he really will have shown that Locke's doctrine of degrees of assent is false. For the degrees Locke is speaking of are degrees of confidence, and these can equally well be described as degrees of doubt. 'Being more confident that . . .' can equally well be described as 'Being less doubtful whether . . .', and 'Being less confident that . . .' as 'Being more doubtful whether'. If Newman can show that whenever we assent, we have to assent with no doubt at all, he will have shown that assent does not admit of degrees in the sense in which Locke thought it did.

The second conclusion which we may draw is more surprising. It is that Newman and Locke are in much closer agreement than Newman thinks. They both agree that there is a common and familiar propositional attitude which does admit of degrees. Locke thinks of it as an attitude of greater or lesser confidence about a proposition and Newman as an attitude of lesser or greater doubt. The difference between them is at least partly one of emphasis. Locke emphasizes the positive—we might almost say the 'life-enhancing'—aspect of this attitude. When he describes it as an attitude of confidence, greater or less, he is pointing out that when we have this attitude to a proposition, we rely upon the proposition to a greater or lesser degree in our subsequent thoughts and actions, and this is why he holds that assent admits of degrees. If I have some confidence that it will be a fine day to-morrow, I can consider various alternative ways of spending to-morrow afternoon, consult maps, get the tank of my car filled up with petrol, spend a little time looking for the field-glasses which I have mislaid somewhere, or a little money buying a new walking-stick if I have lost my old one. These activities and these plans do of course have something tentative and provisional about them. I engage in them 'on the assumption that' to-morrow will be fine, not in the certain knowledge that it will. We might even apply Newman's favourite term 'conditional' to these thinkings and doings which I embark upon. I am well aware, all the time, that to-morrow may not be a fine day after all. I never thought that the weather forecast was infallible, or that the weather-signs I can observe for myself were conslusive. But still, the proposition 'It will be fine to-morrow', though not accepted 'unconditionally', does give me some guidance as to what I should do and what I should think about to-day. I do not just have to wait and see, and fold my hands meantime in a state of inert agnosticism.

But if we prefer to emphasize the 'doubting' aspect of this propositional attitude, as Newman does, we are liable to overlook the important facts which I have just mentioned. We may easily fail to notice that a proposition about which we have some doubt does nevertheless give us some guidance both in thought and in action; that we do nevertheless rely on it in some degree, even though we also have some doubt of it; and moreover, we may fail to notice that this reliance is reasonable, provided it is no greater than the evidence available to us justifies. If we think of this attitude as just a doubting one, we are emphasizing the negative side of it, its shortcomings, so to speak, rather than its advantages, its depressing or devitalizing features rather than its 'life-enhancing' features. It does have these depressing features. It is true that half a loaf is worse than a whole one. If a proposition is of importance to us, whether practically or theoretically, to have some doubt about this proposition is a less desirable state than having no doubt would be—provided that it were reasonable to have no doubt. But it is also true that half a loaf, or even a quarter, is better than nothing.

So far as I can see, Newman fails to notice that propositions about which we have some doubt are nevertheless relied upon in the way I have described, though not of course relied upon absolutely and without reserve. It is this attitude, or rather perhaps the inception of it, which Locke calls 'assent', and it does admit of degrees. Moreover, the rule laid down in his Ethics of Belief does apply here. We ought not to rely, in this sense, upon a proposition 'with greater assurance than the proofs it is built upon will warrant'.[1]

Nevertheless, in Newman's exposition of his own theory of assent there are two points at which he might quite well have

[1] *Essay*, Book IV, Ch. 19, section 1.

admitted the existence and importance of this 'degree-having' attitude to a proposition. He himself holds that what he calls 'inference'—the recognition of evidence, strong or weak, for a proposition *p*—is accompanied by an inclination to assent to *p*, and moreover that this inclination is 'greater or less according as the particular act of inference expresses a stronger or weaker probability' (*Grammar of Assent*, p. 129). He does, of course, insist that we can have such an inclination without actually assenting in his 'unconditional' sense of the word. Nevertheless, he could quite well have admitted that this inclination often results in something else: namely, the taking up of a new attitude to the proposition which we are inclined to assent to, an attitude of relying upon the proposition to some degree, and a disposition to use it, though not without reservations, as a guide to our subsequent thoughts and actions. In the language he himself uses, this attitude could not have been called assent, because it is not in his sense 'unconditional'. But he could quite well have admitted its existence and its importance. In that case, his disagreement with Locke would have been largely a difference of terminology.

Moreover, as we have seen, Newman describes the recognition of reasons for assenting as 'an inferential act' (p. 126). He also says at the beginning of his chapter on Inference that 'Inference is the conditional *acceptance* of a proposition' (p. 197, my italics). Unfortunately, he is more interested in the conditionality than the acceptance. But he might quite well have added that when such acceptance occurs (as it does when we recognize that a proposition *p* is supported in some degree by the evidence we have), it has effects upon our subsequent thoughts and actions which are almost as important as the effects of unconditional acceptance would have been; indeed more important, since we do not so very often have evidence which justifies us in accepting a proposition in this 'unconditional' way, whereas we do quite often have evidence which justifies us in accepting a proposition 'conditionally' (with some degree of doubt or mental reservation, but also with some degree of confidence). And then again his disagreement with Locke would have been, at least partly, a difference of terminology.

The fact remains, however, that Newman did not actually

take either of these opportunities of bringing his own views a little nearer to Locke's. Newman's doctrine, as he himself sees it, is totally opposed to Locke's. Locke maintains that there are degrees of assent, and Newman maintains that there are none.

CONCLUSION

It was suggested earlier that if Newman were right and Locke wrong on the main point at issue between them (does assent admit of degrees?) our human condition would be at once more miserable and more intellectually-disreputable than we commonly suppose.[1] It would be more miserable, because we so often need to be able to assent to propositions on evidence which is far less than conclusive; and therefore we need to be able to assent to them with something far less than total or unreserved self-commitment, if we are to have any guidance for our subsequent thoughts and actions. But Newman tells us that we cannot do it. According to him, the very nature of assent makes it impossible for anyone to assent in this conditional and tentative way. If Newman were right, our situation would also be more intellectually-disreputable than we commonly suppose. In such circumstances, where we have evidence which is less than conclusive, only two alternatives would be open to us: either complete suspense of judgement, or else an assent of the all-or-nothing ('unconditional') sort, which would be unreasonable, because nothing short of conclusive evidence could justify it. We could not be content with the first alternative, which gives us no guidance at all for our subsequent thoughts and actions. We should just have to assent unreasonably, with the clear knowledge, at least sometimes, that our assent *is* unreasonable: for everyone can see, at least sometimes, that the evidence he has for a proposition is less than conclusive, even though it is perfectly good evidence so far as it goes.

But there is a third alternative. We do not always have to choose between an inert agnositicsm—a helpless 'wait and see' attitude—and a total and unreserved self-commitment. When our evidence for a proposition, though not conclusive, is favourable, or favourable on balance when any unfavourable evidence there may be is

[1] P. 133, above.

taken into account, we can assent to that proposition with a limited degree of confidence; and we can then conduct our intellectual and practical activities 'in the light of' the proposition, though not without some degree of doubt or mental reservation. This, surely, is what we find oursleves and our neighbours continually doing. This is what we find when we follow Newman's own plan of 'interrogating human nature, as an existing thing, as it is found in the world . . . and being content with the mind as God has made it'. (*Grammar of Assent*, p. 124.) And on this point, it is surely Newman's view, not Locke's, which must be called 'theoretical and unreal'.

LECTURE 7

HUME'S ANALYSIS OF BELIEF

Hume's analysis of Belief in the *Treatise of Human Nature*[1] is familiar to all students of philosophy, and has been discussed so often that the reader may well think there is nothing more to be said about it. Yet he is, after all, the most celebrated exponent of the traditional Occurrence Analysis of belief and no one has stated it more forcibly than he did. There are other versions of the Occurrence Analysis (possibly better ones) but we must begin with his; and we shall see, I hope, that it is not quite so unplausible as some of his critics suppose.

On the other hand, we can also find in his pages suggestions, at least, of the modern Dispositional Analysis, especially in Sections 9 and 10 of *Treatise*, Book I, Part iii. (It is a mistake to read only Section 7.) The most obvious example is the passage about 'not really believing' in Book I, Part iii, Section 9.[2] We may regard this as a *felix culpa* on his part. It had not struck him, as it strikes us, that these two ways of regarding belief are rather difficult to reconcile with each other, and he himself makes no attempt to reconcile them.

It should also be noticed that in the most 'official' formulation of his theory (Book I, Part iii, Section 7) he says nothing at all about *degrees* of belief. He does not say explicitly, as Newman did later, that assent admits of no degrees. But in this section he writes as if it were degreeless: strangely perhaps, for 'force' and 'liveliness' do admit of degrees. Nevertheless, in his discussion of the Probability of Causes (Book I, Part iii, Section 12) he does admit that there are degrees of belief, and tries to define probability in terms of them. And here, perhaps we have another *felix culpa*.

If we are to be fair to Hume's theory of belief and learn all he has to teach us, there are three preliminary points we must bear in mind. The first is the context (so to speak) of the theory,

[1] My page-references in this lecture are to Selby-Bigge's edition of the *Treatise* (Oxford University Press).

[2] S.B., pp. 113 *ad fin.*-115.

the part which his analysis of belief plays in the whole argument of Part iii of Book I of the *Treatise*. The conclusions he reaches about belief in Sections 7-10 are going to be used later, in his analysis of the Idea of Necessary Connection in Section 14. He finds the problem of Necessary Connection so difficult that he has to begin by 'beating about all the neighbouring fields' in the hope that something useful will turn up.[1] His analysis of belief is the most important part of this preliminary exploration.

Thus we must not be surprised to find that his theory of belief is a somewhat narrow one, applicable to some sorts of belief but not to all. He is thinking most of the time of the sorts of belief which are relevant to his problem about the Idea of Necessary Connection: as when a barking sound, for example, induces the belief that there is a dog in the garden. It is, in fact, the sort of belief which we have when we take a perceived event or situation as a sign of another event or situation which is not at the moment perceived. But this sort of belief—the sort which arises from past experiences of 'Constant Conjunctions' (as when we see a flame and take this as a sign that we shall feel heat if we come nearer), —is not necessarily the *only* sort of belief we ever have, however important it is.

The second point we must bear in mind is this. In his discussion of belief, Hume claims to be asking a question which no philosopher has ever asked before. 'This operation of the mind' he says 'seems hitherto to have been one of the greatest mysteries of philosophy: though no one has as much as suspected that there was any difficulty in explaining it.'[2] Perhaps Hume exaggerates a little. The distinction between Belief and Knowledge has interested philosophers for a very long time, and was indeed first discussed by Plato. But what had chiefly concerned them was the fact that belief is inferior to knowledge, rather than the nature of belief itself.

What is largely new about Hume's discussion is the attention he pays to the phenomenology of belief itself, and not just to the relation between belief and knowledge. And since his problem was a new one, there was naturally no adequate ready-made terminology for discussing it. He points this out himself, and says he will therefore have to formulate his theory in a number of alternative

[1] S.B., p. 78. [2] *Ibid.*, p. 628 (*Appendix*)

ways, and that no formulation he can think of is altogether adequate. We shall be unfair to him (and fail to learn what he is trying to teach us) if we take *one* of his formulations by itself, for example the definition of belief in terms of liveliness,[1] and neglect the other expressions he uses, which are intended to amplify this one and correct any misleading implications it may have. Some of his critics, I think, have made this mistake. He *does* of course say that a belief is 'a lively idea related to or associated with a present impression'; but he uses a number of other words as well, for example 'force', 'solidity', 'firmness', 'steadiness', to describe this peculiar characteristic which he thinks believed ideas have, and other ideas have not.

The third point we must bear in mind is also a terminological one, and this is one which Hume himself did *not* notice. We must not allow ourselves to be misled by his use of the 'idea language'—the terminology of ideas and impressions. It would be too much to say (as some philosophers do) that the idea language should be abolished altogether. But if we use it, we ought to use it much more carefully than Hume himself does. The term 'idea' in Hume can mean either a mental image or a concept (abstract idea) or a proposition (something true or false). It would make no sense to say that a mental image is believed, or disbelieved either. It may of course be used as a symbol (we may think of 'in' or 'with' images, as we may think 'in' or 'with' words) and what is symbolized by it may be believed. But Hume continually says that ideas are the objects of belief, although he also very often uses the term 'idea' in the image sense.

We must allow for this peculiarity in his language; in particular, when he says that believing consists in having a lively idea, we need not jump to the conclusion that by a 'lively idea' he must just mean 'a vivid image'. I think he knew as well as anyone else that we may have vivid images without believing,[2] and that we may believe without having vivid images. He does indeed hold (mistakenly, no doubt) that every concept we have must in the end be cashable by means of images and that if it cannot be so cashed it is not a genuine concept at all. This is the Imagist Theory of

[1] S.B. p. 96.

[2] If he did not, why does he have all this difficulty—admitted, and indeed insisted on, by himself—in explaining to us what this 'manner of conceiving' is?

Concepts which he shares with Berkeley: and even this theory, I think, is not so utterly silly as it is made out to be. (Its defect is not that it is absurd, but that it is too narrow.) But whether true or false, it certainly does not imply that when we have an idea in mind we must be actually imaging, but only that we must be capable of producing appropriate images when needed.

So much for the preliminary points I wanted to mention. To understand Hume's theory of belief, we must remember the context in which he states it, and we must also allow for certain terminological difficulties: partly inevitable ones, arising from the novelty of his problem, and others which he might have avoided if he had used his own idea-language more carefully. Now we are ready to consider his theory, as stated in *Treatise*, Book I, Part iii, Section 7.

HUME'S PROBLEM

Hume's problems in this section may be stated as follows. There are three attitudes we may have towards a proposition. We may believe it; or we may disbelieve it; or we may barely entertain it, without either belief or disbelief. (Entertaining is what he calls 'conceiving the ideas according to the proposition'.[1]) Hume seems to combine the two last—disbelieving and merely entertaining—under the one word 'incredulity'. Plainly they are different, but the difference does not matter for his purpose. What is important for him is the fact that both alike differ from belief. What then *is* the difference between belief on the one hand, and disbelief or merely entertaining on the other: or, as he puts it himself, 'Wherein consists the difference betwixt incredulity and belief?'[2] That is the question which he is trying to answer.

In the first place, it is not a difference in the ideas which are before one's mind. The very same proposition may be disbelieved by someone at one time and believed at another. Again, the very same proposition may be disbelieved by you and believed by me—and merely entertained or considered by a third person without either belief or disbelief. Now suppose I pass from incredulity to belief. What happens? Obviously I do not *add* any new idea to those I was considering before. It is still the very same proposition

[1] S.B., p. 95. [2] *Ibid.*

that I have before my mind. What I believe now is the very same thing that I was incredulous about before.

Hume gives two further reasons for this contention.

(*a*) If belief did consist in adding some new idea to those already before our mind, it would be in our power to believe whatever we pleased. For 'the mind', he says, 'has the command over all its ideas, and can separate, unite, mix, and vary them, as it pleases'.[1] But Hume thinks it obvious that we cannot believe what we please. Belief, on his view, is something which arises in us independently of our choice. Hume gives no examples here. But we can easily think of some. When you look through the window and see rain falling heavily, you cannot help believing that the streets outside are wet. When I see a flame, I cannot help believing that I shall feel heat if I come closer to it. When I hear a barking sound I cannot help believing that there is a dog in the garden.

(*b*) If belief did consist in adding some other idea to those already before the mind, what could this additional idea be? The only possible candidate, Hume thinks, is the idea of existence; but this candidate must be rejected, because there is no idea of existence in the sense in which there is an idea of 'red' or of 'cat'.[2] To put it linguistically, the word 'existence' does not function in at all the same way as words like 'redness' or 'roundness', though grammatically it is an abstract noun as they are. As Hume puts it himself 'The idea of existence is nothing different from the idea of any object'. To conceive of *A*, and to conceive of *A* as existent, are the same thing.[3] 'Any idea we please to form is the idea of a being, and the idea of a being is any idea we please to form.' Hume gives a theological illustration. When I conceive of God, a certain complex idea is before my mind. And when I conceive of him as existent, no new idea has been added to the ideas of omnipotence, omniscience etc. which make up the meaning of the word 'God'. Existence, in more modern language, is not an attribute or characteristic, as omnipotence etc. are. Thus 'When I think of God, when I think of Him as existent, and when I believe Him to be existent, my idea of Him neither increases nor diminishes.'[4]

[1] S.B., pp. 623–4 (*Appendix*).
[2] *Ibid.*, p. 66.
[3] *Ibid.*, p. 94.
[4] *Ibid.*, p. 94.

So far, Hume claims to have shown that believing does not consist in adding some extra idea to those which were before our minds already. When *A* believes a proposition *p* and *B* disbelieves it or just entertains it neutrally, the ideas before their minds are exactly the same, or to put it another way, the state of affairs they conceive of is exactly the same. If it were not, there would be no disagreement between *A* and *B*.

Then what *is* the difference between them—between the belief of the one person, and the 'incredulity' of the other? Hume concludes that the difference can only lie in the manner of conceiving, since what is conceived is the same in both cases.

'RELATIONS OF IDEAS' AND 'MATTERS OF FACT'

Before elaborating this answer, Hume points out (not very clearly) that his problem only arises with regard to propositions concerning matters of fact. It does not arise (he thinks) about *a priori* propositions such as those of Pure Mathematics or Formal Logic (what he calls 'propositions about the relations of ideas') I think his view here is something like this: when a mathematical statement, for instance, is put before us, such as '17 is the square root of 289', the only question which arises is, do we fully understand it or not? (This would apply to mathematical proofs too, which are complex statements of the form '*p* entails *q*'.) If you really do understand the statement '17 is the square root of 289', you *ipso facto* accept it. The contradictory of it ('17 squared does not equal 289') cannot be conceived, because it is self-contradictory. Hume's word for 'self-contradictory' is 'absurd'; it does not make sense to say that 17 squared is not equal to 289. For in mathematics and in the other *a priori* sciences (those which are concerned with 'the relations of ideas' and not with matters of fact) 'true' is equivalent to 'logically necessary', and 'false' to 'self-contradictory'.

With matter of fact propositions, however, it is very different. One of Hume's examples is the proposition 'Caesar died in his bed'.[1] If someone says this to me, I certainly do not assent to what he says. But I do 'clearly understand his meaning' 'and form all the same ideas which he forms'. What he says is false, but it is

[1] S.B., p. 95.

not self-contradictory. In this case the imagination is free to conceive both sides of the question, but with an *a priori* proposition it is not. There is no conceivable alternative to the proposition '17 is the square root of 289'. I think this really amounts to saying that in the *a priori* sciences, such as mathematics, there is no room for belief, as distinct from knowledge. When once you fully understand what is being said, you know either that it is true (i.e. logically necessary) or else that it is absurd (i.e. logically impossible), and there is no room for mere belief at all.

But if this is Hume's view, it needs to be amended a little. In mathematics and other forms of *a priori* thinking there surely *is* room for believing or 'merely believing', as well as for knowledge, because, very often, one does not fully understand the proposition which one is considering; one does not always see all the implications of the relevant definitions, transformation-rules, axioms etc. (Mathematicians themselves speak sometimes of 'conjectures', and they would admit that they sometimes 'have a hunch', i.e. a mild belief, that such and such a proposition is true before they have found the proof.)

But it could be argued, I think, that when someone is said to 'believe' a mathematical or logical proposition (i.e. merely believes it, without knowing it to be true) his belief is not really about the mathematical or logical proposition itself, but about certain words or other symbols. What he is believing is that there is some logically-necessary proposition which these symbols symbolize, without grasping what exactly this proposition is. This is a special case of a very familiar situation, which is vulgarly called 'believing what you do not understand' (or do not fully understand)—as when people are said to believe some doctrine of Theology (or of Physics or Economics) 'without understanding it'. In all these cases, their belief, I suggest, is really about a sentence or other set of symbols: and what they are believing is that there is some important and true propositions which is formulated by the sentence, but they do not know what exactly the proposition is. We all of us operate very often with uncashed or not fully cashed symbols; and we do this in *a priori* studies, such as arithmetic and logic, as well as elsewhere. And that is how belief (as distinct from knowledge) does after all have a place in *a priori* thinking.

BELIEF AS 'A MANNER OF CONCEIVING'

Hume's problem, however, as he sees it himself, is concerned only with empirical propositions. His problem is, 'What is the difference between believing an empirical proposition, and being incredulous about it?' But strictly speaking, even this formulation of the question is too wide. For we also have to exclude propositions about what is sensibly or introspectively evident: statements describing a present sense-impression or a present impression of reflection, in Hume's terminology; for example 'This looks red to me now' or 'I am now feeling frightened'. Here again there is no room for belief, on Hume's view. We are just directly aware of these impressions at the moment when we experience them. His problem really concerns empirical propositions which go beyond what is actually present to sense (or introspection), as when I hear a barking sound and believe that there is a dog outside the door when I do not actually see the dog, or see a flame and believe that it is hot, though I do not at the moment feel the heat.

This is what Hume calls belief about matters of fact. 'Matters of fact' is a technical term of his, meaning empirical facts about something which is not at the moment perceived or introspected. The 'believables' which he is discussing are propositions about matters of fact in this sense of the phrase: and the question he is asking is, what is the difference between belief and incredulity with regard to these propositions?

So far, he has only said that the difference must lie in the manner of conceiving. For when I believe that there is a dog outside the door but you are incredulous about it, there is no difference between the 'ideas' we conceive of. To put it otherwise, what you are thinking of is the same as what I am thinking of. The difference is that you think of it in an incredulous manner and I in a believing manner. Similarly, if I come to believe something which I previously disbelieved or doubted, the change which occurs in me is just a change in my manner of conceiving—not in what I conceive of.

Perhaps we should all agree with Hume so far. Surely he is just saying (in rather peculiar language) that the difference between belief and incredulity is a difference in mental attitude as opposed to a difference in the object? And surely this is perfectly obvious? Perhaps it is, but one may wonder whether it seemed so before Hume wrote. However this may be, he is now going on to tell us what sort of a 'manner of conceiving' belief is; in what way a believed idea differs from one which is not believed. And this is the most important and the most controversial part of his theory.

When we pass from incredulity to belief, the idea which we are conceiving does not alter at all in respect of its content, as we have seen. But, he says, it does become more lively or vivacious. The difference in 'the manner of conceiving' amounts, then, to this: an idea which we believe is conceived in a lively or vivacious manner, or presents itself to our minds in a lively or vivacious way; whereas an idea which is not believed does not present itself to our minds in this lively way, but in a faint or feeble way. As I remarked earlier, it is important to notice that Hume also uses a number of other adjectives (besides 'lively' and 'vivacious') to describe this difference in the manner of conceiving. And he points out himself that none of them are altogether accurate. His hope is that if we consider all of them together, we shall be able to see for ourselves what he is talking about.

I will quote his own words. 'An idea assented to *feels* different from a fictitious idea that the fancy alone presents to us: and this different feeling I endeavour to explain by calling it a superior *force* or *vivacity* or *solidity* or *firmness* or *steadiness*.'[1] He adds that belief is 'that act of mind which renders realities more present to us than fictions, causes them to weigh more in the thought, and gives them a superior influence on the passions and imagination'[2] and further that belief 'makes them [ideas] appear of greater importance; infixes them in the mind; and renders them the governing principles of all our actions.'[3] (here we find a hint, at least, of the Dispositional Analysis of belief).

One may well think that some of Hume's other words—'force' 'solidity' 'firmness' 'steadiness'—are much better than 'liveliness' for describing this difference of feel which there is between ideas which we believe and those we do not believe. It is unfortunate, perhaps, that 'lively' is the one Hume uses, when he wants to give a brief definition of belief ('a lively idea related to or associated

[1] S.B., p. 629 (*Appendix*) Hume's italics [2] *Ibid.*
[3] *Ibid.*

with a present impression').[1] This preference for the word 'lively' has naturally misled his readers, and especially his critics. The word 'lively' is too easily taken in a more or less literal sense to mean just 'vivid'. And so Hume is supposed to be maintaining that believing something just consists in having a vivid mental image. Words like 'solidity' and 'firmness' and 'steadiness'—just because they are obviously metaphorical—do not convey this misleading impression.

But he himself says quite plainly 'I confess that it is impossible to explain perfectly this feeling or manner of conception. We may make use of words that express something near it. But its true and proper name is *belief*, which is a term that every one sufficiently understands in common life.'[2] This is a pretty explicit warning that the words 'lively' and 'vivacious' are not to be taken literally (any more than the words 'force' 'solidity' 'firmness', etc.) and that a 'lively idea' must not be supposed to mean 'a vivid mental image'. If Hume really had thought that believing just consists in having a vivid mental image associated with a present impression, he would not have had all these difficulties in conveying his meaning to the reader. It would not have been in the least 'impossible to explain perfectly this feeling or manner of conception', as he says it is. On the contrary, it would have been quite easy.

Hume illustrates the difference between ideas which are believed and ideas which are not believed by several examples. I shall now mention two of them.

(1) I remember a certain past incident which you have forgotten. I try to get you to remember it too. I describe it to you at length, and still you do not remember, though you understand perfectly what I say (i.e. have the same ideas as I have). But then suddenly some little detail which I mention 'revives the whole, and gives (you) a perfect memory of everything'. And now the very same ideas 'appear (to you) in a new light' and 'have in a manner a different feeling from what they had before'. 'Without any other alteration, beside that of the feeling, they become immediately ideas of the memory and are assented to.'[3]

(2) Two people, *A* and *B*, read the same book. *A* reads it as a

[1] S.B., p. 96. [2] *Ibid.*, p. 629 (*Appendix*).
[3] *Ibid.*, 627–8 (*Appendix*).

romance, and *B* as a 'true history'. The same ideas are before the minds of both. But clearly these ideas feel very different to the two readers. *B* (who reads the book as a 'true history') 'has a more lively conception of all the incidents'. He 'enters deeper into the concerns' of the persons described in the narrative, i.e. I suppose, has stronger emotions about them.[1] Moreover, the direction of his thoughts is affected in a way that *A*'s are not. He is led to consider other propositions which are implied or made probable by what he reads—propositions about the actions or characters of the persons described, about their friendships and enmities, and even about their personal appearance. This illustrates what Hume meant when he said that ideas which we believe 'weigh more in our thoughts' and have 'a superior influence on the passions and imagination' than those which we take to be fictitious.

In considering this rather curious illustration, we must remember that Hume himself was both a historian and a tough-minded lowland Scot. It is possible that a more flightly-minded Celt might react the opposite way. Yet if he did, would he not be at least half-believing the narrative—even though he did 'read it as a romance'?

RELATION TO A PRESENT IMPRESSION

So far then, Hume has argued that the difference between belief and incredulity is a difference in the manner of conceiving, not in the ideas conceived. An idea which we believe feels different from one which we do not believe. This 'feel' or felt quality which believed ideas have cannot be adequately described, though it is familiar to everyone. We may however approximately describe it by saying that an idea which we believe has a liveliness or force or strength or steadiness or solidity, which other ideas have not; adding, that it has an effect upon the subsequent course of our thoughts, and also upon our emotions and our actions, which other ideas have not.

Hume now goes on to complete his theory by explaining how this 'strength' or 'solidity' or 'liveliness' comes into existence: how an idea comes to have this peculiar felt quality.[2] It acquires

[1] S.B., pp. 97–98. [2] Part III, Section 8, *Of The Causes of Belief*.

this liveliness or force, he says, by being related to or associated with a present impression. What sort of relation or association does he mean? It is the sort which arises from past experience of constant conjunctions. Suppose impressions of kind *A* and impressions of kind *B* (flame and heat for example) have been constantly conjoined in my past experience; then if an impression of kind *A* occurs again, it will bring to my mind the idea of *B*. When I now see a flame I shall think of heat.

But this is not all. The impression reminds me of its usual accompaniment. But it does something else as well. The impression, like all impressions, has an intrinsic forcefulness of vivacity. And it communicates some of this forcefulness or vivacity to the idea which is associated with it.[1] (One is reminded of the ghosts in the *Odyssey* which were reanimated by drinking blood.) When I see the flame, I not only think of heat, I think of it in a lively or forceful manner. In other words, I believe that the heat is actually there. The intrinsic liveliness or forcefulness of the sense-impression *A* spreads, as it were, to the idea of *B*, and so the idea of *B* is not just conceived, but conceived in the lively or forceful 'manner' which constitutes believing.[2] In fact, the association due to past constant conjunctions enables an idea to approach in some measure to an impression. When you see the flame, it is almost (though not quite) as if you felt the heat. When you hear the growling sound from behind you, it is almost as if you saw the dog, or felt it biting you.

Seeing is believing, it is said. The remark is obviously false, and Hume does not think it true. Nor does he think that believing is seeing. But he does think that believing approaches in some measure to seeing. When you believe, it is only an idea which is before your mind. But the idea has some of the forcefulness or solidity, the 'feel of reality', which actual sense-impressions have, and it gets this because there is an actual sense-impression present, with which this idea is associated by constant conjunctions.

One may illustrate this last point—about the way an impression communicates some of its forcefulness or vivacity to an idea associated with it by constant conjunction—by an example which

[1] See Hume's 'General Maxim' at beginning of Section 8 '*Of the Causes of Belief*'.

[2] S.B., p. 98.

Hume himself gives in the Appendix[1] (though he uses it for a rather different purpose). If I am looking out of a basement window and see a pair of legs walking on the pavement outside, I shall believe that a complete human being is passing by. For in my past experience the sight of a pair of moving human legs has been constantly conjoined with the sight of a human head, arms and trunk. So when I see the moving legs, I vividly or forcefully conceive of the rest of a human body. And the vividness or forcefulness of this conception approaches the vividness of sensation itself: so much so, that if you asked me, I should almost certainly say that I saw a man walking past.

In strict and sober truth, all I actually saw was a pair of moving legs, and the rest of the man was only conceived of and believed in, not actually seen. But the part which I do see communicates some of its sensational force or vividness to the rest, because of the constant conjunction between moving legs and the rest of a human body which there has been throughout my past experience; so that it really is almost (though not quite) as if I were seeing the man as a whole. Consequently, if the belief turned out to be mistaken—if the thing was not a man at all, but a machine with wooden legs dressed up in trousers—I should be quite inclined to say that my senses had deceived me. This would not of course be true (there would be nothing erroneous about my visual perceptions themselves) but Hume's theory does explain why we are tempted to say it. For in such a case as this, the idea believed is so closely tied to the visual impression that it almost has the vividness or forcefulness of sense-perception itself.

We must now say something more about this associative link between impression and idea which plays such an important part in Hume's theory of belief. As we have seen, he usually holds that it is in the sort of linkage which is produced by experience of constant conjunctions, such as the conjunction between flame and heat. If my experience has been that whenever an event of kind *A* occurs, an event of kind *B* accompanies it, then perceiving an event of kind *A* will lead me to believe in the existence of its 'usual attendant', an event of kind *B*. Moreover, in some passages at any rate, he seems to think that this only happens when there is a causal relationship between the events *A* and *B*, the earlier

[1] S.B., p. 626 (*Appendix*).

of the two events being the cause, and the later the effect. It would not be relevant to discuss Hume's analysis of causation here. It is enough to remind the reader that the necessary connection which we suppose there is between cause and effect is analysed by him in subjective or psychological terms, and is indeed itself defined in terms of belief. We say there is a necessary connection between cause and effect, because when the one event is perceived, we have an irresistible felt inclination to believe that the other event will follow. The impression from which the idea of necessary connections is derived is an 'impression of reflection' (i.e. a datum of introspection). It is the felt passage of the mind from perceiving *A* to believing in the existence of its 'usual attendant' *B*.

In fact, Hume seems to think, usually, (1) that all believing results from experience of constant conjunctions. (2) that therefore all believing is of the sort which occurs in a causal inference: either (*a*) inferring an effect from a perceived cause, as when you see the trigger being pulled and believe that there is going to be a bang; or (*b*) inferring a cause from a perceived effect, as when you hear a bark and believe that there is a dog a few yards away. He says in the *Appendix* 'We can never be induced to believe any matter of fact, except where its cause, or its effect, is present to us'.[1]

But at other times he is aware that this view is going to get him into some difficulties. If believing consists in having a lively or forceful idea associated with a present impression, why must the association be of the 'constant conjunction' sort? There are other relations, beside constant conjunction, which produce associative linkages; namely, the relations of resemblance and of contiguity. If *A* resembles *B*, or *A* has been contiguous with *B* in some past experience of mine, then on perceiving *A* I shall be led to think of *B*. But do associations of this sort produce belief? If not, why not? When *A* leads me to think of *B* because of resemblance or by contiguity, do I think of *B* in the believing way?

For example, there is a cloud in the sky which resembles a dragon. It has a dragon-like shape; so when I see it, I am led to think of a dragon. But do I believe that the cloud is a dragon, or that there are dragons at all? Again, some years ago I drove through Doncaster, and a circus, with a number of elephants,

[1] S.B., p. 623.

was passing along the main street. Here was a relation of contiguity between the houses, pavements etc. and the elephants. I drive through the town again this year, and on seeing the houses, streets etc. I am reminded of the elephants. But do I believe that the elephants are there or that they will shortly reappear? Obviously not. Here is an idea associated with a present impression. But it does not have the liveliness or forcefulness which believed ideas have. Why not?

EFFECTS OF CONTIGUITY AND RESEMBLANCE

Hume discusses this question in Sections 8, 9 and 10 of Book III. That is why he had to write these sections (which I fear are seldom read) as well as Section 7 in which his own theory of belief is stated. First, he argues that the presence of these other relations (resemblance or contiguity) does make belief easier and their absence makes belief more difficult, but they cannot by themselves produce it. Only constant conjunction can do so.

For example, philosophers find it easy to believe in the transmission of motion by impact, because in this case the cause and the effect resemble each other (both are movements); in fact, they find this belief so easy that they suppose, quite falsely, that in this case the effect could be inferred from the cause *a priori* without the aid of experience.[1]

Conversely, they find it very difficult to believe that events in the body can cause events in the mind (or vice versa) because in this case the cause and the effect are so utterly unlike each other: and this, despite the constant conjunction between the two sorts of events which provides such very strong empirical evidence that there is indeed a causal connection between them.[2]

(In fact, the astonishing maxim that causes must always resemble their effects has been regarded by some as a self-evident metaphysical principle, though there is not the slightest empirical ground for it.)

One may offer another, and more commonplace, illustration.

[1] S.B., p. 111. (The word 'apparent' is here equivalent to 'evident'.)

[2] S.B., pp. 246–8 (*Treatise* Book I, Part IV, Section 5 'of the immateriality of the soul').

When you survey the winter landscape, on a cold, dark day, in a snowstorm, don't you find it quite difficult to believe that summer will come again in six months' time, and even a little difficult to believe that it will ever come again? This is because of the contrast, the extreme lack of resemblance, between the present state of affairs which you actually see and feel, and the very different state of affairs you are thinking of. Again, when you come home from a journey abroad (especially if you come by air) you may find it quite difficult to believe that only yesterday you were in Rome—though you quite clearly remember that you were. The contrast between idea and perception is so striking that it almost prevents you from believing what you perfectly well remember. Conversely, you might find it quite easy to believe that you had never been away at all—that yesterday's experience was just like to-day's—though on reflection you can clearly remember that it was very different.

Hume illustrates the effects of contiguity by a curious example about pilgrimages. A pilgrimage to Palestine or to Mecca increases our belief in the events narrated in the Bible or the Koran, and 'has the same influences on the vulgar as a new argument'.[1] This is because the events narrated in the Sacred Book are said to have occurred in or near the places which the pilgrim actually sees. As the vulgar might say themselves, the events described in the Bible seem 'more real' or 'are more real to them' when they have visited Jerusalem, and have seen the River Jordan.

Hume admits, then, that relations other than constant conjunction can strengthen belief, and their absence can weaken it. An idea which is believed will tend to be more lively or forceful, if it is the idea of something contiguous with or resembling what is at present perceived. Indeed, he goes even farther. He thinks that in some exceptional cases an idea can be believed (have a felt forcefulness or liveliness) when it is not related to a present impression at all. He thinks that this happens in madmen[2] (I am afraid he did not notice that there are many different kinds of madness). In madness, he thinks, belief may be produced by purely physiological causes. The 'ferment of the blood and spirits' is such that fact and fiction can no longer be distinguished. Every

[1] S.B., p. 110–11.
[2] Section 10 'Of the Influence of Belief', S.B., p. 123.

idea which comes into the mind is forceful or vivid, and is accordingly believed, no matter whether it is related to a present impression or not. (This is the state of mind which has since been called Primitive Credulity—a state in which every idea which comes into the mind is *ipso facto* believed. I shall have something more to say about it in a later lecture.[1])

Are we to assume, then, that Hume is now giving up the theory of Belief which he holds elsewhere—the theory that believing just consists in having a lively or forceful idea associated with a present impression by a relation of constant conjunction? He has now said, apparently, that sometimes the forcefulness or liveliness is partly the result of another sort of associative linkage between impressions and idea, namely an association by contiguity or resemblance. As we have seen, he admits and even insists that the presence of either of these other relations (contiguity or resemblance) may strengthen or facilitate belief, and their absence may weaken belief or make it more difficult. And in the passage about the madmen, he has gone even further, and has admitted that an idea can be believed (be lively or forceful) when it is not related to a present impression at all. Yet Hume does not seem to have given up his own theory that the liveliness or forcefulness of believed ideas arises from past experiences of constant conjunctions. For he makes constant use of it later, especially in the section on the idea of necessary connection.[2]

JUSTIFIABLE AND UNJUSTIFIABLE BELIEFS

What are we to make of this apparent inconsistency? I think the solution is fairly clear. Hume pretty obviously holds that in so far as the forcefulness or vivacity of an idea depends upon mere resemblances or contiguity, or anything else which is other than constant conjunction, to that extent the belief is subnormal or silly or superstitious or pathological. For instance, the pilgrim may of course be justified in believing what he has read in the Bible; but at any rate he is not justified in believing it more firmly than before, just because he has visited Jerusalem. As a matter of psychological fact, a pilgrimage may 'have the same effect on the

[1] See Lecture 9, pp., 12–18. [2] Book I, Part III, Section 14.

vulgar as a new argument'. But in so far as it does, the vulgar are being silly or superstitious.

Or again, we may consider the two philosophical beliefs which Hume mentions: the belief that motion is transmitted by impact (where cause and effect resemble each other, both being movements) and the belief that bodily changes cause mental ones (where the cause does not resemble the effect at all). Philosophers may in fact believe the first proposition much more firmly than the second. But Hume clearly thinks that this difference between the two beliefs is not justified. The justification for both alike is simply the experience of constant conjunction (observed uniformity of sequence); and it is equally strong in both cases. *A fortiori* the madman's beliefs are silly or subnormal or unjustified, when he believes every idea which comes into his mind, no matter whether it is related to a present impression or not.

According to this interpretation, Hume does want to stick to his original definition of belief as a lively ('strong', 'solid' 'forceful') idea associated with a present impression by a relation of experienced constant conjunction. Only he now wants to say that it is a definition of reasonable or sensible or sane or intelligent belief: and if, or to the extent that, the forcefulness of the idea comes about in some other way, to that extent the belief is unreasonable or silly or unjustified or pathological.

Perhaps Hume would not like using the words 'reasonable' and 'unreasonable' himself, because he tends to associate 'reason' with deductive reasoning, and with the theories of Rationalist philosophers who hold that important truths about matters of fact can be established by purely deductive inference. But actually we all think there is such a thing as inductive reasonableness as well as deductive reasonableness (it is Hume himself who has taught us this) and neither is reducible to the other. And it is perfectly true that for beliefs about matters of fact, the sort of beliefs Hume is here talking about, it is the inductive sort of reasonableness which is relevant. A belief about matters of fact is reasonable or sensible or justifiable, if or to the extent that we are led to hold it by experience of observable regularities—what Hume calls constant conjunctions.

It is sometimes said that Hume's philosophy leaves no room at all for the distinction between reasonable and unreasonable beliefs.

On the contrary, it could be argued, the whole point of the *Treatise*, on its constructive side, is to show what the distinction is. Hume is saying that in the sphere of matters of fact reasonable or sensible or justifiable beliefs are those—and only those—which are based on experienced regularities. On its destructive or sceptical side, on the other hand, the *Treatise* is a criticism of the Rationalistic way of drawing the distinction between reasonable and unreasonable beliefs, which tries to substitute deductive inference for learning from experience. The criticism was greatly needed at the time, and perhaps still is.

If I right so far, Hume's theory of Belief may be summed up as follows:

1. The difference between believing and not believing is a difference in the manner of conceiving an idea, and not in the content of the idea conceived.

2. We can roughly indicate what this manner of conceiving is, by saying that a believed idea is one which feels strong or forceful or lively or solid.

3. Except in the special case of madness, the forcefulness or liveliness of the idea arises from its relation to (its associative linkage with) a present impression; the idea gets its liveliness from its relation to something actually perceived (or introspected) at the moment.

4. In sensible or sober or sane belief, this associative link between idea and impression arises from past experiences of constant conjunctions. The impression *A* enlivens or strengthens the idea *B*, because *A*-like impressions and *B*-like impressions have been constantly conjoined in the past experience of the believer.

5. If, or to the extent that, the associative link between idea and impression is of another sort (if it is just association by resemblance or by contiguity), then or to that extent the belief is subnormal or silly or unjustifiable. And *a fortiori* the belief is subnormal or silly or unjustifiable if the liveliness or forcefulness of the idea does not arise from its relation to a present impression at all, but merely from purely physiological causes (or as Hume might have added, from the effects of hypnotic suggestion).

AN EXTENSION OF HUME'S THEORY

Before criticizing this theory, I want to suggest a slight expansion or extension of it—one which Hume himself (I think) could quite well have accepted. For surely his interpretation of the crucial phrase 'constant conjunction' is too narrow, and consequently his conception of induction is too narrow as well. He seems to hold that the causal sort of constant conjunction is the only sort. And so he is led to say (I have quoted it already) 'We can never be induced to believe any matter of fact, except where its cause, or its effect, is present to us';[1] and again, that causation is the only relation which 'can be traced beyond our senses and informs us of existences and objects which we do not see or feel'[2] (e.g. informs us that there is heat in the neighbourhood of the flame which we see, though we do not at present feel the heat). Consequently, he seems to think that when belief is sensible or sane or justifiable it is always some sort of causal inference, based on past experience of causal regularities.

But if this is Hume's view, it needs to be modified on his own showing, because it will not cover all the examples which he himself gives. Causal constant conjunctions (regularities of sequence) are not the only sort of constant conjunctions we experience. There are also constant conjunctions in which the *conjuncta* are coexistent, not successive—regularities of concomitance, as opposed to regularities of sequence.

Let us consider his own example about seeing the moving legs and believing there is a human body attached to them.[3] No doubt there is a causal relation between the movements of the legs and events going on in the rest of the body (e.g. events in the brain and in the nerves running down the spinal cord). But the ordinary believer knows nothing about these. Yet he believes, and believes reasonably or 'sensibly', that the rest of a human body is there, when he sees no more than the moving legs. The relation on which his belief is based is a relation of constant concomitance or coexistence, not of constant succession. Whenever he has previously seen a pair of moving legs, they have been spatially (not temporally) conjoined with a head, arms and trunk.

[1] S.B., p. 623 (*Appendix*) [2] *Ibid.*, p. 74. [3] *Ibid.*, p. 626 (*Appendix*).

It is true that Hume only uses this example once. But if we consider another, which he uses frequently, the one about flame and heat, it is not clear that this is a case of regular sequence either. On the face of it, it too is a case of constant concomitance or coexistence. And if we do start asking causal questions and consult the physicists or the chemists, they certainly will not tell us that the flame is the cause of the heat—at any rate not if you mean by 'the flame' the bright flickering thing which you actually see (which is what Hume himself means by it). They will say that both the flame and the heat are concomitant or coexistent effects of a common cause—namely the chemical process of combustion, which causes both light rays and heat rays to be radiated concomitantly.

It is easy to think of other examples. When I see a chimney pot, I believe that there is a fireplace somewhere underneath it. When I see a wall in the distance, I believe that it is hard; i.e. that these visible qualities are accompanied by the tangible quality of hardness. When I look at the sea I believe that there is land on the far side of it, beyond the horizon. Again, let us consider what happens when we recognize an object as being a cat, or as being a piece of ice. Such recognition is made possible by past experience of constant conjunctions. When I recognize something as a cat, all I see, perhaps, is a tabby-coloured thing with a round face and two ears; on seeing this, I believe that it has many other feline characteristics as well, e.g. soft fur, a liking for milk, a tendency to pursue mice, a capacity for purring. I believe this, because these characteristics have constantly accompanied that sort of shape and colouring in my past experience.

This is obviously an inductive belief, something learned from experience; it is just the sort of case which fits Hume's theory very well. It is very plausible to say here that an idea (that of cathood) is made lively or forceful by its relation to a present impression, and that this comes about through past experiences of a constant conjunction. But the constant conjunction in this sort of case is not a causal one. It is a constant concomitance, a regularity of coexistence, and not a regularity of sequence.

Moreover, in all these examples, the belief is sensible or justifiable, or reasonable: reasonable, that is, in the inductive way. It is a belief about a matter of fact, and a result of learning from experience. But the experience, in these cases, is an experience of constant concomitances, not of constant sequences. We are making an inductive inference, but it is not a causal inference. Hume does seem to think that all inductively-established beliefs are causal ones. But one can see nothing in his own empiricist principles which obliges him to hold such a narrow view of induction and of beliefs about matters of fact (such a narrow view, if you like, of learning from experience). And his own phrase *constant conjunction* can perfectly well be made to cover constancy of coexistence (constant concomitance) as well as constancy of succession. So in what I have just been saying, I have not been making an objection against his theory of belief, but merely suggesting a quite easy and obvious extension of it—an extension, too, which seems to be demanded by some of the examples he gives himself.

Before leaving this point, we may notice that it is relevant also to what he says about beliefs based on mere contiguity. What is 'contiguity' but a kind of concomitance or coexistence? Is there really anything wrong (silly, pathological) about beliefs based on mere contiguity? Nothing; unless the contiguity is irregular or inconstant, as for example when I believe that there is a bull behind this hedge now, merely because I once saw a bull there. But if I had walked down the lane many times in the past, and had always seen a bull behind the hedge, that would be quite a good ground for believing that there is a bull there now.

Similarly if very extraordinary events were always happening in Jerusalem or near the River Jordan, then a pilgrimage to Palestine would quite justifiably strengthen the pilgrims' belief in the Biblical narratives. But actually, of course, in most cases where belief is strengthened by the effects of contiguity, the contiguity is not constant or regular. Your belief in the reality of King Arthur may be strengthened by a visit to Caerleon, because he is supposed to have held his court there. But there is no regular or constant contiguity between persons or events of the Arthurian type and that particular part of Monmouthshire.

Thus, if I am right, the distinction Hume wants to make between sensible or sane or justifiable beliefs and silly or superstitious or pathological beliefs should be formulated as follows:

1. There are beliefs arising from experience of constant conjunctions, either conjunction of the causal sort, or conjunction of the concomitance sort. These beliefs, and these only, are sensible or sane or justifiable.

2. There are beliefs arising either (*a*) from mere resemblance, or (*b*) from conjunctions which are only occasional, not constant, (that is what 'mere contiguity' amounts to), or (*c*) from purely physiological causes, as in madness. These are silly or superstitious or subnormal or pathological.

We ourselves might prefer to formulate his distinction in more familiar or 'ordinary' language. We might wish to say that beliefs arising from experience of constant conjunctions (whether causal conjunctions or not) are reasonable; and if, or to the extent that, a belief arises in some other way, i.e. is independent of experience of constant conjunctions, then (or to that extent) it is unreasonable or non-reasonable. But in that case we must of course remember that the reasonableness, or lack of it, which is here in question is inductive reasonableness, not deductive. For the beliefs Hume is talking about are beliefs concerning matters of fact. A reasonable person, in this sense, is one who learns from experience and believes accordingly.

'Common sense' (at least in one usage of the term) is another name for this inductive sort of reasonableness. If we say that 'Mr. A has no common sense' we often mean that in forming his beliefs he is unaffected by or indifferent to his own experience of constant conjunctions. Similarly if we say to someone 'Use your common sense', this amounts to saying 'Recall to your mind the now-relevant part of what you have learned from experience'.

THE WEAKNESSES OF HUME'S THEORY

We may now turn to the weaknesses of Hume's theory. The first and most obvious one is that it is a very narrow theory, as I hinted at the beginning. It fits some beliefs very well, and they are important ones too, but by no means all. And even if we extend it a little, in the way I have just suggested—by widening Hume's own notion of constant conjunctions—it is still a very narrow theory. Even within the sphere of 'matters of fact' there is a very important class of beliefs which Hume's definition of belief does not fit, namely, *general* empirical beliefs: for example, the belief that all men are mortal; that water expands when it freezes, that wood is combustible. In fact any inductive generalization will do as an example: and we ought to include among such generalizations not only propositions of the form 'All *A* is *B*'. 'No *A* is *B*', but also propositions of the form 'Most *A*'s are *B*', 'Few *A*'s are *B*', 'about 70 per cent of *A*'s are *B*', etc. (e.g. 'Most Englishmen enjoy watching cricket'.).

It is very odd that Hume's theory of belief will not apply to inductive generalizations, because he was so particularly interested in induction. He obviously thinks that we do believe many inductive generalizations, and is more concerned than any other philosopher before him to enquire what the justification for them is. Nevertheless, his own theory of belief (so far as I can see) will not apply to inductive generalizations at all. It will not apply to *general* beliefs about matters of fact, but only to beliefs about particular matters of fact. This is because he insists that an idea which we believe must be related to or associated with a present impression.

Let us consider the generalization 'Water always expands when it freezes'. If we are willing to use Hume's 'idea' language, we can agree that the (complex) idea conveyed by this sentence presents itself to our minds in a lively or strong or solid or forceful manner. This proposition 'feels' very different from a generalization we do not believe, e.g. 'All swans are black' 'Glass is a good conductor of electricity'. So this part of Hume's theory—his contention that believing is 'a manner of conceiving' and his attempt to indicate what this manner of conceiving amounts to—applies well enough. But though the idea or set of ideas conveyed by an inductive generalization does have this character of strength or forcefulness or solidity, where is the relation to a present impression?

I can believe that water always expands when frozen, even though I am not now seeing or touching any water. No doubt some sense impression will be present when I consider this proposition. Sense impressions are always occurring so long as one is awake and conscious. When I consider this generalization about the freezing of water, I may be seeing a desk and hearing the sound of the traffic in the street outside my window. But the sense-impressions I happen to be having at the time are entirely irrelevant to this belief. If the relation to a present impression is essential (as Hume says it is) I could indeed believe that this freezing water which I see or touch is expanding or will shortly expand, but not that water in general expands when frozen. Similarly, to take his own favourite example, I could believe that this flame which I see across the room is hot, but not that all flames are hot.

GENERAL BELIEFS AND HABITS OF BELIEVING

Now some followers of Hume (and possibly Hume himself) might try to get out of this difficulty by saying that there are no general beliefs, but only habits of singular belief. This is the line taken by F. P. Ramsey in his interesting and intriguing essay 'General Propositions and Causality'.[1] According to Ramsey, we do not really believe that all flames are hot: the truth is only that we have a habit of believing that each particular flame which we see is hot. The actual believings are all of them concerned with actually perceived particulars. Again, on this view one does not actually believe that all men are mortal. The truth is only that whenever one sees some particular man, one will believe him to be mortal. Thus in all our actual believings (as opposed to mere habits of belief) the idea believed would be related to a present impression.

We notice that there is a suggestion here of the Dispositional Analysis of belief, since a habit is one kind of (acquired) disposition. One could quite well reformulate Ramsey's theory by saying that he does not so much want to abolish general beliefs—which was the way I put it just now—but wants to give a dispositional analysis of them, as opposed to an occurrence analysis. Nevertheless, this theory of Ramsey's is not what is ordinarily called the Dispositional Analysis of Belief, but only a restricted and incomplete version of it.

It is not a Dispositional Analysis of Belief as such, but only of one sort of beliefs—namely general beliefs, where the propositions

[1] *The Foundations of Mathematics*, pp. 237–255.

believed are inductive generalizations. Its restricted character is clearly shown when we consider what these habits or dispositions are which he is talking of. They are themselves habits of *believing*, dispositions to believe. There would be an obvious absurdity (a vicious circle) in suggesting that all belief is just a disposition to believe. Ramsey does not fall into this obvious error. He is not suggesting a dispositional analysis of singular beliefs, e.g. the belief that this man whom I see is mortal, or that this freezing water which I touch is expanding. He holds that singular beliefs, such as these, are actual introspectible occurrences.

So much to make clear what Ramsey's theory is. According to him, what is called a general belief is really a habit of forming singular beliefs; or, as he also says, a rule for forming singular beliefs (something like a recipe in a cookery-book). Quite possibly Hume himself would have accepted this. It is quite in line with his own doctrine that induction is a matter of custom or habit; and that what we learn from experience of constant conjunctions is certain habits of expectation—for example, we learn to expect that whenever a particular flame is seen, it will be hot. But attractive though this theory is (and very convenient for white-washing Hume, as we should all like to do), there are serious difficulties in it.

If it were correct, it is not at all clear how we could use general beliefs as premisses in reasoning, or how there could be logical relations between them, e.g. compatibility or incompatibility. If you believe that whales are mammals, and I believe that they are fish, here are two general beliefs which are incompatible, inconsistent with each other. But it does not make sense to say that a habit of mine is inconsistent with a habit of yours—or consistent with it either. To put the same point rather differently, we all suppose that inductive generalizations are true or false. And a habit is not true or false; nor is a recipe in a cookery-book—though it may be expedient, or inexpedient, to act upon it.

Again, if we consider our mental attitude to inductive generalisations, it seems obvious that we assent to them, or dissent from them, in just the same way as we assent or dissent to singular empirical propositions. In fact, we believe them (or disbelieve them) in just the same way as we believe or disbelieve other empirical propositions.

It is indeed true that a dispositional analysis of *all* beliefs, including singular ones like 'that flame over there is hot', is very plausible, and we shall see presently that there are hints of it in Hume himself. But this half-way house, which combines a dispositional theory of general beliefs with an occurrence theory of singular beliefs, is not a satisfactory position to stop in, though it looks attractive at first sight. On the contrary, one has to go the whole hog, either one way or the other; and either say that '*x* believes *p*' is always an occurrence-statement about him, no matter what sort of a proposition *p* is; or else say that it is always a dispositional statement about him, no matter what sort of a proposition *p* is.

If this is right, we shall just have to conclude that *general* beliefs about matters of fact fall outside the scope of Hume's theory altogether; for the reason I gave before, that though here too the proposition which we entertain is conceived in a lively or forceful manner, it is not related to a present impression.

Hume's theory of singular beliefs—e.g. the belief that 'That flame over there is hot'—might still be correct, of course. Beliefs of this kind are certainly very important, and play an enormous part in our lives. And if Hume's theory does give the correct analysis of them, this is a very remarkable achievement. Only, he has not succeeded in giving us what I think he claims to give, namely an analysis of *all* belief about matters of fact, but only about one sort of belief about matters of fact—the sort in which one actually perceived event or situation is taken as a sign of some other event or situation which we do not perceive at the moment. This, then, is one ground for saying that Hume's theory of belief is a narrow or restricted one, though within its own limits it might still be substantially correct.

BELIEFS TO WHICH HUME'S THEORY DOES NOT APPLY

The narrowness of Hume's theory may also be brought out in a different way as follows: his theory only applies to what one might call automatic beliefs: beliefs which arise in us immediately, as soon as the appropriate sense-impression occurs, without any previous process of questioning or deliberation or weighing of evidence for and against, and without any consideration of alternatives to the proposition believed.[1]

When I see a flame ten yards away and believe that it is hot, I do not weigh the evidence for and against the proposition 'It is hot'. It never even occurs to me to ask whether it might be anything else. The logically-possible alternatives that it might be cold or cool instead, or that it might have no temperature-quality at all, just do not present themselves to my mind. It is true that in a sense I have evidence for the proposition which I accept in this automatic and unquestioning manner, and very good evidence too, the evidence of past constant conjunctions. I have seen a great many flames in the past, and every one of them felt hot when I was near enough to it to feel it at all.

But though in a sense I have good evidence for the propositions I believe, I do not consider this evidence at the time. I do not recall these past conjunctions of flame and heat, nor notice their relevance to the present situation. Quite obviously, I do not recall all of them. You might expect perhaps that I should recall one or two of them at any rate, and possibly also have a dim recollection that there have been a great many others. No! nothing of the kind happens. I do not actually recall any past examples of the conjunction of flame and heat, though no doubt I could recall many if I tried. I might recall one or two if the conjunction (though constant) was a relatively unfamiliar one: for instance if I had only recently begun to notice that ice floats in water (I might have lived most of my life in a tropical country, so that I never saw any ice before this winter). But when the conjunction is very familiar, like the conjunction of flame and heat, we certainly do not recall any previous examples of this constant conjunction. When we see a flame now, we just jump immediately to the conclusion that it is hot without recalling any past experiences at all.

Hume emphasises this point himself in Book I Part iii, Section 8. 'The past experience, on which all our judgements concerning cause and effect depend, may operate on our mind in such an insensible manner as never to be taken notice of, and may even

[1] In a way Hume insists upon this narrowness himself in his section *Of the Reason of Animals* (Book I, Part III, Section 16). He is saying there that the human beliefs he has been analysing are the same sort of beliefs as animals have or may be supposed to have.

in some measure be unknown to us.'[1] He illustrates this by the example of a traveller who 'stops short in his journey upon meeting a river in his way'[2] 'Can we think' (says Hume) 'that on this occasion he reflects on any past experience, and calls to remembrance instances that he has seen or heard of, in order to discover the effects of water on animal bodies?' Obviously he does nothing of the kind. Just seeing the water there in front of him is quite enough to make him believe that if he walks into it, he will sink. In such a case, and in innumerable others, 'the mind makes the transition' (from the perception to the consequent belief) 'without the assistance of the memory'.[3]

But obviously there are beliefs which are arrived at in a very different way; cases where we do consider alternatives, where we do attend most carefully to the evidence *pro* and *con.*, try very hard to recall any past experience which may be relevant; and then, but not till then, we make up our minds (as we say) to accept the proposition *p*, and reject the alternative propositions *q* and *r*. The most obvious example is a jury considering its verdict; or again a doctor making a difficult diagnosis, or a barrister arriving at an opinion on a very intricate legal question.

Or let us consider the belief of a classical scholar, that Homer was a historical person and really did write the *Iliad* and the *Odyssey*. This scholar may have spent half a lifetime studying the question, considering and reconsidering the evidence on both sides, continually hunting for fresh evidence. At least, after many years of thought and study, he 'makes up his mind' about the question. He passes from doubt and suspense of judgement to belief. This is very unlike the automatic and almost instantaneous process which Hume describes.

Moreover, a belief of this kind certainly does not consist in having a lively or forceful idea related to a present impression, any more than the general beliefs do which I mentioned before, e.g. the belief that water expands when frozen. It is a lively or forceful idea, if you like. No doubt the idea (proposition) 'Homer was a historical person' does now feel different to the classical scholar from the way it felt before, when he had not yet made up his mind. And we may try to describe this difference by saying that the idea is now lively or strong or forceful in a way it was not

[1] S.B., p. 103. [2] *Ibid.* [3] *Ibid.*, p. 104.

before. But here again no present impression enters into the situation. No doubt the scholar is experiencing sense impressions since he is awake and conscious. When he at last gives his assent to the proposition 'Homer was a historical person' he is seeing a wastepaper basket, and feeling rather cold, and hearing the coo of a pigeon outside the window. But these 'present impressions' have nothing whatever to do with his belief.

So much for the narrowness of Hume's theory. There are types of belief to which it will not apply at all; though it applies very well to one very important type of belief, namely the sort of belief which one may call sign-cognition—taking one perceived event or situation as a sign of another, because of past experience of constant conjunctions.

But it is a mistake to suppose that this is the only sort of belief we have.

HUME AND THE DISPOSITIONAL ANALYSIS

You will remember that the central topic of these lectures was to be the examination and comparison of two very different ways of treating belief: the traditional Occurrence Analysis in which belief is regarded as an introspectible happening, and the modern Dispositional Analysis.

It is pretty clear that Hume himself is, in this respect at least, a Traditionalist. He does think that believing is an introspectible experience. He insists that a proposition which we believe feels different to us from a proposition we do not believe, and he tries his best to indicate what this difference of 'feel' amounts to, by the use of words like 'lively' 'strong' 'forceful' 'vivacious' 'solid' 'firm' 'steady'. These words of his are certainly intended to indicate an introspectible quality or characteristic, or an introspectibly-detectable way in which a believed idea presents itself to the mind.

Nevertheless, if we consider the literal meaning of these adjectives, we notice that all of them, except perhaps 'lively', are names of causal properties: that is, taken literally, they are dispositional words. If we attribute force to something, we are speaking of the amount of movement it is capable of producing in other things. If we call something 'firm' or 'steady', that means literally that it has the capacity of resisting disturbing agencies of one sort or another. The word 'solid' too is usually a causal-property word, equivalent to something like 'capable of resisting penetration (or deformation)', though sometimes, as Locke noted, it is the name of a tangible quality.[1] It is quite obvious that 'strength' is similarly a causal-property word: and even 'lively' (or 'vivacious') could be a causal-property word, though it might also mean perceptible or introspectible vividness. For instance, we might say that this kitten is a lively or vivacious creature, and this could be truly said of it even though it is fast asleep at the time.

So there is at any rate a hint or suggestion here that believed ideas differ from others in the effects they are liable to have on us—and not (or at any rate not only) in some introspectible quality they possess. And this is something much more like the Dispositional Analysis. Thus in Professor R. B. Braithwaite's version of the Dispositional Analysis (which I shall consider later[2]) believing that a flame is hot consists in being disposed to act as if this proposition were true. It might be suggested that this is what the 'forcefulness' or 'strength' of the believed idea would amount to—its tendency or liability to affect one's actions (where 'tendency' and 'liability' are dispositional words).

Moreover, though Hume himself obviously intends to use these causal-property words ('strength' 'force' 'steadiness' etc) in a metaphorical way to indicate an introspectible felt quality, he does also emphasise the effects which believed ideas have on us, and unbelieved ideas have not. Belief, he says, gives ideas 'more force and influence' 'makes them appear of greater importance' 'infixes them in the mind' and 'renders them the governing principles of all our actions'. He also says that belief 'gives them (ideas) a superior influence on the passions and imagination'—an influence which mere fictions do not have.[3]

Perhaps his own view is, that though we do have such dispositions when we believe some proposition (are disposed to 'take the proposition seriously', to act, and also to draw inferences as if it

[1] *Essay*, Book II, Ch. 4.
[2] In Vol. 2, Series II, Lecture 1 'Believing and Acting "as if"'.
[3] S.B., p. 629. (*Appendix*.)

were true) these dispositions are merely consequences of the peculiar introspectible quality or 'feel' which the proposition has. Nevertheless, it is a very natural suggestion that believing something just consists in having these dispositions, that coming to believe something just consists in acquiring them (in acquiring a tendency to take a proposition seriously both in thought and in action) and ceasing to believe it consists in losing them. That is why I say that there are at least hints in Hume of the Dispositional Theory, though the theory he actually holds is the traditional Occurrence Theory, which treats belief as a special sort of introspectible happening. Hume also has some interesting things to say about a topic which cannot very well be discussed at all if we accept a pure and simple occurrence analysis: namely half-belief.[1] *Treatise* Book I, Part iii, Section 10 (rather misleadingly entitled 'Of the Influence of Belief') contains a discussion of one important sort of half-belief, the sort of half-belief or near-belief which we sometimes have when we read the works of poets and dramatists.

[1] See Series II, Lecture 4.

LECTURE 8

TRADITIONAL OCCURRENCE ANALYSIS (I)

THE ENTERTAINING OF PROPOSITIONS

We have now at last reached the 'central topic' of these lectures—the examination of two very different analyses of belief, the Traditional Occurrence or Mental Act Analysis on the one hand, and the modern Dispositional Analysis on the other.

In this lecture and the next I shall try to state the traditional Occurrence Analysis. I want to state it as plausibly as I can. We may still have something to learn from it, and should not just reject it out of hand, as many contemporary philosophers are inclined to do.

Now if we are to make the Occurrence Analysis plausible we need a terminology which will not prejudice us against it. We could of course speak of 'belief-occurrences' or 'occurrent believings' or 'acts of believing'.[1] But such language is technical and artificial, and gives critics an opportunity to say that the occurrences which these queer phrases purport to describe are obviously fictitious entities. As Professor Ryle has pointed out, it sounds very odd indeed to say 'at half past three, I was engaged in believing that Oxford would win the Boat Race'.

But fortunately there is another word available. Several of the Occurrence theorists have used it, and I have been using it myself quite often already. This is the word 'assent'—used by Locke, by Newman, and occasionally by Hume. The word 'assent' is quite naturally used in an occurrent sense, to denote an introspectible mental event or mental act which can be more or less precisely dated. It does make sense to say that I assented to a proposition p at half past three today. (As the corresponding occurrence-word for disbelieving we may use the verb 'to reject'.)

[1] Russell, for example, says, 'Believing seems the most "mental" thing we *do*' (*Analysis of Mind*, Lecture XII *ad init.* [my italics]).

Let us say then that the Occurrence Analysis of belief is primarily an analysis of assenting.

If this terminological recommendation is acceptable, the first point to consider is, what we assent to, or what is the object of the act of assenting. What we assent to, it would be said, is always a proposition—something which is either true or false. And in order to assent to a proposition, or indeed in order to reject it, or again, in order to doubt it, or wonder about it, one has to entertain that proposition, or have it in mind, or think of it. So the first thing we have to do is to consider what entertaining a proposition is.

Assenting to a proposition is, of course, something more than just entertaining it. But entertaining it is an essential precondition for assenting to it—or for rejecting it either, or for questioning it, or for taking up any other mental attitude about it. The 'priority' here involved is logical, not temporal. It may happen, sometimes, that a proposition is assented to as soon as it comes into your mind at all—whether it comes there as a result of mental processes of your own, or because of what you hear someone else say, or of what you read. The important point is that in assenting to it one must also be entertaining it, whether the assent comes at once, as soon as the entertaining begins, or only comes later when one has already been entertaining the proposition for some time.

There are, however, a number of different cognitive acts or attitudes concerned with propositions; 'propositional attitudes', as Russell calls them. Assent is one of them. But there are others, for instance, questioning, supposing, wondering, doubting, imagining (in the sense of imagining that . . .). In all of them there is a common factor, and this is what is called 'entertaining a proposition'. What distinguishes assent, supposal, questioning, etc. from one another is some further attitude over and above the bare entertaining which is the common element in them all. Likewise, if I change from one of these attitudes to another—for instance, if I first feel doubt about a proposition *p*, then suppose it for the sake of argument and finally assent to it—the entertaining of *p* continues through this change of attitudes. Again, if I assent to *p* and you reject it, we must both entertain the proposition *p*. To that extent, your attitude is the same as mine; and if it were not, we could not disagree. Alternatively, the relation between entertaining and these further attitudes may be brought out by the use of adverbs (cf. Hume's phrase 'manner of conceiving'). One may entertain a proposition doubtingly, or wonderingly, or assentingly.

We may notice in passing that the entertaining of propositions also enters into many of our conative and emotional states. When I desire, or hope, or fear that there will be kippers for breakfast, I am entertaining the proposition 'There will be kippers for breakfast' and having an additional attitude towards it; though this time the additional attitude is not a purely cognitive one, as it was in my previous examples. The old-fashioned way of putting this is to say that conative and emotional states 'have objects' or are 'directed upon something'. One does not just hope, or wish or feel anxious. One hopes for something, wishes for something, feels anxious about something.

Sometimes the object of an emotion is an actually-existing thing, or event, or state of affairs. For instance, I am afraid of the Alsatian dog which I see rushing towards me, or distressed at the fact that you are angry with me. But quite often, the object of an emotion is something which does not actually exist. 'They were afraid where no fear was' (i.e. when there was in fact nothing to be afraid of). And in desire this is always so. What one desires, the 'object' of desire, is something which does not yet exist. It may even be something which cannot exist. I may wish that I had a happy day yesterday, instead of a wretched one. It is now too late for yesterday's happiness to exist. But still, in order to have this wish, I must entertain the proposition 'Yesterday was a happy day for me'.

So much to illustrate the importance of what is called 'the entertaining of a proposition'. It plays a fundamental part not only in our cognitive life, but in our emotional and volitional life as well. One might almost be inclined to define a rational being as a conscious being capable of entertaining propositions.

It is a curious question whether there is such a thing as bare or pure entertaining; just 'thinking of' a proposition without any further attitude at all, either cognitive or emotional or volitional. I am inclined to say that there is, though it is not very common. It seems to me that sometimes when I understand a sentence which I hear or read or which floats into my mind, I entertain a proposition in a perfectly neutral way, without either assent or dissent, doubt or supposal, hope or fear, desire or aversion.

But it is not necessary for our present purpose to decide this question. It is sufficient if we agree that we do very frequently entertain propositions, and that this entertaining is the common factor in the various cognitive, emotional, and volitional attitudes which have been mentioned.

WHAT IS ENTERTAINING A PROPOSITION?

We have now to ask what entertaining a proposition is. This may seem rather a queer question. In a way, everyone knows already what it is to entertain a proposition. The entertaining of propositions is the most familiar of all intellectual phenomena. It enters into every form of thinking and into many of our conative and emotional attitudes as well. Indeed, one might be inclined to say that it is the basic intellectual phenomenon; so fundamental that it admits of no explanation or analysis, but on the contrary all other forms of thinking have to be explained in terms of it.

I have some sympathy with this view. Perhaps all one can do is what I have tried to do already: give you instructions to enable you to identify for yourselves the occurrence which this technical phrase 'entertaining a proposition' denotes. Still, let us see whether any further elucidation is possible. (In what I am going to say I shall confine myself to the entertaining of empirical propositions.)

The first suggestion which occurs to us is this: entertaining a proposition *p* is knowing what it would be like for an indicative sentence *s* to be true—without necessarily believing (still less knowing) that the sentence is true. If you entertain the proposition 'It is raining', you know what it would be like for this sentence to be true; you know what sort of an actual situation would be described by this sentence. But to state this view fairly, we ought to add something. It is possible to entertain a proposition in a non-verbal way, by means of mental images, or again by means of pictures or diagrams or gestures or dumb show—whether one produces the pictures, gestures etc. oneself, or observes those produced by other people.

So the right way to put this view is as follows: entertaining a proposition *p* is knowing what it would be like for an indicative sentence *s* to be true, or for some non-verbal symbol equivalent to it to be true. If it is a sentence, you know what sort of a situation would be described by the sentence; if it is a visual image or a picture, you know what sort of a situation would be correctly represented or depicted by the image or the picture.

But in future, to avoid making things too complicated, I shall speak mostly about knowing what it would be like for an indicative sentence to be true, and shall ask you to remember for yourselves that we can entertain at least some propositions in non-verbal ways as well.

As we have seen, one can entertain without assenting. But one cannot assent without entertaining, if the traditional analysis of belief is right. So if we are to understand the traditional analysis of belief, we must try to isolate the entertaining from the further attitude which has to be added to it when we also assent to what we entertain (or when we dissent from it, or reject it).

Let us consider the sentence 'There is a mouse in the bathroom'. If you understand that sentence when you read it, or hear it uttered, or utter it or write it yourself, you are entertaining the proposition 'There is a mouse in the bathroom'. (To put it in a more old-fashioned way, you are 'having the idea' or 'having the thought' of a mouse's being in the bathroom.) The proposition might quite well be true—mice do sometimes go into bathrooms—and equally it might be false. You have no reasons for accepting it, and no reasons for rejecting it. You just entertain it without either belief or disbelief. But though you certainly do not know that the proposition is true (nor even believe it to be true) surely you do know what it would be like for it to be true? You do know what sort of a situation the sentence would describe.

If, however, you do *not* know what it would be like for a certain sentence to be true, then you are hearing or reading that sentence without understanding. For you, it is 'mere words', and in hearing it or reading it, uttering it or writing it, you are not entertaining any proposition at all, though other people may charitably suppose that you are. It is the same when you see a picture or diagram or map or piece of dumb show without knowing what sort of situation would be correctly represented or depicted by them. Here again, in seeing these visible objects (or in having similar visual images of your own) you will not be entertaining a proposition. The same applies if you yourself provide the picture or diagram or map or piece of dumb show.

This requirement, that to understand a sentence we must know what it would be like for the sentence to be true, has some resemblance to the Verification Principle laid down by the Logical Positivists. But it is much less stringent. Knowing what it would be like for an indicative sentence to be true does not entail that one knows of any way of finding out whether it is in fact true, nor that anyone else does. Sometimes, of course, we do know of a way of finding this out. In the example about the mouse in the bathroom we obviously do. We just have to go and look. But quite often we ourselves do not know of any way of finding out whether there actually is the situation which the sentence would describe or the map or diagram would depict.

Even if someone else knows of a method of verifying the sentence (some very clever scientist or archaeologist perhaps)—or if someone is going to discover a method of verifying it some day, it does not follow that you and I have or know of such a method. An instance would be 'It rained three hours ago on the planet Neptune'. We know what it would be like for this sentence to be true; what sort of a state of affairs would be correctly described by this sentence. It may be that some very clever astronomer or physicist knows of a method of verifying it, or will some day discover one: for example, he may have succeeded in discovering that it is always raining on Neptune, which entails that it must have been raining there three hours ago. Or again, he may now know or some day discover a method of getting some evidence for or against the truth of this sentence, even though not conclusive evidence. (This would be so-called 'weak' verification.) But most of us know of no method of finding out whether this proposition is true; and yet we can entertain it perfectly well—we do know what sort of a situation this sentence about rain on the planet Neptune would describe.

Let us agree, then, that if a man entertains a proposition *p*, he does have to know what it would be like for a sentence *s* (or other equivalent symbol) to be true. He has to know what sort of a situation this sentence would describe. The difficulty, however, is that this does not take us all the way. The knowledge of what it would be like for a sentence or other symbol to be true is a necessary condition for entertaining a proposition, but not a sufficient one.

For the word 'know' is (at least usually) a dispositional word; but entertaining a proposition is an occurrence—or as old-fashioned philosophers would have said, it is a mental act. Your entertaining of the proposition 'There is a mouse in the bathroom' is something that happens now, when you hear me utter the sentence; or perhaps a little time afterwards. (It may take a little time for the meaning of a sentence to 'dawn on you', or to 'sink in'.) But in any case, entertaining is something which happens. It is an event, or occurrence. But knowing something is not an event or occurrence, at least in the way the word is ordinarily used (though some philosophers in the past have talked about 'acts of knowing').[1]

There would be a similar difficulty if one said (as some would) that entertaining a proposition consists just in understanding a sentence or other symbol; for the word 'understand', too, is most commonly used in a dispositional sense. If we do want to define 'entertain' in terms of 'understand', we shall have to use the verb 'understand' in an occurrence sense, to mean something which happens at a particular moment, or something which someone does at a particular moment (an 'act' of understanding). And then it would be necessary to ask what sort of an event or activity this can be.

It would surely be very odd to say that you did not understand the sentence about the mouse in the bathroom before you heard me utter it, and that your understanding of it ceases a minute or two later, when you cease to attend to this sentence about the mouse, and think of something else. Perhaps the best way to use the word 'understand' in this context is to use it adverbially. You hear my sentence about the mouse understandingly, or with understanding. But I suggest that this is only another way of saying that you know what it would be like for the sentence to be true. And as we have seen already, this is indeed a necessary condition for entertaining a proposition, but not a complete account of what entertaining is, because entertaining is an occurrence.

[1] See Series I, Lecture 1, pp. 44–5.

CONSIDERING AND REALIZING

Shall we say, then, that when you entertain a proposition you are 'realizing', or, 'actually realizing', what it would be like for an indicative sentence, or some non-verbal equivalent for it, to be true? (This rather tiresome and rather colloquial word 'realize' is sometimes used by contemporary philosophers as the occurrence-word corresponding to the dispositional word 'know'.) Or again, shall we say that when you entertain a proposition, you are considering what it would be like for a sentence to be true, considering the sort of a situation the sentence would describe? Considering is certainly an occurrence, or perhaps we should rather say an activity. It is something that happens at a particular time.

The trouble, however, is that both these words—both 'consider' and 'realize'—say rather too much. The word 'consider' suggests that when you entertain a proposition you must be pondering on or ruminating about the situation which the sentence would describe—thinking it over, as we say. Considering the proposition 'there is a mouse in the bathroom' involves attending to some of the consequences which would follow (either certainly or probably) if this sentence described an actual situation. It also involves asking questions and thinking of possible answers to them. Thus if there is a mouse in the bathroom, it must have got in somehow. Did it come in through the door, or through a hole in the wainscoting? Or perhaps it was brought in by the cat and then escaped from him? Or again, our considering may involve asking practical questions. What would be the best way of getting the mouse out again, since it is a nuisance if it is a permanent inhabitant of the bathroom?

The word 'realize' suggests something similar. To realize what it would be like for this sentence about the mouse to be true, you do have to survey at least some of the consequences which would follow (certainly or probably) if the sentence described an actual situation. And to realize fully what it would be like, you would have to 'think out' all the consequences, positive and negative, certain or probable, which would follow if the sentence described an actual situation.

There is another important point about this 'realizing' which we may easily overlook. Most of the indicative sentences which we understand have some degree of generality about them; indeed they all have. They describe something, but they do not describe it in full detail, with complete specificity. They leave alternatives open. It follows that many different states of affairs would be correctly described by the same sentence, though certain common features would be present in them all.

Thus our sentence 'There is a mouse in the bathroom' does not specify just whereabouts in the bathroom it is. (In the bath? Under the wash-basin? Just inside the door?) Nor does it specify what the creature is doing—running about or sitting still, awake or asleep—nor how large a mouse it is, nor whether it is a young one or an old one, nor even whether it is a house mouse or a field mouse. Realizing at all fully what it would be like for the sentence to describe an actual situation involves taking account of these alternatives, all of which are consistent with the sentence's being true. The same applies to considering what it would be like for the sentence to be true, at any rate if one considers at all fully what it would be like.

No doubt we do sometimes entertain propositions in this sort of way, considering or realizing fairly fully what it would be like for the relevant sentences to be true. But this is not essential to entertaining, nor is it at all usual. Ordinary entertaining is something much more cursory, much less thoughtful than this. Remember how quickly one can read. (Reading is entertaining propositions conveyed by written words.) Or think how one can follow a very rapid sequence of spoken sentences. I suppose that a rapid talker can easily utter twenty sentences in a minute, and yet we can manage to understand what he says, at least sometimes. That is, we manage somehow to be aware of what it would be like if each of his sentences were true, although they succeed each other so quickly. Or again, when we think in words ourselves, or in images either, how very quickly the words or the images succeed each other[1]. Yet we *are* thinking. We are producing the words or the images understandingly; that is, we are entertaining a series of propositions.

In all these cases of rapid understanding, we are in some sense being aware of what it would be like for each of the sentences

[1] Cf. the phrases 'swift as thought' 'wind-swift thought'.

(or other symbols) to be true. We are being aware of what it would be like for each of them to describe an actual situation. But we are certainly not considering what it would be like if each of them were true. Nor are we realizing what it would be like in the ordinary sense of the word 'realize'. And if we did have to consider or to realize, this rapid understanding of sentences we hear or read or produce for ourselves would be quite impossible. We should be like a revered Oxford teacher of mine when he read a philosophical book. He was such a careful and conscientious thinker that he felt bound to consider very carefully and to realize very fully what it would be like for each sentence to be true, and to think out all its consequences both positive and negative. It took him so long that he hardly ever got beyond the end of page two.

ENTERTAINING AND 'INSPECTING'

Our conclusion so far is this: it is not sufficient (though it is true) to say that when we entertain a proposition we know what it would be like for a certain indicative sentence (or other equivalent symbol) to describe an actual situation, because the word 'know' is a dispositional word, whereas entertaining is an occurrence. On the other hand, when we look for a suitable occurrence-word, neither 'realize' nor 'consider' seems quite right. They suggest that entertaining is a much more thoughtful and a much more lengthy process than it usually is. 'Realize', moreover, is itself often a dispositional verb. ('Of course, I realize that this country's economic situation is a very difficult one: but still . . .')

It is indeed very difficult to decide what is the best word for what we want. We could say, perhaps, that when we entertain a proposition we are being aware (possibly for a very short time) of what it would be like for an indicative sentence or other symbol to be true. Or again, we could say that for a time we actually have in mind what it would be like for the sentence to be true or for it to describe an actual situation. But what kind of awareness is it, or in what way do we have this in mind? It is extremely difficult to answer these questions, though the entertaining of propositions is something so familiar to us that it seems perfectly simple and obvious. And in a way (as I hinted at first) no-one can tell you what kind of an awareness or 'having in mind' it is, when you are being aware of what it would be like for a sentence or other symbol to describe an actual situation, or are having this in mind. There is something ultimate and unanalysable here, which can only be indicated and not explained. As I suggested earlier, the entertaining of propositions is the basic intellectual phenomenon.[1]

But perhaps two points may be made about it. The first is a negative one. Though we cannot say fully what entertaining is like (because there is nothing else which it is quite like) we can mention something which it is *not* like. It is not very like inspecting an entity, inspecting something. It is worth pointing this out, because some philosophers (Bolzano and Meinong, for instance) have supposed that propositions are timeless and subsistent entities, and that when we entertain a proposition we are inspecting one of these entities. The word 'subsistent' is used to indicate the peculiar sort of 'being' which propositions are supposed to have. They do not exist as tables or persons do, nor do they happen as lightning-flashes do. They are timeless and non-spatial. So we are invited to say that they subsist. And Meinong tells us that we must try to get rid of our prejudice in favour of the actual—as Plato also told us long ago, in rather different words.

Others, again, e.g. Stout and Broad, have held that entertaining a proposition consists in inspecting a subsistent possibility, a possibility which there is though it need not ever be actualized. Thus there is the possibility that fifteen resident cats live in New College kitchen (though in actual fact there are only two). And when you entertain the false proposition 'there are fifteen resident cats in New College kitchen' you are supposed to be inspecting this unactualized possibility.

There is no doubt a temptation to speak of entertaining—and other forms of thinking—in this quasi-visual way, as if it were a kind of seeing. 'Inspecting' is a visual word; so is 'intuiting'. Again, we often say 'I see now what you mean', and we say this even when we do not believe what he has said. Sight is our most important source of information about the world, and it is very natural to describe thinking in terms of visual metaphors, as if it were a kind of intellectual seeing or gazing.

[1] P. 192 above.

The danger is that these metaphors may be mistaken for an explanation, and thereby prevent us from trying to notice for ourselves what thinking actually is. When we do try to do this, to attend to what is actually going on in us when we entertain propositions, we find that it is not at all like looking at something—taking a brief look at something with our intellectual eyes, or giving it a long stare, when we entertain a proposition in the 'considering' manner which I described earlier.

Perhaps it will be said that image-thinking is rather like looking at something, even though verbal thinking is not. And one must agree that imaging (visual imaging) does indeed resemble seeing. And one must agree, too, that it is possible to entertain propositions (or some propositions) by means of images. But entertaining a proposition by means of images does not just consist in having these images, still less in inspecting the images which one has. One must also be aware of, or have in mind, what sort of actual situation would be depicted or represented by these images. If images are used for entertaining propositions, the images have to be understood (or interpreted, if you like) and not just contemplated. And the same applies when we entertain a proposition by means of public visible entities or happenings—for example, by means of pictures or diagrams or dumb show, or indeed by means of written words. To entertain a proposition we must understand or interpret these things that we see.

So much for my negative point: entertaining a proposition is not like inspecting something. We must not allow ourselves to be misled by the visual metaphors which we often use in describing thinking, and must not take them for more than they are worth. If we take them literally, or anywhere near literally, we shall give a quite unrealistic account of what entertaining actually is.

ENTERTAINING AND READINESS

But there is also a positive point, which it is not at all easy to state clearly. You will remember my discussion just now of considering and realizing (considering what it would be like for a certain sentence to be true; realizing as fully as you can what it would be like). I said that entertaining is not ordinarily so thoughtful—

nor so lengthy—a process as this. Ordinarily it is a much briefer and less laborious thing, sometimes almost instantaneous.

Nevertheless, though such considering and realizing does not ordinarily occur when we entertain a proposition (and certainly need not occur), it is not irrelevant to the analysis of entertaining. Even in ordinary entertaining, however rapid and cursory it may be, there is a *readiness* to do some considering or some realizing, a readiness to consider what it would be like for the sentence to describe an actual situation, or to realize what the situation described would be like, though as a rule this considering or realizing does not actually occur.

Moreover, this readiness is not something purely and simply dispositional. It is not just that we are capable of considering or realizing what it would be like for the sentence (or other symbol) to be true; though we do of course have to possess this capacity if we are to entertain the proposition. The readiness I speak of is rather like being poised to run in a certain direction, if need arises; this is something more than just having the capacity to run—and also something less than actually running. This readiness to consider or to realize is something actually felt or experienced. It is a feature—and an important one—of the actual experience of entertaining. It is part of what we mean by saying that we are 'being aware of', or 'having in mind', what it would be like for the sentence to describe an actual situation.

I find it difficult to give any further account of what this felt or experienced readiness is (though I think we are all perfectly familiar with it). All I can do is to reformulate my point in more technical phraseology: when we entertain a proposition our capacity for considering or realizing what it would be like for a certain sentence to describe something is always subactivated, though it is only completely activated or rather special and rare occasions.

Moreover, a readiness of another sort is also a part of the experience of entertaining a proposition: a readiness to recognize a situation such as the sentence describes, if we should happen to observe such a situation. And this readiness again is something more than just a capacity. The capacity to recognize a mouse-in-the-bathroom situation is something you have all the time. You have had it ever since you first learned the meaning of the words 'mouse' 'bathroom' and 'in'. From that time onwards, it has always been true of you that you have the capacity of recognizing that there is a mouse in the bathroom if ever you happened to see one there.

But when you are actually entertaining the proposition 'there is a mouse in the bathroom', it is not merely that you are capable of recognizing a situation which would make that sentence true; you are ready to exercise that capacity—even though you disbelieve the proposition, and therefore do not at all expect that the need or the possibility of recognizing the described situation will in fact arise. And this readiness too, like the other (the readiness to consider or to realize what it would be like for the sentence to be true) is something actually experienced or felt or 'lived through', a part of what it actually 'feels like' to entertain a proposition.

The readiness to consider what it would be like for the sentence to be true is, roughly, a readiness to attend to the consequences which would follow (certainly or probably) if the sentence were true. This attention to the consequences is also what is usually meant by 'realizing' what it would be like for the sentence to be true.

But sometimes, I think, 'realizing' may just mean being ready to recognize a verifying situation, if there should be one. In that case if we are ready to recognize a situation which would make the sentence true, this would be equivalent to saying that we do realize what it would be like for the sentence to be true—not merely that we are ready to realize this.

I have already complained that 'realize' is a vulgar and illiterate word, and I doubt whether it can be pinned down to any precise sense. Still another sense it sometimes has is cashing the sentence by means of images, and/or feeling in some degree the emotions you would have if the situation described did actually exist, and you did actually witness it. (Cf. 'I did not realize till now what is meant by saying "There is an inflation going on" ' or 'I did not realize till now what is meant by "the blocking of the Suez Canal" '.)

However this may be, and whether we use the word 'realize' or not, these two readinesses are present whenever we entertain an empirical proposition: the readiness to follow out the consequences there would be if the sentence described an actual situation, and also the readiness to recognize the situation described, if we were to encounter it.

But I do not claim that entertaining is nothing but these two readinesses combined. I think that there is something about it which cannot be explained or analysed at all, but only indicated. Nor is this surprising. No one can explain to you what it is like to have the thought of something if you do not know already. And entertaining a proposition is just what ordinary people call 'having the thought of' some situation or state of affairs, without necessarily either knowing, or even believing, that the state of affairs actually exists. So much—too much, perhaps—for the entertaining of propositions. It was necessary to consider this difficult subject first, before discussing the traditional theory of assent, since one cannot assent to a proposition unless one entertains it.

LECTURE 9

TRADITIONAL OCCURRENCE ANALYSIS (II)

ASSENT AND BEING UNDER AN IMPRESSION THAT

We have seen that in the traditional Occurrence Analysis of belief, attention is concentrated on a special sort of mental occurrence or mental act, which may be called assenting To assent to a proposition, we have to entertain that proposition; and in the last lecture I tried to say what entertaining a proposition amounts to. Assent, in the traditional theory, consists in taking up a further attitude to an entertained proposition. We have now to consider what happens when we assent to a proposition as well as entertaining it.

In the traditional theory it is usually held that assent admits of degrees. Though Newman, as we have seen, denies this, most other exponents of the Occurrence Analysis have accepted it, as Locke does. The usual view is that when we give our assent to a proposition, we give it with a greater or smaller degree of confidence. I have already said a good deal about this, and need not say much more about it now; I will just remind you of the traditional view that a rough scale of degrees of assent can be constructed, ranging from suspecting or surmising at the bottom end, to absolute sureness or complete conviction at the top end, with various degrees of opinion in the middle.

It is a curious question whether this series of degrees should be regarded as a continuous one: that is, whether between any two degrees of assent there must always be another. I do not see why it need be regarded as absolutely continuous. It is more plausible to suppose that confidence rises or falls in small finite jerks, as the intensity of sensations is supposed to do.

I will just add that there is another difference of degree which should be mentioned. We may assent very firmly to a proposition to-day, we may even be absolutely convinced of it; and yet to-morrow we may assent to it much less firmly or even withdraw our assent altogether, although our evidence for the proposition has not altered in the meantime.

In other words, assent may have different degrees of tenacity or stability over a period of time, as well as different degrees of intensity at any given moment. I shall have to consider this later, in Series II, when I discuss the relation between belief and action. The notion of the stability or tenacity of assent is relevant when we ask how a man can assent to a proposition *p*, and yet behave, in practice, as if *p* were false. For the moment we may put it this way: an act of assent (or assent occurrence) may be more confident or less; a habit of assent may have various degrees of stability or tenacity. For the present, it is the act of assent or assent-occurrence that we are concerned with.

The next point is that assent (whatever degree it may have) is the culmination, as it were, of a process: we might almost say, the resolution of a kind of conflict. Assent, at least when reasonable, is preceded by a state of wondering or questioning, in which several alternative propositions are before the mind, together with the evidence for each of them. There must be at least two, *p* and not-*p*, and there may be more: not-*p* may cover quite a large range of alternatives, *q*, *r*, etc. During the preliminary stage of wondering or questioning, we sit on the fence, as it were, between these alternatives. As we fix our mind on the evidence in favour of *p* we may have an inclination to assent to *p*; and then, turning our mind to the evidence for *q*, we may have an inclination to assent to *q* instead. But though we may have these inclinations to assent this way or that, we do not yet actually assent. We remain in a state of suspended judgement.

This state of suspended judgement may last only for a very short time. On my way to deliver a lecture I wonder whether my watch is slow. I look at the clock in the corridor and my state of wondering and suspense of judgement is very quickly terminated. But in other cases the state of suspended judgement may last for a very long time, because the evidence is indecisive, or because there is too little evidence either way, or again, because there is too much, and it is not clear whether on the whole it favours *p*, or *q*, or *r*. The question just has to be left unsettled for the time being, because there are other more urgent matters to be attended to;

and when we start wondering about it again, tomorrow or next week, perhaps, we still cannot settle it. We may even remain in a state of suspended judgement about it for the rest of our lives, as the life-long Agnostic does about the question whether God exists.

But still, the state of wondering and suspended judgement, long or short, does often come to an end. We do eventually assent to one of the alternatives. We come off the fence on one side. We prefer or plump for one of the alternatives, accept it or commit ourselves to it, and reject the others; and if we are reasonable, we accept the one which is supported, on balance, by the evidence we have been considering and reject those which are not.

It is important to notice the preferential character of assent. One result of it is that we cannot believe without also disbelieving. If we accept this proposition, we are also rejecting that one. Assenting is something two-sided or two-faced. In assenting to *p*, one *ipso facto* dissents from its alternatives *q* and *r*; at any rate this is what we do if, or to the extent that, we are assenting reasonably. This is why we find it natural to describe assent in the language of choice. We speak not only of deciding *to*, (i.e. deciding to do something) but also of deciding *that*. After waiting for him for 1½ hours, I decided that John had missed the train. We also speak of 'making up our mind *that* . . .' as well as 'making up our mind *to* do something'. After some doubt, I made up my mind that the bird was a lesser spotted woodpecker.

Assent, then, is in some respects analogous to decision: and the process of wondering and evidence-weighing, which precedes reasonable assent, is in some respects analogous to practical deliberation, where we consider several alternative actions and try to estimate the weight or force of the reasons for doing this one or that one.

Moreover, as I said before, assent can also be viewed as the resolution of a conflict.[1] We describe it as 'making up our mind' because our mind has primarily been, as it were, divided; we had some inclination to assent to *p*, and also some inclination to assent to *q*, when *p* and *q* are mutually incompatible propositions.

We may summarize this account of assent as follows:

[1] It is this aspect of the situation which Hume mentions, too briefly, in the Appendix to the *Treatise*, pp. 625–6 (Selby-Bigge's edition).

1. Assent is the taking up of an attitude towards an entertained proposition.
2. This attitude has two different features or components (*a*) Preference; (*b*) Confidence.

(*a*) *Preference*

Because of its preferential character, assenting always includes dissenting. In assenting to *p*, we *ipso facto* dissent from or reject its alternatives *q* and *r*. Perhaps it was this preferential character of assent which led Newman to say that assent is unconditional,[1] and that 'There is no medium between assenting and not assenting.' If you assent at all, you do have to make up your mind between two or more alternatives. You cannot 'have it both ways'; you must decide in favour of this alternative or that.

It is true that you may withdraw your decision later: you may even withdraw it half a minute after you made it. But then you are ceasing to assent; you are returning to the state of wondering or suspended judgement, 'sitting on the fence' again. But in so far as you do assent to *p* rather than *q*, and for as long as you assent to it, it *is* *p* that you decide for. You cannot partially decide for *p*, or half-choose it. This follows analytically from the concept of 'choosing'. You are rather like a motorist who comes to a fork in the road. He can stop at the fork as long as he pleases. But if he goes on, he must choose between this road and that.

(*b*) *Confidence*

But though when we prefer or plump for *p* and reject *q* it is *p* that we prefer and no half-way house is possible about that, we may still have great confidence or little about the alternative preferred. We may rely upon it whole-heartedly, with no mental reservations at all. Then we have assented with complete conviction. Or we may rely upon it with considerable confidence but with some mental reservation, and then our assent is what we call 'Having the opinion that' or more usually 'Thinking that' (as opposed to 'Being convinced that'). Or finally, the confidence we have about *p* may be small, although *p*—as opposed to *q* or *r*—still is the alternative which we prefer. This is what is traditionally called 'suspecting that', and is the lowest degree of assent.

[1] See Lecture 6 above.

As I have mentioned before, some exponents of the traditional view have described confidence as a feeling: Cook Wilson,[1] for instance, calls it 'a feeling *sui qeneris*'. Walter Bagehot[2] calls it 'the emotion of conviction'. Hume holds that a proposition which we believe feels different to us from one we do not believe. It has a feel of strength or force or vivacity about it, and in his discussion of probability he maintains that this 'feel' may vary in degree.[3]

This part of the traditional theory has been criticized, notably by Professor William Kneale.[4] Perhaps confidence should not be called a feeling, still less an emotion. But provided we are willing to speak of acts of assenting at all, or assent-occurrences, it does seem to be true that we can assent more confidently or less; the question whether confidence should or should not be described as a feeling can be postponed until later. I shall have something more to say about it in Series II.[5] It is one of the issues we have to consider when we try to decide between the Occurrence or 'Act' Analysis, on the one hand, and the Dispositional Analysis on the other.

As you may have noticed for yourselves, contemporary philosophers have a certain hostility towards the concept of 'feeling' as such; and perhaps this hostility has gone a little too far. For the moment let us leave the matter there, and just say that in the traditional Occurrence Analysis it is usually held that there are degrees of assent, and that we assent more confidently to some propositions and less confidently to others.

'BEING UNDER AN IMPRESSION THAT. . .'

It will be seen that in the analysis of Assent which I have just been stating, reasonable assent is taken as the typical case. Here assent is preceded by a state of wondering or questioning, where we consider several alternative propositions, together with the evidence for each of them. Our assent, when given, is assent upon evidence, or reasoned assent.

[1] *Statement and Inference*, Vol. 1, p. 102.

[2] *Literary Studies*, Vol. 2, pp. 412–21, 'The Emotion of Conviction'. See also below, pp. 212–216.

[3] *Treatise*, Book I, Part III, Section 12.

[4] *Probability and Induction*, pp. 13–18.

[5] See Series II, Lecture 2 — where Kneale's criticisms are discussed. (pp. 282–5).

But it happens sometimes, indeed quite frequently, that we accept propositions in a very different way from this. We accept them in an *unquestioning* manner; we just 'take it for granted' that *p*, without question or doubt, and without any previous process of weighing the evidence *pro* and *con*.

To complete this account of the traditional Occurrence Analysis, we must therefore consider a kind of appendix to it. This is concerned with the state of mind which Cook Wilson called 'Being under an impression that . . .'.[1] (His disciple Prichard called it 'Thinking without question'.) Cook Wilson's own example, which I shall elaborate a little, is this: I see walking in front of me in the street a man who resembles my friend Tom in build and clothing. He is tall and rather stout, as Tom is; he has a dark blue overcoat and reddish hair, as Tom has; he walks with a slightly rolling gait as Tom does. I quicken my pace and go straight up to him, and then 'without hesitation perform some act which it would be a liberty to take with anyone but an acquaintance'.[2] But then I find that this person is not my friend Tom at all. He is a complete stranger. Covered with confusion, I apologize and say 'I am so sorry, I thought you were my friend Tom Postlethwaite'.

Now in what sense did I think that the man was my friend Tom? As we have seen, the phrase 'think that . . .' is often used to express the intermediate degree of belief, the degree which is called 'opinion'. But was this an opinion? Did I weigh the evidence for and against, and then assent with a mild degree of confidence? No, not at all. I just saw the man's back, and 'jumped to the conclusion' that he was my friend Tom, without any consideration of alternatives, without any weighing of evidence *pro* and *con*, and without any doubt. My visual percept simply recalled my friend Tom to my mind, and caused me to 'be under the impression' that the man *was* my friend Tom. One might also say 'I took it for granted that the man was Tom'. One might add, perhaps, 'it never even occurred to me that it might be someone else'. (This is the point of Prichard's term 'thinking without question.')

But surely we did have some evidence that the man in the street

[1] *Statement and Inference*, Vol. I, Part II, Ch. 3, pp. 109–113.

[2] *Loc. cit.*, p. 109. According to an Oxford tradition, Cook Wilson slapped the man on the back.

was our friend—not conclusive evidence by any means, but evidence all the same? Cook Wilson's reply to this, if I interpret him correctly, is that there was indeed evidence available to us (the observed facts about the colour of the man's overcoat, the colour of his hair, his height and girth, his gait) but we did not *use* it as evidence.[1] For us, on this occasion, these percepts do not function as evidence, though for someone else, who is attentive and wide-awake, they might have. For us, in the unquestioning state of mind in which we are, they are merely associative cues. The blue overcoat, the bodily shape, the gait, the reddish hair *remind* us of our friend Tom, they cause the proposition 'This is Tom' to come into our mind, and we then accept this proposition without question or doubt. It never even occurs to us that the proposition might be false.

This state of mind, whatever name we choose for it, is very common. When one sees an approximately transparent liquid in a bath, one nearly always takes for granted that it is water. Conceivably it might be sulphuric acid, but one does not apply litmus paper to make sure. Because it looks like water one 'takes' it to *be* water in a completely unquestioning manner. If you give me something which looks like a pound note, I do not inspect it carefully with a magnifying glass to make sure it is not a forgery. Our ordinary attitude to testimony[2] is much the same, for instance when someone tells me 'It is still raining' or 'I met Jane at a tea-party yesterday'. It is only in rather special circumstances that one weighs the evidence about the speaker's veracity, asks oneself 'Is he likely to be telling the truth?' and then arrives at the rational opinion that he is telling it. Our usual attitude is to take for granted the veracity of other people's statements, and to accept their testimony 'without question' unless their testimony is very improbable on the face of it, or we already have reason to think them very unreliable people.

Moreover, Cook Wilson's example might lead us to suppose that when we are under an impression that *p*, the proposition *p* is invariably false (as it was in this example). But as he points out himself, at the end of the chapter, there are numerous instances

[1] *Statement and Inference*, Vol. 1, p. 113. 'The reason in such a case is not a conscious reason for us, in the sense of a premiss from which we infer.'

[2] See Lecture 5, above.

in which this state of mind 'does not attract attention, because, though unwarranted, it does not lead to a mistake'.[1] When I am under an impression that *p*, *p* may very well be true; and very frequently, it is in fact true. In 9 cases out of 10, perhaps, the man I take (in this unquestioning manner) to be an acquaintance really is the man I take him to be. And in 999 cases out of a 1000 when I am 'under an impression that' the liquid in the bath is water, it actually *is* water.

It is however true, and important, that this state of mind may easily lead us into error. And when it does, the error we fall into is something quite different from a mistaken opinion. In opinion, we are aware already that the proposition assented to may be false, and that the evidence for it, though favourable, is not conclusive. So if it turns out later than the proposition is false, we are indeed surprised, but we do not experience the peculiar kind of 'shock' which we have when the man in the blue overcoat turns out to be a complete stranger. This is something we were not at all prepared for (as we would have been, if our state of mind had been one of reasonable opinion). It is almost as if the universe itself had 'let us down', since it never even occurred to us that the proposition we accepted might turn out to be false.

According to the traditional Occurrence Analysis, there are two factors in assent, preference and confidence. It will be noticed that both are absent in 'being under an impression that . . .'. When I assent to a proposition *p*, I prefer it to its alternatives. Not only *p* but also other propositions *q* and *r* are before my mind, and I decide in favour of *p*, in preference to *q* and *r*. But in the situation we are now discussing there are no alternatives before the mind. In the example about the man in the street, the proposition 'That is Tom' is the only one which occurs to me. It 'never even enters my head' that the man might be someone else. There cannot be preferring when there are no alternatives (or rather, when we are aware of none), nor can there be consideration of grounds for preferring this alternative to that. As Cook Wilson says 'there is a certain helplessness'[2] about this state of mind.

More surprisingly, perhaps, the second factor in assent, confidence, is lacking as well. What is characteristic of this state of unquestioning acceptance is the absence of doubt or diffidence.

[1] *Statement and Inference*, Vol. 1, p. 113 *fin.* [2] *Ibid.*, p. 112.

And whereas confidence, according to the traditional account of assent, is something which varies in degree, there are no degrees at all in 'being under an impression that' as Cook Wilson describes it. The feeling of doubt or diffidence is totally absent.

On this view, reasonable assent, even reasonable but incorrect assent, is something of an achievement. It takes a certain amount of effort to consider alternatives, to weigh the evidence for and against each of them, before giving assent to one of them. And—equally important—it takes a good deal of effort to refrain from assenting when the evidence is conflicting, or when there is too little evidence to justify assent at all.

'PRIMITIVE CREDULITY'

Can we throw any further light on this state of unquestioning acceptance, which Cook Wilson called 'being under an impression that . . .'? We have seen that if the traditional Occurrence Analysis of assent is correct, we do not assent to a proposition when we accept it in this unquestioning way. Then how does this unquestioning acceptance differ from pure and simple entertaining? We spoke about jumping to a conclusion. The sight of the blue overcoat, reddish hair etc. suggests (by association) 'That is my friend Tom'. Now this does explain why that particular proposition—rather than some other one—comes into my mind at that particular moment. But even so, why should I accept it? Why should I not just entertain it in a neutral way, without either accepting or rejecting it? The jump is explained in this associative way, but not the fact that it is a conclusion which is jumped to. Concluding, even of this not-very-rational kind, is something more than mere entertaining, though in order to conclude that p we do of course have to entertain p.

Some philosophers have tried to explain this phenomenon by referring to a tendency of human nature which they call 'primitive credulity'. The phrase was invented by Alexander Bain, but something like the doctrine of primitive credulity is already to be found in Spinoza, as William James points out. James himself appears to accept it (*Principles of Psychology*, Vol. 2, pp. 287-9). But perhaps the clearest and most forceful exposition of it is in an essay by Walter Bagehot called 'The Emotion of Conviction' (*Literary Studies*, 3rd Edition, 1884, Vol. 2, pp. 412-21).[1]

According to these philosophers—I shall use their own terminology for the moment—the natural tendency of the human mind is to believe any idea which comes before it, unless and until that idea is contradicted directly and obviously by sense-experience; it is a 'natural' tendency, in the sense that such a belief comes into existence unless and until there is some special factor to inhibit it. As Bagehot puts it himself 'My theory is, that in the first instance a child believes everything' (*op. cit.*, p. 417). All sorts of queer beliefs flourish side by side in the mind of the primitive adult or the civilized child. Any idea which comes into their minds is at once believed, unless it very obviously clashes with perceived facts. Moreover, as Bagehot remarks (p. 419) even the mind of the civilized adult operates in this way in dreams; and also, we might add, when he is under hypnosis.

Thus, according to this doctrine, what needs explanation is not belief but rather the absence of belief—suspense of judgement, the questioning attitude when one weighs evidence and considers alternatives. Belief is the primitive and the 'natural' state for which we have a strong and spontaneous inclination. So the existence of this unquestioning acceptance (called by Cook Wilson 'Being under an impression that . . .') ought not to surprise us. It is just a manifestation of Primitive Credulity. What ought to surprise us is the fact that we sometimes manage to avoid it.

What are we to say of this doctrine? Clearly there is some truth in it. But before we try to decide how much, it would be well to alter the terminology which these philosophers use. As you will have noticed, it is much the same as Hume's. The 'believing' which is manifested in primitive credulity is not at all like the assent which is analysed in the traditional Occurrence Analysis. It is just the unquestioning acceptance of an idea: and by 'idea' they mean what we have been calling 'a proposition'. (Strictly, perhaps, an 'idea' should be a proposition symbolized by mental images; but in their usage it also includes propositions formulated in words.)

Their doctrine, then, in my own terminology, comes to this:

[1] It is most unfortunate that this brilliant little essay is omitted from the Everyman edition of *Literary Studies*.

the human mind has a spontaneous (unacquired) tendency to accept without question any proposition which is presented to it; and this tendency operates as a matter of course, unless there is something else to hold it in check. The power of suspending judgement, of asking questions and weighing evidence, the power on which reasonable assent depends, is not something we possess from the beginning. It is an achievement, which has to be learned, often painfully. To put it in another way: the attitude of 'being objective' about a proposition which comes before one's mind and assenting to it only if the evidence which one has is on balance favourable to it, and then only with that degree of confidence which is warranted by the evidence, and of suspending judgement unless and until these conditions are fulfilled—this attitude is something which 'goes against the grain' of our natural tendencies.[1] We have to acquire this attitude of being 'objective' and impartial, much as we have to acquire the power of controlling our instinctive desires.

No doubt every sane adult does acquire this power of suspending judgement in some degree (indeed, it is one of the essential constituents of sanity); but not necessarily about all subjects, nor at all times. Many a man can suspend judgement and weigh evidence very well about matters which fall within his own personal experience, or about matters on which he is an expert; and yet outside this field he may remain, as we say, 'childishly credulous'. Moreover, this critical and questioning frame of mind is not only an achievement, it is a somewhat precarious one. Most of us can suspend judgement and weigh evidence when we are healthy and wide-awake, but not so easily when we are tired, or ill, or frightened, or angry. We quite often slip back into the state of primitive credulity under the stress of emotional excitement or fatigue; and as Bagehot says, we all slip back into it when we are dreaming.

I suggest then, that Cook Wilson's 'Being under an impression that . . .' may be regarded as a relapse into this state of primitive credulity. When we jump to a conclusion, a proposition is brought into our minds by association or by some other non-logical

[1] Most of us rather dislike 'sitting on the fence' in a state of suspended judgement, or even disapprove of it. Lloyd George is supposed to have said of a political colleague 'He has sat on the fence so long that the iron has entered even into his soul'.

process. And if we are not wide-awake and on our guard (as we quite often are not) our spontaneous tendency to accept the proposition has free play; there is nothing to inhibit our primitive credulity, and so we accept the proposition in an unquestioning and undoubting way, without noticing what we are doing (or rather, without noticing what is happening to us).

As has been suggested already, the surprising thing, according to this account of the matter, is that quite often this unthinking acceptance does not occur and reasonable assent, in accordance with the evidence, does occur instead; or suspense of judgement, if the evidence is too weak or too conflicting to justify either assent or dissent.

We might explain this, as Bagehot does, by supposing that our primitive credulity has been to some extent chastened or disciplined by adverse experience. Propositions accepted without evidence are very often falsified, at any rate when they are propositions about easily observable matters of empirical fact, and this painful experience of falsification tends by degrees to *inhibit* our primitive credulity. If it be asked why falsification should be painful, or why it should matter to us at all whether a proposition we have accepted is false or true, the reply is that however credulous we are, we also have a desire for the truth both as a means and as an end. So as a result of this painful experience of falsification, we learn by degrees to restrict our spontaneous inclination-to-believe, and to adopt the more 'canny' policy of believing only those propositions which the available evidence favours. The point of this policy is that these are the propositions which are likely to be true. (That they are the ones which are likely to be true follows analytically from the definition of 'evidence for'. To say that there is evidence E for a proposition p is to say that since E is the case, p has some likelihood of being true.)

Nevertheless, this painful and salutary lesson is never completely learned by any human creature. The policy of believing only in accordance with the evidence can be maintained only by constant effort. The price of maintaining it is 'eternal vigilance', as has been said of freedom. Even the most rational man cannot always keep it up. We all relapse at times into the state of primitive and uncritical credulity in which we accept propositions in an undoubting and unquestioning way: and that is why there is such a state as 'being under an impression that . . .'. It must be pointed out that these speculations about primitive credulity are not to be found in Cook Wilson's own writings, nor in those of his disciples. So far as I am aware neither he nor his disciples mention 'primitive credulity' at all.

IMPRESSIONS AND ESTIMATES

So far, my own aim has been just to expound this final part of the traditional Occurrence Analysis of belief, this Cook Wilsonian appendix, as it were, on 'Being under an impression that' or 'Thinking without question', and to state it as plausibly as I could. It cannot be denied that Cook Wilson has here put his finger on something important and interesting, something, too, the existence of which must be acknowledged (in one form or another) whatever analysis of belief we accept, and even if we have to conclude in the end that the whole traditional way of treating belief is mistaken, or inadequate.

Nevertheless, there are some criticisms which are bound to occur to us. We are inclined to say that Cook Wilson has exaggerated the difference between the two states of mind he distinguishes, reasonable belief on the one hand and 'being under an impression that . . .' on the other. And might there not be intermediate cases between the two? To be clear about these questions we need to consider different types of example. His own example, the mistake about the man in the street, is highly relevant; but there are others.

When we make a slip in a piece of deductive reasoning, an arithmetical calculation for instance, our state of mind *is* entirely different from the one in which we are when we have a reasonable but mistaken opinion, and our error is rightly described as 'a failure to think'. Here we are just 'jumping to a conclusion' in an unreasonable, or rather, a non-reasonable way. (It is not that we are 'reasoning badly'. The trouble is that at a certain stage in the process we are not reasoning at all.) But in Cook Wilson's own example, about the man whom we mistake for a friend, it is not nearly so clear that our state of mind is *completely* different from one of reasonable belief, though of course it is not completely reasonable either. There is really no denying that in this case we do in some sense 'have evidence' for the proposition we unquestioningly accept, weak though that evidence may be. Moreover, there is no denying that in some sense we accept the proposition 'because of' this evidence which we have. What is wrong with us is the unquestioning way in which we treat the evidence. We fail to consider that there might be adverse evidence as well: e.g. the fact that to-day is Tuesday and our friend is nearly always away from Oxford on Tuesdays, or just the fact that two different men often look very much alike from the back.

There are other states of mind which are quite clearly intermediate between Cook Wilson's two extremes. Indeed, we sometimes use Cook Wilson's own word 'impression' for describing states of mind which are at any rate partially reasonable.

We sometimes ask another person 'What is your impression of Mr So and So?' or 'What impression have you formed of him?' For instance, we might be enquiring of the Warden of St Benedict's College about one of his undergraduates, and the reply we receive is 'My impression is that intellectually he is low Third Class, but in character as sound as a bell'. Sometimes we treat such answers with respect and attach considerable importance to them. The 'impression' need not be about a person. It might be about a place ('What was your impression of Guatemala?'). Or it might be about a whole class of persons or a whole class of material objects. 'My impression is that Oxford undergraduates work much harder than they did thirty years ago.' 'My impression is that most metals conduct electricity.' On the other hand, when we say, as we sometimes do, 'My general impression is . . .' we might be referring to an individual person or place or object. This is because inductive generalizations can be made about an individual entity, for example, 'John usually goes to Church on Sundays' 'It rains nearly every day in the Lake District' and these 'general impressions' are akin to them or are, as it were, an inexplicit form of them.

Again, let us consider the process which is called 'estimation'; for instance estimating how far away a certain hill is which you see ('about $1\frac{1}{2}$ miles') or estimating on a foggy day that the range of visibility on this part of the road is between 80 and 100 yards. A more painful example is the mark which an examiner gives to a candidate's paper. All these estimates are no doubt fallible. But again, we think it proper to pay some attention to them, and *faute de mieux* we are willing to rely upon them in our actions and take quite important practical decisions on the strength of them.

We may also consider the unsupported *dicta* of experts. For instance a classical scholar says 'This line cannot have been written by Virgil even though it does occur in quite a good manuscript of the *Aeneid*.'

In all these cases, the interesting point is that these people cannot produce evidence for their impression or their estimate. At any rate they cannot produce nearly enough evidence to justify it, and quite often they cannot produce any evidence at all. Why then do we rely on such impressions and estimates—our own or other people's—to the extent that we do, and why do we think it reasonable to rely on them? Because there is a sense in which such impressions and estimates *are* quite often based on abundant evidence, although the speaker cannot state the evidence, either to others or to himself, or at best can only state a very little of it. One may have evidence, though one cannot give it.

What has happened is roughly this. The speaker has in fact had a number of experiences (very many, perhaps) which are relevant to the question you ask him. These experiences have accumulated over a considerable period of time, and each of them has had an effect upon his mind, though he cannot recall most of them or even perhaps any of them. It is the cumulative effect of these past experiences which determines the 'impression' which he has concerning the person or thing or class of things or persons, about which you ask him, or the 'estimate' which he makes. In this respect, his state of mind does resemble reasonable belief. In one sense of the word 'have' he really does have a great deal of evidence for the impression or the estimate which he imparts to us.

But in another respect, his state of mind differs from reasonable belief. Although he has this evidence and his impression or estimate is in accordance with it, he cannot *recall* this evidence or state it (not even to himself) or, at the best, he can only recall a very little of it.

When we ask him 'What is your impression of *x*?' or indeed when he asks himself, he just finds himself inclining to a particular answer, perhaps very decidedly, but he cannot say why. He cannot 'justify' his answer or his estimate, or at best can only give a very incomplete justification of it. He cannot *give* the evidence which (in a way) he has. Sometimes, moreover, this state of mind comes even closer to reasonable belief. The impression or estimate need not be an absolutely unquestioning one. The man may consider several alternative answers, when we ask him for his impression of so and so or his estimate of such and such. 'Let me think', he says, or 'Give me a little time to think'. What sort of thinking does he do? Rather an odd sort. He considers various alternative answers, dwells upon each of them for a time, and then selects the one which 'feels right'. What he is really doing is to allow time for his relevant past experiences to work upon him. For he does 'retain' them, even though he cannot recall them individually, and they can still have effects upon his present consciousness.

Consequently his answer, when he gives it, does have the preferential character which belongs to reasonable assent. We cannot quite say that he decides for p rather than for q. 'Decide' is too active a word. It would be nearer the truth to say that p recommends itself to him more than q does. Furthermore, in this type of case (where the man says 'Give me a little time to think') the other feature which reasonable assent is supposed to have, namely a feeling of confidence which varies in degree, is often present also. The impression or estimate need not be absolutely undoubting, as it is in Cook Wilson's 'being under an impression that'. The speaker may say 'My strong impression is that . . .'. Or he may say 'That is my impression, but of course it is no more than an impression'. In the same way, an estimate (e.g. about the range of visibility on a foggy day) may be more confident or less. It may be made with very little confidence indeed, thereby resembling the lowest degree of reasonable assent. 'The best estimate I can make is that it is about 80 yards, but I may easily be wrong.'

I hope it has now been shown that there are intermediate cases between Cook Wilson's two extremes, reasonable belief or opinion on the one side, and 'being under an impression that . . .' on the other. Cook Wilson has made a hard and fast distinction, a distinction of black and white, where in fact there are many shades of grey in between.

But still, we should not have been able to see that there are these intermediate cases, or to appreciate their interest and importance, if he had not drawn our attention to the great difference there is between the two extremes. His doctrine of 'being under an impression that' was therefore a very notable addition to the traditional Occurrence Analysis of belief.

LECTURE 10

THE FREEDOM OF ASSENT IN DESCARTES AND HUME

What is the relation between belief and will, or more generally, between belief and the conative side of our nature? On this question there is an interesting conflict of opinion between Descartes on the one side and Hume on the other. It is convenient to begin with Hume's view (reversing the historical order) because it is a very natural and plausible one.

In a well-known passage in the *Appendix* to the *Treatise of Human Nature*[1] Hume says plainly that belief is something involuntary. He is arguing against the theory that believing consists in adding some other idea to those which are already before one's mind. His answer to it is this: 'The mind has the command over all its ideas, and can separate, unite, mix and vary them, as it pleases; so that if belief consisted merely in a new idea annexed to the conception, it would be in a man's power to believe what he pleased.' He obviously regards this as a *reductio ad absurdum* of the theory which he is criticizing. He goes on to say quite explicitly that belief consists in 'something that depends not on the will' and that it arises 'from certain determinate causes and principles of which we are not masters'.

Assent, then, according to Hume, is something wholly involuntary. We may illustrate his view by an example which he uses elsewhere, about flame and heat. If I see a flame over there, on the far side of the room, I cannot help believing that the flame is hot. I cannot prevent the idea of 'heat over there' from presenting itself to my mind in a lively or forceful manner. And if the idea does present itself to my mind in this lively or forceful way, that is the same as saying (in Hume's view) that I believe it or assent to it. So in a case like this, I just have to assent to the proposition 'That flame over there is hot'; I cannot help it. I have no choice about it.

[1] Clarendon Press edition (ed. Selby-Bigge) pp. 623 *fin.*–4.

Descartes, however, in an equally celebrated passage in the *Meditations* (Meditation IV)[1] appears to reject this doctrine quite flatly. Descartes' word for assent is 'judgement'. (Sometimes he calls it 'affirming or denying'.) And the whole point of Meditation IV is to maintain that judgement is an act of free will. It might seem to follow from this that it *is* in our power to assent to whatever we please—just what Hume denies.

I am not sure whether Descartes does want to go quite as far as this. In actual fact, at any rate, it seems perfectly clear that we cannot assent to any proposition we please, just by an act of will here and now. Consider the proposition 'Pigs have wings'. Is it really in one's power to assent to this proposition just by an act of free choice? Or again (to alter Hume's example a little), suppose you see a house which is on fire. You look into a room from outside, through the window, and see the furniture and the floor blazing, and hear the flames crackling. Is it in your power to assent to the proposition 'the room is confortably cool'? You may very much wish that you could, because you would like to save a valuable picture which is hanging on the wall. But obviously you cannot assent to this proposition, however much you might wish to. On the contrary, you cannot help believing that the room is intensely hot.

Nevertheless, it *is* sometimes possible to induce oneself to assent to a proposition by a long series of voluntary efforts, even though it is not in one's power to assent to it by a single act of will here and now. To put it another way; belief can be voluntarily cultivated, at least sometimes, though it cannot be instantaneously produced just by a single *fiat* of will. This is why people sometimes request us or entreat us to believe things. When someone says 'I never meant to do it, please do believe me' (or even 'You have got to believe me', 'You must believe me'), perhaps he is requesting or commanding something which is at the moment quite impossible. The story he has told us may be so extraordinary that we just cannot accept it here and now. Nevertheless, we may manage to accept it later if we try hard enough and long enough. Indeed, he himself might say 'Please *try* to believe me'.

The important point here is that the direction of our attention

[1] *Philosophical Works of Descartes* (edited by Haldane and Ross, Cambridge University Press 1911), Vol. 1, pp. 174–7.

is to a considerable extent under our voluntary control. For example, it may be difficult to believe an undergraduate's story when he says he fell asleep in the train on the way back from London, missed the connection at the junction, and woke up to find himself at Bristol instead of Oxford. Still, we reflect afterwards, he has told us the truth more often than not on past occasions, and on this occasion he told his story with an air of ingenuous sincerity. He is not a very good actor either, as we saw from his performance in the College play last term. And after all, people do fall asleep in trains sometimes.

In other words, what we do is to direct our attention to the favourable evidence, the evidence for the proposition we were asked to believe, and avert our attention from the evidence against it. This is something which we can voluntarily do, if we try hard enough and go on trying. And as a result, we may be able in the end to assent to the proposition without any difficulty, though it was quite beyond our power to do so at the beginning. Thus assent may be voluntary in the long run, at least sometimes, even though in the short run it is quite beyond our voluntary control.

You may think that the procedure I have described is indeed a charitable one (at least in this example), a case of trying to 'believe the best' of another person and succeeding; but you may also think that from an intellectual point of view it is somewhat disreputable. The point is, however, that this procedure—disreputable or not—is sometimes effective. So in some cases, at least, it is in a man's power to 'believe what he pleases', at any rate in the long run; and therefore Hume must be wrong when he says, without any qualification, that belief is something 'that depends not on the will'. And Descartes is at least partly right when he says that judgement (assent) is an act of will. At any rate, he is right in maintaining that assent is to some extent under our voluntary control, in the long run even if not immediately; and we still have to admit that he is right about this, even if we reject his ultra-libertarian conception of the will.

I will just add that the process of voluntarily directing our attention is not always an intellectually disreputable or unreasonable one. By directing our attention to the favourable evidence, we may discover that there really is a good deal more evidence for the proposition than there seemed to be at first sight. We may be led to recall relevant facts which had not previously occurred to us, for example, that the undergraduate is an unusually sound sleeper, so that his story of not waking up at the junction might quite possibly be true.

What *is* intellectually disreputable is to direct your attention in such a way that you end by forgetting about the unfavourable evidence altogether. One ought to direct attention to the unfavourable evidence too; and then one may find that there is also more of that than one supposed.

But when Descartes maintains that assent is an act of will, what chiefly interests him, of course, is the negative side of this doctrine: not so much that it is in our power to assent as we choose, but that it is in our power to withhold assent as we choose. The important point about this 'freedom of judgement', in his eyes at least, is that it is a freedom to suspend judgement. The only limitation on it is that we cannot help assenting to propositions which we 'clearly and distinctly perceive to be true'. We do have to assent to propositions which are self-evident. It is not so much that a man can believe what he likes; it is rather that (with this exception) he can always refrain from believing, if he likes. In all other cases, however plausible a proposition may be, however strongly or forcefully or vivaciously it presents itself to one's mind (as Hume would put it), one can always suspend judgement about that proposition, and just consider it in a neutral way, neither accepting it nor rejecting it. This is the kind of 'freedom of judgement' which Descartes is most anxious to maintain; and this is the most important part of his doctrine that assent is a matter of free will. If assent is a matter of free will, we are always free to refuse assent as well as to give it, except when the proposition we are considering is one which we clearly and distinctly perceive to be true.

This doctrine is an essential precondition for Descartes' Method of Doubt. We obviously cannot use this method unless it is in our power to suspend judgement about many propositions which we ordinarily believe. Descartes thinks that if we are able to withhold assent, by a voluntary effort, it is always in our power to avoid assenting erroneously. When we do fall into error it is our own fault. We need not have assented to a proposition which turns out later to be false.

A consequence of this, to which Descartes himself attaches

importance, is that God is not responsible for our errors, whereas we should have to say that God *is* responsible for them, if we did not have this freedom to assent or to withhold assent as we choose. God is no more to be blamed for our erroneous assents than for our immoral actions. In the one case as in the other, it was in our power to refrain from making the wrong choice. In either case, the responsibility is ours. Each of us is personally responsible for his beliefs, as he is for his actions; whereas, if Hume were right, the notion of personal responsibility would have no application to beliefs at all.

From this, again, a further conclusion has sometimes been drawn, though not by Descartes himself: namely, that we deserve to be chastised for our intellectual errors, no less than for our moral delinquencies, and that it is no excuse in either case to say 'I couldn't help it'. This is a most alarming contention, which could easily be used to justify all sorts of political and religious persecution. We may hope, for Descartes' sake, that it does not really follow from his doctrine of the freedom of assent. I shall return to this question later.[1]

But is it always in our power to withhold assent from propositions which are not self evident? In the example mentioned before about the burning house, *is* it in our power to abstain from assenting to the proposition that the room full of flames is very hot? Can we help believing this, whether we like it or not? Can we suspend judgement about it, however hard we try? To take a less exciting example, can we help believing that the wall over there is hard? It may seem obvious that we cannot.

But even if we are incapable of withholding assent from these propositions here and now, there is still something which we can voluntarily do. We can train ourselves by degrees to suspend judgement about the whole class of inductively-supported propositions concerning matters of fact, propositions which acquire their 'force' or 'vivacity' (as Hume would put it) from a long experience of 'constant conjunctions'. Descartes could still maintain that in the long run, though not immediately, it is in our power to withhold assent even from such propositions as these. After all, as Hume himself admits or indeed insists, these inductively-supported

[1] P. 238, below.

propositions are not logically necessary. It is conceivable that they might be false. Not only that. Some propositions supported by pretty strong inductive evidence do in fact turn out to be false, even though they present themselves to our minds with a 'feel' of forcefulness or vivacity, for example, the celebrated propositions that all swans are white; or that no creature with fur lays eggs (the duck-billed platypus does); or that what looks like water is water (it may be a mirage). Nor does Descartes claim that his Method of Doubt, which requires such suspense of judgement, is an easy one to use. On the contrary, he insists himself that a considerable amount of voluntary effort is required and has to be continued over quite a long period of time.

We should also notice that it is only suspense of judgement which Descartes is concerned with, not suspense of action. He is not recommending us to follow the example of the ancient sceptic Carneades, who had to be led about by the hand, to prevent him from walking into fires or over cliffs. And surely it is in our power to act as if a proposition were true without assenting to it, and even to act resolutely as if it were true. No one would deny, of course, that it is in our power to act so, when the proposition is one which we have no inclination to believe. This is something which actors and hypocrites manage to do quite easily. But Descartes maintains that it is in our power to combine these two attitudes—suspense of judgement and a decision to act 'as if'—where the proposition is one which we have been in the habit of believing all our lives, for example, the proposition that walls are hard, or that dogs bite. He says that it is in our power, though it is not at all easy. We may notice that the same is said by mystics about the 'spiritual exercises' which they recommend; and indeed the Cartesian Method of Doubt could itself be regarded as a kind of 'spiritual exercise'.

THE RELEVANCE OF SOME PSYCHOPATHOLOGICAL PHENOMENA

Before we decide that Descartes is mistaken, perhaps we might do well to consider certain phenomena of psychopathology, which do at least show what human nature is capable of, in the way of withholding assent from propositions which most men believe. In this respect, human nature is capable of more things and stranger things than common sense philosophers suppose, and even than Hume supposes.

There are propositions which the ordinary person might say he cannot help believing, for example the proposition that other human beings have thoughts and feelings as he has himself. And yet in some forms of mental disease people do refrain from assenting to these 'obvious' propositions. They are quite seriously not convinced that other human creatures are conscious beings, who have thoughts and wishes and feelings and sense-experiences. Or again, they are not convinced that walls are solid or even (sometimes) that there is a material world at all. Indeed, they sometimes go even further than Descartes recommends when he is describing his Method of Doubt. They not only suspend judgement about these propositions, but refrain at least sometimes, from acting as if they were true (for example they treat another human organism as if it were not conscious).

So Hume must be wrong if he thinks, as he apparently does, that assent to such propositions is absolutely unavoidable, that no-one can *help* believing them—whatever difficulties we may have, in our philosophical moments, in finding any good reason for doing so. For here are people who do not believe these propositions, but are in a state of suspended judgement about them. To these people it seems a perfectly serious possibility that these 'obvious' propositions might be false.

Of course, their attitude of suspended judgement is not altogether the same as the one Descartes has in mind. When such people refrain from assenting to these propositions which everyone else believes, their suspense of judgement is not a matter of conscious choice. It is not an exercise of what Descartes calls 'free will'. So far as their consciousness goes, they just find themselves unable to assent to these propositions which everyone else believes. It is not just that they cannot help suspending judgement about them; they cannot help suspecting that these propositions may very well be false. Their non-assent, then, is not something consciously and freely decided on; and in that important respect it differs from the non-assent (or suspense of judgement) which Descartes is talking about, the suspense of judgement which is an essential part of his Method of Doubt.

But perhaps this is not the whole story. First, we may point out that according to some theories at any rate (theories of the psycho-analytical type) this pathological suspense of judgement, though we cannot call it voluntary, is not wholly involuntary either. There is a sense in which these people suspend judgement (withhold assent) because they want to, though this 'want' is an unconscious one, that is, a desire which they have but are unaware of having. They want to escape from what other people call 'the real world'—the world in which there are things and persons independent of oneself, things and persons to which one must adapt oneself practically, and also emotionally, a process which is often troublesome and sometimes very painful. So they want this world of things and persons to be something whose existence is uncertain and questionable. Thus there is a sense in which they withhold assent from these 'obvious' propositions because they prefer to withhold it, though this preference is not a matter of conscious choice.

'BE MAD IN ORDER TO BE WISE'

Descartes himself, of course,—unlike Leibniz—had no conception of unconscious or even subconscious mental processes or states. That is one of the major weaknesses of his philosophy of mind. Still, these pathological cases are relevant to his doctrine of the Freedom of Assent. As I have said already, they do at least show —contrary to the view of Hume and of some modern common sense philosophers—that human beings really are capable of withholding assent from propositions which most people believe with complete conviction. Moreover, it seems that motivation has something to do with this suspense of judgement. There is at any rate something conative or volitional about the non-assent which occurs in these pathological cases.

Well, what these mentally diseased persons achieve from unconscious motives (motives they are not themselves aware of, and are even unable to be aware of) *we* might be able to achieve by conscious choice and effort. And what they achieve from interested motives, from a desire to 'escape from reality', we might be able to achieve from disinterested ones—from a desire to find which of the propositions we ordinarily assent to are worthy of assent, or can be reasonably assented to.

There *is* something resembling madness in the Cartesian suspense of judgement. Critics of Descartes are right in pointing out that his Method of Doubt does require us to suspend judgement about propositions which all sane people believe in the ordinary affairs of daily life. Nevertheless, the difference of motives (between the insane persons we have mentioned and the Cartesian doubter) is after all rather important. Descartes' motive is a desire to know: the insane person's motive is a desire *not* to. And another important difference, as I have said, is that Descartes consciously decides to suspend judgement, in a wide-awake manner, well aware of why he does it; whereas the insane person suspends judgement without being aware of why he does it, and has no conscious control of his assenting or non-assenting.

If you like paradoxes, what Descartes says is 'Be mad in order to be wise': not in order to escape from reality (or from disagreeable duties to your neighbour), but in order to find out, if you can, what sort of a real world there is, and what propositions can be reasonably believed about it. The best way, he says, of achieving these aims is to become conscious of your freedom in assenting: to realize, by actually doing it, that you *are* free to withhold assent if you choose; that you *need* not give your assent to any proposition if you find no good reason for doing so. I see nothing silly in this programme; and I think that when Descartes emphasizes this autonomy of rational beings, their freedom to assent or not as they see fit, he has put his finger on something important, which empiricist philosophers have tended to neglect.

Locke, it is true, does seem to agree with Descartes on this point. The 'Ethics of Belief' which he states in Book IV of the *Essay* seems to presuppose a theory of the freedom of assent. But later empiricists, for the most part, have not paid much attention to this part of Locke's philosophy, or have rejected it. We have seen that Hume explicitly rejects the doctrine of freedom of assent, and maintains on the contrary that belief is something wholly involuntary. We have also seen that Newman (whom one may count as an empiricist) makes a brilliant and savage attack on Locke's version of the Cartesian doctrine.[1]

[1] *Grammar of Assent*, ch. 6. See Lecture 6, above.

If I may continue to talk about the history of Philosophy for a moment, I should like to suggest that this issue about the freedom or non-freedom of assent has some bearing on a complaint which has sometimes been made against the empiricist philosophy—the objection that the empiricists conceive of the human mind as 'purely passive'. There is a good deal of confusion in this criticism. One may point out, for example, that the antithesis between 'active' and 'passive' is a somewhat slippery one, and moreover that both 'active' and 'passive' are highly emotive words as these critics of empiricism use them.

Nevertheless, this traditional objecton to empiricism is not wholly pointless. The empiricists have not always been clear about the distinction between the mental processes which just go on in us automatically, and those which are rationally and consciously controlled. To put it in an exaggerated way, they tend to regard the human mind as if we were half asleep all the time. So we are, much of the time. We do spend a good part of our lives behaving, and thinking, in a more or less habitual way.

But we are not always in this condition. It is in our power to wake up, to become self-conscious and clearly aware of what is going on in us (or at least of some of the things which are going on in us) and to criticize and evaluate it: to ask ourselves what reason there is for believing something we find ourselves believing, or what good there is, either moral or prudential, in some action we find ourselves doing or about to do. And then, if we see fit, we can decide, at least sometimes, to give up this belief and either suspend judgement or adopt some other belief instead; and similarly, to abandon this action, and either do nothing, or do something else instead. Moreover, these decisions are sometimes effective.

It is as if we had the power of intervening, consciously and rationally, in our own mental processes, and of altering the course they take. And this is one of the excuses for the talk about 'two selves', a 'higher' self and a 'lower' self, which bothers some philosophers so much. Still, everyone knows that we can do the things I have just been trying to describe, however difficult it is to talk sense about them. And my suggestion is that the empiricists have on the whole tended to emphazise these facts too little; whereas the rationalists—or at any rate Descartes and Leibniz—

and Kant too, who is a rationalist in his moral philosophy—have perhaps emphasized them too much.

The relevant antithesis, however, is not that between 'active' and 'passive' (as in the traditional criticism of empiricism which I mentioned). It is rather the antithesis between two sorts of activity, automatic and unchosen activity, and reasonable self-conscious activity, when the course of our thoughts and of our actions is controlled by conscious decisions.

Or again (if I may continue a little longer with these rather high-flown considerations) perhaps we might put the point this way: There are two types or levels of 'autonomy' or 'freedom' in the human mind, and consequently two types or levels of 'responsibility'. In the first, it is simply that the *ἀρχή κινήσεως* is *ἐν ἡμῖν* (as Aristotle puts it), 'the cause of what happens is in ourselves'. We behave as we do because of our desires or our habits; we believe as we do because of our past experience of constant conjunctions, or because of our desires again, or because we have got into the habit of believing what our teachers told us.

But there is another sort of autonomy which we only have when we consciously decide what to do, and consciously decide what propositions to assent to. We may sometimes consciously decide to assent or to act unreasonably. But this sort of 'chosen' unreasonableness is something different from the unchosen unreasonableness which we display when we assent stupidly or act foolishly without being clearly aware of what is going on in us. Of course, we are responsible for these unchosen stupidities or follies or wrongdoings. These unchosen assents or actions were ours and we must take the blame for them. But if we assent or act 'with our eyes open', as a result of a conscious decision, we are responsible for our reasonableness or unreasonableness in a new way, or to a degree we were not before.

'CLEARLY AND DISTINCTLY PERCEIVED'

So far I have been arguing that there is a good deal to be said for Descartes' doctrine of the Freedom of Assent. But the use which he himself makes of it is another matter, or (if you like) the use which he recommends *us* to make of this freedom of assent which he claims we possess. Here he lays himself open to very serious criticisms, as recent philosophers have pointed out. According to Descartes, a reasonable person will assent only to those propositions which he clearly and distinctly perceives to be true. He will withhold assent from all other propositions (even though he may go on acting as if they were true, *as a thinker* he will suspend judgement about them). For this is the only way in which he can avoid assenting erroneously. What sort of proposition can be clearly and distinctly perceived to be true? Sometimes Descartes is thought to say that the only propositions in this privileged class are logically necessary ones.

He does, of course, lay great stress on the clearness and distinctness of mathematical propositions, and especially of the simpler sorts of mathematical entailments which can be comprehended without the aid of memory. But he does not really hold that logically-necessary propositions are the *only* ones which can be clearly and distinctly perceived to be true. Some contingent propositions are also admitted to this privileged class: for example the contingent proposition 'I am now thinking'. There are also propositions (equally contingent) concerning the ideas which I have at present in my mind. These ideas may or may not correspond to anything in the extra-mental world, but at any rate it is evident that I do have them. Let us call these 'inspectively-evident propositions'.

Thus he holds, I think, that there are two sorts of propositions which are clearly and distinctly perceived to be true. (1) *logically necessary* propositions, or rather those logically-necessary propositions which are simple enough to be grasped without the aid of memory. (2) *inspectively evident* propositions about one's own mental processes and about the ideas one has in one's own mind. And his view is that in order to avoid error, we ought to assent only to propositions which fall into one or other of these two classes, and that we ought to withhold assent from all other propositions—unless or until we can see that some of them follow logically either from a necessary proposition, or from an inspectively evident one, or from some combination of the two. This is his recommendation for the use we should make of the Freedom of Assent which he claims that we have.

But what makes this policy reasonable? Descartes' answer is, that it is the only one which will save us from assenting mistakenly. It is, so to speak, an insurance policy against error—and he claims that it is the only possible insurance policy for this purpose. We might be inclined to reply that it is reasonable, at least sometimes, to take the risk of assenting mistakenly. Taking this risk, and accepting the consequences, is sometimes the best way of finding out what the facts actually are. But let us suppose that we do wish to avoid error at all costs. Even so Descartes' recommendations for avoiding it involves him in very great difficulties.

SOME DIFFICULTIES IN DESCARTES' ARGUMENT

For we must ask *how we know* that we are liable to fall into error, if we do assent to propositions which we do not clearly and distinctly perceive to be true. Unless we do know this, or at least have good reasons for believing it, Descartes' insurance policy is pointless, and there is no reason for limiting our assents in the way he recommends. For example, how do I know that I run the risk of being mistaken if I assent to Hume's proposition 'That flame over there is hot'? It is true we know *a priori* that this proposition may conceivably be false. Its falsity would involve no contradiction. That is, it is not a logically necessary proposition. And it is not an inspectively evident proposition either, as 'There now appears to me to be a flame over there' is. But though it may conceivably be false that the flame over there is hot, or even that there is a flame over there at all, it does not follow from this alone that either of these propositions is in the least *likely* to be false—as Moore has pointed out. If you claim that there is a finite probability of its being false, and therefore there is a risk of being mistaken if one assents to it, you must give grounds for making this claim.

'Well', you may say (as Descartes himself does) 'Propositions of this sort, which I have believed in the past—empirical or contingent propositions going beyond what is inspectively evident—have quite often turned out to be false. So I run the risk of being mistaken again if I assent to such a proposition now.' This argument is very plausible. But there are two difficulties in it.

(*a*) How do you know that its premiss is true? (*b*) If it is, why should it be relevant to the conclusion (viz. that I am likely to be mistaken again if I go on assenting in the way I have in the past)?

Let us first consider the premiss. If you do know that you have held false beliefs in the past (have assented mistakenly)—as of course you do—you can only know this by memory. But according to Descartes' own principles, all memory judgements are fallible. No memory-proposition can be clearly and distinctly perceived to be true.

He is somewhat embarrassed about this point, because on the face of it memory is needed for all deductive reasoning except the very simplest. For example, to follow the reasoning in Pythagoras' theorem—to see that if something is a Euclidean right angled triangle, the square on the hypotenuse *must* be equal to the sum of the squares on the other two sides—you must remember the earlier steps in the argument in order to see that the conclusion is entailed by them. But he thinks this difficulty can be got over by training yourself to keep all the steps of the argument in mind at once (itself an inductive claim). And I think he does want to stick to his contention that all memory-judgements are fallible.

Now if they are, I cannot know that I have held false beliefs in the past. No doubt I am strongly inclined to believe this proposition about my own past beliefs. But after all, it *is* only a memory proposition, and I do not clearly and distinctly perceive it to be true. So according to Descartes' principles I ought to withhold assent from this proposition about my past beliefs. Nothing compels me to assent to it, however much I may be inclined to. So, if I am reasonable, should I not suspend judgement about it?

Thus the premiss of Descartes' argument—the proposition that I have often assented erroneously in the past—is one which he is not entitled to assert on his own principles. He can indeed assert that this proposition about his own past mistakes is being entertained by him, and also that he feels an inclination to believe it. For these are things which are inspectively evident. But he is not entitled to assert to the proposition itself, because it is a memory-proposition, and therefore not one which he can clearly and distinctly perceive to be true.

Moreover, in order to know that we have assented mistakenly in the past, we really need to use memory twice over. First we must be able to remember that we really did assent to a proposition *p* on some past occasion. But this is not all that we have to remember. For secondly, if I claim to know not only that I did assent to this proposition on some past occasion, but also that the proposition turned out to be false, I must remember that the actual facts were other than I had believed them to be.

To take an example of Descartes' own, he believed that a tower which he saw in the distance was round, because it looked round from the place where he was. He must be able to remember that he did believe this. But before he can assert that this was an erroneous belief, he must be able to remember that the tower turned out later to be square and not round at all. And here, we may notice, we should have to assume that some perceptual propositions—propositions about material objects (not just about sense-data) can be known to be true. To take another example, I myself used to believe that all rooks are black. How do I know that this belief of mine was mistaken? Because I remember seeing a pale-cream coloured rook one day on the top of Elsfield Hill.

So much for the premiss of Descartes' argument. He is not entitled to assert that he has often made mistakes in the past, if the class of propositions to which we may reasonably give assent is as restricted as he claims it is. For in order to assent that he has often made mistakes in the past (or even that he has ever made any mistakes at all) he must be able to remember what some of his past beliefs were, and also to remember that the facts turned out to be different from what he had believed them to be.

DESCARTES' RELIANCE ON INDUCTION

Now I turn to the second difficulty in Descartes' argument. However much I know about my own past mistakes, why should this knowledge be relevant to the conclusion Descartes wishes to draw—namely that if I give assent to similar propositions in future, I am likely to be mistaken again? The difficulty, from Descartes' point of view, is that this is an inductive argument, an argument from observed cases to unobserved cases. Because some past beliefs of sort *A* have turned out to be incorrect, it is likely that other beliefs of sort *A* will also be incorrect. That is the argument, and it is clearly an inductive one.

Now the trouble with an inductive argument, as Hume pointed out, is that the conclusion is not entailed by the premiss. There is no contradiction in supposing that the conclusion might be false although the premiss is true. And this is still so, when the conclusion takes the form of a probability statement, as it does here (some propositions of sort *A* have been false, therefore there is a probability that other propositions of sort *A* will also be false).

So here Descartes seems to be in a very awkward dilemma. This inductive proposition 'Because past beliefs of sort *A* have sometimes been erroneous, there is a probability that future beliefs of sort *A* will sometimes be erroneous'—is *not* one which we can clearly and distinctly see to be true, since the premiss does not logically entail the conclusion. It would seem, then, that Descartes ought to withhold assent from it. Yet if he does, he can give no reason for what I called his insurance policy—his policy for avoiding error by confining his assent to propositions which he clearly and distinctly sees to be true.

If we are to refuse to assent to inductive arguments (on the ground that their premisses do not entail their conclusions) the fact that beliefs of sort *A* have often been erroneous in the past is no reason whatever for supposing that future beliefs of sort *A* are sometimes likely to be erroneous too. On the other hand, if Descartes is willing to accept inductive evidence as relevant in *this* case (when he is recommending a policy for assenting) he can have no good ground for refusing to accept it in other cases. And then the policy he recommends is too narrow. It cannot then be reasonable to assent *only* to logically necessary propositions and inspectively evident ones, and to withhold assent from all others.

I am not saying that there is anything inconsistent about the policy itself. But I am saying that it is inconsistent with the reason which he gives for it, because this is an inductive reason; and also (as I mentioned earlier) because the facts which he appeals to are facts about the past and require that we should assent to memory propositions, which we have no right to do if we follow the policy of assenting he recommends—and to some perceptual propositions too, for example 'The tower is square, though it looked round from a distance'.

If I am right, it follows that his insurance policy for avoiding error is too narrow; and he has himself admitted this, first by assenting to memory-propositions about his own past errors, and secondly by assenting to an inductive argument from past errors to the probability of future ones.

So much for the way Descartes applies his doctrine of the Freedom of Assent, or, if you like, the way he recommends us to use the freedom of assent which he claims that we have. In recommending that we should withhold assent from (suspend judgement about) all propositions except those which we clearly and distinctly perceive to be true, he has too narrow a conception of reasonableness—too narrow a conception of what constitutes a good ground for assenting. We may have good grounds for assenting to memory propositions, perceptual propositions, and inductively-supported propositions—with greater or less confidence, according to the strength of the evidence. It is not true that the only good grounds we can have for assenting to a propositions are that it is either logically-necessary, on the one hand, or inspectively evident on the other.

Moreover, in the reasons he himself gives for recommending that we should limit our assents in this way, he assumes that inductive arguments can give good grounds for assent, and also assumes that some memory propositions and some perceptual propositions may be properly assented to: assumptions he cannot consistently make, if his own recommendations are correct.

CAN WE BE REASONABLE ALL THE TIME?

But of course Descartes' doctrine of Freedom of Assent might be true, and important too, even though he himself mis-applies it. Nevertheless, there is one rather serious qualification to be made. Descartes is right in insisting that we do have the power of withholding assent from a proposition if we see no good reason for assenting to it. It is in our power to wake ourselves up and decide consciously whether to assent or to suspend judgement.

But though we have this power, can we exercise it at all times? He seems to assume that we can, if only we will make the effort. 'Just pull yourself together' he seems to say 'and everything will be all right.'

The trouble is, I think, that Descartes regards human beings as more mature and grown up, so to speak, than they actually are. We are not capable of maintaining ourselves continuously in this wide-awake and fully conscious state which he describes—neither with regard to our assents nor yet with regard to our actions—though we *are* capable of getting ourselves into it for short periods, and this is an important fact about us which empiricist philosophers have tended to neglect—despite Locke's remarks on the Ethics of Belief in Book IV of the *Essay*.

I said earlier (somewhat extravagantly perhaps) that empiricist philosophers tend to write of the human mind as if we were always half asleep. Descartes tends to make a different and to some extent opposite mistake. He seems to assume, not indeed that we are always wide awake, but that we could always be, by a mere effort of will. The trouble is that we can sometimes be wide-awake (more often that we actually are) but not always.

Nevertheless, it is important to emphasize that we do have the power of waking ourselves up and deciding consciously and autonomously whether to assent or not, even though we are not capable of maintaining ourselves in that state all the time. After all, we are rational beings, though it is beyond our power to be wholly rational all the time. But even if it were in our power to be wholly rational all the time, it still would not follow that there is anything morally blameworthy about assenting unreasonably (against the evidence or without regard to the evidence) or that we ought to be chastised for doing so.[1] There is nothing wicked about such assents. It is however true, and important, that unreasonable assent is contrary to our long-term interest. It is to our long term interest to believe true propositions rather than false ones. And if we assent reasonably (i.e. in accordance with the evidence), it is likely that in the long run the propositions we believe will be more often true than false.

[1] See p. 225, above.

AN INCONSISTENCY IN HUME

To return now to the conflict between Descartes and Hume concerning the Freedom of Assent: it is worth while to point out that though Hume does say that belief is wholly involuntary—'depends not on the will', arises from principles 'of which we are not masters'—yet he is not wholly consistent about it.

First, what we may call his own philosophical practice seems to contradict his anti-Cartesian theory. If anyone ever went in for Cartesian doubt on the grand scale, surely Hume did. In his sceptical mood, he himself practises Cartesian suspense of judgement, perhaps even too successfully (for instance in Book I Part IV of the *Treatise*).

In that mood, he certainly does refrain from assenting to the propositions which he says elsewhere that we cannot help believing. And his motive is precisely the one Descartes recommends. He abstains from assenting to these propositions because he can find no good reason for assenting to them. And he confesses himself that his belief in them can only be restored by 'carelessness and inattention', or by returning to the activities and interests of ordinary life, such as playing backgammon or dining with his friends.[1] These words seem to denote a slipping back out of the wide-awake and fully conscious condition in which Descartes thinks we have to be, if we are to exercise our freedom of assent.

Secondly, in his less sceptical moods Hume is willing to divide our beliefs about matters of fact into two classes. On the one hand, there are the beliefs which have strong inductive support, based on a long experience of constant conjunctions; on the other, there are beliefs which have very little inductive support or none at all.

He does not go so far as to call the first sort of beliefs reasonable ones, as we probably should. We should be inclined to say that they are reasonable in the inductive way, and should reject the assumption that the deductive criteria of reasonableness are the only ones. Nevertheless (in this less sceptical mood) Hume clearly does think that there is a distinction between sensible or

[1] *Treatise* (ed. Selby-Bigge), pp. 218, 269.

sober or sane beliefs on the one side, and silly or superstitious beliefs on the other.

Not only that: he clearly thinks that it is better to hold sensible beliefs, those which have strong inductive support from past experience (of constant conjunctions), than to hold superstitious or silly ones which have very weak inductive support or none at all. Of course, it might be better to abstain from holding silly or superstitious beliefs—it might be better to withhold assent from propositions which have no inductive warrant—and yet we might be incapable of withholding it. Habit or education might be too strong for us. But clearly this is not what Hume thinks himself, at any rate in the *Enquiry concerning Human Understanding*. In the last four pages of the *Enquiry*.[1] He offers us what one may call a policy for believing. So far as propositions concerning matters of fact are concerned, the policy consists in putting all one's money on inductive evidence; and the only *a priori* propositions we are allowed to assent to are deductively-established propositions about 'quantity and number'. He does not just describe this policy, which he calls 'mitigated scepticism'. He recommends us to adopt it. If so, he must surely think that it is in our power to refrain from assenting to propositions, unless and until we find that they have the kind of support which the policy requires.

He is now assuming (just like Descartes) that it is at any rate in our power to abstain from assenting if we choose. This policy for believing was part of a whole 'way of life', too—a way of life which he actually practised, and which helped to make him the admirable and charming person that he was. Hume, perhaps, was a bit of an Existentialist in this part of his philosophy.

The policy he recommends may or may not be a good one. Some of the beliefs he would regard as superstitions may have more to be said for them than he allows. But that is not the question we are discussing. The relevant point at present is merely that he does recommend a policy for assenting: and thereby admits that we do have that freedom to withhold assent from some propositions and give assent to others, which Descartes claims we have.

[1] *Enquiries* (Clarendon Press, Ed. Selby-Bigge), pp. 162–5.

SERIES II

LECTURE I

THE DISPOSITIONAL ANALYSIS: INTRODUCTION

THE TWO ANALYSES CONTRASTED

So much for the traditional Occurrence Analysis of belief. It is now almost universally rejected, at any rate in the English-speaking philosophical world. As we have seen, there are several different versions of the Occurrence Analysis. Locke's version differs from Newman's, and Hume's version is very different from Cook Wilson's. But the contemporary view is that all of them are mistaken. All of them start off on the wrong foot, so to speak, by trying to answer a question which should never have been asked. It is absurd to ask what kind of a mental occurrence believing is, or what kind of a mental act it is, because believing is not any kind of mental occurrence or act.

It would be admitted, I think, that entertaining a proposition *is* a mental occurrence and that we may call it a 'mental act' if we please. But (it would be said) when a man believes some proposition which he is now entertaining, there is not some special sort of event or act occurring in his mind over and above the event or act of entertaining. The additional factor, which makes the difference between bare or neutral entertaining and believing, is something dispositional.

It would also be admitted that coming to believe a proposition, and ceasing to believe it, are mental occurrences, though not necessarily introspectible ones. Or perhaps we should call them processes, for a belief can be acquired over quite a long period of time, and can also be lost gradually. At any rate, both coming to believe and ceasing to believe are happenings. But the belief itself is not a happening: any more than a taste for oysters is, though this too is something which is acquired and may later be lost, and both the acquisition of it and the loss of it are happenings.

So the Dispositional Analysis does not deny that there are

mental occurrences nor that they are relevant to the analysis of belief; or at least it need not, though it has sometimes been stated in a purely Behaviouristic form. But it does deny that belief is itself an occurrence or mental act. A belief, according to this analysis, is something which we have or possess for a period, long or short, not something which happens to us, or something which we 'mentally do', as the phrase 'mental act' might suggest. In this respect (it would be said) belief is like knowledge. Both 'know' and 'believe' are dispositional words; and the 'acts of knowing', which philosophers used to discuss in former days, are just as mythical as 'acts of believing'.

But the difference between the two analyses of belief is not quite so clear-cut as it looks. Even those who think that believing is a mental occurrence or mental act must admit that the word 'believe' is quite often used in a dispositional way. For many years I have believed, on the authority of my teachers, that Rome was founded in 753 BC. But it certainly is not true that all through those years this proposition has been continuously present to my mind in a forceful or vivid manner, or that an act of assenting which has this proposition for its object has been going on in me all the time. If there are indeed occurrent believings or acts of believing, they can only occur at times when a person is actually thinking of or entertaining the proposition believed. And if his belief still exists at other times, as some of our beliefs certainly do, we must admit that the word 'believe' does have a dispositional use, and is in fact used in this way very frequently. Otherwise, we should have to say that when I am not actually thinking of the proposition 'Rome was founded in 753 BC' I no longer believe it; and every time we fall asleep we should lose most of the beliefs which we had during our waking hours, or even all of them.

It follows that the Occurrence Analysis (or at least any plausible version of it) agrees with the Dispositional Analysis on a most important point. According to both analyses, the verb 'to believe' *can* be used in a dispositional way and must be so used quite frequently; and the same is true of such phrases as 'suspect that', 'be of the opinion that', 'be convinced that', which indicate the various degrees a belief may have. However devoted we are to the Occurrence Analysis, we must admit that some statements of the form '*x* believes that *p*' do have to be analysed in a dispositional way.

But of course there is still a very great difference between the two analyses. According to the Occurrence Analysis, the word 'believe' does have an occurrent use as well as a dispositional one. Moreover, 'as well as' does not put the point strongly enough. According to the Occurrence Analysis, the occurrent use of 'believe' is primary, and the dispositional use is derivative; a belief, in the dispositional sense, is a disposition to have actual belief-experiences, occurrent believings, when and if appropriate conditions are fulfilled. Whenever during the past fifty years I have actually entertained the proposition 'Rome was founded in 753 BC', this proposition presented itself to my mind in a vivid or forceful way (as Hume would put it), or an act of assenting took place in me which had this proposition for its object (as Locke or Newman put it). Moreover, at any other time during those years it was true of me that if I *had* been entertaining this proposition at that time, it *would* have presented itself to my mind in a strong or solid or forceful manner, as Hume would say, or an act of assenting to the proposition *would* have taken place in me, as Locke or Newman would say.

In the Dispositional Analysis, on the contrary, it is held that the word 'believe' (and other kindred expressions such as 'think that . . . ' or 'be convinced that . . . ') has *only* a dispositional use. The disposition which we attribute to someone when we say he believes a proposition *p* does of course have its characteristic sort or sorts of occurrent manifestations. Various events are liable to happen in him which would not have happened if he did not believe this proposition. What sort of events they are, we shall see later. But none of these occurrent manifestations are themselves believings. According to the Dispositional Analysis there are no occurrent believings, or rather it makes no sense to say that there are.

It would follow that in this respect the verb 'to believe' differs from some other psychological verbs, for instance the verb 'to fear'. It can truly be said of me that I fear adders, or have a fear of adders, though there are no adders in this neighbourhood at present. But when someone says this of me, he is saying that whenever I do encounter an adder I experience actual feelings of fear, and if I had been seeing an adder now, I should have been experiencing such feelings now. Again, we may say of someone that he is indignant about what has recently happened in Borneo, and this statement may be true of him when he is not thinking of these events at all. But if we make this statement about him, we are saying that whenever he does think of them, he experiences an actual feeling of indignation. Both the verb 'to fear' and the verb 'to be indignant' have an occurrent use as well as a dispositional use. In this respect they are unlike the verb 'to believe', if the Dispositional Analysis of belief is correct: the word 'believe', which we use for describing the disposition, cannot also be used for describing any of the actual occurrences by which the disposition is manifested. It has only a dispositional use.

THE DISPOSITIONAL ANALYSIS: SOME LOGICAL CONSIDERATIONS

When we say that *x* has a disposition *D*, for instance that an object is elastic or soluble in water, or that a person is timid or friendly, what kind of a statement of this? The usual answer is that it is equivalent to a series of conditional statements. If *x* were in circumstances c_1, an event *A* would occur in *x*; if it were in circumstances c_2, a different event *B* would occur in *x*, etc. Thus when we say that *x* is elastic, we are saying that if it were stretched, it would return to approximately its original length when released, and if it were bent, it would return to approximately its original shape when released. We are not of course saying that it *is* actually being stretched or bent, or even that it ever has been stretched or bent, or that it ever will be: though if it never had been actually bent or stretched, or at least if things like it never had been, we should have no means of knowing that these conditional propositions are true of it.

Next, it is important to notice that temporal predicates apply to dispositions and not only to occurrences. We are liable to overlook this. Assuming, rightly, that there are very important differences between dispositions and occurrences (or between disposition-statements and occurrence-statements) we conclude, wrongly, that they have nothing in common at all.

Or, if we do not make this mistake, we tend to assume that the only temporal predicate which applies to dispositions is the predicate of permanence. The dispositions of *x*, we think, last as long as x does, whereas the occurrences which happen to it are momentary or at any rate have a brief duration. But that is a mistake too. Some dispositions, both of things and of persons, are permanent in this sense, though it is not always easy to discover which are the permanent ones; but others have a beginning and an end, as occurrences have. For example, this rubber band is elastic as present. But when it is heated to a high temperature, or is exposed for some days to strong sunlight, it loses its elasticity.

So in the conditional statements which describe a disposition we have to mention a period of time. If between t_1 and t_2 x were in circumstances c_1 an event A would occur in it. If between t_1 and t_2 it were in circumstances c_2, and event B would occur in it, etc. The period between t_1 and t_2 may cover the whole duration of x's existence; on the other hand, it may be quite short. The dispositional property of being good to eat only belongs to a plum for a few days, between the time when it gets ripe and the time when it goes rotten; and a piece of toast only has this property for an hour at the most. Or again, let us consider the dispositional property of being adhesive. A piece of sealing wax has this property for a very short time, while it is held in the candle-flame and for perhaps ten seconds afterwards. (Its adhesiveness *is* a dispositional property. The sealing wax has it, for that short period, even though it is not actually used for sealing up a parcel or an envelope.)

It is important to remember this when considering beliefs. Some of our beliefs do last for a very long time. Archibald acquired his Marxist beliefs when he was a schoolboy, forty years ago, and he has retained them ever since. But there are beliefs which are very short-lived indeed. On a warm and sunny afternoon, a motorist may believe that there is a pool of water on the road ahead. But a second or two later, he ceases to believe this, and is convinced that it was a mirage. When I got up in the morning I believed that to-day was Thursday. But I ceased to believe this as soon as I looked at the newspaper at breakfast. If beliefs are dispositions, it is important to notice that some of them are relatively short-lived dispositions, unlike many of the other dispositions of human beings such as avarice or audacity. And unless we think that there are innate beliefs, no beliefs at all are dispositions which a person has throughout the whole duration of his existence. All of them are acquired at some time or other, though once they have been acquired, some of them may continue as long as the person does who has them.

EPISTEMOLOGICAL CONSIDERATIONS

These logical properties of the dispositional analysis of belief have important epistemological implications, and perhaps rather disturbing ones. If '*A* believes that *p*' is a dispositional statement about *A*, how is it possible to know or find out that *A* does believe that *p*? On the traditional occurrence analysis, there is always one person, namely *A* himself, who can find this out directly, by introspection. All he has to do is to consider the proposition *p* and notice what is going on in his mind. Does he or does he not have the experience of assenting to the proposition? If he does have this experience, he believes the proposition: if not, he does not believe it. (It does not follow that he disbelieves it. To find out that he disbelieves it, he must either have an experience of 'rejecting' it, or an experience of assenting to its contradictory, not-*p*.)

Or again, as Hume would put it, he has to consider the proposition *p* and notice the way in which it presents itself to his mind. Does it present itself to his mind with a 'feel' of solidity or forcefulness or strength? If so, he believes the proposition; if not, he does not.

In the same kind of way, by introspection of his occurrent belief-feelings, he can know directly what *degree* of belief he has with regard to the proposition *p*—whether he believes it with full conviction, or is nearly sure about it but not quite, or believes it only in a mild degree ('I think that *p*') or in a very mild degree ('I suspect that *p*'). All he has to do is to consider the proposition and notice what degree of confidence he feels about it.

Other people, of course, do not have this direct knowledge of *A*'s beliefs. They can sometimes infer what *A*'s beliefs are, by observing his actions, his utterances, or perhaps his emotional symptoms (e.g. the indignation or discomfort he shows when the proposition *p* is denied by someone else, the surprise he shows when *p* turns out to be false). But such inferences, according to the traditional theory, are not always very reliable. Only the believer himself is in a position to know directly what his beliefs are. If others wish to find out what they are, the simplest thing is to go and ask him. He may give an insincere or dishonest reply. But at any rate he knows directly what the right answer is, and no one else does.

But if '*A* believes that *p*' is a dispositional statement about him, the situation is entirely different. *A* himself is no longer in a privileged position. Any knowledge he can have about his own dispositions is as indirect as the knowledge which other people can have about them. A disposition, whether it belongs to an inanimate object or to a person, whether it is one's own or someone else's, is not something which can be known 'just by inspection' either of the introspective or the perceptual kind. The events which are occurrent manifestations of it might be 'inspected', or some of them might be, but that is all.

A dispositional statement, as we have already seen, is equivalent to a series of conditional statements (not just one conditional statement, but a series of them). And at least some of these conditional statements have unfulfilled if-clauses; they are what logicians call 'counter-factual conditionals'. This rubber band was about an inch long when we first saw it. Then someone took it in his hands and stretched it to about twice that length, and when he put it down again it returned to approximately its original length and shape. We say that this rubber band is elastic, that it has been so for a considerable time and will remain so for a considerable time. But when we say this, we are saying that the same thing *would* have happened if it had been stretched in a similar degree a minute earlier and then released, and *would* be happening now if it were to be stretched and released now, and will happen again if it is stretched and released at 2 a.m. tomorrow morning, though it is almost certain that no such events are actually going to occur at such an unlikely hour.

We see now that these conditional statements are much like those to which we commit ourselves when we accept a causal law: except that in this case the conditionals (including the counter-factual ones) are about one single entity—this rubber band—whereas in a causal law they are about a class of entities. Of course, there are also universal dispositional statements, for example 'all salt is soluble in water', 'No serpent is liable to catch measles'. But we are concerned at present with dispositional statements which we make about an individual entity, especially about an individual human being.

The reason why such dispositional statements cannot be established by 'direct inspection' is now fairly obvious. They are inductive statements. It is a defect of some of the older treatments of induction that inductive statements about individual entities were neglected: for example 'John nearly always goes to church on Sundays', 'My car does about 40 miles to the gallon', 'Oxford is usually cold in February'. Scientists indeed are not much interested in inductive statements of this kind. But it would be a mistake to think that induction only goes on in scientific laboratories (if indeed it does go on there, which some authorities on scientific methodology deny). What we call 'knowing a person well' consists very largely in having made a number of fairly well-established generalizations about him in particular. We do not often make them in a conscious and reflective manner. They just grow up in us by degrees, as a result of our familiarity with him, so that we are not surprised, or are less surprised than strangers would be, by what he says and does, or by the emotions or wishes which he has in various sorts of circumstances. The same applies to 'knowing oneself' if we take this to mean 'knowing what sort of a person one is'. I learn by an inductive process that I am timid or resentful and very liable to put the blame on others when things go wrong.

Now if the dispositional analysis of belief is correct, statements of the form '*x* believes that *p*' are somewhat similar to these. We may describe them as inductive hypotheses. As we have seen already, their scope or subject-matter is restricted in two ways. Each of them is a hypothesis about just one individual, and each of them applies only to a limited period of time, though we may not be able to say accurately what its limits are. This period of time may extend into the future, but the more remote the future is, the more precarious our hypothesis becomes.

BELIEVING AND ACTING 'AS IF'

But what exactly is the content of this hypothesis? To put it in another way, what is a person disposed *to*, when he believes a proposition *p*? What are the characteristic manifestations of this sort of disposition, if they are not occurrent believings or it makes no sense to say they are? One answer is that they are actions: to believe a proposition is to be disposed to act as if the proposition were true. This is the simplest version of the Dispositional Analysis, and it is so plausible (at least at first sight) that it has found expression in a familiar proverb 'Acts speak louder than words'.[1]

Let us begin by considering this 'acting as if' analysis of belief. You will find an exposition of it in Professor R. B. Braithwaite's article 'The Nature of Believing' in the *Proceedings of the Aristotelian Society* for 1932-3 (pp. 129-46). I shall make some references to this article, though it should be pointed out at once that Braithwaite's views on belief have altered very considerably since he wrote it. Moreover, the theory stated there is rather less radical than the one I wish to discuss. In this article Braithwaite makes two important concessions to the traditional occurrence analysis. First, if I interpret him correctly, he thinks that a sense can after all be given to 'I am now believing that *p*' provided that I am now actually entertaining the proposition *p and* it is also true of me that I have a disposition to act as if *p* were true (p. 132). Secondly, he admits that we do sometimes have occurrent belief feelings when we entertain a proposition, though he also thinks that no such feelings occur if our belief amounts to complete conviction (p. 142).

I propose to ignore these two concessions. The theory I wish to discuss is a pure or unmixed acting-as-if theory of belief. Anyone who holds it would indeed have to admit that entertaining is somehow relevant to the analysis of belief. However regularly one acted as if *p* were true, one could hardly be said to believe it unless one had actually entertained it at least sometimes. For many ages many people acted as if a diet rich in vitamins were conductive to health. But they were not in a position to *believe* this at a time when vitamins had not yet been discovered and the very concept of 'a vitamin' did not yet exist. Nor are they in a position to believe it at present if they have never even heard of this concept.

Let us suppose, however, that someone who has heard of it does actually entertain the proposition 'a diet rich in vitamins is conducive to health': he entertains it for ten seconds this morning,

[1] See below, pp. 256–9.

and it is also true of him that he is disposed to act as if it were true. (He eats two oranges every day.) If we accept the Acting-as-if Analysis, are we compelled to say that during those ten seconds the man is 'engaged in believing' this proposition about vitamins, as Braithwaite apparently would? Let us also suppose that he believes the proposition with something less than absolute conviction. If we accept the Acting-as-if Analysis, are we also compelled to say that he has, or is quite likely to have, occurrent belief-feelings about the proposition during those ten seconds? It is at any rate instructive to consider a radical version of the Acting-as-if Analysis in which no such concessions are made, and when I speak of the Acting-as-if Analysis in future, it is this radical version that I shall have in mind.

We may formulate it thus: believing a proposition consists just in being disposed to act as if the proposition were true, where the proposition is one which is actually entertained sometimes by the person who is disposed to act on it. (He need not necessarily entertain it at the time when he is acting as if it were true, nor yet at the time when he is about to act in this way.)

Such an analysis of belief seems very plausible and very easy to understand. But when we consider it, we soon find ourselves confronted by questions which are difficult to answer. Let us begin with the most obvious one.

THE MEANING OF 'AS IF *p* WERE TRUE'

How are we to interpret the crucial phase 'as if *p* were true'? The subjunctive 'were' might suggest that *p* is actually false. Your dog is not at all dangerous really, though I habitually act as if it were whenever I encounter it. But when we say 'he believes that the dog is dangerous' there is no suggestion that the proposition believed is false. It might perfectly well be true. Again, 'he acts as if . . . ' might suggest that he is pretending or shamming. For example 'he sometimes acts as if he were a lunatic, but in fact he is as sane as you or I'. But in 'he believes that *p*' there is no suggestion that he is pretending.

'He acts as if *p* were true' does not *entail* that *p* is false, nor yet that he is pretending. Nevertheless, it is liable to suggest one or other of these two thoughts to a person who hears this statement or reads it; and we must resolutely ignore both of them if we are to understand the Acting-as-if Analysis of belief. No doubt we can ignore them, and we will now proceed to do so. But we should be told that we have to.

A more serious difficulty is this. When it is said that someone acts as if a proposition *p* were true, for example the proposition 'it is going to rain', we might quite well take this to mean 'he acts as a person would who *believes* that *p* is true'. (He takes his umbrella with him when he goes out of the house.) This is quite a natural way of explicating the somewhat mysterious phrase 'as if *p* were true'. But according to that interpretation, the acting-as-if analysis of belief would of course be circular.

Are we saying, then, that he acts as if *p* were *in fact* true? But this will not do either. Let *p* be the proposition 'Vladivostok is a large town'. I have long believed this proposition, and doubtless most of you believe it. Do we have a disposition to act as if it were in fact true? If we have, it does not prevent us from acting on many occasions exactly as we should act if the proposition were in fact false. If Vladivostock were a tiny village, or even if there had been no such place as Vladivostock at all, many of us would be doing exactly what we are doing now.

Why is this? It is because the proposition 'Vladivostok is a large town' has no practical relevance for us, and never has had any. Still, it *would* have practical relevance for us, if we ever had occasion to go to that part of the world, and would have had practical relevance for us in the past, if we ever had had occasion to go there. So when we say of someone 'he has a disposition to act as if *p* were true', perhaps we mean that he would act in this way, *if* the question whether *p* is true or false were practically relevant to some action of his? Not quite. For it is not enough that the proposition *p* is in fact relevant, in this practical way; to the circumstances in which we are. We might be unaware that it is relevant.

For example, a man believes firmly that toadstools are poisonous. Yet he eats a toadstool which is served up to him for breakfast, and it makes him very ill. He did not want to be ill. Far from it. He ate a larger breakfast than usual in order to do a good morning's work afterwards. Surely he acted as if the proposition 'toadstools are poisonous' was false, and he acted in this way in a situation to which that proposition was highly relevant? He did, but he was not aware that it was relevant. He believed that the object on the plate was a mushroom.

It seems, then, that a person who does act as if a proposition *p* were true has to *believe* that the question 'is *p* true or false?' is relevant to the achievement of his purpose in the situation in which he is, or rather, in the situation as he *believes* it to be. But in that case, the Acting-as-if Analysis is open to a very serious objection. To explain what is meant by 'acting as if a proposition *p* were true' we have to introduce the concept of belief over again. If so, the Acting-as-if Analysis of belief is circular.

'ACTING-AS-IF' AND PRACTICAL REASONING

Let us see whether we can avoid this difficulty by a reformulation of the Acting-as-if Analysis. The source of the difficulty is fairly obvious. When a man is said to be acting as if *p* were true, it is not only the belief that *p* which is manifested in his action. His action is a manifestation of several beliefs at the same time, and the belief that *p* is only one of them.

Perhaps it will be helpful to consider some remarks which F. P. Ramsey makes about the relation between belief and inference in his essay 'General Propositions and Causality' (*The Foundations of Mathematics*, pp. 237-55) especially as he himself accepted a form of the Acting-as-if Analysis. The view which he suggests might be formulated thus: when we come to believe a proposition *p*, we add it to our stock of premisses.[1] So long as our belief continues, this proposition is available to us as a premiss in our inferences, and our belief that *p* is occurrently manifested whenever we do actually use *p* as a premiss in some inference which we make: and not only when we use it as our sole premiss, but when we use it as *a* premiss, along with some other premiss or premisses also contained in our 'stock'.

The Acting-as-if Analysis can now be formulated without circularity as follows: when we say that a person believes a proposition

[1] Ramsey himself does not actually use these words, so far as I have been able to discover. But he does speak of 'adding a proposition hypothetically to [one's] stock of knowledge' (p. 247 n.) and he also says 'it belongs to the essence of any belief that we deduce from it and act on it in a certain way' (p. 251 *ad. fin.*).

p we mean (1) that *p* is a member of his stock of premisses (2) he is disposed to use it as a premiss in his practical reasoning or practical inferences, inferences whose conclusions, if put into words, would be of the form 'let me therefore do *x*' as opposed to 'therefore *q* is true'. It may well be that he cannot ever draw a practical conclusion from any one of these premisses alone. He may always have to use two of them, or more, in combination, and one of them may only have been added to his stock of premisses a moment ago (e.g. 'there is ice on the road'). But still any one of the propositions in his stock of premisses has the status of *a* potential premiss in some possible piece of practical reasoning; and that is what we should have to mean by saying that he believes it, if the Acting-as-if Analysis of belief is correct. So far as I can see, there is no circularity in the Acting-as-if Analysis when it is reformulated in this way.

We speak sometimes of 'acting upon' a proposition, or acting 'in the light of it', or 'taking account of it' in deciding what to do; and this revised version of the Acting-as-if Analysis could be put in an untechnical way by saying that a proposition which we believe is one of those propositions which we are disposed to take account of in our practical deliberations. 'Taking account of it' does not entail that it is ever the only proposition which we take account of. To answer the practical question 'what am I to do?' we might always have to take account of several propositions; and in any action which we perform, we might have to act 'upon' or 'in the light' of several propositions, and not just of one.

Assuming that this is the best way to state the Acting-as-if Analysis of belief, we may now consider an example which supports it. This afternoon you intend to go to a village ten miles away, and you believe that the bus will be crowded. Then you will do your best to arrive early at the bus station. Or you will make the journey on a bicycle. Or you will get a lift from a passing motorist. Or you will start your journey very much earlier and walk all the way. In doing any of these actions you are using the proposition 'the bus will be crowded' as a premiss in a piece of practical reasoning or inference-guided conduct. You are acting 'in the light of' this proposition or acting 'upon' it. You are not just making bodily movements of one sort or another. You are acting thoughtfully or intelligently.

'ACTS SPEAK LOUDER THAN WORDS'

There is another type of case which appears to support this analysis of belief. We sometimes find that a person claims to believe a proposition *p* or professes to believe it; and yet, in circumstances to which the proposition is obviously relevant, he acts as if it were false. For instance, he says he believes that no one can do a good day's work unless he has had a good night's sleep. Yet on Monday night he sits up playing Bridge until 1.30 a.m., although he knows that he has a very heavy day's work on Tuesday; and he repeatedly acts in this way. We are inclined to say of such a person that he does not really believe what he says he believes. He does not act 'upon' or 'in the light of' the proposition which he claims to believe.

Obviously there is a good deal of truth in such cynical remarks about 'not really believing'; all of us are very familiar with this situation in which someone says he believes a proposition *p*, but fails to act as if it were true. And we do quite often judge of a man's beliefs—his *real* beliefs as opposed to his professed ones—by observing the way he acts. 'Acts speak louder than words.' 'It is what a man does, not what he says, which shows what he really believes.'

In a moment of unusual candour, one may even apply this criterion to one's own beliefs. For example, when someone asks me to lend him a valuable book of mine, I may say (even to myself) 'I am quite sure he will remember to return it'. All the same, I write my name and address on the flyleaf before I hand the book over to him.[1]

But though these observations about 'not really believing' do in some respects support the Acting-as-if Analysis, in other respects they do not.

Anyone who insists in this way that 'acts speak louder than words' will get himself into difficulties if he also holds that 'acting as if *p* were true' includes *speaking* as if *p* were true.

For as these examples are supposed to show—indeed, that is the whole point of them—that one may speak as if *p* were true

[1] Something more will have to be said later about this concept of 'not really believing' when we discuss Half-Belief. See Lecture 4, below.

when one does *not* believe it, or does not really believe it. There is no difficulty about ordinary liars, perhaps. They do speak publicly as if a proposition *p* were true when they do not believe it. But it could be argued that they speak privately, to themselves, as if it were false; that it is private or inward speech (sub-vocal speech or verbal imagery) which counts; and that someone who speaks privately, to himself, as if *p* were true really does believe it. The difficulty is not so much about liars as about self-deceivers: people who say to themselves, as well as to others, 'I believe that *p*' when their actions show that they do not believe it. Probably there is some degree of self-deceit in most of us.

The position is, then, that sometimes a man who speaks as if a proposition were true does believe it, and sometimes he does not; it is even possible that he does not believe the proposition although he speaks privately, to himself, as if it were true. And this is the difficulty we get into, if we maintain (as some acting-as-if theorists might) that acting as if *p* were true includes speaking as if it were true.

'NATURAL' OR UNSTUDIED SPEECH

It has been suggested, however, that we can get round this difficulty by drawing a distinction between two sorts of speech: natural or spontaneous or unstudied speech on the one hand, and careful or guarded speech on the other.[1]

It is then maintained that one of the actions which manifests your belief that *p* is speaking in a natural or spontaneous or unstudied manner as if *p* were true. (This could perhaps be stretched to cover what one may call *automatic* speech: what a person says when he is drugged or drunk or half asleep, or what he says in slips of the tongue, or slips of the pen, when he is awake.[2]) In all these cases one is speaking without self-concern, if I may put it so —without asking oneself what impression one is making on other people. Perhaps when a person speaks in this way, what he says does always accord with what he 'really' believes?

[1] See G. Ryle *The Concept of Mind*, pp. 181–5.

[2] Cf. *In vino veritas*, though *veritas* here primarily means sincerity about one's wishes and emotional attitudes, rather than sincerity about one's beliefs.

Sometimes it does, but not always. There is such a thing as unconscious self-deceit, pretending, even to oneself, that one's beliefs are different from what they actually are, without being aware that one *is* pretending. When this happens, other people may be able to discover, by observing one's conduct, that one is thus deceiving oneself. But it is much more difficult for them (and for oneself too) to make the converse discovery, that is, to establish conclusively that one is speaking 'naturally' or 'spontaneously' or 'without self-concern'. And this is what matters in the present argument.

In actual fact, I think, we are inclined to argue the other way round—from the beliefs which a man is *already* known to hold, to the 'naturalness' (or otherwise) of the way he speaks. In other words, we have an inclination to define 'natural speech' or 'spontaneous speech' in terms of belief: speaking naturally or spontaneously is saying what you do really believe. But if so, it would of course be circular to define belief itself, wholly or partly, in terms of 'natural' or 'spontaneous' speech.

There is another difficulty in the doctrine that speaking as if *p* were true is just a special case of acting as if *p* were true. It is this. Although speaking, even speaking privately and sub-vocally, is indeed a kind of action, it is very different from other kinds of action; and consequently the phrase 'as if' has a different meaning, when it is 'speaking as if' that we are discussing, from the meaning which it has when we are discussing other sorts of action. When I say (in a natural or unstudied manner) 'it is going to rain soon' I am indeed speaking as if the proposition 'it is going to rain soon' were true. And when I take my umbrella or my mackintosh down from the peg, I am moving a material object from one place to another as if this same proposition about the weather were true. But in the second case I am using this proposition as a premiss in a piece of practical reasoning or drawing a practical inference from it (that to avoid getting wet I must take an umbrella or a mackintosh with me when I go out); whereas in the first case, when I merely say to others or to myself, 'it is going to rain soon' I need not be using the proposition as a premiss at all. Of course, I *may* be using it as a premiss in an argument to show that the meteorological forecast in the morning paper is not infallible. But I need not be using it as a premiss in any piece of reasoning, either theoretical or practical. I may be just expressing my belief. And expressing a belief is very different from acting upon it, as I do when I take the umbrella down from the peg.

A philosopher of 'Ordinary Language' might also draw our attention to another point about the phrase *as if*. If we used this phrase about someone's utterances—e.g. 'he talked as if it were going to rain'—we should usually mean not that he actually said 'it is going to rain', but that he said something else, such as 'the barometer has been falling all day' or 'you will need an umbrella when you go out'. That is, he asserted some *other* proposition *q*, which would be rendered true, or highly probable, if *p* were true, but he did not assert *p* itself. In short, in this (ordinary) use of the phrase 'speaking as if *p*' or 'speaking as if *p* were true' it is implied that the speaker was using *p* as a premiss for an inference, without actually uttering the sentence '*p*' itself. He was *not* actually expressing his belief that *p*, though we can infer that he holds it.

'NOT REALLY BELIEVING'

So much for the difficulties which arise when 'acting as if *p* were true' is taken to include speaking as if *p* were true. We may now return to the inference from 'he does not act as if *p* were true' to 'he does not really believe *p*'. As we have seen, the fact that we do often make this inference is one of the most persuasive arguments in favour of an Acting-as-if Analysis of belief. But the inference is often a good deal more precarious than it looks.

Let us first consider a complication which Braithwaite himself points out. The purpose of the agent must be taken into account (his 'needs' as Braithwaite calls them[1]) before we decide that he does not really believe what he claims to believe.

For example, a man says he believes that coal gas and air form an explosive mixture. One evening, as he is passing the cellar door, he notices a peculiar smell. He goes in there and lights a match, and then there is an explosion. We are inclined to say 'You can see that he did not really believe this proposition about coal gas and air: for when it came to the point, he did not act as if it were true. Acts speak louder than words.'

[1] *Proceedings of the Aristotelian Society*, 1932–33, pp. 134–5.

But if we do say this, we may easily be mistaken. It depends what his purpose was. It may be that he wanted to commit suicide, or to blow up the house in order to get the insurance money or because he so much disliked its Ruskinian architecture. Supposing he did want to do any of these things, he acted as if the proposition about coal gas and air was true; and in that case he ought to infer not that he 'did not really believe' the proposition, but that he did believe it.

Let us assume, however, that he did not want to commit suicide or to do anything else which an explosion would facilitate. Even so, his action fails to prove that he did not believe the proposition. For the proposition 'coal gas and air form an explosive mixture' is a *universal* proposition. The sentence formulates a general law. And though he believed the general law and had not at all lost this belief, he may have failed to recognize that it applied to this particular case.[1] Perhaps he had a heavy cold and could not smell very well. Or he may have failed to recognize what sort of smell it was. Having had a purely literary education, he has never learned to distinguish this sort of smell from others. It was just 'a stink' to him.

'LOSING ONE'S HEAD'

But we must also consider another and perhaps more interesting possibility. When the man struck the match and caused an explosion, he may have been flustered or frightened. Perhaps when he smelt the smell in the cellar he 'lost his head', as we say. He did not at all wish or intend to cause an explosion. But because he lost his head, he did just the thing which was bound to have that result.

The very existence of this phrase 'losing one's head' seems to refute the doctrine that a person's actions are infallible signs of his beliefs. For the phrase was invented to cover the case where a man does believe a proposition, but fails to act on it—owing to fear, anger, anxiety, astonishment or some other 'disconcerting' emotional state (another is excessive eagerness to 'do something about' the situation at once).

A person may believe a proposition *p*; he may also believe, and believe correctly, that he is in a situation to which *p* is relevant.

[1] Cf. Aristotle, *Nicomachean Ethics*, Book VII, ch 3.

And yet, under stress of emotion, he fails to act upon this proposition. He fails to use it as a premiss in his practical inferences. He even acts as if it were false, or as if it were not relevant to the situation in which he is. When other people hear that he has acted in that way, some of them are sure to say that he did not 'really' believe the proposition *p* at all, even though he has spoken sometimes as if he did. But instead of saying that his action shows the absence of the belief, one might equally (or better) say that it shows the presence of another disposition in him, an emotional disposition such as excitability, or a tendency to get into a panic in sudden emergencies. By this account of the matter, the man's belief was really there. He did not just claim or profess to believe that coal gas and air form an explosive mixture. He really did believe it, and he still believed it even at the moment when he failed to act upon it. The belief was still there, but it was inhibited, prevented from manifesting itself, by the emotions which the situation aroused; and this, surely, is just what 'losing one's head' amounts to.

So if we *must* make some cynical comment on such a person, one who loses his head in circumstances of this kind, the appropriate comment is that his character is weak or unstable. Indeed, part at least of what we mean by saying that a person's character is weak or unstable is that in emotion-arousing situations he is likely *not* to act in accordance with propositions which he does quite genuinely believe.

Perhaps it will now be agreed that the relation between belief and action is more complicated than a simple Acting-as-if Analysis of belief might suggest. Many of our beliefs certainly do manifest themselves in our actions; and certainly this is a very important fact both about belief and about action. But before we can infer from a man's actions to his belief or absence of belief that *p*, we must take into account the following factors:

(1) his purposes, which may possibly be queer or eccentric ones, quite different from the purposes we ourselves should have if we were in his situation;

(2) his belief, or failure to believe, that the situation is one to which the proposition *p* is relevant. *He* may believe that *p* is relevant to the situation, when *we* believe or even know that it is not. He may believe that it is not relevant to the situation, when we believe or even know that it is;

(3) the strength or weakness, the stability or instability, of his character—the degree to which he is capable of 'keeping his head' in a situation of this particular sort, or rather in a situation which he himself believes to be of this sort.

ACTING AS IF *p* WERE TRUE WHEN ONE DOES NOT BELIEVE IT

We have seen that a person may fail to act as if a proposition were true, even though he does believe it. He may also act as if a proposition were true even though he does not believe it. Here we must distinguish between 'not believing that *p*' and 'believing that not-*p*', though in colloquial English the two phrases are often used as if they were equivalent.

Let us first consider an example in which there is no belief either way, the neutral state of suspense of judgement. An Oxford teacher of mine once betted on a horse because its name was 'Aristotle'. He was a man eminent for his good sense, who subsequently became the Head of his College. He was well aware that a horse's name, however distinguished, has no relevance, either favourable or unfavourable, to the creature's chances of winning a race. He did not believe the proposition 'Aristotle will win' (though he did not disbelieve it either) and then he proceeded to act as if the proposition were true.

Perhaps it will be said that this action was 'not serious' and therefore does not count. But if what a man does is an infallible sign of what he believes, there could not be any un-serious actions at all. It is notorious, however, that un-serious actions do sometimes occur, even in our serious-minded age; and there was a time when they occurred quite frequently. Moreover, if the word 'serious' is introduced into the acting-as-if analysis of belief, we get into a logical difficulty. Suppose we said that believing a proposition consists in being disposed to act as if it were true when (and only when) one is acting seriously. What is meant by 'acting seriously'? Surely it can only mean 'acting in accordance with one's *beliefs*'; and that would make the Acting-as-if Analysis circular.

But it is also possible to act as if *p* were true when one disbelieves the proposition *p* (or believes its contradictory, not-*p*, if the reader prefers to put it that way). This may be illustrated by a well-known story about King Canute. Canute's courtiers asserted that he ruled the sea, from which it would logically follow that the sea would obey any command that he might give it. Canute did not believe this. Not only so; he disbelieved it. And he then proceeded to act as if it were true. He sat on this throne in Chichester Harbour when the tide was coming in, and commanded the sea to go back; and the sea took no notice whatever of his command. He acted as if a proposition were true when he disbelieved it, or rather, because he disbelieved it and wanted, if possible, to disprove it.

A somewhat similar procedure is an important part of scientific method. One of the best ways of disproving a hypothesis is to act in accordance with it, and show that the predicted consequences of it do not in fact occur. This illustrious Anglo-Scandinavian monarch may perhaps be regarded as one of the founders of Scientific Empiricism.

Perhaps it will be said that when Canute did this he was acting as if the proposition 'Canute rules the sea' were *false*. In a way, he was. Certainly he was acting as a highly intelligent man would act who wished to prove that the proposition was false. But if we take this line about the example of Canute, it only shows what an ambiguous criterion this acting-as-if criterion of belief is. For here the very same action can be described in two mutually incompatible ways: *either* as an example of acting as if a proposition *p* were true, *or* as an example of acting as if *p* were false. A man disposed to act as if the courtiers' hypothesis were true might be expected to do what Canute did; and a man disposed to act as if the hypothesis were false (provided he was intelligent enough) might also be expected to do what Canute did.

PURELY THEORETICAL BELIEFS

The Acting-as-if Analysis also gets into difficulties about beliefs which we hold in a purely theoretical way, without ever having occasion to act on them. (It must be remembered that speaking and writing do not count here as actions. That was the point of the remark 'acts speak louder than words'.) Those beliefs which never manifest themselves in our actions at all may be called 'purely theoretical' for brevity's sake, though this adjective applies to the believing rather than the propositions believed, which may quite well be propositions about matters of fact. It is obvious that such beliefs exist. Everyone has some beliefs which are purely theoretical in this sense, and some people have a great many.

For example, I myself believe, on the authority of geologists, that in a remote geological epoch this country was not yet an island, and there was a continuous land-bridge between it and the Continent where the Straits of Dover now are. It is no doubt conceivable that circumstances might arise in which one would act as if this proposition were true. If one were a palaeontologist, one might investigate the sea-bottom outside Dover Harbour in the hope of finding fossils of extinct land-animals there. But in point of fact, no such circumstances have ever arisen in my own case, nor in the case of many thousands of other people who hold this belief. Neither they nor I have ever in fact acted as if this proposition about the remote past were true; yet there is no doubt that we do believe it.

It is true that if we are greatly *interested* in some proposition about the past, our belief may well affect our actions. For example, we believe that Alexander the Great invaded India in the fourth century BC, and that there were Greek-speaking people in India and in Bactria for a century or two afterwards. I myself happen to be interested in these events and in their consequences. So if there were an exhibition of Greco-Buddhist sculpture in London, I might quite well travel to London in order to have a look at it. On the other hand, I should do no such thing if there were an exhibition of fifteenth century printed books. I do believe firmly that printing began in the fifteenth century, but am not particularly interested in this proposition. In any case, it is quite impossible that we should 'do something about' *all* the propositions we believe even when opportunities arise for doing it. *Non omnia possumus omnes.*

Now certainly it does not follow from the Acting-as-if Analysis that anyone who believes a proposition does in fact act as if the proposition were true, but only that he *would* act thus *if* circumstances were to arise to which the proposition were (for that person) practically relevant, and would have acted thus if such circumstances had ever arisen since the time when he first acquired his belief. Beliefs which are never in fact acted upon might perfectly well exist, if the Acting-as-if Analysis is correct. The difficulty is that there would be no way of discovering that they exist. Neither the believer himself, nor others, could possibly find out that he does believe some propositions (very many, perhaps) in this purely theoretical way. It is all very well for him to say to others, or even privately to himself, 'I believe that *p*'. But this, according to the Acting-as-if Analysis, is very weak evidence for the hypothesis that he does believe it. We must have deeds, not words; and so must he, if he is to find out what his own beliefs are. Yet in point of fact, each of us is quite sure that he does believe many propositions in this purely theoretical way, and that many propositions (not necessarily the same ones) are believed in this purely theoretical way by others.

Moreover, beliefs held in this purely theoretical way need not be beliefs about the past. There are many other examples: beliefs about the remote future, such as the belief that some millions of years from now the earth will be too cold to be habitable; beliefs about objects which are remote in space, for instance the belief that there are albatrosses in the South Atlantic, or that there are mountains at the South Pole; beliefs about very general causal laws, for instance the belief that when a particle moves with a velocity approaching the speed of light, its mass increases.

It is true that any one of these beliefs might very well manifest itself in the actions of the appropriate scientific specialists. Such beliefs might determine what apparatus these men install in their laboratories, what experiments they undertake, what expeditions they made to remote parts of the earth's surface or (some day) to remote parts of the solar system. Nevertheless, these beliefs can be held, and are held, by laymen like ourselves, who never have any opportunity of acting on them; and since we never do in fact act as if these propositions were true, neither we ourselves nor others who observe our actions would be entitled to affirm that we do believe them, if the Acting-as-if Analysis is correct. But actually we know very well that we believe them. How do we know this? Is it possible that we just know it by introspection, as the traditional theories of belief maintained? How very upsetting that would be!

Finally, the Acting-as-if Analysis may be criticized for taking an unduly narrow view of human nature, and of the motives which make us believing beings. One of these motives undoubtedly is that we wish our actions to be successful. We often have to act without knowledge of some of the relevant circumstances; and we very seldom, or never, know (in any strict sense of the word 'know') what the results of our action are going to be. We often have to use a proposition as a premiss in our practical reasoning without knowing it to be true. When someone gets into a train at Oxford in order to attend a committee meeting in London, he cannot know that he will arrive in time or even that he will arrive at all. He has to be content with believing, on the authority of the railway time-table (which is by no means infallible), that the train will reach London not much later than the time-table said it would.

But this practical motive, this desire that our actions should be successful, is not the only motive we have for acquiring beliefs. There is also the desire for knowledge for its own sake. Knowledge is something which we value as an end in itself. It is good to know how things are. But here again, we often find that knowledge in any strict sense of the term is not available. All the same, the desire for knowledge is still there, and belief is a partial satisfaction of that desire; a second-best, but much better than nothing. That is why there are purely theoretical beliefs, which make no difference to our actions.

It is therefore not so very surprising that theory which defines belief as a disposition to act as if a proposition were true is not altogether satisfactory. It is indeed true, and important too, that many of the propositions which we believe are used as premisses in our practical reasoning. One of the functions of belief is to provide us with guidance in our actions and our practical decisions. But this is not its only function. Another is to give a partial and second-best satisfaction to our desire to know how things are.

LECTURE II

ANOTHER VERSION OF THE DISPOSITIONAL ANALYSIS

The 'acting as if' version of the Dispositional Analysis of belief is no doubt the simplest, but it turns out to be too simple. There is a certain narrowness about it. Why should we suppose that a person's overt actions are the only occurrent manifestations of his beliefs? If a belief is a disposition which a person acquires at a certain time and retains for a certain period, it is surely a multiform disposition which manifests itself in many different ways, and not only in the actions which he does.

First, we notice that inaction, as well as action, can be a manifestation of belief. For example, my passenger has the map, but for the past twenty minutes he has not even opened it. He just sits there, doing nothing about it. Thereby he manifests his belief (possibly an incorrect one) that we are on the right road. Again, by sitting quietly in the waiting room, doing nothing, I manifest my belief that the train will not arrive just yet.

This is our first step beyond the too narrow and restrictive Acting-as-if Analysis, and the reader may think it is a very little one. If the acting-as-if philosophers themselves failed to take it, perhaps that was no more than an oversight on their part. For it might well be said that inaction, as well as action, is a form of conduct, at any rate when it is belief-manifesting inaction and not just a bodily quiescence resulting from purely physiological causes.

We take a much bigger step beyond the Acting-as-if Analysis when we notice the close connection there is between belief and some emotional states.

Let us first consider hope and fear. It might be thought that epistemology has no relevance to the study of emotions. But epistemological questions, and even logical ones, do arise about hope and fear. We notice at once that both verbs, 'to hope' and 'to fear', can govern that-clauses. We also notice that hopes and fears can be reasonable or unreasonable. There are groundless hopes, and even absurd ones (for example, the hope that we shall some day visit Utopia). But there are also reasonable hopes, and it may still have been reasonable to entertain them even though they were eventually disappointed. One may have good grounds for fear too, and one may still have them even though all was well in the end. (The ice was thin, and I feared that it would break, but in fact I got across it safely.) On the other hand, some fears are unreasonable or groundless: which does not of course imply that they are not 'really' fears, or that they do not matter to the person who feels them.

BELIEF AND HOPE

It is indeed obvious that hope and belief are closely connected.[1] If we hope that *x* will happen, we must at least believe that it is possible that *x* will happen. Once we are convinced that the thing hoped for is impossible, hope vanishes away. To abolish our hope, it is enough to be convinced that what was hoped for is *logically* impossible (e.g. the squaring of the circle, which was hoped for long ago). But if our hope is to be retained, we must believe that the thing hoped for is causally possible also. I may be very fond of the sunflower in the garden, but I cannot very well hope that it will say 'good morning' to me. It is no doubt logically possible that a sunflower should speak, but I do not believe that it is causally possible.

In very difficult and dangerous situations when 'we hope against hope', as we say, it is enough to believe that the event hoped for is at any rate causally possible. If there is just a chance that I shall get over the top of the slippery wall before the wolf catches me, I still hope that I shall manage to do it. But normally (as the phrase 'against hope' suggests) we believe more than this. We believe, with some degree of confidence, that the thing hoped for will actually happen. We at least suspect or surmise that it will (these are the traditional words for the lowest degree of belief).

[1] Cf. J. Harrison *Christian Virtues*, Aristotelian Society Supplementary Volume, 1963, pp. 80–1, and J. M. O. Wheatley, 'Wishing and Hoping', *Analysis*, June 1958.

We may go farther and have the opinion that it will. We may even be almost sure that it will happen; this is what we call a 'very confident hope'.

But if we are absolutely sure that the event will happen and have no doubts about it at all, then again we cease to hope: not because we despair, but because we have gone beyond hope into something better. We cease to hope, because we are now *more* than hopeful. We do not hope for a certainty, or for what we consider to be such. Does anyone hope that the sun will rise next Wednesday? A philosopher might, if he is rather sceptical about induction. He might also say that other people ought, or 'ought only', to hope that the sun will rise next Wednesday, because he thinks they have no right to be sure that it will. But they pay no attention to his admonitions. Try as they may, they cannot hope for this event, because they cannot get rid of their complete conviction that it is going to happen.

So far, then, it seems that hope lives in the intermediate region between two opposed convictions. The person who hopes must not be absolutely sure that the event will not happen; but neither must he be absolutely sure that it will. Some degree of incertitude is a characteristic feature of hope.

But there is another belief-factor in hope: the valuational belief that it will be a good thing if *x* happens (whether good in itself, or good as a means). One does not hope that *x* will happen if one believes it would be a bad thing for *x* to happen, or even if one believes it would be neither good nor bad. Here the situation is quite different. Let us consider a politician who is completely sure that it will be a good thing if his party wins the next election. Obviously this does not prevent him from hoping that his party will win. On the contrary, we might be tempted to think that this conviction is a necessary condition for his hope. At any rate, if he only suspects that his party's victory will be a good thing, or thinks so without being anything like sure, we should probably say 'he half-hopes' or 'he has some inclination to hope', rather than 'he hopes'. Perhaps if we are to hope that *x* will happen, it is enough to be nearly sure that it will be a good thing if *x* happens. But ordinarily, I think, when we hope that *x* will happen, we *are* convinced (rightly or wrongly) that it will be a good thing if *x* happens. So there is an important difference between the two beliefs which we must have if we are to hope for something. There must be some degree of incertitude in our factual belief, the belief that *x* is going to happen. But in our evaluative belief, the belief that it will be a good thing if *x* does happen, there need be no incertitude at all; and if there is any, it is likely to be slight.

Finally, we may notice that the incertitude of our factual belief makes it possible for us to have hopes about the unobserved present, and even about the past. Usually we are unsure about the unobserved present, and often we are unsure about the past. For example, I can hope that my remarks yesterday evening did not cause offence to anyone, because I am not sure what affects they had on my audience. John has been ill, but I hope he is perfectly well by now. I can have this hope so long as I am not absolutely sure what his present state of health is. Did we win the boat-race this afternoon? So long as no news has reached me about the result of the race, I can hope that we did win.

Such hopes may seem paradoxical. Ordinarily our hopes are concerned with the future. It might be suggested, then, that when I say 'I hope that John is perfectly well by now' I am really hoping that evidence *will* be forthcoming which will show that he was indeed perfectly well at the time when I made my remark; and that in the same way, I hope to receive evidence later that what I said yesterday evening caused no offence.

On the contrary, it does not feel like this at all, even though in some of these examples I do *also* hope that future evidence will be forthcoming. (For instance, I hope that the evening paper will inform me that we did win the boat-race.) When I hope that John is now well, it feels like a hope about what now is. When I hope that my remarks yesterday caused no offence, it feels like a hope about what formerly was—the state of mind of my audience yesterday evening.

Moreover, so far as the hoping person can tell, there may be very little likelihood that such future evidence will be forthcoming. He may even be quite sure (correctly or not) that he is never going to get any; and as we have seen, this makes it impossible for him to hope that he will get it. There may be some chance of receiving information which will show that my remarks yesterday did not in fact cause offence. But I might have a similar hope about something I said at a meeting thirty years ago; and it is much too late to hope that evidence will be forthcoming which will show that I caused no offence on that occasion.

BELIEF AND FEAR

We may now turn to the relation between fear and belief. We tend to think of hope and fear as a symmetrical pair, as if fear were the same attitude as hope but with a 'change of sign' (like the change from + to −); or as if the only difference between hope and fear was the difference between *pro* and *con*. There is indeed a difference of this kind between them. When we hope that *x* will happen, we believe that it will be a good thing if *x* happens. When we fear that *x* will happen, we believe that it will be a bad thing if *x* happens. If you and I have both promised to play cricket this afternoon, I hope that it will rain this afternoon, whereas you fear that it will.

We can also detect some important resemblances between the two emotions so long as we confine our attention to fear *that* . . . Some degree of incertitude is a necessary constituent of both. Unless one has doubts about the reliability of induction, one does not fear that the sun will fail to rise next Wednesday, any more than one hopes that it will rise. More paradoxically, perhaps, if one is quite sure that some very unpleasant event will happen, one can no longer fear *that* it will happen, any more than one can hope that some very pleasant thing will happen when one is quite sure that it will.

For the past twelve hours the conscience-stricken schoolboy has feared that the Headmaster will summon him for an interview to-morrow. But now the matter is settled. The summons has come, and this fear 'that' is abolished. It is not that the boy's fear has been abolished altogether. Far from it. But it assumes a different (and worse) form. Fear 'that' the interview will happen is replaced by fear 'of' the interview itself. He contemplates this future event with fear and trembling. Nevertheless, he does not, and even cannot, continue to fear *that* it will occur. He may now have other fears 'that', for example the fear that he will be beaten or that he will be expelled from the school or that he will disgrace himself by shedding tears, since he cannot be sure that these things will happen in the course of the interview, but only that there is an appreciable probability that they will. But the particular fear 'that' which he previously had—the fear that the interview would take place—really has been abolished, just as hope is abolished when we come to be sure that the event hoped for is actually going to happen.

Again, fear 'that' can be extended to the unobserved present, and even to the past, as hope can. As I can hope that John is quite well by now, I can fear that William is still pretty ill. As I can hope that my remarks yesterday evening caused no offence, I can fear that those I made a week ago did cause great offence. And here again, there has to be some degree of incertitude. If I am quite sure that William is still pretty ill, I can be very sorry that it is so, but I cannot fear that it is so. Nor can I fear that my remarks caused offence if I have conclusive evidence that they did. I can only regret very much that I made them.

But now we encounter a complication. One might say to another person (not to oneself) 'I fear that *p*' when one is quite sure that *p* is true. For example the newsagent at the railway station, when asked for a copy of to-day's *Times*, might say 'I am afraid that we have no copies left; we sold the last one an hour ago'. Or again, when I am asked 'Who did it?' I may reply 'I am afraid that I did'. But there *is* some incertitude here: not about the fact itself, but about the way one's hearer will take it. The newsagent fears that you will be distressed to hear that there is no copy left. I fear that you will be shocked to hear that I am the person who did it. If the speaker were quite sure that his information would distress or shock his hearer, he would put his remark differently. He would say 'I am very sorry to have to tell you that . . .' instead of 'I am afraid that . . .'.

FEAR 'OF' AND FEAR 'THAT'

So far, then, there are important parallels between hope and fear. But it would be a great mistake to suppose that the only difference between them is the difference between *pro* and *con*. For one thing, fear is a more passive attitude than hope. We can be frightened *by* something, made or forced to fear. But there is nothing which is related to hope as being frightened is related to fear. We can hope but we cannot be 'be-hoped'. We may no doubt be encouraged or persuaded to hope; but we can resist such encouragements and persuasions, and we often do. Hope is more autonomous than fear. It is not just something which we suffer. Consequently, fear is even more liable to be unreasonable than hope is. The mere thought of something can frighten us, though there is no evidence at all that it is going to happen.

There is another difference, and it is more relevant to our discussion. Fear is not always fear that. . . . One can also fear an entity—a wolf, or a precipice, or a headmaster. One can fear an event, either an event which is actually happening, such as the thunderstorm which is now going on, or a future event (e.g. the interview with the headmaster to-morrow) if one is absolutely sure that it is going to happen. And here the passive character of fear is most obvious. These entities or events frighten us. They *make* us afraid.

To put it in another way: hope is always a propositional attitude. It is always hope that . . . Hopes 'of' and hopes 'for' are quite easily reducible to hopes 'that'. The hope of victory is just the hope that our side will win. Belinda hoped for a pony (you have given her a donkey instead). But her hope for a pony was the hope *that* she would have a pony, or *that* she would be presented with one. Fear can be a propositional attitude too (fear that . . .) but it need not be. There is also fear of . . . , where the 'object' of our fear is not a proposition but an entity or an event. We fear the wolf. But we cannot hope the Siamese cat; or rather, it makes no sense to say we can, though we can very well hope *that* this agreeable creature will visit us again some day.

Consequently, fear 'of' is not abolished by certitude, as fear 'that' is. I do not fear the wolf any less because I am sure that it is now there in front of me. The schoolboy does not fear to-morrow's interview any less when he is quite sure that it is going to happen. This certitude does indeed deliver him from his previous fear *that* the interview would happen. But, as we have seen, his fear 'that' is replaced by something worse—fear 'of'. One does not hope for a certainty. But it might be said that unpleasant certainties are what we fear most of all. Indeed, fear 'of' may be so intense that we are beyond the use of that-clauses altogether. Our intellectual powers are for the time being paralysed. This is what happens in the extreme fear which we call 'terror'.

There are other questions which would have to be considered in any complete account of the epistemology of hope and fear. For instance, can one both hope that *x* will happen and fear that it will happen? Presumably one can, if one believes that the happening of *x* would be a good thing in some ways but a bad thing in others. In the middle years of the fourth century a patriotic Christian might both hope and fear that Julian would be the next Emperor. Again, what should be said about the odd but morally respectable phenomenon of hope on behalf of another person? ('I hope for his sake that he will win the prize.') We may even have such hopes—and fears too—when the other person is fictitious and known by us to be so, for instance when we are reading a novel or watching a play. Indeed, we may go farther and 'identify ourselves' with the other person, as if his hopes and fears were our own.

It would not be relevant to discuss these questions here. Enough has been said to show that hope and fear are ways in which a person's beliefs are manifested. Hopes and fears are quite important 'belief-indicators'. It is not true, then, that action is the only belief-indicator we can find, nor even that action and inaction are the only ones.

We can also notice something else which the Acting-as-if Analysis omits. Hope and fear, like other emotional states, are something more than modes of bodily behaviour. Fear is, no doubt, more 'bodily' than hope. At any rate, in fear 'of' there are very noticeable bodily symptoms, though they are less easily noticeable in fear 'that'. But neither fear nor hope is reducible to a conjunction or series of outward and publicly-observable bodily states. Both have an inner aspect as well. We must feel them or 'live through them' at first hand if we wish to know what they are like. Moreover, if we wish to discover *what* a person is afraid of, or what his fears 'that' are concerned with, it is appropriate to go and ask him. His introspective report may not be decisive (there are what we call 'unconscious fears') but at any rate it is relevant evidence. And certainly it is relevant evidence if we wish to learn what he hopes for. Indeed, it is almost the only evidence we can get, since hope—unlike fear—does not show itself by any obvious bodily symptoms.

So if a person's hopes and fears throw some light, at any rate, on his beliefs, *A*'s own introspective evidence is not, after all, quite irrelevant to the question 'Does *A* believe that *p*?' If we wish to answer that question, we may have to consider what goes on in *A*'s own inner life. Here it is worth noticing that even action itself has an 'inner aspect' too. Even if belief were purely and simply a disposition to act as if a proposition were true, inward and private events would still have some relevance to the analysis of belief. Bodily movements do not count as actions unless the agent has the appropriate kinaesthetic sensations. Otherwise, his bodily movements would just be physical happenings, like the movements of a clockwork mouse across the table, and we could not say that he made them. But these kinaesthetic sensations are private experiences of his own. If he were to report to us that he did not feel any such sensations while his bodily movements were taking place, we could not say that he was acting as if such and such a proposition were true; he was not performing an action at all. Moreover, to know just what it is that he is doing we must know what his purpose is. We can often guess for ourselves what it is; but sometimes we guess wrong, and then we draw mistaken inferences about his beliefs (as in the example of the man who struck a match in the cellar, pp. 259–60, above).[1] So there is some point in asking him what his purpose was. Here again his introspective evidence is not decisive (there are what we call 'unconscious purposes') but it is at any rate relevant to the question 'what is he doing?'—or more vulgarly, 'what on earth is he up to?'

BELIEF AND SURPRISE

It is however conceivable that there might be intelligent creatures who neither hope nor fear. Some human creatures have wished, or professed to wish, to be 'free' both from hope and from fear; and if this wish were fulfilled, they would still be capable of holding beliefs. But there are two other feeling-states which are more closely connected with belief. They are surprise and doubt. Indeed, they are so closely connected with belief that we find it very difficult to conceive of a believing being who is incapable of feeling them. If there were such a creature, belief, for him, would be something very different from what it is for us.

We might describe surprise and doubt as 'cognitive feelings'.

Traditionally there is a third member of this peculiar class of feelings: the feeling of confidence. Its status is much more controversial, and its existence has sometimes been denied. But let us first consider surprise. No one will deny that we do sometimes experience surprise.

Perhaps it would be a little strange to say that surprise is an emotion, as hope and fear are. But it is certainly something that we feel. Sometimes it has organic repercussions too. At any rate, intense surprise can have them; we may gasp with surprise. And of all feeling-states, surprise is perhaps the one which is most closely connected with belief. It is the feeling which we have when some proposition which we believe turns out to be false. We also feel some surprise, though not so much, when we come across evidence against some propostition which we believe, even though this adverse evidence is by no means conclusive. If I believe that a colleague has gone away for the week-end, I am a little surprised to see a light in his rooms when I walk across the quadrangle on Saturday evening.

The connection between belief and surprise is so close that we sometimes express our belief that *p* by saying 'I should be surprised if not-*p*'. We can also indicate the degree of our belief by specifying the degree of surprise we should feel if *p* were to be falsified. The lowest degree of belief, traditionally called 'suspecting that . . .', is indicated by saying 'I should be just a little surprised if not-*p*'. The middle degrees ('thinging that . . .' or 'having the opinion that . . .') are indicated by saying 'I should be a good deal surprised if not-*p*'. When we are very nearly sure but not quite, we say 'I should be greatly surprised if not-*p*'. The highest degree of belief (conviction, being absolutely sure) is not usually indicated at all. When I am quite sure that we shall arrive by 7 o'clock, I usually just say 'we shall arrive by 7 o'clock', if I say anything. But perhaps you ask me whether I am absolutely sure about it; and then I reply 'I shall be very surprised indeed if we don't'.

Moreover, if a person *is* surprised when a proposition *p* is falsified, this is about the strongest evidence we can have that he did, until then, believe the proposition for some period of time; and the degree of his surprise is about the strongest evidence we can have concerning the degree of his belief.

But are there perhaps two different kinds of surprise, not only the surprise of falsified belief, but also the surprise of sheer novelty? In the latter case, it might be said, what clashes with, or is removed by, the newly-ascertained fact is not a previously held belief, but sheer ignorance. The first European who observed a duck-billed platypus was no doubt much surprised to find a furry four-legged oviparous creature with a beak like a duck. (It is called *ornithorhynchus paradoxus* to this day.) Did he believe beforehand that no such creature existed, and was his surprise due to the empirical falsification of this negative proposition which he had, until then, believed? Surely it is more likely that he had never even conceived of such a creature at all? In that case he could not have believed beforehand that no such creature existed, and the surprise which he felt could not have anything to do with the empirical falsification of a proposition previously believed.

We have to admit, I think, that any belief of his which was refuted by these surprising observations was an 'implicit' or 'tacit' belief. The propositions 'no furry four-footed creature is oviparous' and 'no furry four-footed creature has a beak like a duck' were taken for granted by him, or assumed without question, without being explicitly assented to. But still, it was not true that he considered this strange creature with a completely open mind, as the phrase 'sheer ignorance' might suggest. His previous observations of various members of the animal kingdom, and what he had been taught about them or read about them, determined the way he 'approached' the creature which he saw. A child of two years old would not have felt surprise when he saw his first duck-billed platypus. For him, it would have been no odder than anything else. When everything is new, nothing is surprising.

It is, however, possible to resist or suppress one's surprise. That is what the old lady did who exclaimed 'There's no such animal!' when she was shown a giraffe at the zoo. If I interpret the story rightly, she embraced the hypothesis that she was having a visual hallucination. No doubt she was confronted by a choice of evils. But it was too much to have to give up her belief that all the species of quadrupeds in the animal kingdom were represented in pictures of the animals going into Noah's Ark (no dappled quadruped with a very long neck and two small horns on its head was among them). It was better and more comfortable to suppose that she was now having an hallucination. This is an excellent way of protecting one's beliefs against empirical refutation. The lady was strong-minded enough to make use of it there and then. We cannot always manage that. But a day or two afterwards, when the memory of some belief-refuting experience has faded a little, we can often persuade ourselves that we must have been dreaming when we had it.

BELIEF AND DOUBT

Surprise is something which we feel, and it is so closely connected with belief that the rather paradoxical phrase 'cognitive feeling' is quite naturally applied to it. Much the same could be said about doubt. This too is closely connected with belief; and since doubting, like surprise, is an inward experience which we 'live through', we are quite willing to say that we *feel* doubt about something, not merely that we have it. If we believe a proposition *p*, we feel surprised when it turns out to be false. But even when it has, as yet, been neither verified nor falsified, we feel doubt of other propositions which would be improbable if *p* be true. We do, of course, have to notice that they *would* be improbable if *p* be true, and conceivably we might fail to notice this. But sometimes it is very obvious. For instance, I have lost my umbrella, and I believe that I left it behind in the bus yesterday afternoon. Then I doubt the proposition 'I shall get it back again'. I do not go so far as to disbelieve this proposition, not yet at any rate, since articles left behind in buses are very occasionally recovered by their owners. Doubting is not the same as disbelieving, though sometimes, for courtesy's sake, we may say to another person 'I doubt it' when in fact we firmly disbelieve it, as we may also say 'I think so' when in fact we are perfectly sure that it is so.

Still, there is a connection between doubting and disbelieving, and a feeling of doubt might be described as a felt inclination to disbelieve. But it is not a merely wishful inclination, or at any rate it need not be. There are indeed persons who enjoy doubting for doubting's sake, as there are others who find doubting almost unbearable. But if and so long as we do believe that *p*, it is reasonable to doubt another proposition *q* which would obviously be rendered unlikely if *p* be true. Doubt of *q* is something we are rationally committed to, so long as we do believe that *p*. It is, however, open to us to doubt *p* itself instead. For example, I am sure that it will continue to rain all day. Then at 1 p.m. it is reported to me that the wind has already veered a point or two. Either I must doubt this report (does my informant really know the difference between 'veering' and 'backing'?) or else I must doubt whether the rain *is* going to continue all day; or at any rate, if I accept the report, I must 'reduce' my belief from a conviction to an opinion, and hold it with less confidence than I did.

We see from this example that there is a direct connection between doubt and surprise, as well as a connection between each of them and belief. What I doubt is also what *would* surprise me, if it were true. For our present purpose, however, the most important point is that the doubts which a person feels throw some light on his beliefs, as his surprise does also, and moreover that doubt, like surprise, is something inward and introspectible. It may sometimes manifest itself by hesitant action. But if we wish to know whether a person doubts a proposition, we usually have to go and ask him. This is true of the milder degrees of surprise too. Intense surprise ('being astonished that . . .') is likely to show itself by publicly-observable bodily symptoms; but even then we may have to go and ask the person what it is that he is astonished at.

THE FEELING OF CONFIDENCE

No one would deny that surprise and doubt are relevant to the analysis of belief; and it is quite natural to describe them as feelings. But what is to be said about the feeling of confidence? It has been thought that the feeling of confidence varies in degree, and that the different degrees of it may be used to define the different degrees of belief, from barely suspecting that . . . at the bottom end of the scale to complete conviction at the top, with the various degrees of opinion in between. On this view, the maximum degree of confidence is expressed by saying 'I feel sure that . . .'.

If we accept the Dispositional Analysis of belief, we cannot take over this traditional doctrine just as it stands. But the feeling of confidence might still be relevant to the analysis of belief, even though that analysis takes a dispositional form. It might still be true that anyone who believes a proposition has a feeling of confidence when he actually entertains that proposition; and moreover, that anyone who has a higher degree of belief with regard to *p* than he has with regard to *q*, feels *more* confidence when he actually entertains the proposition *p* than he feels when he actually entertains the proposition *q*. To put it in another way, the feeling of confidence which a person has when he actually entertains a proposition might still be an important 'belief-symptom', so important that if it were absent we should conclude that he did not really believe the proposition. (Cf. the absence of surprise when the proposition is falsified.)

But is there such a feeling at all? The view that there is has been severely criticized by some contemporary philosophers, for instance Professor William Kneale (*Probability and Induction*, ch. 2). We shall consider his criticisms later.[1] But before we do so, it is worth while to mention one or two linguistic points.

On the traditional view, the highest degree of confidence is expressed by saying 'I feel sure that . . .'. But we notice that in everyday English there is also a rather different use of 'feel sure'. It is quite usual to say 'I feel much more sure of this than of that'. Here there seem to be degrees within the feeling of sureness itself. Yet we might add 'All the same, I do not feel absolutely sure of either'. And now feeling sure does not admit of degrees; instead, there are degrees of approximation to it.

This double usage of 'feel sure' might trouble a philosopher. But we can find analogues for it. 'This line is straighter than that: all the same, neither of them is quite straight.' 'Your cup is fuller than mine, but yours is not quite full.' 'You were more punctual than I was, but neither of us was absolutely punctual.' 'This duster is much cleaner than that one, though neither of them is quite clean.' We also notice that confidence itself is sometimes spoken of as if it did *not* admit of degrees. 'How confident are you that it will go on raining all day?' 'I do not feel completely confident about it, but I think it will.' For ordinary everyday purposes, we often do not find it necessary to distinguish very sharply between degrees of approximation to *x* and degrees of *x* itself. But for philosophical purposes we do need to distinguish between

[1] Pp. 282–5, below.

them; and it seems better (dare one say, more accurate?) to treat 'confidence' as something which does admit of degrees, and sureness as something which does not. The more confident we are, the nearer we are to sureness: sureness is the maximum degree of confidence. At any rate this is the usage I propose to adopt.

There is another linguistic point which is worth considering. We often speak of confidence as if it were a *pro*-attitude. It certainly is when we have (or feel) confidence 'in' another person. We may also have (or feel) confidence 'in' an instrument or a device. I have not much confidence in my watch—it is often five minutes slow—whereas I have a good deal of confidence in the College clock. Confidence 'in' is closely connected with belief 'in', a topic which we shall have to discuss later.[1] For the present, however, we are only concerned with belief 'that'. Are we to say that the confidence which enters into it is likewise a *pro*-attitude? And would it follow from this that whenever we believe a proposition, we wish it to be true? Is all believing, or all believing 'that', a kind of wishful thinking? Obviously it is not. However addicted we are to wishful thinking, we are often nearly sure, or even quite sure, that a proposition is true when we would much prefer it to be false.

But still it does seem a little odd to say 'I feel very confident that we shall lose the game' or 'I feel pretty confident that the Judge will send me to prison for five years'. Do they hope to lose the game? Does the accused man want to be sent to prison for five years? The answer to both these questions might conceivably be 'Yes'; and if it is, we shall no longer be puzzled. The other side have lost all their matches so far. It would be nice if they could win for once, and we are almost sure they will. There is something to be said for going to prison; it gives one an opportunity for meditation, and it is a way of atoning for one's offence. But such wishes are unusual, and what are we to say when they are absent—when there is no wish at all to lose the match or to be sent to prison?

Let us consider another example, an extreme example which makes the difficulty still more obvious. When the little boy is terrified of the bogey-man in the dark cupboard, should we say he feels confident or very confident that there is a bogey-man inside?

[1] See Lecture 9, below.

He does feel nearly sure that there is, or even quite sure. But does he feel any confidence at all? We might be inclined to say that confidence is the last thing he feels.

There is indeed some connection between confidence and courage, or at any rate between confidence and boldness, the readiness to take risks or to 'have a go', cost what it may. Confidence is a manifestation of vitality (perhaps the little boy is rather deficient in that valuable quality) and a confident person is likely to be energetic and enterprising, for good or ill. But this is what we call *self*-confidence. It is a kind of trust in oneself or in one's own capacities, somewhat like the trust one may have in another person. It is related to belief 'in' and not to belief 'that'. The highest degree of it is what we call 'being sure of oneself'.

The little boy is far from being sure of himself. In this alarming situation, he has no trust at all in his own capacities. If we say of him 'confidence is the last thing he feels', it is *self*-confidence that we speak of, as we quite often do when the word 'confidence' is used. And though he has little self-confidence, or none at all, he may still feel very confident about the proposition 'there is a bogey-man in the cupboard'. It is this propositional or 'epistemic' confidence which concerns us now, and not self-confidence; and it was this 'epistemic' confidence which the footballers expressed when they said 'we feel confident that we shall lose the game' and the accused man expressed when he said 'I feel confident that the Judge will send me to prison'.

KNEALE'S CRITICISMS

But whatever complexities there may be in our ordinary use of the words 'confident' and 'sure', we are perfectly willing to speak of *feeling* confident (not only of being confident) and of *feeling* sure (not only of being so). We are also perfectly willing to speak of feeling more confident about one proposition than we feel about another. The traditional doctrine about a feeling of confidence which varies in degree is supported by the evidence of ordinary language, for whatever that support may be worth.

Nevertheless, it has been held that there is no such feeling, even though we do ordinarily speak as if there were. Let us now consider Professor William Kneale's discussion of this question (*Probability and Induction*,[1] Part I, Section 4, 'The Nature of Opinion'). He has made some formidable objections to the traditional doctrine. It is true that his main aim in this chapter is to criticize another traditional doctrine, the view that probability is to be defined in terms of degrees of confidence, whereas we are concerned with the doctrine that degrees of belief are to be defined in terms of them. Again, the distinction which he has in mind is the distinction between opinion and knowledge, whereas we are concerned with the distinction between opinion and conviction (being sure that . . .). There is still an important difference between opinion and conviction even when the conviction does not amount to knowledge, as it often does not. When I am, or feel, sure that *p*, *p* may in fact be false; and even if it be true, I may not have conclusive reasons for believing it. We are also concerned with the distinction between opinion and suspecting that . . ., which Kneale does not discuss. (Perhaps he would regard suspecting that . . . as the weakest variety of opinion.)

But although the doctrine I am discussing is not the main target of Kneale's criticism, he does make some shots at it, and it may well be thought that he hits the bull's eye. Confidence is supposed to be something which we feel. But he himself can discover no such feeling when he is rationally opining (p. 14). Perhaps we need not discuss the rather unplausible view which he then proceeds to criticize. It is concerned with the measurement of probability. Probabilities are measured by fractions; but can we really suppose that for every degree of probability between 0 and 1 there is a corresponding degree of felt confidence? (p. 15). Degrees of belief might still be definable in terms of degrees of confidence even though degrees of probability are not. And if we do wish to define degrees of belief in this way, we are not compelled to suppose that the series of degrees is continuous. The degree of felt confidence, and the degree of belief likewise, might rise by finite jerks or jumps as we pass along the series, from suspecting that . . . at the bottom to conviction at the top.

On the same page, however, Kneale makes a remark about knowledge which is very relevant to the question we are discussing. 'It is obvious that knowledge itself is not accompanied by

[1] Oxford University Press, 1949.

confidence. When we realise that $2 + 2 = 4$, we do not sweat with any feeling of supreme intensity' (p. 15, *ad fin.*). Here again, what Kneale has in mind is the contrast between knowledge and rational opinion. But what he says about knowledge could be applied to any conviction, whether it amounts to knowledge or not. Whatever proposition we are sure of, whether true or false, *a priori* or empirical, whether our sureness is reasonable or unreasonable, do we find ourselves 'sweating with a feeling of supreme intensity' when we entertain that proposition? Conceivably we might, when we have just *come* to be sure about something, like Archimedes when he rushed out of the bath shouting 'Eureka!' But then it is the coming to be sure, perhaps after a long period of doubt and unsuccessful enquiry, which has this strong feeling-tone, accompanied very likely by organic sensations, as the phrase 'sweating with' suggests. The sureness, once we have it, and have got used to having it, is no longer manifested in this exciting way.

Why then do we speak of 'feeling confident'? Kneale's answer is this: 'When we speak, as we admittedly do, of feeling confident, we are referring, I think, to the absence of serious doubt or questioning from our minds, much as when we speak of feeling tranquil we are referring to the absence of uneasiness'[1] (p. 16). And he agrees that doubt itself can properly be described as something which we feel, since there is at any rate a feeling-element in it, 'a feeling of frustration and restlessness' (*ibid.*)

As we have seen, Kneale is mainly concerned here with degrees of probability. But what he has said suggests a way of reformulating the traditional doctrine about degrees of belief: or rather, perhaps, a way of turning it upside down. Where the traditional doctrine speaks of degrees of confidence, should we speak of degrees of doubt instead? A person who merely suspects that p feels a good deal of doubt about the proposition p, when he actually entertains the proposition. In the middle degrees of belief (traditionally called 'opinion') he feels some doubt about the proposition p, but not so much. Within opinion itself there are

[1] Kneale himself does not wish to *define* opinion in terms of doubt, though he agrees that 'anyone who opines feels some doubt about what he opines' (*op. cit.*, p. 16). I think this is because he is concerned only with the distinction between rational opinion, on the one hand, and knowledge on the other; and not with the distinction between opinion, whether rational or not, and conviction whether rational or not.

degrees, and he might express these by saying how much doubt he feels: some doubt, a little doubt, and just a very little doubt when he is nearly sure but not quite. Finally, the highest degree of belief (conviction, being quite sure) would be expressed by saying 'I do not feel any doubt at all that *p*'. Conviction, then, so far from being a feeling of supreme intensity, would be the absence of a feeling: the complete absence of any feeling of doubt. In this way, we might hope to dispel the mystery which has somehow gathered round the traditional doctrine of 'a feeling of confidence which varies in degree'. Feeling more confidence is turned into feeling less doubt, and feeling less confidence into feeling more doubt. And the supposed supreme degree of confidence, conviction, just consists in feeling no doubt at all.

CONFIDENCE AND DOUBT

This is a very attractive proposal. Doubt is something which is perfectly familiar to everyone. Doubt *is* something which we feel, or at any rate it is something which we experience or 'live through'. We all know what it is like to doubt, and some of us enjoy it. How happy we should be if everything we say about confidence could be said, and said more clearly, by talking about doubt instead!

But can it? Let us consider conviction. Believing a proposition *p* with conviction (being completely sure that *p*) cannot just consist in not having any feelings of doubt about *p*. There are many propositions which a person feels no doubt about, because he has never considered them at all. If you have never heard of Great Snoring, you do not feel any doubt about the proposition 'Great Snoring is a village in Norfolk'.

Indeed, there are propositions about which one cannot feel any doubt, because one cannot even entertain them. (It is worth while to mention this, because a state of conviction or complete sureness is sometimes expressed by saying 'I cannot doubt that . . .'.) For instance, there are many propositions in Higher Mathematics which I myself cannot doubt, because I cannot at all understand the technical symbols in which they are formulated. The most I can manage to be convinced of is that some necessary truths or other are formulated in this (to me) unintelligible manner.

So we must obviously make some reference to entertaining, if conviction (being sure that . . .) is to be defined in terms of absence of doubt. For instance, we might say 'whenever *A* entertains the proposition *p*, he does not feel any doubt about it'. And this would indeed be true of him, so long as his conviction continues, and provided that it is what we call a 'conscious' conviction.[1]

We encounter other difficulties when we consider the lower degrees of confidence, those which we are supposed to feel in suspecting and in opinion. Ordinarily we are quite content to say 'I feel more confident about *p* than about *q*'. For instance, I feel more confident about the proposition 'it will rain some time to-day' than I feel about the proposition 'it will rain within the next hour'. Are we to say, instead, that I feel less doubt about the first proposition than I feel about the second? It is true that I do. But if we stop at that point in our analysis of 'feeling more confident . . . than . . .' we have left something out. For here again, I might quite well feel less doubt about *p* than I feel about *q* without believing either of them. I greatly doubt the proposition 'some human being will visit Sirius some day'. I also doubt the proposition 'some human being will visit the planet Neptune some day' and I doubt it a good deal less. But I do not believe either of them. It may be that it would be reasonable for me to believe the second one, at any rate with the lowest degree of belief ('suspecting that . . .'), if I were better informed about the technology of space-travel. But as it is, I doubt the first more than the second without believing either of them. In the same way, a sceptical person might doubt the existence of telepathy and he might doubt the existence of telekinesis still more, without believing that either of them exists.

It seems, then, that degrees of belief cannot be *defined* in terms of degrees of doubt. It is indeed true, and relevant, that when we are more nearly sure of *p* than of *q*, we feel less doubt about *p* than we feel about *q*. But 'being more nearly sure of . . .' cannot be equivalent to 'being disposed to feel less doubt about . . .'; and 'being quite sure of . . .' cannot be equivalent to 'being disposed

[1] On 'unconscious' beliefs, see below, Lecture 3, pp. 299–301.

not to feel any doubt about . . .'. Something relevant is being said when these analyses are offered, but something else which is equally relevant is being omitted.

It is not just that there is less doubt in some cases than in others, and that in complete conviction (being absolutely sure that . . .) there is no doubt at all. There is something else which counteracts the doubt. In conviction this anti-doubting factor is completely victorious. Doubt is squeezed out altogether. In opinion, it is not squeezed out altogether. Some doubt is still felt, even in the higher degrees of opinion, when the 'opined' proposition is actually being entertained; but the anti-doubting factor has the upper hand. It still has the upper hand in suspecting that . . ., but only just. Its victory is 'a very near thing'. The victory may be short-lived too. Suspecting is a less stable state of mind than opinion. We easily slip out of it into the neutral state of suspense of judgement. Then we just wonder whether *p* is true or false. Sometimes we go farther, and being to suspect that not-*p*, whereas we had previously suspected that *p*.

What is this anti-doubting factor? It is exactly what we call 'confidence', and it has to be mentioned, under some name or other, in any tolerable analysis of the degrees of belief. If, or to the extent that, our believing is reasonable, the degree of confidence varies with the strength of the evidence we ourselves have for the proposition believed, while the degree of doubt varies with the strength of the evidence we ourselves have against the proposition. (As has been pointed out before, it is the evidence we ourselves have which is relevant here, not merely the evidence which 'there is', nor the evidence which other people have.)

But does it follow from this that confidence is something which we 'feel', as doubt is? Let us confine ourselves, for the moment, to the lower degrees of belief, from suspecting that . . . at the bottom to being nearly, but not quite, sure at the top (that is, to beliefs which fall short of conviction). There is a sense in which all of them are conflict-situations. At any rate, this is true of *coming to* suspect that . . . and coming to have the opinion that . . . And this conflict is something which we feel; it is even agonizing sometimes. If we do eventually arrive at a more or less stable state of suspecting that . . . or of having the opinion that . . . , the conflict is terminated. But a certain state of tension remains between the two opposing factors, doubt and confidence. One side has gained ground, the other has lost it. But both still retain their hostile posture, because neither has achieved a decisive victory. Each is still exerting pressure on the other. It is this state of tension which we 'feel' when we suspect that p or have the opinion that p; and we still feel it a little in the highest degree of opinion (when we are very nearly sure, but not quite). We can describe our condition either by saying how much confidence we feel or by saying how much doubt we feel. But if we are to be explicit we ought to mention both.

This is the conclusion we reach if we use the word 'feel' in an emotion-like sense. Now let us consider conviction. In *this* sense of the word 'feel', it is true that in the state of conviction (being completely sure that . . .) there is no feeling at all. There may well have been some while we were coming to be sure. But once we *are* sure, and so long as we remain so, there is no feeling at all, in this sense of the word 'feel'. Being sure is not a conflict-situation, and there is no felt tension in it.

But the word 'feel' also has a wider sense than this. It is applied to any mental state or mental process which is introspectible. What is felt, in this sense, is what can be (though it need not actually be) an object of introspection; what we feel is just something which we 'live through'. We may recall Samuel Alexander's distinction between 'enjoyment' and 'contemplation'. 'Feeling', in this sense, is equivalent to what he called 'enjoying'. Emotions themselves are often lived through, though not always, if there are what we call unconscious emotions (e.g. unconscious fears). But they are certainly not the *only* mental states or happenings which are lived through.

Now is being sure something which can be felt in this sense of the word 'feel' (the 'living through' sense) though in the emotion-like sense it cannot? I suggest that it is. As we have seen, in ordinary everyday speech we are perfectly content to speak of 'feeling sure' as well as 'being sure'. If you ask me whether I feel sure that it is going to rain, and I reply that I do, are we bound to suppose that my reply is false? It would have to be, if the truth is that I have no feeling at all about the proposition 'it is going to rain' in any sense of the word 'feel'.

Sureness is indeed the absence of a feeling, if the word 'feel' is used in its emotion-like sense. Sureness is a state of mind in which conflict or tension is absent. But it might still be a state of mind which is lived through or 'enjoyed' by the person who has it; and that, I suggest, is the sense which the word 'feel' has when a person says 'I feel sure'. (Cf. 'Did you feel very frightened?' 'No, oddly enough I felt perfectly calm at the time'.) Feeling sure *is* rather like feeling calm, or feeling tranquil as Kneale puts it.[1] But he is mistaken in supposing that feeling tranquil is just the absence of uneasiness. It is a positive state which we sometimes 'live through'. Should we wish to say that when a man feels well, the truth is only that he does *not* feel at all ill?

[1] *Probability and Induction*, p. 16.

LECTURE 3

THE DISPOSITIONAL ANALYSIS: INFERENCE AND ASSENT

BELIEF AND INFERENCE

Another important manifestation of belief is inferring, drawing inferences from the proposition believed. (We may recall Ramsey's view that when we come to believe a proposition we add it to our stock or premisses.[1]) The Acting-as-if Analysis does make room for this belief-manifestation. Acting as if a proposition were true amounts to using it as a premiss in one's practical reasoning. But why only in one's practical reasoning? Propositions which we believe are used as premisses in inferences of all kinds, not merely in practical ones.

But if we wished to say that believing a proposition *is* (among other things) a tendency to draw inferences from it, our analysis of belief would apparently be circular, since inferring itself is one way of coming to believe. Perhaps we may put it this way: the belief that *p* has a tendency to spread itself or extend itself to other propositions which follow from *p*, whether with certainty or with probability.

This 'extensibility' of belief is a most important property of it. If a person claims to believe a proposition, but fails to believe even its most obvious consequences (e.g. shows no surprise at all when one of them is falsified) we are inclined to doubt whether he does believe the proposition. At 2 p.m. he says he believes that the Front Quadrangle of the College is square; but two minutes later, when he walks round it, he is not at all surprised to find that its North side is three yards longer than its East side. Clearly there is something paradoxical here which needs explanation. It might be that by the time he began to walk he had lost his belief that the Front Quadrangle is square. Or perhaps he believed that it was indeed square at 2 p.m., but also believed that college quadrangles are liable to change their shapes very quickly, as

[1] See Series II, Lecture 1, above, p. 254.

clouds do. Colleges are queer places, and all sorts of strange things are liable to happen there.

The most likely explanation, however, is that he was not in full possession of his wits at the time. He was tired, frightened, flustered or half-asleep, and therefore failed to notice that the observations he made during his walk 'had any bearing on' the proposition he believed. No one is in full possession of his wits all the time. It is also true that the appreciation of the logical relations between propositions varies greatly between different people, even when all of them are in full possession of whatever wits they have.

But normally, when we believe a proposition, our belief does extend itself to at least some of the consequences of the proposition. We need beliefs because we need guidance not only in our actions but in our thoughts also. We are interested in the question 'What am I to think?' as well as in the question 'What am I to do?' To put it another way, when we believe a proposition *p* we are interested in the question '*p*, so what?' And 'so what?' does not only mean 'so what am I to do?' but also 'so what else am I entitled (or obliged) to believe?'

This tendency to draw inferences from the proposition believed does have something to do with the 'cognitive feelings' we have been discussing (surprise, doubt and confidence). What spreads itself or extends itself from the proposition believed to its consequences, or at least to its obvious consequences, is the whole complex disposition which we call 'believing', and this includes the disposition to have the feelings we have discussed. If the consequences are not only obvious, but also follow with certainty from the proposition believed, the belief-disposition remains intact, as it were, when it spreads or extends itself to these consequences. In that case, a person who merely suspects that *p* will merely suspect that *q*; a person who believes with considerable confidence that *p* (has the opinion that *p*) will have an equally strong or firm opinion that *q*; and a person who is completely sure that *p* will also be completely sure that *q*. Moreover, whatever degree of surprise he is disposed to feel if *p* should turn out to be false, he is disposed to feel the same degree of surpirse if *q* should turn out to be false.

But if we are aware that *q* is only a probable consequence of *p*, our degree of belief is lower with regard to *q* than it is with regard to *p*. Our belief does spread itself or extend itself to *q*, but in a diluted or weakened form. Let us suppose that we are in the Lake District. It is raining heavily and we are quite sure that the heavy rain will continue all day. If it does, the brook at the bottom of the garden will probably be impassable by this evening. This happens quite often, though not always, when there is heavy rain in these parts. Then, if we are reasonable and in possession of our wits, we shall opine, or perhaps only suspect, that the brook will be impassable by then. We shall not feel quite sure about it, though we do feel quite sure that the rain will continue all day. It is a possibility to be reckoned with and taken seriously, but we do not feel sure that it will actually happen. If it does not, we shall be somewhat surprised, but not astonished, as we shall be if the rain stops at lunch-time.

Let us now suppose that *p* itself is only something I suspected and that *q* is only a moderately probable consequence of it. I suspect, for example, that the cat has gone out for the night; and if he has, it is not unlikely that he is in the garden of the house across the road. Even here there is some spreading of my (weak) belief-attitude from *p* to *q*. But by the time it reaches *q* it is still more diluted, and shows itself only in my considering the *question* 'whether *q*?' and not in any belief about the answer. That is not much, but still it is something. It is some gain to have discovered at any rate one question which 'arises' from our suspecting that *p*. Even when the extension of belief occurs in this, its weakest and most diluted form, it is not to be despised.

If the case where *q* follows from *p* with certainty may be represented by saying *p* confers a probability of 1 upon *q*', we may sum the matter up like this:—the manner in which our belief that *p* spreads itself or extends itself to another proposition *q*, which is a consequence of *p*, depends upon two factors taken together: (1) the degree of our belief that *p* (2) our estimate of the degree of probability which *p* confers upon *q*. If we do not or cannot estimate this degree of probability at all, our belief does not spread itself to *q* at all. If, or in so far as, we estimate it incorrectly, as we may, our belief does spread itself to *q*, but this extension of it to *q* is unreasonable, even though the belief that *p* may be perfectly reasonable.

If the Dispositional Analysis of belief is correct, we shall certainly have to say that this 'spreading' of belief from a proposition to its consequences is one of the most important ways in which such a disposition is occurrently manifested. This, I think, is what we have in mind when we speak of 'relying' on a proposition. When we believe a proposition we rely upon it. This is not quite a tautology, equivalent to 'when we believe a proposition, we believe it.' The word 'rely' makes explicit something which might have been overlooked. A proposition is relied upon when it is available to us as a premiss for inferences, whether theoretical or practical.

Our beliefs are like posts which we plant in the shifting sands of doubt and ignorance. They are fixed points or stable landmarks; and once they are there, we are able to make short journeys into the surrounding wastes, planting another post or two as we go. That is why the loss of a belief can be such a serious matter for us. We have lost something which we have been using to find our way about a wilderness. We are in a state of 'bewilderment'.

This spreading of belief from one proposition to another may be experienced or lived through by the believing person. There is an experience called 'inferring' or 'drawing a conclusion'. But sometimes we just find ourselves feeling confident of the conclusion, or feeling surprised when it is falsified, though we did not actually experience any process of inferring. The conclusion 'drew itself', as it were. We did not consciously draw it. For instance, if I believe that one of my colleagues went to New York the day before yesterday, I feel surprised when I meet him in Oxford this evening, though I did not consciously infer that he was unlikely to be back so soon.

Nevertheless, it is an important fact about the autonomous character of rational beings that we can, if we wish, inhibit or suspend this extension of belief from one proposition to another, until we are satisfied that *q* is indeed a consequence of *p*, and satisfied also about the strength of the logical connection between them. Does *p*, which we believe already, render *q* certain? If it does not, what degree of probability, if any, does it confer upon *q*? In such a case the conclusion certainly does not 'draw itself'. We may even be tempted to say of such a self-critical and consciously supervised inference that here, at any rate, inferring is something which we *do*, as the phrase 'making an inference' might suggest. There is indeed something voluntary about it. It is an exercise of our freedom. The initial suspension or inhibition is voluntary; and so is the attention we give to the logical connection between the proposition already believed and the other proposition to which our belief would have 'spread' if we had allowed it to. And after that, our freedom is exercised again in our willingness to be guided by the strength, be it great or little, of the logical connection between the two propositions, and to conclude accordingly. For instance, we notice that *p* makes *q* very likely, but does not make it certain. Then, though we feel absolutely sure that *p*, we shall not allow ourselves to feel absolutely sure that *q*, but only to have a pretty confident opinion that *q*.

So much for inferring. We have only been concerned with it in so far as it is one very obvious way in which our beliefs are occurrently manifested. As Ramsey pointed out, every proposition which a person believes is for that person a potential premiss, so long as his belief continues; and when it actually functions as a premiss, whether consciously or not, whether in a self-critical way or not, his belief with regard to it is occurrently manifested.

BELIEF AS A MULTIFORM DISPOSITION

In these two lectures we have considered a good many different sorts of belief-manifesting occurrences. It should now be clear that if '*A* believes that *p*' is a dispositional statement about *A*, the disposition we attribute to him is a multiform disposition, which is manifested or actualized in many different ways: not only in his actions, not only in his actions and his inactions, but also in emotional states such as hope and fear; in feelings of doubt, surprise and confidence; and finally in his inferences, both those in which a belief just 'spreads itself' from a proposition to some of its consequences (certain or probable), and those in which the inference is a self-conscious and self-critical intellectual operation.

Some of these belief-manifestations are public, or public in principle, though not necessarily public *de facto*. But others are inward and private. They take place in the 'inner life' of the believer. If we wish to know what they were, we have to ask him, as indeed we sometimes have to ask him about those which are in principle public, since they are not always public *de facto*. Moreover, even those which are public *de facto*, such as the actions we see him performing, do also have their 'inner' or private aspect. Actions, or at any rate normal actions, have to be experienced by the person who does them. The Acting-as-if Analysis, incomplete as it is, is still more incomplete if action is 'reduced' to observable bodily movement, or inaction to observable bodily quiescence.

If one may dare to say so, the 'inner life' does matter. Certainly we cannot ignore it when we are trying to understand what it is to believe something. And if we think of these various sorts of belief-manifestations as belief-*symptons*, by means of which another person can find out what *A*'s beliefs are, or what degree of belief he has concerning this or that proposition, we certainly have to consider not only overt and public symptoms but private and purely introspectible ones as well: for instance, the private feeling of slight surprise which *A* experienced when it did not rain after all.

It may well seem to you that the belief-manifestations we have discussed are a 'pretty miscellaneous lot'. Indeed they are, and others might well have been added to the list. Anger, for example, can be a manifestation of belief. I am angry with you about something which I believe you said or did (or omitted to say or do). Perhaps my belief is incorrect, and then I am angry with you 'under a misapprehension'. All the same, my anger is a manifestation of my belief. Again, belief sometimes shows itself by the distress or dismay one feels when others deny the proposition believed, or express doubt of it, or say 'only an idiot could believe a thing like that'. For we have a certain attachment to propositions which we believe, and we may still have it even when we should much prefer them to be false. Something like the principle 'Love me, love my dog' applies to them.

But, after all, the miscellaneous character of belief-manifestations is one of the most interesting and important things about them. If *A* holds some belief, many *different* sorts of happenings in *A*'s history, both overt happenings and purely private and introspectible ones, are tied together or made explicable by the fact that he holds it. If the Dispositional Analysis of belief is correct, believing must be a multiform disposition. That is why the acting-as-if version of the Dispositional Analysis is too simple and too narrow.

BELIEF AND ASSENT

In this long and laborious attempt to reformulate the Dispositional Analysis, we have so far said nothing about the event which is the main topic of the traditional Occurence Analysis, the mental event (or mental act) described as 'assenting to a proposition'. If believing is to be conceived as a disposition, is it among other things a disposition to assent to the proposition believed? Another topic which we did not discuss is the distinction between reasonable and unreasonable belief. What does the Dispositional Analysis make of this important distinction? There is a connection between these two questions, as we shall see.

There certainly is a mental event which can be quite naturally described as assenting to a proposition. Moreover, it is often a purely inward event. It need not necessarily be expressed by means of bodily behaviour, for instance by saying 'Yes, I think so' or 'I am sure it is so', or writing a sentence down on paper and underlining it in green ink.

As we have seen, a person who believes that *p* is disposed to use the proposition *p* as a premiss in his inferences. Now when the inference is of a conscious and explicit kind, it is not enough to say (though it is true) that he believes the premiss; nor is it enough to say (though this also is true) that his belief spreads itself or extends itself to the conclusion. He has to *assent* to the premiss and he has to assent to the conclusion, if the inference is to be a conscious and explicit one. And it is not very extravagant to describe these two events as 'mental acts' or 'acts of assenting'. If believing is a disposition which we have with regard to a proposition, it certainly is (among other things) a disposition to use that proposition as a premiss. And when we do actually use a proposition *p* as a premiss in some conscious and explicit inference, the disposition is manifested by this important sort of mental occurrence or mental act.

The assent to the conclusion *q* is likewise a mental occurrence or mental act. But it is not an occurrent manifestation of a belief which we already have. It is the initiation of a new one. By assenting to the conclusion *q* we have acquired a new disposition, which is liable to manifest itself by various sorts of mental and psycho-physical occurrences thereafter; and further acts of assenting to *q* may be among them. For one thing, *q* itself has now been added to our 'stock of premisses', and we may have occasion to use it, in its turn, as a premiss in some conscious and explicit inference.

If the inference from *p* to *q* is a valid one, the belief that *q* which we have thus acquired is a reasonable belief. But what shall we say if the belief that *p* is itself unreasonable? Conceivably, it might be just a piece of 'wishful thinking'. For instance, I believe (on no evidence at all) that I am going to win £1000 in next week's lottery; and from this I infer that by the end of next week I shall have more than enough money to buy a new car which costs £800. It might be said that in believing this conclusion I am just as unreasonable as I am in believing the premiss. And yet, so long as I do believe the premiss, it would be unreasonable of me *not* to believe the conclusion. Perhaps we may say that it is 'conditionally reasonable' to believe the conclusion.

But conditionally reasonable believing is not the only sort of reasonable believing. If it were, every reasonable belief would have to be acquired by means of inference from something we believe already. There is, however, another way of acquiring reasonable beliefs. We can acquire them by considering *evidence.* (The four most important types of evidence are the evidence of sense-perception, of self-consciousness, of memory, and of testimony.[1]) This way of acquiring reasonable beliefs is the primary one. It provides us with the premisses which we may subsequently use for acquiring other beliefs by means of inference.

Nevertheless, this reasonable procedure of considering evidence, and believing accordingly, does resemble inference in one important respect. When we infer *q* from *p* in a self-conscious and self-critical way, our belief that *q* is initiated by a conscious act of assent. The same thing happens when we acquire a new belief by examining the evidence. We acquire it by assenting to that proposition which is supported (on balance) by the evidence which we have.

[1] See Series I, Lectures 4 and 5.

Here too, our assent is an introspectible mental event and can be quite naturally described as a 'mental act'. Here too, it initiates a disposition which we did not have before. For instance, as a result of this assenting, we are now disposed to feel surprise if the proposition to which we have assented turns out later to be false, to use the proposition thereafter as a premiss, and to feel doubt of any other proposition which would be very improbable if the proposition assented to is true.

Here, then, is the connection between assenting and reasonable believing. Both in the primary sort of reasonable believing which depends on the examination of evidence, and in the derivative or inferential sort which we called 'conditionally reasonable', a belief is acquired by means of a special sort of mental event or act. We need a name for this mental event or act; and 'assent' (or 'assenting') is the most suitable one.

We cannot just call it 'coming to believe'. For one thing, we may come to believe a proposition in an unreasonable way; and then, this multiform disposition which we call 'believing' is not initiated by any conscious mental act. Unreasonable beliefs come into being in a 'behind the scenes' manner. The believer does not notice himself acquiring them. He acquires them without knowing what is happening to him.

Secondly, assenting also occurs when the disposition has already been established; and not only when the proposition believed is being used as a premiss in some inference, theoretical or practical, but on other occasions too. For instance, if someone asks me (or I ask myself) whether I do believe the proposition *p* or whether I 'really' believe it, I may consciously and attentively entertain the proposition *p*; and then I may find myself assenting to it. It is true that this does not completely settle the question whether I do believe that *p* or do 'really' believe it. It might be that I am in the curious state called 'half-belief' which we shall discuss later.[1] (Some events in my history, both overt and introspectible, may suggest that I do believe the proposition, while other events in my history suggest that I do not.) But still, the fact that I consciously assent to the proposition here and now when I entertain it attentively is *some* evidence—and quite strong evidence—that I do believe the proposition. If we wish to find out

[1] See Lecture 4, below.

whether a person believes that *p*, there really is something to be said for going and asking him.

THE OCCURRENCE ANALYSIS RECONSIDERED

The traditional Occurrence Analysis of belief was certainly mistaken when it described belief as an introspectible mental event or mental act. Nevertheless, the mental events or acts which its exponents refer to do occur, and they are relevant to the analysis of belief. Only, it is a mistake to say that these mental events or acts *are* beliefs or believings. I suggest, therefore, that we ought to be more indulgent to the traditional Occurrence Analysis than we are. If we were willing to be very indulgent indeed, we might even say that its mistake was mainly a mistake of idiom. Philosophers do use language in odd ways, especially when they are trying to say something which is very difficult to say at all. But still, they may manage thereby to draw our attention to some important question which we should not have considered otherwise. In this case the question is 'In what way are introspectible events relevant to the analysis of belief?'

Hitherto, I have been emphasizing the differences between the traditional Occurrence Analysis and the modern Dispositional Analysis, as if we had to choose between the two. The situation is not quite so bad as that. The differences are there, and if we do have to choose, we must prefer the Dispositional Analysis. But still, up to a point, we may have it both ways. Much of what is said in the traditional Occurrence Analysis can be incorporated into the Dispositional Analysis. Mental events which can quite properly be described as 'assents' or 'assentings' really do occur; and they certainly are relevant to the analysis of the complex and multiform disposition which we call belief, whether we are considering the initiation of such a disposition, or the occurrent manifestations of it when it has been acquired. For once in a way, let us rejoice in complexity.

UNCONSCIOUS BELIEFS

Finally, our discussion of assenting may help us to understand how there can be 'unconscious' beliefs. When we say that *A* has an unconscious belief that *p*, we mean that all or most of the other manifestations of a belief that *p* do occur in him, but he does *not* assent to the proposition *p* when he entertains it and attends to it, and perhaps he even rejects it. He is surprised when presented with evidence which suggests that *p* may after all be false, and quickly forgets that adverse evidence. He acts as a person would act who used *p* as a premiss in his practical reasoning, but does not notice that he *is* acting as such a person would. He may also show the emotional symptoms of a belief that *p*, for instance a fear of some unpleasant event which would be unlikely to happen unless *p* were true. But when he actually entertains and attends to the proposition *p* (as he has to, when we ask him 'Do you believe it?') he does not assent to the proposition and his answer is 'No, of course not'. And he makes the same answer to himself, when he asks himself that question.

Assenting to a proposition is certainly a very important symptom of belief, as we have seen; and we might be inclined to say 'since he does not assent to the proposition when he entertains it, he obviously does not believe it'. Yet he does show many of the other symptoms of believing it, including some of the introspectible ones. It cannot be denied that he is at any rate in a belief-like state with regard to this proposition. It is better, then, to use a terminology which emphasizes the striking resemblances which there are between this man's state and the state of the normal believer. We do this by saying 'he unconsciously believes that *p*'. The other alternative, of refusing to say that he believes it, has the defect of drawing our attention away from some interesting and puzzling phenomena which we need to understand.

For similar reasons, it seems perverse to deny that there can be unconscious wishes or unconscious fears (as philosophers sometimes do) by insisting on terminological rules which would make it nonsensical to use such expressions. If we insist on such a narrow and rigid terminology, we deprive ourselves of insight into the complex facts of human nature, by depriving ourselves of the linguistic tools which are the most handy ones for describing them and discussing them.

I conclude then that there are unconscious beliefs; '*A* believes that *p*' can still be true, even though *A* does not assent to the proposition *p* when he entertains it and attends to it. We may, if we please, regard this as no more than a terminological recommendation. But I hope it has been shown that there are reasons for making it.

It is not very surprising that we should find the term 'unconscious belief' useful. Everyone has many beliefs about other human beings, and some of them are closely connected with his moral dispositions. Among these beliefs of his, there may well be some which suggest pretty strongly that he has an uncharitable attitude towards some other person or persons. So he has a strong motive for concealing from himself the fact that he holds such beliefs. The same is true of a person's beliefs about himself. For example, it has been said that no one is indispensable, and most of us would agree with this remark. Nevertheless, it is quite easy for a person to believe that he is an exception to this general rule; to believe, for instance, that he is himself an indispensable member of some institution to which he belongs, even though no one else is. If he were to acknowledge that he does hold this belief, he might well have to admit that he over-estimates his own mertis or capacities, and also perhaps that he underestimates the merits or capacities of others.

No one likes to admit that he has such morally-reprehensible attributes as conceit or unfairness, and therefore we are all reluctant to admit that we have the kind of beliefs which a person with these attributes is likely to have. If we were to recollect some of our past sayings and doings and some of our own past introspectible states, and I ask 'what do all these add up to?' it would become obvious that we do hold some belief which it is painful or shameful to acknowledge. But either we fail to recollect these phenomena which have occurred in our own past history; or if we ever do, we fail to consider them together, and therefore fail to notice 'what they all add up to'.

LECTURE 4

HALF-BELIEF[1]

The concept of half-belief has not been much discussed by philosophers. But it is familiar to all of us. We quite often say of another person that he half-believes such and such a proposition though he does not wholly believe it. Sometimes we even say such things about ourselves, usually in the past tense. 'I see now that at that time I only half-believed what he told me.' I did not quite believe it, but I did not disbelieve it; and yet I was not in a state of suspended judgement about it either. My attitude was one which came fairly close to believing and yet did not go all the way; or it had some of the characteristics of believing, but lacked others. Again, when we make the too-familiar accusation 'He does not really believe what he says he believes', it would sometimes be more accurate, as well as more charitable, to say that he does half-believe it.

Let us begin by distinguishing half-belief from two other attitudes with which it might possibly be confused. The first is believing mildly, with a relatively low degree of confidence. The second might be called 'believing half of . . .'.

With regard to the first, I assume, as before, that Locke and his followers are right in maintaining that there are 'degrees of assent'. (*Essay* Book IV chapters 15, 16 and 19.) As we have seen, the lowest degree is traditionally called surmising or suspecting, and the highest degree is called conviction. Between these two extremes there are the various degrees of opinion, most commonly expressed by saying 'I think that . . .'. I do think that it will be a fine afternoon though I am by no means sure about it. Or again, I am nearly sure that it will be fine, but not quite sure.

[1] This lecture is a revised version of the orally-delivered Gifford Lecture on Half-Belief. It was read at the joint session of the Aristotelean Society and Mind Association at Reading in 1964 and printed in the Aristotelean Society Supplementary Volume for 1964. It is reprinted here with the kind permission of the Editor.

The image we have here is of a graduated scale, where 0 is suspense of judgement and 10 is absolute conviction. We need some such picture if we wish to say, as Locke in effect did, that there are two questions (not just one) which we must ask when we are considering whether a particular belief is reasonable First, we must ask whether the believer has evidence for the proposition believed. If he has none, his belief is obviously unreasonable. But his belief may still be unreasonable even though he does have some evidence for it. We must also consider the degree of his belief. He may believe more firmly than his evidence warrants. For instance, he may be in a state of absolute conviction, when his evidence is only sufficient to justify a moderately confident opinion. Indeed, this is probably the commonest form of unreasonable belief. We do not so very often believe on no evidence at all, but we quite often believe more firmly than the evidence warrants.

Now suppose I believe with only a moderate degree of confidence that I shall get a reply to my letter by to-morrow morning's post. I think it will come, but I am not by any means sure. There is nothing partial or 'half-ish' about this attitude of mine. For example, I do not show the symptoms of belief in some circumstances and those of disbelief or doubt in others. My attitude of mild confidence remains the same throughout the day, unless or until the evidence alters. Of course I should lose it, or at any rate it would be diminished in degree, if I learned at tea-time that my correspondent was in bed with influenza. But then I should have acquired a new and relevant piece of evidence.

It must, however, be admitted that such a moderately confident opinion could be called 'half-belief' or 'mere half-belief', if we rejected Locke's doctrine of degrees of assent, as Newman did (*Grammar of Assent*, ch. 6).[1] If belief is a matter of all or nothing, and we are not allowed to say that you believe unless you are in a state of total conviction, it does of course follow that opinion is not believing. It would only be a kind of second-rate or partial approximation to that much admired state of absolute conviction, and someone might call it half-belief to show what a poor thing he thinks it is. But this is not the ordinary usage of the term 'half-belief'. Moreover, it seems quite clear that there are degrees of *something* in our acceptance of propositions, whether we call them

[1] See Series I, Lecture 6.

degrees of confidence or not. We do not have to choose between absolute conviction on the one hand and hopeless agnosticism on the other. We can accept propositions with moderate confidence on evidence known to be less than conclusive, and make use of these propositions, for what they may be worth, for the guidance of our thoughts and of our actions. Locke's doctrine of degrees of assent, and the 'Ethics of Belief' which goes with it, was no arbitrary invention, as Newman seems to think. Locke was merely codifying the principles which reasonable men have always followed ever since history began.

BELIEVING HALF OF . . .

We may now consider 'believing half of'. We believe not only single propositions (e.g. 'it will go on raining all day') but also sets of propositions. Do you believe what William said? Yes, I do. But what he said consisted of a large number of propositions, a long story perhaps; and I believe the whole lot. Someone else, however, or myself in a cooler hour, might believe some of those propositions and disbelieve others, and entertain still others neutrally, neither believing them nor disbelieving them. In that case he might perhaps say that he half-believed William's story. But it would be more accurate to say that he believed half of it or part of it. (Throughout our discussion the word 'half' must not be taken with strict arithmetical literalness.)

A more important case, perhaps, is the one where the set of propositions in question is not just a series, but an organized or systematic body of propositions, a theory of some kind. For example, it is said that there are, or have been, people described as Christian Communists. It would be misleading to say that they half-believed the Marxist world-outlook; and if we said that they 'partly' believed it, we should have to mean that they wholly believed some parts of it (e.g. Marx's economic theory, his theory of social structure, his economic interpretation of history) but wholly disbelieved other parts of it. Since they were also Christians, we must suppose that they altogether disbelieved Marx's Atheistic metaphysics, and his materialistic theory of human personality. Whether their attitude was a reasonable or self-consistent one is of course another question. The more tightly organized and systematic a body of propositions is, the more difficult it is to accept some parts of it and reject others without falling into a logical inconsistency somewhere. But clearly this attitude of 'believing half of' does exist, and it is psychologically possible to hold it (though perhaps logically reprehensible) with regard to a systematically organized body of propositions.

It is worth while to add that just because half-believing and 'believing half of' are different, they can be combined. I may half-believe the first half of William's story, but disbelieve the second half altogether. Someone might half-believe Marx's theory of social classes, but reject all his other doctrines completely.

SOME EXAMPLES OF HALF-BELIEF

So much for what half-belief is not. First, it must be distinguished from believing mildly, and secondly from 'believing half of . . .'. If we wish to understand what it is, the best plan is to consider a number of examples. Half-belief is a fairly common phenomenon. We may have half-beliefs about many different subjects. Some of these subjects are of great importance and others are trivial.

Let us begin with the most important case of all, religious half-belief. Here is a man who half-believes the basic propositions of Theism. (We will suppose that he half-believes them all, in order to avoid complications about 'believing half of . . .'.) What makes us say that he only half-believes them?

The position seems to be that on some occasions he acts, feels and thinks (draws inferences) in much the same way as a person who does believe these Theistic propositions. But on other occasions he acts, feels and thinks in much the same way as a person who does not believe them, or even as a person would who had not heard of them at all. For instance, it seldom occurs to him to say his prayers except on Sundays. He does not usually forgive people who have wronged him, and he hardly ever turns his other cheek to the smiter. Yet when he is in Church on Sundays it is very different. He not only behaves outwardly as a pious person would. He also assents inwardly to what is said or sung, and really does have the appropriate emotions of reverence, contrition and thankfulness. Indeed, when those positive symptoms occur in him (including the private and introspectible ones) they may well be symptoms not of a mild belief but of a strong one. Perhaps they occur on other occasions too, for example when he is reading a book of popular theology in the evening, or arguing about its contents with an Agnostic neighbour who has come in to have coffee with him.

It would not be fair to describe this man as a hypocrite, someone who pretends or professes to believe what he actually disbelieves or doubts. Nor would it be fair to say that his religion is just a matter of outward conformity. He resembles a hypocritical conformer in some ways, but not in others. For he really does assent to these theological propositions on some occasions; and then he not only behaves outwardly, but also thinks and feels inwardly, as a genuinely religious person would. His religious attitude is not just a pretended one. But it is, so to speak, a part-time one. It is operative only in some parts of his life but not in others. He is seldom in it except on Sundays.

We may also have half-beliefs about much less important matters. All the same, such trivial half-beliefs are interesting both to the philosopher and to the psychologist. For example, there is the half-belief that it is unlucky to walk under a ladder or to start a journey on a Friday. 'Unlucky' is presumably to be interpreted as a probability-word. Walking under a ladder is supposed to increase the probability that something disadvantageous will happen to one within—say—the next twelve hours. Again, there is the very common half-belief that 13 is an unlucky number, for example that evil consequences of some kind will probably follow if you spend a night in a room or a house whose number is 13. In some British hotels the room between No. 12 and No. 14 is called '12A'. I recently heard of a block of new flats where the flat between No. 12 and No. 14 was called '57' (presumably because $5 + 7 = 12$, and No. 57 was regarded as a kind of variant for No. 12). Another example is the curious superstition about touching wood. 'Have you ever had trouble with the brakes of this car?' 'No, touch wood' the driver replies. Some people do actually touch wood when they say this, or fumble about in their pockets to find a pencil, and they feel quite uncomfortable if there is no wood within reach. They have a half-belief that if wood is not touched, the disadvantageous event which has been mentioned is more likely to occur. Again, someone may have a half-belief that the churchyard is haunted. He does not mind walking through it in daylight or in company, but he avoids walking through it alone on a dark night.

AESTHETIC HALF-BELIEF

We may perhaps find examples of rather a different kind if we consider activities which are not wholly serious, such as reading novels or watching plays or cinematograph films. To put it more technically, let us consider one very familiar form of aesthetic experience and ask whether half-belief is an element in it.

There are of course several different types of aesthetic experience, and perhaps aesthetic theorists have sometimes overlooked these differences, which may account for some of the rather extraordinary things they have said. I cannot see that half-belief plays any part at all in the experience we have when we enjoy a landscape painting, or when we enjoy an actual visible landscape in the physical world. Perhaps it plays no part in a very musical person's appreciation of music, and he just enjoys a very complex pattern of sounds. But certainly there are aesthetic experiences which have a propositional character, experiences in which the entertaining of propositions plays an essential part. The propositions are conveyed to us by means of spoken or written words, or sometimes by means of pictures, as in a silent film, or by means of visible actions or gestures, as in a pageant.

What is out attitude to these propositions? Is it at least sometimes an attitude of half-belief? Sometimes it does seem to be a belief-like attitude, which has at any rate something in common with half-belief, though 'near-belief' might perhaps be a better name for it.

It would be generally agreed that if we are to appreciate a novel or a play there must be what Coleridge called a 'willing suspension of disbelief'. But one may suspect that there are some people for whom this suspension of disbelief is not enough. For them, it is only the first stage, and they pass through it into a more positive attitude: not quite an attitude of belief, but something near it. In their case, there is indeed a voluntary suspension of disbelief when they open a novel and begin to read Chapter I, or when the curtain goes up at the theatre. But afterwards, when they have become absorbed, as we say, in the novel or the play, the state they are in is not merely an absence of disbelief, but something more, and something more positive. It is a state in which they almost believe (for the time being) that the events narrated by Sir Walter Scott did really happen as he described them, or that Hamlet's father really was murdered by Hamlet's uncle. They do not quite believe it, but neither do they just refrain from disbelieving it.

Of course, we must not suppose that everyone who goes to a theatre or reads a novel gets into this attitude of near-believing. No doubt there are highly civilized and highly intellectual persons who do not. Probably they do not get beyond suspension of disbelief, and do not need to. For them the neutral state of neither believing nor disbelieving may well be sufficient to enable them to follow the story with interest and attention.

But there are others, more naive or less hard-headed, for whom mere suspension of disbelief is too cold and *too* neutral an attitude, and if they remained in it they could not enjoy the story they are reading or the play they are seeing. These people get 'carried away', as we say, by the story or the play: carried away into a state which does resemble belief, though it is not complete belief.

There are other ways of describing this state of mind: for example, 'while Tommy is reading a novel or when he is at the cinema he isn't in the real world at all'. This is a rather picturesque way of saying that he *is* in the state of near-belief we are discussing, a state of near-belief with regard to propositions which do not correspond to actual facts. Again, one of the many things we might mean by calling a person 'imaginative' is that he has a tendency to slip into belief-like states of this kind. The trouble with Tommy is that he is such an imaginative boy.

To turn to examples of a rather different kind, let us consider what is called 'make-believe'. The reader will remember the child who plays bears in Professor Ryle's *Concept of Mind* (p. 258). We will suppose that the game is to pretend that the fur rug on the drawing room floor is a bear. At first there is not even a suspension of disbelief. There is only acting 'as if'. This is how I interpret

Ryle's statement that 'the child . . . knows, while in the well-lit drawing room that he is only playing an amusing game'. He disbelieves the proposition 'that is a bear' though he does his best to behave as he thinks a person would who believed it. But later he goes off to a solitary landing, and now he 'feels faint anxieties'. A suspension of disbelief seems to have occurred on the way, though not exactly a willing one. And finally, 'in the darkness of a passage' he 'cannot be persuaded of his safety'. Apparently he has ended by half-believing that there *is* a bear in the house. Or perhaps when he got as far as the landing, he was already in a state of half-believing, and by the time he reached the dark passage he fully believed. As Ryle himself points out, 'make-believe is compatible with all degrees of scepticism and credulity'.

It may be added that half-belief seems to occur sometimes when a person is dreaming or hallucinated, though not of course always. (Usually there is full belief; and occasionally there is full disbelief—the man is quite sure that the experience is 'only a dream' or 'only a hallucination'.)

One might also suggest, though with hesitation, that some mentally disordered persons (not all) are in a state of half-belief about their own 'fantasies' or 'delusions'—the curious and complicated sets of propositions, often ordered in a surprisingly systematic way, which they enunciate to anyone who is willing to listen to them. No doubt such a person does not disbelieve the propositions he asserts. He is not just a liar. And certainly he goes beyond entertaining them in a neutral manner, neither believing nor disbelieving. Yet perhaps he does not wholly believe them either, though he comes a good deal nearer to full belief than the novel-readers and play-goers mentioned before. Possibly a similar state or half or three-quarter belief may also occur in the lighter stages of hypnosis, though not in the deeper ones.

DISCUSSION OF THESE EXAMPLES

If I am right so far, there are many examples of this queer state of half-belief, and we can find them in several different departments of human experience. What are we to make of them?

Perhaps it will be suggested by someone that what I have called half-belief is after all just *belief*, though it may often be belief of an unreasonable kind. For instance, it might be said that the rather unsophisticated or over-imaginative novel reader just believes what he reads in the novel. We should have to add, of course, that his belief is only temporary. It ceases, or quickly fades away, when he shuts the book or when a visitor comes to see him. But many beliefs are short-lived, and this does not prevent them from being perfectly good beliefs while they last. For a time I believed that the train would arrive punctually. But I ceased to believe so when it had taken an hour to cover the first 20 miles.

Again, it might be suggested that the man who avoids walking under ladders does just *believe* (however unreasonably) that walking under ladders has bad consequences, and the man who touches wood does believe that touching wood averts misfortune.

After all, these people act as if they believed, and they often go to considerable trouble in consequence. They step off the pavement into a muddy street or even into a street full of traffic, to avoid the ladder; they hunt about in their pockets in order to find a pencil or other wooden object which they can touch, or go a very long way round to avoid walking through the churchyard in the dark. Moreover, they show the emotional symptoms of belief, for example discomfort or unrest if there is no wood within reach or no way of avoiding the ladder. Our novel-reader or play-goer shows them too. He is moved to tears, as we say, and quite often this is literally true; tears do actually run down his cheeks.

Of course, these people will not admit that they do believe these propositions; not even to themselves, and still less in public. Such an admission, in a scientific age, would be too disreputable, and is only to be expected of someone who has almost heroic candour and strength of mind. But one may hold beliefs, permanent or temporary, without admitting even to oneself that one holds them.

This proposal to dispense with the concept of half-belief altogether (for that is what it comes to) can be made to look plausible, because there really are people who wholly believe what most people only half-believe. No doubt there are some who do wholly believe that their chances of suffering misfortunes are increased if they walk under a ladder or spend the night in room No. 13: they wholly believe it, though they will not admit that they do. And there may be a few who are in a similar state of complete belief when they are reading a novel or watching a play, though they would not admit it either.

But I do not think that this is the usual situation. Let us consider the man who is watching a play. His emotions and his behaviour are in some ways like what they would be, if he believed that the events represented on the stage were really happening. So are his intellectual activities too. He asks himself questions about what he sees and hears ('Can it be that the private secretary was the murderer after all?') or he considers what inferences might be drawn. ('It looks as if Hamlet had studied metaphysics when he was at the University of Wittenberg.') But though the man's emotions, behaviour and intellectual activities are like what they would be if he believed, the likeness is not complete. He is in a state resembling belief. But he keeps this state of his in a watertight compartment, as it were. When the heroine falls into the clutches of the villain, he does not rush out of the theatre and ring up the police. He is emotionally moved, and perhaps strongly moved, but not quite in the way he would be if the events witnessed were taken by him to be 'real life' events. His emotions are genuine enough. He does really feel them and is not just pretending. All the same, they are not wholly serious. And his intellectual activities—the questions he asks himself and the inferences he considers—are not wholly serious either, though he may put quite a lot of thought into them. (A parallel case is the literature on the early career of Sherlock Holmes.)

Again, the ordinary person who avoids walking under ladders does not seriously believe that walking under ladders does any harm, or at any rate he does not believe it with complete seriousness. We notice that if it is very important for him to get to his destination quickly (for example, he will miss a train if he does not hurry) he does not seem to mind the ladder at all. He sees it—there it is, in front of his nose—but he goes straight under it without hesitation. He himself, if he thinks about his experience afterwards, will be able to notice that he felt no qualms at all about doing the thing which he ordinarily avoids so carefully. It is the same with the child who was playing bears. You go and find him in the dark passage and inform him that Christmas presents are to be opened downstairs, and his fear of the bear vanishes away.

A half-belief, then, seems to be something which is 'thrown off' when circumstances alter. In some sorts of contexts one is in a belief-like state with regard to a proposition, but in others one disbelieves it or just disregards it. Or perhaps we should say that in some contexts to which the proposition is relevant one is in a belief-like state about it, but in other contexts to which it is equally relevant one disbelieves it or disregards it ('There is a bear in the hall' is very relevant if one has to go downstairs). In both sorts of contexts, the evidence for the proposition—if there is any—remains the same, and the probability of the proposition is as great, or as little, as it was before. But with the change of context your belief-like attitude to the proposition disappears. It may return later when the context changes back again. This is what happens to the religious half-believer discussed earlier.[1] Next Sunday his belief-like attitude will revive.

IS HALF-BELIEF UNREASONABLE?

Finally, we may ask whether it can be reasonable to hold a half-belief. We commonly use two criteria for deciding whether a belief is reasonable. First, there is the evidential criterion, the one which Locke emphasized in his 'Ethics of Belief'.[2] A belief is reasonable if it is supported by the evidence which the believer has, and if the degree of his belief corresponds to the strength of the evidence. Secondly, there is the consistency criterion. In a reasonable man, any belief which he holds during a given period is consistent with all the other beliefs which he holds during that period.

Now some of the half-believers we have discussed have no evidence, or only very weak evidence, for the propositions which they half-believe. There is not really very much evidence that spending a night in bedroom No. 13 is likely to lead to unfortunate consequences. To be sure, I may have a puncture when I continue my journey next day. But the frequency of punctures does not seem to be appreciably greater for drivers who have spent the previous night in a room or house numbered 13 than it is for drivers in general. Again, when we are watching Shakespeare's *Julius Caesar* and the actor playing the part of Caesar says 'The Ides of March

[1] See pp. 305–6, above. [2] See Series I, Lecture 6.

are come' this is very poor evidence for the proposition 'to-day is the Ides of March'; and the child in the dark passage has very little evidence for the proposition that there is a bear in the house.

Nevertheless, a half-believer might quite well have good evidence for a proposition which he half-believes. To judge from their conduct, many people only half-believe that exercise is conducive to health, or that one is less likely to do a good morning's work if one has gone to bed at 2 a.m. But there is strong evidence for both these propositions. Again, on a dark, cold, dreary day in mid January some people can only half-believe that five months hence there will be some days when the afternoon temperature will reach 70° F. Yet there is good evidence for this proposition. The case of the religious half-believer is a specially complicated one because it involves half-believing 'in' as well as half-believing 'that'. He not only half-believes that God exists; he half-believes *in* God as well. But it would be rash to suppose that there cannot be any good reasons at all for holding either of these half-beliefs.

Half-believers, then, need not necessarily offend against the evidential criterion of reasonableness. But they do at first sight appear to offend against the consistency criterion. In some contexts, the half-believer acts, feels, and draws inferences as if *p* were true, and in other he acts, feels and draws inferences as if *p* were false, although the evidence for *p* (strong or weak) has not altered at all in the meantime.

But is this unreasonableness? It could equally be said, and perhaps better, that a half-believer is in some degree a dissociated or disintegrated personality. To put it very crudely, with one part of his mind, the part which is operative in circumstances *A*, *B* and *C*, he believes such and such a proposition: with another part of his mind, which is operative in circumstances *D*, *E* and *F*, he does not believe it or even disbelieves it. There is nothing very shocking in this suggestion. No one, perhaps, is a completely integrated personality in all respects and in all circumstances.

Even so, we might be inclined to say that half-belief is 'a bad thing', something dishonourable to human nature or unworthy of a rational being. No doubt we are justifiably ashamed of some of our half-beliefs. One should not even half-believe that it is disadvantageous to walk under ladders, if there is no evidence to support this proposition. But I cannot see that there is anything shameful about aesthetic half-beliefs, for example the half-belief that to-day is the Ides of March, although all the available evidence shows that it is the 9th of November. As to the religious half-believer, it is presumably a 'sign of grace' that he does at any rate half-believe that God exists, and moreover half-believes *in* Him. What he should be ashamed of is that he does not believe wholly.

Moreover, if we were unable to hold half-beliefs, it would be much more difficult for us to change our convictions. And surely it is sometimes a very good thing to change them. In order to be 'converted' from believing not-*p* to believing *p*, it is almost inevitable for many people that they should first pass through an intermediate stage of half-believing *p*. This is most obvious where *p* and not-*p* are not just single and isolated propositions but organized systems of propositions ('theories' or 'outlooks'). For then our belief is liable to influence a large part of our conduct and our emotional attitudes. But the same is true sometimes where the belief which has to be changed is of a less complex kind: for example my belief that So-and-So disapproves of me, if he is a person whom I have much to do with.

In such cases as these, it is no simple matter to give up one belief and change over to another, however strong the evidence is which suggests that such a change is called for. No doubt it is easy enough to give up the belief that it will remain fine all the afternoon. We do not need to pass through an intermediate stage of half-believing that it will rain before tea-time (though even here, we sometimes do). But this is not true of all changes of belief.

It would be a mistake, then, to say without qualification that half-belief is 'a bad thing', interesting only as a pathological phenomenon. There are occasions when it is a very good one.

LECTURE 5

NEWMAN'S DISTINCTION BETWEEN REAL AND NOTIONAL ASSENT

The *Grammar of Assent*[1] is not much read by philosophers, unless they are interested in the philosophy of religion. The book is indeed concerned with the philosophy of religion. We might even say that it is one of the classics of that subject. But it is an epistemological book as well. The distinction Newman draws between real and notional assent is not only a distinction between two ways of assenting to religious propositions. The propositions assented to might be propositions about almost any subject matter, and many of Newman's own examples are not concerned with religion at all. Much the same could be said of several other doctrines propounded in this book, for example in ch. VI 'Assent considered as unconditional',[2] in ch. VII 'Certitude' and in ch. IX 'The illative sense'. The *Grammar of Assent* is one of the very few full-length books in English on the epistemology of belief.

I have discussed ch. VI in Series I, Lecture 6. Here Newman is criticizing Locke's Ethics of Belief. His contention is that assent does not admit of degrees, and that Locke must therefore be mistaken in recommending that the degree of our assent to a proposition should be proportional to the strength of the evidence we have for the proposition assented to. I tried to show that on this important issue Locke was more nearly right than Newman was.

I now turn to another doctrine of Newman's, his distinction between notional and real assent in *Grammar of Assent* ch. IV. But as we shall see, it is also necessary to consider ch. I–III, on the apprehension of propositions; and at the end I shall say something about ch. V, Section I ('Belief in one God') where Newman

[1] My page references in this lecture are to Longmans edition of 1947. This edition is the only one which has an adequate index. The paperback edition (Image Books, New Nork 1955, introduction by Etienne Gilson) has only an index of proper names.

[2] See Series I, Lecture 6.

illustrates his conception of real assent by applying it to religious belief.

The distinction between notional and real assent had not been made before, though we may perhaps find some faint hints of it in Hume's *Treatise*.[1] It is Newman's most original contribution to the epistemology of belief. But as we have seen already, the *Grammar of Assent* is not an easy book to understand, in spite of —or even because of—the brilliant style in which it is written; and this is certainly true of the chapters with which we are now concerned. When we have read them, we sit back and ask ourselves 'What does it all come to?' The question is not easy to answer. Still, we must try to answer it. For this much, at any rate, is clear: Newman is here drawing our attention to a distinction which is interesting and important. It does make a very considerable difference whether we assent to a proposition in what he calls the 'real' way, or in what he calls the 'notional' way.

NEWMAN'S USE OF THE WORD 'REAL'

Our first difficulty is concerned with the word 'real' itself. Despite Newman's un-technical style of writing, he uses this word in a technical sense, or at least in a sense which is strange and unfamiliar to his modern readers, though it may not have appeared so to his own contemporaries. (The *Grammar of Assent* was published nearly a century ago, in 1870.) For example, it must not be supposed that when we give a notional assent to a proposition we are not really assenting. Our assent may be perfectly genuine and sincere; and according to Newman there are some types of propositions (conditional propositions, for instance) which can only be assented to in a notional manner. Nor must it be supposed that when we give a real assent to a proposition, there has to be a real state of affairs which makes the proposition true. We may give a real assent to a proposition which is false, and it need not even be a proposition about an entity which is itself real. A child might give a real assent to the proposition 'the bogey-man in the shoe-cupboard has black eyes'.

[1] *Treatise* Book I, Part 3, Sections 9 and 10 (pp. 114–15 and pp. 122–3 in Selby-Bigge's edition).

Indeed, this antithesis between 'real' and 'unreal', which immediately comes to our minds when a distinction is drawn between what is real and what is other-than-real, does not seem to occur to Newman's mind at all. He uses the word 'real' in its etymological sense, derived from the Latin *res* ('thing'). By 'real' he means something like 'thingish'. As we shall see, he often describes real assent as 'assent to things', and contrasts this with 'assent to notions'. His book was addressed to educated readers, and in 1870 nearly all of them had had a classical education, like himself. In their minds, as in his, there would be a very firm association between the English word 'real' and the Latin word *res*. They would have no inclination to think that if a man assents in an un-thingish manner he is not assenting at all or is only pretending to assent. Newman could not be expected to foresee that one day he would have readers, and highly educted ones too, who are wholly or almost wholly unacquainted with the Latin language. Perhaps we might put it this way:—in real assent, as Newman uses the term, we assent to something which is thought of in a concrete manner; in notional assent, we assent to something which is thought of in an abstract manner.

But although Newman's use of the word 'real' is strange to us, we must use the word in his sense when we are discussing his doctrine. He has the privileges of a pioneer. He was the first person to draw the distinction between these two different ways of assenting, and thereby he made his most important contribution to the philosophy of belief. Ever since, the distinction has been called by the name which he chose to give it. We must use his term 'real assent' and try not to be misled by it. We shall not be misled by it, if we remember that 'real' in his sense is connected with what is 'thingish' or concrete.

THE APPREHENSION OF PROPOSITIONS

In the first three chapters of the *Grammar of Assent* Newman is mainly concerned with what he calls 'the apprehension of propositions' and with the relation between apprehension and assent. It is important to consider what he says about the apprehension of propositions, because he holds that the difference between real and notional assent is a derivative one, a consequence of the difference between real and notional apprehension. If you apprehend a proposition in the real way, you also assent to it in the real way, if you assent to it at all; and if you apprehend it in the notional way, you also assent to it in the notional way, if you assent to it at all. Or rather, if *at a given time* you apprehend a proposition in the real way, you also assent to it in the real way, if you do at that time assent to it (and similarly for notional apprehension and assent).

For it is perfectly possible that one's way of apprehending a proposition may change. What I used to apprehend in a purely notional manner, I may later apprehend in a real manner. The converse change is also possible. What I used to apprehend in a real manner, I now apprehend in a notional manner. The change, either way, is especially liable to happen with religious propositions, the ones which interest Newman most. A young man, brought up in a pious family, may have a real apprehension of the proposition 'God loves us all' and may also give a real assent to it. But later, by the time he is fifty years old, his apprehension of this proposition has ceased to be real and has become notional instead; and though he does still assent to the proposition, his assent is now a notional one. Conversely, a person may have assented to the proposition 'God loves us all' for a great many years. But hitherto he has always apprehended it in a notional manner, and therefore his assent to it could only be notional. But then, suddenly or gradually, he finds himself apprehending it in quite a different way. It 'becomes real to him', as we say, or 'comes home to him', or 'comes alive for him' in a way it never did before; and then he gives a different sort of assent to it, what Newman calls a real assent.

Moreover, the mode of apprehension varies not only with time but also with the context of discussion. For instance, there is a difference between the way we apprehend propositions about God when we are praying to him or thanking him or asking his forgiveness, and the way we apprehend them when we are discussing theology. In a theological discussion, or in a philosophical one, these propositions are apprehended in a notional way; in prayer or worship they are apprehended in a real way. Fortunately, there is nothing to prevent a theologian (or a philosopher of religion) from being a religious person as well. Indeed one suspects that he has to be, if he is to understand what he is talking about. Nevertheless, as Newman insists, there is a difference between these two attitudes. The theological attitude is notional, and we may add that the philosophical attitude is notional too; the theological attitude is real (thingish, concerned with the concrete.) In both attitudes there are propositions concerning God to which one assents, and in both the assent may be perfectly sincere. But in theology (or in the philosophy of religion) our assents are of the notional kind, while in religion itself they are of the real kind. Theorizing about religion, however sincerely or however correctly, is not the same thing as being religious.

Let us consider a secular example, since the religious mode of apprehension is nowadays so unfamiliar to most of us, and it is hard for us to imagine what it would be like to apprehend propositions about God in a real manner or to assent to them in a real manner. Let us consider our apprehension of propositions about a foreign country which we have never visited. We are all familiar with the proposition 'The United States is a very large country' and we all assent to it. But this proposition comes home to us in a new way when we actually go to the United States, and travel all the way across it by train from the Atlantic coast to California. (The journey takes $3\frac{1}{2}$ days.) We now give a real assent to that propositon, as opposed to the notional assent as given before, whom it was merely something that 'every schoolboy knows'.

APPREHENDING AND ENTERTAINING

But what exactly does Newman mean by his term 'apprehension of a proposition'? 'Apprehension' is a word which is not much used by philosophers nowadays. In the school of Cook Wilson, it was the act-word or mental occurrence word corresponding to the dispositional word 'know'. When you come to know something for the first time, or recall something you already know, you are said by these philosophers to be apprehending it. This is not Newman's sense of the word 'apprehend'. There is this much resemblance, that in Newman, as in Cook Wilson, 'apprehension' denotes a mental occurrence or mental act. But in Newman apprehension is connected with understanding rather than knowledge, and what is understood is a sentence, or rather a true-or-false sentence. As far as one can see, Newman does not distinguish, as some philosophers have, between true-or-false sentences on the one hand and propositions on the other. In his usuage, a proposition just *is* a true-or-false sentence. And his doctrine is that there are two ways of understanding such a sentence, a real (thingish) way and a notional way, or two ways of 'taking' it. He does not, however, wish to say this about all true-or-false sentences. An *a priori* sentence such as '17 is a prime number' or 'if *p* entails *q*, then not-*q* entails not-*p*' can only be understood in the notional way if it is understood at all. Moreover, he seems to hold that any *conditional* sentence can only be understood in the notional way, even when it is a sentence concerning concrete objects, e.g. 'if the kitchen door is open, the cat has already eaten the fish'. Certainly he holds that inference is a purely notional activity, and that a proposition of the form 'because *p*, therefore *q*' can only be assented to in a notional manner.

But in his discussion of real and notional assent, he is mainly concerned[1] with sentences about matters of fact and existence, to use Hume's phrase, though he takes a more liberal view than Hume does about the types of entity which may be meaningfully said to exist. These are the true-or-false sentences which can be understood in either way, either notionally or really, and can therefore be assented to in either way; whereas those which are about 'the relations of ideas' (to use Hume's terminology again) can only be understood in the notional way, and therefore our assent to them, if we do assent, can only be notional. Or perhaps we should say that Newman is mainly concerned with sentences which at least *purport* to be about matters of fact and existence; for as we have seen, they may be false, however real (thingish) our apprehension and assent may be.

It can now be seen that Newman's technical term 'apprehension of a proposition' means much the same as the modern technical

[1] Perhaps not exclusively. In one passage (*G. of A.*, p. 67) he appears to say that moral and political principles can be the objects of real assent: see p. 336, below. Cf. also his remarks on *dulce et decorum est pro patria mori*, apprehended in a notional way by Horace but in a real way by 'a Wallace or a Tell' (*G. of A.* pp. 8 *fin*–9).

term 'entertaining a proposition'.[1] There are many different attitudes which we may have towards a proposition: not only assent and dissent, but also doubting, questioning, wondering about, supposing for the sake of argument ('If *p*, what would follow?') and the neutral state of suspense of judgement. Entertaining is the common factor in them all. What I formerly doubted or suspended judgement about, I now assent to. But I am still entertaining the same proposition, though my attitude to it has altered. Again, if you and I disagree about a proposition *p*—you accept it and I reject it—the same proposition must be entertained by both of us. Otherwise we should not be disagreeing. Moreover, there may be a third person who neither accepts the proposition nor rejects it, but just considers it neutrally in a state of suspended judgement. He disagrees with both of us; or rather, he does not agree with either of us. But this somewhat awkward relation of non-agreement could not hold between him and us, unless all three of us entertained the same proposition.

If I am right so far, Newman's view comes to this:—There are two different ways of entertaining propositions about 'matters of fact and existence'. They may be entertained either in a real manner or in a notional manner. The same proposition may be entertained in a real manner by one person, in a notional manner by another person. Moreover, the same person may entertain it in a real manner at one time, in a notional manner at another time. When someone entertains a proposition in a real manner, he must also assent to it in a real manner, if he assents to it at all. Likewise, if he entertains a proposition in a notional manner, he must also assent to it in a notional manner, if he assents to it at all. As the entertaining is, so also is the assent, if assent there be.

[1] Newman himself once uses the word 'entertain'. In *G. of A.*, p. 5 he speaks of 'three modes of entertaining propositions, doubting them, inferring them, assenting to them'. But surely there must be more modes than three. Moreover his use of the word 'inference' is puzzling to his modern readers. Often he seems not to distinguish between 'because *p*, therefore *q*' and 'if *p*, then *q*', and calls both of them inferences. Cf. *G. of A.*, pp. 137–8 (example of the consumptive patient).

IMAGES AND 'REAL' APPREHENSION

Perhaps we can now see what Newman means by his technical phrase 'apprehension of a proposition'. But he also holds that there are two different ways of apprehending propositions about matters of fact and existence, a real way of apprehending them and a notional way. What is the difference between them? This is the most important question we have to consider. If we can answer it, we shall also be able to understand his distinction between real and notional assent.

To elucidate his distinction between the two sorts of apprehension, Newman makes use of the rather questionable phrase 'standing for'. The terms of which the proposition is composed may be taken in two different ways, either as standing for 'things' or as standing for notions. If we take them as standing for things, we apprehend the proposition in the real way. If we take them as standing for notions, we apprehend it in the notional way. And 'the same proposition may admit of both these interpretations at once, having a notional sense as used by one man, and a real as used by another'. For example, Horace's words '*Dum Capitolium scandet cum tacita virgine pontifex*' are notionally apprehended by a schoolboy who can translate them accurately, and 'has an abstract hold upon every word of the description'; but they were apprehended in a real way by the poet's contemporaries who had actually seen the pontiff climbing the Capitol, accompanied by a silent Vestal Virgin.[1]

Evidently the word 'things' has to be understood in a rather wider way: not only because persons (e.g. the Pontiff and the Vestal Virgin) have to be counted as 'things', but because qualities and relations must apparently be counted as 'things' too (e.g. the silence of the Vestal Virgin, and the relation of 'being accompanied by'). Still, we could say that for Horace's contemporaries all these words stood for concrete realities, or at any rate had a concrete sense.

Moreover, the 'things' which the terms in the proposition stands for need not be present to our senses at the time when the proposition is being apprehended, and often they are not. Indeed,

[1] *G. of A.*, p. 8.

most of the propositions which we entertain, even when they are propositions about perceptible objects, are about objects *not* at the moment present to our senses. One of Newman's examples is 'London is on fire' (p. 21). We can entertain this proposition, and entertain it in the 'real' manner, when we are many miles from London, and are not seeing or feeling or smelling any fire. How do the terms of this proposition manage to stand for 'things', as they must if we are to apprehend the proposition in a real manner? It now turns out that this relation of standing for 'things' is an indirect one.[1] According to Newman there are, as it were, two stages in it. In the first stage, the terms composing the proposition stand for *mental images*, and in the second stage these images in their turn stand for 'things'. Newman is not as clear as we could wish about the difference between these two stages. He sometimes describes real assent as 'assent to images'. But if that were all, its 'thingish' character would vanish. Both in apprehension and in assent, the function of the images must surely be to represent things other than themselves. In Newman's own very wide sense of 'things', I suppose we could just say that mental images are themselves 'things', because they actually exist or occur in our minds. Indeed, Newman himself says something rather like this of memory-images. 'They are things still, as being reflections of things in a mental mirror' (p. 19). Nevertheless, as the word 'reflections' shows, their function is to represent things other than themselves.

What of notional apprehension? Might there also be two stages here? Suppose I have never seen a Comprehensive School, still less have I been inside one. I think of it just as a school which contains pupils of many different sorts and degrees of intellectual attainment. I read in the newspaper that a Comprehensive School has just been opened at Eccleshall, a place I have never visited, and all I know of it is that it is somewhere in the Midlands of England. I can only apprehend this proposition in a notional way, and my assent to it (if I do assent to it) can only be of the notional kind. For me, the terms of which this proposition is composed 'stand for notions'. But do these notions, in their turn, stand for something else, as the images do when one's apprehension is real? Not quite. But still, a notion can apply to

[1] *G. of A.*, 19 *et seq.*

something. It can have instances. And these instances, if it has them, are what Newman calls 'things'. A Comprehensive School is a thing, in his wide use of the term 'thing', and so is Eccleshall, wherever it is. An event, such as the opening of a school, would also count as a 'thing'; at any rate, it is a concrete reality. It would seem, then, that even in notional apprehension we might sometimes be apprehending 'things'. True, we should apprehend them indirectly, by apprehending notions first. So it might seem that the difference between the two is only this: images can resemble things, whereas notions can have things for their instances. But as we shall see, Newman thinks there is another difference as well, and a very important one: images have a psychological power which mere notions have not. That is why he is so much concerned with images, and describes real assent sometimes as 'assent to images'.

Indeed, the most remarkable feature of Newman's discussion of real and notional assent is the importance he attaches to mental images. It is true that the word 'image' widens its meaning somewhat in the later stages of his argument.[1] But at the present stage of it, he is clearly speaking quite literally about mental imagery.

NEWMAN'S ACCOUNT OF HIS OWN MENTAL IMAGERY

The numerous examples which he gives on pp. 19–24 make it obvious that his own mental imagery was exceptionally copious and vivid. For instance, he tells us that when he is in a foreign country, he is able 'to conjure up before him the vision of his home'. 'I see those who were once were there and are no more; past scenes, and the very expression of the features, and the tones of the voices, of those who took part in them, in a time of trial or difficulty. I create nothing; I see the facsimiles of facts' (pp. 19 *fin*–20). The tones of the voices must have been conveyed to him by auditory images, not visual ones. He goes on to mention other auditory images ('I can bring before me the music of the *Adeste fideles*, as if I were actually hearing it') and moreover images of smell 'I can bring before me . . . the scent of a clematis as if I were in my garden'. He has images of taste too, for instance of 'the

[1] See below, pp. 340–4, 347–8.

flavour of a peach as if it were in season'. Such an image, he adds, need not be in any sense an abstraction 'Though I may have eaten a hundred peaches in times past, the impression which remains on my memory of the flavour, may be of any of them, of the ten, twenty, thirty units, as the case may be, not a general notion distinct from every one of them' (p. 20).

He does not seem to have what are called generic images, for instance a visual image of a typical cat or a taste-image of the flavour of a typical peach. Nor does he mention either tactual or kinaesthetic imagery. He does not say, for example, that he can 'bring before him' the feel of velvet when he is not actually touching any velvet; nor that when he is sitting quietly in his study he can bring before him the bodily feelings which he had when climbing a steep mountainside.

He does appear to say, however, that he has images of introspectible events ('our past mental acts of any kind'), and speaks of 'the vivid image of certain anxieties and deliverances' which never fades away from the mind, as the memory of countenances and places may well do. But this paragraph is difficult to interpret, and perhaps the word 'image' is not here being used literally.[1]

If one happens to be interested in mental imagery, one finds this autobiographical passage most fascinating, and wishes greatly that other writers had given such a full account of their own imagery. But we must notice that it *is* an autobiographical passage. We must not assume that everyone else has the remarkable imaging powers which Newman evidently had. It looks as if Newman himself did make this assumption, or at any rate assumed that the mental images which other people have were pretty similar to his own. Such an assumption was made by almost all philosophers upon the epoch-making researches of Francis Galton. Galton's book, *Inquiries into Human Faculty* was first published in 1883, thirteen years after *The Grammar of Assent*. Galton adopted a very simple plan, so simple that it took a man of genius to think of it. If we wish to know what mental images other people have, why not write round to them and ask them? He did so, and the results

[1] *G. of A.*, pp. 20 *fin.*–21. What does he mean by 'an apprehension of the memory of those definite acts'? Is it a memory-apprehension of them? Or is 'the memory of them' what is apprehended? In that case it might just possibly be called 'an image of them'.

were surprising. For instance, some people, when asked to describe their visual image of their own breakfast-table, were unable to understand what they were being asked to do. Apparently they had no visual imagery at all. They supposed that phrases like 'having an image of one's breakfast table' were rather extravagant metaphors. Others, however, produced long and detailed descriptions. It turned out also that most peculiar visual images occur in some people's minds when they think of the series of numbers, or of the days of the week (each day has its colour).

Again, Newman himself says that visual images are the most vivid of all.[1] This may well be true of many people, but it cannot be true of everyone, if some have no visual images at all. And in those who do have them, they may be faint and fleeting and poverty-stricken, or highly schematic—very far from being the detailed reproductions of past visible scenes which Newman describes in the passage about his visual images of his home. On the other hand, their auditory images may be vivid and detailed.

More important, it seems that some people's imagery is almost entirely verbal. They 'think in words', that is, by means of images of words (auditory or kinaesthetic) and not at all, or hardly at all, in images of the objects or events which these words denote. They remember in words too. It is natural to suppose that the notional way of apprehending, and of assenting, is connected somehow with thinking in words.

Newman did not consider such people, who may well be particularly numerous among the learned. Would he hold that they are incapable of real assent, and can only apprehend propositions (and therefore can only assent to them) in the notional manner? And are we to suppose that they, for their part, would be quite incapable of understanding the distinction between 'notional' and 'real' which he is trying to explain?

Are we also to suppose that these purely verbal thinkers are incapable of being religious, though quite capable of being theologians? In Newman's view, religion, or at any rate personal religion, requires a real assent to at least some propositions concerning a Divine Being or Beings. Of course these verbal thinkers

[1] 'The memory preserves the impress, *though not so vivid*, of the experiences which come to us through our other senses also.'
G. of A., p. 20, my italics.

might sincerely assent to such propositions, even though their assent was purely notional. Notional assent can perfectly well be sincere. It need not be what Newman calls mere 'assertion'. But according to him it lacks the heart-felt character, the force and cutting-edge, if I may put it so, which real assent has; and as we shall see later, he thinks that real assent owes its forcible nature to the part which mental images play in it. And they have to be images of 'things', not just images of words.

THE FACULTY OF COMPOSITION

We may now return to Newman's own account of mental imagery in *Grammar of Assent*, ch. III. The images hitherto described were reproductions of particular past experiences. But on p. 22 he goes on to discuss 'an inventive faculty or faculty of composition'. By means of this, we are able 'to follow the descriptions of things which have never come before us, and to form out of such passive impressions as experience has heretofore left on our minds, new images, which, though mental creations, are in no sense abstractions, and though ideal, are not notional'. What Newman says here reminds us of Locke's account of the 'compounding' of complex ideas out of simpler ones. But there is one important difference. Newman distinguishes sharply, as Locke did not, between images on the one hand and concepts on the other, and makes it quite clear that the *composita* (the results of the composition-process) are images. Of course, there might also be complex concepts; indeed it is certain that there are. But Newman is not here discussing them.

But what are we to make of the 'impressions' (here qualified as 'passive') out of which these new images are formed? Clearly Newman is not using the term in Hume's sense. Hume's impressions are brief occurrences, whereas Newman's impressions persist through time. Past experience has 'left' them on our minds, and there they stay. These impressions, I think, are not themselves images. Instead, they are what are now called memory-traces. That is what the word 'passive' suggests. And Newman assumes that these traces are mental, more or less persistent modifications of the mind, not of the brain. They are left 'on our minds'. He would not deny, perhaps, that there are persistent modifications of the brain which are correlated with them. But no one who believes in personal immortality, as Newman clearly did, can admit that memory-traces are purely and simply modifications of the brain. For if they were, personal identity could not continue after the brain has disintegrated.[1]

To return to phenomenological considerations: it is pretty clear that we do not in fact 'compound' complex images by literally putting simpler ones together. The new and complex images come into out minds ready-made, so to speak, aroused perhaps by the words of some vivid writer, although we have never ourselves perceived any such object or event as the words describe. Nevertheless, such an image of a complex object or event (let us call it *ABC*), an object or event which we have never ourselves perceived, could not come into our minds at all unless we *had* perceived at least one object or event which was *A* and at least one which was *B*, and at least one which was *C*. And not only must we have perceived each of them; each of them must have left a more or less permanent 'impression' on our minds, what I have just called a memory-trace.

Whatever we think of the puzzling word 'impression', which Newman uses in several other passages,[2] it is worth while to mention some of the examples he gives to illustrate his remarks about the faculty of composition. 'I may never have seen a palm or banana [i.e. banana tree], but I have conversed with those who have, or I have read graphic accounts of it, and from my own previous knowledge of other trees have been able . . . to light up such an image of it in my thoughts, that, were it not that I was never in the countries where it was found, I should fancy that I had actually seen it' (p. 22).

Newman gives three other examples, more striking and more surprising. 'I am able as it were to gaze upon Tiberius as Tacitus draws him and to figure to myself our James the First as he is painted in Scott's Romance.[3] The assassination of Caesar, his *Et tu, Brute*, his collecting his robes about him, and his fall under

[1] Even if the brain were re-integrated (traces and all) at the 'General Resurrection on the Last Day', personal identity could not continue in the period between death and the Last Day.

[2] *G. of A.*, pp. 20, 21.

[3] *The Fortunes of Nigel.*

Pompey's statue, all this becomes a fact to me and an object of real apprehension.' He continues 'Thus it is that we live in the past and in the distant' (pp. 22–3). The word 'live' is of some importance. One of the characteristics of real apprehension, and of real assent also, is the 'warm' or 'vital' character which they have, the appeal they make to our emotions. We not only think of the past and the distant, as we should if our apprehension of the narratives of travellers or historians were purely notional. We are interested in the past and the distant, they move us, we are as it were personally involved in them; and this is because we are able to form composite images of things, persons, and happenings which we have not ourselves perceived.

Newman then says that this faculty of composition has rather narrow limits. 'It is mainly limited, as regards its materials, by the sense of sight' (p. 23). We notice that the passage quoted just now is full of visual words: 'gaze upon', 'draws', 'figure to myself', 'painted'. It seems, then, that when we live in the past and the distant, we do it mainly by using the memory-traces of past visual experiences and compounding new visual images out of them (though I suppose Newman did have a composite auditory image of Caesar's *Et et, Brute*).

Again we have to ask whether this is just an autobiographical fact about Newman himself. If someone had only very faint and poor visual imagery, would he find it difficult to 'live in the past and the distant'? And what if he lacked visual imagery altogether, like some of Galton's correspondents? Would he be unable to live in the past and the distant at all? Or could he manage it in a purely verbal way, just by describing distant scenes and long-past events to himself in words, provided that these verbal descriptions were sufficiently specific and detailed? Perhaps we should draw a distinction between 'imaging' on the one hand and 'imagining that' or 'imagining as' on the other.[1] 'Imagining that' (which can be done in a purely verbal way) might be able to take over at least some of the tasks which Newman here assigns to visual imagery of the composite kind.

Newman also holds that the faculty of composition is hardly at all applicable to the impressions (memory-traces) of introspectible events. It is difficult, he says, 'to apprehend by description images

[1] See also pp. 340–4, below.

of mental facts of which we have no direct experience'. For example 'Not all the possible descriptions of headlong love will make me comprehend the *delirium*, if I have never had a fit of it'. Again 'we meet with men of the world who cannot enter into the very idea of devotion . . . because they know of no exercise of the affections but what is merely human' (p. 24). We may add that this inability is not confined to 'men of the world'. There seem to be psychologists, sociologists (and even, perhaps, philosophers) who cannot enter into this idea either.

CAN ASSENT BE WHOLLY UN-NOTIONAL?

More will be said later about Newman's treatment of the imagination, and about the distinction between imaging and imagining 'that' or 'as'. But before we return to this subject, which is crucial for the understanding of his doctrine of real assent, we should ask whether his own distinction between 'real' and 'notional' is quite so hard and fast as he maintains.

There are indeed assents which are in no way 'real' (thingish, imaginative), for instance our assent to the *a priori* truth 'if *p* entails *q*, not-*q* entails not-*p*.' But however concrete the subject-matter of a proposition is, can we entertain that proposition in a completely un-notional way, or assent to it in a completely un-notional way?

Let us consider an example in which our assent to a proposition is as 'real' (thingish and imaginative) as any assent can be. We entertain the proposition 'a passenger train is now standing at the down platform of the railway station', and we assent to it on the authority of the railway time-table. Newman's rather strange phrase 'assent to things' fits this example fairly well. At any rate, the station could be described as 'a thing', and so could the down platform. The train too could be described as a set of 'things' joined together by couplings which are themselves 'things'. Moreover, his rather strange phrase 'assent to images' also fits fairly well, in the sense that some people when they hear or read this sentence would no doubt have visual images of the platform, the railway-carriages and the engine, and these images might well be vivid and full of detail. Since the 'things' in this case are not actually being perceived, Newman supposes that we can only assent in the real or thingish way by first assenting to images.[1]

But however clear and vivid these images might be, it is not sufficient just to have them and contemplate them. Moreover, it is not literally true that we assent to the images themselves. What we assent to is the proposition 'there is a state of affairs which these images accurately represent'. The difficulty is not that this proposition may be false. Newman himself admits that real assents can be mistaken. The difficulty is that this proposition has to be apprehended in a notional manner, or at any rate there is something notional in our apprehension of it. Let us consider the phrase 'there is a state of affairs which . . .'. Could anything be more notional than this? Perhaps it is misleading to ask what it 'stands for'. But if someone does ask, we shall have to say that it stands for a *logical* concept.

I would suggest that there is something incurably notional about the entertaining of propositions.[2] There can be no propositions unless there are concepts. Moreover, among them there have to be *logical* concepts. Or at any rate, in expressing any proposition we have to use logical words such as 'all', 'some', 'a', 'whenever', 'there is', 'if', 'not'; and we also have to know how to use them. It surely cannot be true, as Newman seems to say, that a proposition can consist of nothing but singular terms. His example is 'Philip was the father of Alexander'.[3] 'Philip' is indeed a singular term, and so is 'Alexander'. But it is very odd to say this of 'father of', which denotes a relation, and moreover a relation which has very many other instances. And what of the words 'was' and 'the'? These again are logical words. Their function is to convey the logical structure of the proposition.

There is one logical concept to which Newman pays a good deal of attention, namely 'if' or 'if . . . then'; and I hope I am not being unfair to him if I say that he rather dislikes it. (This is because any proposition into which it enters can only be apprehended and assented to in a notional manner.) But strangely enough, he says hardly anything about 'not', and very few of the propositions he uses as examples are negative. Would he perhaps have held that

[1] Cf. above, pp. 322–4.

[2] Indeed Newman himself says that real assent is 'in itself an intellectual act' (p. 68).

[3] *G. of A.*, p. 8.

all negative propositions are likewise notional, that is, can only be apprehended and assented to in the notional manner? He does not say, what we might have expected him to say, that assent has a contrary, dissent, and that the function of the word 'not' is to express dissent. His view is, I think, that 'not *p*' is equivalent to 'it is false that *p*'. But if so, we must ask whether 'it is false that *p*' can be apprehended and assented to in the 'real' manner. Presumably it cannot; for it would seem that 'false' is a notional predicate, incapable to being cashed by means of images.

REFORMULATION OF THE REAL-NOTIONAL ANTITHESIS

But if there is something incurably notional about the entertaining of propositions, and consequently about the assent to them, it does not follow that Newman's distinction between real and notional assent must be abandoned. He has over-stated his case a little, as anyone might who has something new to say. He has set up a hard and fast distinction of kind, where there is in fact a rather complicated distinction of degree. There are assents of the sort he calls 'real' ('thingish') in which the imagination plays an essential part. But it is a mistake to suggest that notions play no part in them at all. The entertaining of propositions is a concept-using activity.

Moreover, when we do use images to 'cash' these concepts, the extent to which we use them varies greatly from time to time and from person to person. Two persons *A* and *B* may both use visual imagery to cash or illustrate the proposition 'there was a fox in the garden yesterday evening', and both may assent to it. Let us suppose that *A* actually saw the fox yesterday, while *B* only hears and believes *A*'s report of it to-day. Yet it may well be that *A*'s image is faint and schematic, even though it is a memory image; whereas *B*'s is vivid and detailed, even though he had to use his 'faculty of composition' to produce it, just as Newman did when he 'as it were gazed upon Tiberius'. Shall we say, then, that *B*'s assent is *more* 'real' (more concrete or thingish') than *A*'s though *B* never saw the fox and *A* did?

The person who has the more detailed and vivid images may also have the more inaccurate ones. Perhaps the fox which *A* saw was young and reddish, and his faint and schematic image represents the scene correctly as far as it goes. But *B*'s vivid and detailed image represents a fox which is greyish and elderly. What shall we say then? That *B*'s assent, though 'more real' than *A*'s, was also less correct, partly though not wholly mistaken? Not necessarily. A person who habitually has vivid and detailed imagery may learn to discount it or make allowances for it. He may recall that it has sometimes led him to make mistakes in the past, for instance when he visualized the buildings and quadrangles of Oxford as a schoolboy. When at last he came up to the University, he found the place a good deal less glamorous than these images suggested. So in this example of the fox he says to himself 'The situation my friend has described to me was something like the one which my present visual image so vividly depicts, but not necessarily exactly like it'; and that, if one may put it so, is a highly notional thing to say. An image is present in his mind, and a decidedly 'thingish' one (realistic, detailed, vivid). But his assent to his friend's report is more notional than real, though there is something real about it too, since he does have this image.

The conclusions we may draw are these: (1) It is a mistake to say that real assent and notional assent are different in kind, since we cannot entertain propositions at all without using concepts ('notions'). It follows that there are no assents which are wholly *un*-notional.[1] (2) Some assents are 'real' or 'thingish', and it is true that the imagination plays an essential part in them. (3) But this 'real' character, which some assents have, varies very considerably in degree, and is not a matter of all or none. Instead of asking 'Was his assent real?' we ought to ask 'In what degree was it real, if it was real at all?' (4) Finally, as Newman himself insists, there are very many assents which are purely or wholly notional, in no degree 'real' or 'thingish', in that no images play any part in them, other than images of words or of numerals or of technical symbols such as the symbols of algebra. If we wish to sum the whole matter up in the form of a brief antithesis, it is not an antithesis between real assent on the one hand and notional assent on the other, but between assent which is in some degree real or 'thingish', and assent which is wholly or purely notional.

[1] Newman seems to admit this in one passage which I have already quoted. Real assent, he says, 'is in itself an intellectual act' (p. 68).

If these conclusions are justified, they do rather 'take the edge off' the sharp contrast which Newman wishes to draw. But the distinction between real assent and assent which is purely or wholly notional might still be an important one, even though no assent is wholly un-notional, and even though the real or 'thingish' character which some assents have is a matter of degree. It might still be true that in so far as it is real, assent has a psychological force or power which purely notional assent has not, and has a much greater influence on our emotions, our actions and our characters. It might still be true that in many different sorts of human activity, and not in religion only, the faith which is said 'to move mountains' is acquired and maintained by means of real assents and not by purely notional ones. It might also be true that a man's real assents, if he utters them or even if they are just inferred from his conduct, have an influence on other men which his purely notional assents do not have. As Newman himself puts it, a person's real assents, unlike his purely notional ones 'form the mind out of which they grow, and impart to it a seriousness and manliness which inspires in others a confidence in its views'. But as he is careful to point out, these effects of real assent, both personal and social, need not always be desirable. Real assents, he says, create not only 'heroes and saints, great leaders, statesmen, preachers and reformers, the pioneers of discovery in science' but also 'visionaries, fanatics, knight-errants, demagogues and adventurers'.[1] He might also have pointed out that they are by no means absent in persons suffering from mental disorders. *Cortuptio optimi pessima.*

THE PASSION FOR THE THEORETICAL

But is it true that purely notional assents can never have effects like these? There is a state of mind, or even a habit of mind, which might be called 'a passion for the theoretical' or 'an enthusiasm for abstractions'; and there are some persons whose whole

[1] *G. of A.*, p. 67. Compare Hume, *Treatise* Book I, Part III, Section 10, 'a vigorous and strong imagination is of all talents the most proper to procure belief and authority' (Clarendon Press, ed. Selby-Bigge, p. 123). According to Newman, real assent always has an imaginative character.

lives are dominated by it. They are moved, stirred to their depths, by the contemplation of propositions which have to be entertained in a wholly notional manner, if entertained at all. They have a love of inference for its own sake; and inference, according to Newman, is a wholly notional activity. They spend sleepless nights and laborious days trying to decide whether *q* does follow from *p* or not. Validity and consistency are to them almost as food and drink are to others. What Newman sometimes calls assent to things and sometimes assent to images plays no part in these activities (unless it be to answer purely incidental questions like 'where have I put my pencil?') The extreme example of such a type of mind is a pure mathematician who is wholly devoted to his subject. His conduct, and the way he spends his time and his energies, are profoundly affected, or even dominated, by the purely notional apprehension of propositions, by his assent (purely notional) to some of them, and by his indecision or doubt (equally notional) about others.

This is an extreme example, because pure mathematics is of all subjects the most notional and is not at all concerned with concrete entities, what Newman calls 'things'. There are other sorts of learned investigation in which 'assent to things' plays an indispensable part. It obviously does in the Natural Sciences and also in historical enquiries of any kind. Nevertheless, all types of learned persons are greatly concerned with inferences, not merely in the sense that they have to make inferences in the course of their work, but also in the sense that they are moved by them or excited by them. The question 'If *p*, what follows?' is never far from their minds. They may spend hours, or even years, in trying to answer it; and if they succeed, the answer is something which can only be apprehended in the notional way.

What are we to make of this passion for the theoretical? It is not very uncommon; and Newman seems to have left no room for it, though he himself must have been moved by it when he was writing this book. A philosophical analysis of assent is not something which can itself be the object of real assent. Shall we say that pure notions (abstractions not cashable by images) can sometimes have the psychological power which images have? We must agree with Newman that images do have it, or at least that imaginative activities have. But do notions sometimes have it too? If so, the distinction between real and notional would still be an important one, but not quite so important as he suggests. At any rate, there is a difficulty in his doctrine which he has failed to consider.

Perhaps this is because he says so little about evaluative judgements. He does say something. As has been pointed out already, he seems to hold that moral and political principles can be objects of real assent.[1] And as we shall see later, he discusses the phenomena of conscience in ch. 5, section 1 ('Belief in One God'). It might be suggested that the learned persons whose emotions and conduct I have described do give a real assent to some propositions which others assent to in a purely notional manner, but that these are *value*-propositions: for example 'it is good to discover the truth about complex numbers', 'it is better to be clear than muddled about the nature of abstract ideas', 'it would be nice to know what inferences can safely be drawn from the remarks of Gildas about the state of Roman Britain in the first quarter of the fifth century'. Everyone who considers such value-propositions as these might be prepared to give some sort of assent to them. But in most persons it would be a very cool and off-hand sort of assent, of a purely notional kind, and they certainly are not prepared to 'do something about it'. Nevertheless, there are some persons who do assent to one or another of these value-propositions in a real and not merely notional way, and therefore *are* prepared to do a great deal about it. In order to give such real assent, perhaps they have to imagine to themselves what it would be like to achieve one or another of these purely theoretical goods, and to triumph over all the obstacles which make such an achievement very difficult, though this imagining could hardly be done by means of visual or auditory or tactual imagery.

In some such way, it might be argued that it *is* real assent, after all, which provides the motive power for the laborious activities of these learned persons, even though the activities themselves are largely, or even wholly, concerned with what is 'notional'.

[1] Cf. the passage quoted above (p. 334) in which he mentions 'heroes and saints, great leaders, statesmen, preachers and reformers' (*G. of A*. p. 67).

THE PSYCHOLOGICAL POWER OF IMAGES

How then does real assent come to have the psychological power which purely notional assent has not? Newman's answer is 'because of the part that images play in it'. As we have seen, he sometimes says that real assent just *is* assent to images, though he also calls it 'assent to things'. I take his view to be that it is the use of images which gives an assent its 'thingish' character or prevents it (shall we say, saves it?) from having the wholly notional character which very many of our assents inevitably have. For real assent, according to Newman, is relatively rare. 'On only few subjects have any of us the opportunity of realizing in our minds what we speak and hear about'.[1]

But why should the use of images make so much difference to the character of our assent? We begin to see why if we consider a striking passage about religious assent on pp. 43–5. Here Newman says that religion too may be made a subject of notional assent 'and is especially so made in our own country'. 'Theology, as such, always is notional, as being scientific; religion, as being personal, should be real, but except within a small range of subjects it commonly is not real in England.' For most Englishmen religion consists mainly in Bible-reading, and the doctrine of Divine Providence is 'nearly the only doctrine held with a real assent by the mass of religious Englishmen'. For the most part, 'it is not a religion of persons and things, of acts of faith and of direct devotion; but of sacred scenes and pious sentiments' (p. 44). These words were written in 1870. One trembles to think what Newman would have said of the state of religion in England today. Or could it be that, in the small minority who have any religion at all, the proportion of real assents to notional ones is now somewhat higher?

However this may be, Newman claims that religion is something very different in Catholic populations 'such as those of mediaeval Europe, or the Spain of this day, or quasi-Catholic as those of Russia'. Among them, he says, 'assent to religious objects is real, not notional. To them the Supreme Being, our Lord, the Blessed Virgin, Angels and Saints, heaven and hell, are as present as if they were objects of sight' (p. 43).

[1] *G. of A.*, p. 27.

The important phrase here is the last one, 'as present as if they were objects of sight'.[1] The word 'present' perhaps has a double meaning: its temporal meaning of 'actually existing now' and its epistemological meaning of 'present to the mind'. At any rate, when these supernatural beings are present to someone as if they were objects of sight, he does not treat them as negligible or irrelevant. He has to take account of them both in his actions and in his emotional life. They matter to him, as they would not if his assent to their existence were purely notional. There might be some superstition and some anthropomorphism in the religious assents of a nineteenth century Spanish peasant. Perhaps Newman himself would admit that there might be. But still there may well have been a force and vividness in these assents which Newman seldom found in the religious assents of Victorian Englishmen; and the religion of the Spanish peasant was no doubt a religion of 'acts of faith and direct devotion'.

Is this because the Spanish peasant was 'assenting to images' and the Englishmen were not? According to Newman it is; or at any rate he thinks that the religious assents of the Spanish peasant were in some way imaginative whereas the Englishmen's were not.

Let us turn to the section called 'Notional and Real Assents contrasted' (Ch. IV, Section 3). Here Newman is discussing the relation between assent and action. He says of real assent 'it is in itself an intellectual act, of which the object is presented to it by the imagination; and though the pure intellect does not lead to action, nor the imagination either, yet the imagination has the means, which pure intellect has not, of stimulating those powers of the mind from which action proceeds . . . the images in which [real assent] lives, representing as they do the concrete, have the power of the concrete upon the affections and passions' (p. 68).

We must admit, I think, that Newman's main contention here is correct. It is true, and important too, that the imagination 'has the means, which pure intellect has not, of stimulating those powers of the mind from which action proceeds'. It should be noted, however, that there are not only outward actions (which consist, roughly in moving pieces of matter about). There are also inward actions, if one may call them so. The 'acts of devotion'

[1] Cf. the question 'Can I believe as if I saw?' which Newman tries to answer in Ch. V, Section 1 (discussed below, pp. 345–7).

which Newman mentions need not necessarily be manifested by any bodily movement, and frequently are not. Prayer may be silent, and need not be done on one's knees. Religious meditation is a purely inward activity. The same can be said of less reputable sorts of meditation. A person may work himself up into a state of bitter resentment just by ruminating privately upon some injury which he believes has been done to him. There is even such a thing as inward conduct, since the direction of our attention is to some degree under our voluntary control. The phrase 'the inner life' denotes something real and important, especially (but not only) when we are discussing religion. A person's real assents, and the psychological power which their imaginative character gives them, are manifested not only by what he does publicly, but also by the direction his private thoughts take, even though he tells no one else about these thoughts and no one observing him from without is able to discover what they are.

THE PERSONAL CHARACTER OF REAL ASSENT

Newnan has said earlier that real assents 'are of a personal character, each individual having his own and being known by them'.[1] They are what distinguish him from other men; they are characteristic of him as an individual. Notional assents, on the contrary, are shared by many different people. So we learn little about a person as an individual by considering his notional assents. 'Notional apprehension is in itself an ordinary act of our common nature'. But to give real assents 'we have to secure first the images which are their objects, and those are often peculiar and special. They depend on personal experiences, and the experience of one man is not the experience of another.' Real assent, then, 'thwarts rather than promotes the intercourse of man with man' (p. 64).

It may happen, however, that a number of different persons do have similar personal experiences, and therefore have similar images, even though the images which *A* has are the products of *A*'s own personal history, and the images which *B* has are the products of *B*'s own personal history. And so it may turn out that there are images 'possessed in common', and therefore apprehen-

[1] *G. of A.*, p. 63.

sions and assents (i.e. real assents) which are likewise shared by several different persons, even though each of these apprehensions and assents is still a 'personal characteristic' of the person apprehending and assenting. Such an image, common to a number of persons and yet the product of the personal experiences of each of them, 'would necessarily be a principle of sympathy and a bond of intercourse . . . far stronger than could follow upon any multitude of mere notions which they unanimously held' (p. 66). Such common images are the foundation of what we now call 'like minded groups'.

It is not easy to understand how a mental image could be literally common to a number of different persons 'the same in all' (p. 66) and yet a 'personal result' of the personal experience of each. There is some mix-up of numerical and specific identity here. Nevertheless, though my image is numerically different from yours, the two images might be sufficiently similar to be used for cashing or illustrating or 'bringing home to us' the same proposition. And then both of us will apprehend that proposition in a 'real' manner, and both of us will also assent to it in a 'real' manner if we do assent ot it.

IMAGING AND IMAGINING

Is this or something like this what Newman intends to say when he speaks here of 'images possessed in common'? Or has the word 'image' changed its meaning? When Newman first introduced the subject of images in ch. 3 he was clearly using the word 'image' in the sense it has usually had in the writings of philosophers and psychologists. This is shown by the examples he gives in the passage already quoted, where he describes his own mental imagery.[1] But by the end of ch. 4 the reader begins to suspect that the word 'image' *has* altered its meaning, or at any rate that another sense of it has crept in alongside the first.

This second sense of the word is something like the one which has now become regrettably common among ourselves, as when politicians and journalists speak of the 'public image' of British Railways and urge those who direct that institution to improve

[1] *G. of A.*, pp. 19–24 (see pp. 324–30, above).

'its public image' or even just 'its image'. It is not easy to understand what this image is supposed to be. But it seems to resemble a set of propositions rather than an image. And certainly it is very unlike what Newman describes when he speaks of the visual image he has of his home when he is in a foreign country. For instance, it would not be appropriate to ask whether the image of British Railways is visual or auditory or tactual or kinaesthetic. Some phrase like 'think of as . . .' would have to be used in describing it. Most members of the British public think of British Railways as an institution whose trains are unpunctual, its carriages dirty, its relations with its employees bad, and whose principle of operation is 'higher fares for worse services'. This 'thinking of . . . as' is something more than mere neutral entertaining of these propositions, but something less than conscious and explicit assent to them. It might perhaps be described as half-belief. Almost every traveller, in his more reflective moments, can recall travelling in at least some punctual trains, some years in which there were no railway strikes, and some cases when fares were raised but services remained just about as good or bad as they were before. Yet the propositions out of which this so-called 'image' is constructed do have considerable social and political importance; and many of us do act and feel (and vote) much as we should act, feel or vote if we did give a conscious and explicit assent to them.

The important point for our present purpose is that such an 'image' has very little to do with mental imagery. A person does not need to be a good visualizer in order to have the image of British Railways which has just been described. Nor does he need to have auditory images of the clanking sound which ancient railway-carriages make when they pass over railway tracks which have not been repaired for many years, nor kinaesthetic images of those weary walks he has taken up and down the platform while waiting for unpunctual trains to arrive. The propositions of which this so-called image consists may be entertained in a purely verbal manner. In this 'public relations' sense of the word 'image', an image is something more like a concept, though a concept unreflectively acquired, unreflectively applied, and confused rather than clear.

One hesitates to accuse so eminent a thinker as Newman of using the word 'image' in this somewhat disreputable sense, and certainly he does not always use it in this sense. In many passages he is certainly speaking quite literally of mental imagery. But he does use the verb 'to image' and the verbal noun 'imagination'; and in some of his examples, though not in others, 'imagination' seems to denote something different from having mental imagery. For instance: 'what imagination does for us is to find a means of stimulating those motive powers [i.e. those which manifest themselves in our actions]; and it does so by providing a supply of objects strong enough to stimulate them'. His examples of such objects are 'the thought of honour, glory, duty, self-aggrandizement, gain, or on the other hand of Divine Goodness, future reward, eternal life, perseveringly dwelt upon'.[1] We may agree that the thought of any one of these can stimulate the motive powers he speaks of. But such thoughts are surely concepts, not mental images.

Or are we to suppose that mental imagery has to be used when such thoughts are 'perseveringly dwelt upon'? Certainly if the thought of honour or of self-aggrandizement is to affect a person's conduct and his emotional life, it is not sufficient that this thought should just pass through his mind occasionally. He must sometimes consider 'what it would be like' to behave honourably in difficult circumstances, or what it would be like to have attained a position of power whose holder is envied, admired, or feared by others. He may perhaps consider particular examples: the honourable behaviour of someone he has known, the methods by which some political leader acquired and kept the power which he had. He may try to put himself in the shoes of such persons or to identify himself with them. Moreover, the persons whom he considers may be wholly fictitious. He may have read of them in some poem or novel. He may even have invented them for himself. And even if they are real persons—even persons whom he has actually known—the details of what they may be supposed to have done or felt or said at such and such a crucial point in their careers will have to be filled in by his own imagination, when he tries to dwell perseveringly upon the thought of being an honourable person, or a person who seeks self-aggrandizement and keeps it when he has got it.

We can therefore agree that imagination does play a very im-

[1] *G. of A.*, p. 63.

portant part in this procedure of perseveringly dwelling upon a thought or concept, at any rate when these thoughts are of a secular sort ('honour, glory, self aggrandizement, gain').[1] But what kind of imagination is it, or what sense does the word 'imagine' have? If a person is very deficient in mental imagery, is this important kind of perseverance beyond his power? To put it very crudely: suppose he just tells stories to himself, true or fictitious, many different ones, and all of them *ad rem*, but does not illustrate them with mental pictures (because he cannot) nor yet with auditory images of the voices of the *dramatis personae* (because he cannot do that either). He cannot visualize the boy standing on the burning deck, nor form an auditory image of Richard III saying 'Off with his head!' Shall we say that he is not really dwelling upon the thought of honour or of self-aggrandizement, no matter how copius and how persevering his private story-telling is?

On the contrary, he *is* dwelling upon this favourite thought of his, and perseveringly too, even though he uses no mental imagery in doing so, except images of words; and the effects of his perseverance will show themselves eventually in his actions and in his emotional life. Perhaps we may put it in this way: what matters most is the degree of detail or specificity which these imaginative ruminations have. One must consider in detail what it would be like to behave honourably in some specific situation, or to succeed in some specific scheme of self-aggrandizement (as Richard III did when he succeeded in having himself crowned King of England). But the details need not necessarily present themselves to one's mind in the form of mental imagery. If they do present themselves in that form, the psychological effects of this process of 'dwelling upon' a thought or concept may well be greater. But surely the effects of it are not negligible if one dwells upon the thought or concept in a purely verbal way, provided that one does so by considering *instances* (real or fictitious) of this concept, and describing them to oneself in detail.

Shall we say, then, that there are two senses of the word 'imagine': a sense in which it means imaging (having mental

[1] For the religious ones which Newman also mentions, the thought of the Divine Goodness, etc., see below, pp. 345–8, on the acquisition of 'an image of God'.

imagery) and a sense in which it means imagining *that* . . . or imagining *as*? We do need to draw some such distinction, and Newman himself has not drawn it. For instance, a person who is dwelling on the thought of honour may imagine himeslf *as* refusing to betray a friend or comrade despite the threat (or the blandishments) of the Secret Police. He may imagine *that* he is being interrogated by them, and that he is behaving as a very honourable person would, by answering no questions and at the same time telling no lies. He may 'fill out' the scene with a good deal of detail much as a novelist might, actually formulating to himself the questions which the hard-faced Police Chief asks and the inducements which his smooth-faced Adjutant offers. All this he may do just by using words. They will probably be imaged ('silent') words, not actually uttered or written down. But still he need have no images at all of the persons, objects or events which these words describe.

Nevertheless it is perfectly possible, and probably very common, for imaging and imagining 'that' (or 'as') to occur together. One may actually picture some part of the scene in the police court, in visual images, and then 'eke out' these images by means of words. Perhaps we are not good enough visualizers to form a clear image of the Police Chief's face, though Newman himself could no doubt have done it. So we use words to help us out: 'heavy-jowled', 'short snub nose', 'unblinking gaze'. And perhaps our auditory images of the remarks we suppose him to utter do not accurately reproduce the tone of voice in which such a person might be expected to speak. To remedy this defect, we have to resort to words again: it is like the bark of an Alsatian dog.

Moreover, these two activities of the imagination, imaging and imagining *that*, have a common origin. Both are dependent on memory. Neither could exist unless we had the power of 'retaining' past experiences. Both imaging and imagining *that* are ways in which this retention of past experiences is occurrently manifested. Or, as some would put it, neither of these activities of the imagination could exist unless past experiences left 'traces' in us, which persist long after the experiences themselves have ceased. As we have seen, Newman himself sometimes speaks of 'impressions' (occasionally of 'impresses'), and appears to use this word in the sense of memory traces.

'AN IMAGE OF GOD'

Both the strong and the weak points in Newman's account of images come out in Section 1 of Ch. 5, 'Apprehension and Assent in the matter of Religion'. The title of Section 1 is 'Belief in one God'. Newman's aim here is not to prove the existence of God, but to show 'how we gain an image of God and give a real assent to the proposition that He exists'.[1] This is not just an isolated passage in which Newman's picturesque style of writing has run away with him. The strange and difficult idea of an image of God occurs frequently in this Section, and is indeed the main topic discussed in it. In one passage he even calls this image 'a picture' ('the picture of a Supreme Governor, a Judge', etc.) and refers us in a footnote to the pages in ch. 3 about the formation of composite images—pages in which he is quite clearly talking about mental imagery, and not about imagining 'that' or imagining 'as'.[2]

Moreover, in this Section he twice uses the verb 'to image'. In one of these passages he speaks of 'imaging the thought of God in the definite impressions which conscience creates',[3] as if he were already aware of the distinction which we ourselves should make between 'imaging' and 'imagining that'. (The phrase 'the thought of' is also worthy of notice. It suggests that when we apprehend a proposition in the real manner, there is still something notional about our apprehension. I have tried to show earlier that there must be.)[4]

The question which Newman wishes to answer in this Section is first formulated on p. 78. 'Can I attain to any more vivid assent to the Being of a God than that which is given to the notions of the intellect? . . . Can I believe as if I saw?' It will be remembered that in an earlier passage Newman has told us of people to whom the Supreme Being and other supernatural beings are 'as present as if they were objects of sight'.[5] But how can we believe as if we saw, since no man hath seen God at any time?

Newman's answer, to put it very crudely, is this: first he points out that when we are said to 'see' ordinary human persons, the

[1] *G. of A.*, p. 80.

[2] P. 84. The pages referred to in his footnote are pp. 22, 23.

[3] P. 84, second paragraph. Is this the first occurrence of the verb 'to image, in English?

[4] Cf. pp. 330–2, above.

[5] *G. of A.*, p. 43.

sense in which we 'see' them needs some analysis.[1] Secondly he suggests that though we do not see God, there is a sense in which we have heard Him very frequently: not indeed with our outward ears, but inwardly, in the phenomena of moral experience. Everyone has a conscience, and we all find it natural to speak of the *voice* of conscience. It is 'a voice, or the echo of a voice imperative, and constraining, like no other dictate in our experience' (p. 82). It is imperative, in that it tells us what to do and what not to do: constraining, in that it threatens us with disagreeable consequences if we disobey. These threats are no idle ones either. If we do disobey we have what is called a bad conscience. We 'suffer various perturbations of mind . . . which may be very considerable . . . and their contraries when the conscience is good, as real though less forcible' (p. 82).

What is this voice which issues commands and threatens sanctions? Surely it must be the voice of a personal being, a Lord and Master to whom we are responsible. Such emotions as shame, which we all feel when we disobey the voice of conscience, can only be felt towards a personal being. We do not feel shame towards a horse or a dog (p. 83). Again ' "the wicked flees, when no man pursueth"; then why does he flee? Who is it that sees in solitude, in darkness, in the hidden chambers of the heart?' The Lord and Master who speaks to us in the voice of conscience is one whose knowledge has no limits. He must be supernatural and Divine (p. 84).

At first, he presents himself to us as one whom we fear. But later we come to love him as well. For what he commands us to do is always good. We ourselves approve of the actions commanded, and we still approve of them when we disobey. So we acknowledge that he is our good Lord and Master, and we begin to love him, because goodness is the proper object of love (pp. 86–7).

This, in outline, is Newman's answer to the question 'Can we believe as if we saw?' It is not merely that we can have a notional apprehension of these propositions about God. We can have more.

[1] P. 78 'The evidence which we have of their presence lies in the phenomena which address our senses, and our warrant for taking those for evidence is our instinctive certitude that they are evidence': see also pp. 84–5, on the 'instinctive' character of this certitude.

We can have a real apprehension of them as well. We can entertain them in an imaginative way, and not merely in a notional way. And then, if we also assent to them, we shall be assenting to 'an image', and we *shall* believe as if we saw, or at any rate as if we heard a person speaking to us. 'The phenomena of conscience, as a dictate, avail to *impress the imagination with the picture* of a Supreme Governor, a Judge, holy, just, powerful, all-seeing, retributive'; and this is 'the creative principle of religion, as the moral sense is the principle of ethics'. On the same page, he uses the phrase mentioned earlier, 'imaging the thought of Him in the definite impressions which conscience creates'.[1]

Let us recall that Newman is not here offering us a proof of the existence of God. (If he had been, we should have to consider various difficulties and objections to it.) But he says quite explicitly that this is not what he is doing. He only claims to show how propositions concerning God and his attributes can come to be entertained in a 'real' and not merely notional manner. Suppose that someone is already familiar with the propositions which Theists believe, but entertains them in a purely notional way, and assents to them in a purely notional way, as many Theists do. Then reflection on the phenomena of conscience—on his own personal memories of his own first-hand experience of them—might well enable him to 'image the thought of God in the definite impressions which conscience creates'. He will no longer think of God as a remote and inaccessible Supreme Being, but as his own Lord and Master, his good Lord and Master too, one who has addressed him very frequently, one with whom he has personal relations. Then he will no doubt entertain propositions about God in a 'real' manner, and not in a wholly notional manner as he did before.

It is a little strange to say, as Newman does, that such a person has acquired 'an image' of God, and still stranger to call it a picture. And though Newman speaks of 'imaging the thought of God in the definite impressions which conscience creates', it turns out that this 'imaging' does not consist at all in having or inspecting mental images, not even in having or inspecting a 'composite' image such as Newman discusses in his passage about

[1] P. 84, my italics. Here we must remember Newman's distinction between religion and theology.

the faculty of composition.[1] What Newman calls an image of God is not at all like a visual image of a unicorn, or the visual image of a banana tree which one might be able to form though one has never actually seen such a tree. On the contrary, it is something acquired by means of imagining *as*. By reflecting on his own moral experiences, the person whom we are discussing is enabled to imagine God *as* being his Lord and Master, *as* being one with whom he has personal relations, and *as* being a proper object both of fear and of love.

This conclusion seems to be confirmed by the example Newman himself uses to illustrate his discussion of the image of God. On p. 86 he gives us a wonderful phenomenological description of the religious consciousness of a child. 'Supposing he has offended his parents, he will all alone and without effort, as if it were the most natural of acts, place himself in the presence of God and beg of Him to set him right with them. Let us consider how much is contained in this simple act . . . it involves the impression on his mind of an unseen Being with whom he is in immediate relation . . . of One whose goodwill towards him he is assured of, and can take for granted—nay, who loves him better, and is nearer to him, than his parents . . . of One who can hear him, wherever he happens to be, and can read his thoughts . . . of One who can effect a critical change in the state of feeling of others towards him.' In short, 'this child has in his mind the image of an Invisible Being, who exercises a particular providence among us, who is present everywhere, who is heart-reading, heart-changing, ever-accessible, open to impetration'.[2]

Everyone who believes in God would wish to resemble this child. As a piece of religious phenomenology, the passage is beyond praise. But still, we must ask whether the word 'image' can bear so great a weight. The gift which this charming and pious child has is not a gift for forming visual images, nor auditory nor kinaesthetic ones. We may properly describe him as imaginative. But the imagination which he uses so well is imagining 'as' or 'imagining that'.

[1] *G. of A.*, pp. 22–4.

[2] *Ibid.*, p. 86.

LECTURE 6

SELF-VERIFYING BELIEFS

In this lecture I shall discuss a paradoxical class of beliefs to which William James drew attention in his essay *The Will to Believe*. He claims that there are situations 'where faith in a fact can help create the fact'.[1] But one of them had been noticed some nineteen centuries earlier by Vergil. He says of one of the crews competing in a boat-race *possunt quia posse videntur*, 'they can because they think they can'.[2] If a lecture required a text, like a sermon, these words of the illustrious poet would serve the purpose very well. Obviously there is something paradoxical about them. Can it ever be true that 'thinking makes it so'? We ordinarily suppose that facts are independent of our beliefs. Facts are what they are, we say, no matter what anyone believes. Someone's belief that it is raining has no tendency whatever to make it true that it is raining (nor, of course, to make it false either).

But perhaps this is not quite the right way to formulate our ordinary view of the matter. For example, it is a fact that at 5.30 p.m. I open my front door and walk down the road to the post-box, and the state of affairs comes about because of a belief which I have, my belief that the post-box will be cleared at 5.45 p.m. In this kind of way, innumerable facts clearly are dependent, or partly dependent, upon people's beliefs, since our beliefs affect our actions and our actions cause changes in the world. Our ordinary assumption is not so much that facts in general are independent of beliefs in general, but rather that the fact which verifies a belief is independent of that particular belief. That the post-box *is* cleared at 5.45 p.m. is something completely independent of my belief that it is, though not independent of other beliefs, for instance those held by post office administrators about the time it takes to transport letters from here to the sorting office and from there to the railway station.

[1] William James: *Selected Papers on Philosophy* (Everymans Library), p. 119.
[2] *Aeneid V*, line 231.

Again, I believe that there are several motor cars now passing down the High Street in Oxford in a westerly direction. Let us suppose that there are in fact fifteen motor cars doing so, which makes my belief correct. This fact is no doubt dependent on other people's beliefs, for example the belief (correct or not) held by one of the drivers that this is the quickest way to the railway station, and the belief (correct or not) held by another that he will enjoy the musical comedy which he believes is going to be performed at the theatre this evening. But the fact that the motor cars are moving in this way is completely independent of *my* belief.

In short, we ordinarily suppose that the state of affairs which makes a particular belief correct or incorrect (verifies it or falsifies it) is entirely independent of *that* belief, though it may sometimes be dependent in some degree upon other beliefs—namely, when the state of affairs in question is one which human actions can influence. 'Nothing is made true', we say, 'simply by the belief that it is so. Believing a proposition *p* has not even a tendency to make *p* true, nor to make it false either.' This is what we ordinarily assume; and this assumption does seem at first sight to be an essential ingredient in our notion of 'objectivity' or 'objective reality'. The objective is what is so, no matter what beliefs anyone holds about it. This is part, at least, of what we mean when we speak of 'hard' facts. I once heard a philosopher say 'the objective is the objectionable'.[1] It is objectionable because it so often falsifies our beliefs, and also in another way, because it so often prevents our wishes from being fulfilled. It is a fact that it is a cold day, whether you like it or not. It is a fact that I am still sitting in the train at 11.30 p.m., though I should much prefer to be in bed.

But these assumptions about 'objectivity' seem to be contradicted by examples like the one quoted from Vergil 'They can do it because they think they can'. Here the very fact which makes the belief correct seems to be dependent, or partly dependent, on the belief itself. Or, as James puts it, 'faith in a fact' has apparently 'helped to create that fact'.

[1] This remark, I think, was made by Professor J. A. Smith of Oxford in a lecture which I attended as an undergraduate.

OTHER EXAMPLES

Let us now consider some other examples. The paradoxical phenomenon which we are discussing is not at all uncommon.

1. Some years ago a paragraph appeared on the sports page of a Sunday newspaper. Its title was 'Failure in the foursomes. Beaten because they expected it'. This resembles Vergil's case. Believing that you will fail can cause you to fail, just as believing that you will succeed can cause you to succeed.

2. If you believe that you are going to get hurt (for example in a game of mixed hockey) the chances are that you *will* get hurt. So just don't think about it at all.

3. If the patient believes that he will be well again a fortnight from now, this makes it more likely that he will be well again by then.

4. Suppose you have to walk across a narrow plank over a small river. If you believe that you are going to fall off into the water, you probably will fall off. On the other hand, if you believe you are going to get across safely, the chances are that you will in fact get across safely.

5. If a large number of business men believe that there is going to be a slump or a devaluation of the currency, this makes it likely that there will in fact be a slump or a devaluation of the currency.

The same phenomenon can be noticed when the proposition believed is negative; or, if one likes to put it so, disbelief can be as effective as belief. When the competitors in the golf match expected to be beaten, we could equally say that they expected *not* to win or draw; and that the business men just mentioned believe that economic prosperity will not continue, or that the currency cannot be maintained at its present value for much longer.

Or let us consider another patient who believes that he will not get well for a very long time. This belief does seem to retard his recovery. He remains ill for more than a month, whereas most people with his physical symptoms are completely restored to health in three weeks.

Again, the man confronted by the plank across the river may be in a state which is the exact converse of the one described by Vergil. He is quite sure that he cannot possibly walk across it, even though he has just seen his companions do it, apparently without any difficulty. He cannot do it, because he believes he cannot.

This kind of belief-induced inability may take a more general form. Robert seldom succeeds in any of his undertakings because he has no belief in his own capacities. Whenever any task confronts him, or at least any important task, he believes that he cannot manage it, and because he believes this, he cannot in fact manage it.

Beliefs of this paradoxical kind need a special name. Let us call them self-verifying beliefs. Let us say that a belief is self-verifying if the belief that *p* either makes *p* true or at any rate increases the probability of *p*. (Perhaps you do not actually fail in your undertaking, but the belief that you are going to fail makes it appreciably more likely that you will.)

It is important to include this second case, when the probability of a proposition is increased in some degree by someone's believing the proposition, because even this appears at first sight to contradict our ordinary assumptions about the relation of beliefs to facts, and to be inconsistent with our ordinary notion of 'objectivity'. If believing a proposition *p* has even a *tendency* to make *p* come true, the truth or falsity of *p* cannot be wholly independent of the belief that *p*.

In the example about crossing the plank, perhaps the man who believed that he could do it fell off into the water all the same. But he did get more than half way across, whereas the men who believed they could not do it just remained standing on the bank.

Perhaps the patient does not actually recover from his illness. But the paradox we are discussing still arises, if his belief that he was going to recover made his recovery more likely, or less unlikely, than it would have been otherwise. And we may have evidence that it did have this effect. The patient eventually died of his disease; but he lived longer than a patient with this type of illness would normally be expected to live.

OVER-CONFIDENCE

Before going further, there is a difficulty, or complication, which we must consider. Are these not cases where a belief, so far from being self-verifying, is actually self-falsifying? Surely this is the characteristic feature of the state of mind called over-confidence? For instance, it might be said, an undergraduate who believes very firmly that he will get a First Class in his final examinations is likely, for that very reason, *not* to get one. It might even happen that because of this belief of his he fails to get a degree at all.

Again, I once heard a doctor remark 'One can make out a good case for saying that belief that you will recover makes it more likely that you will not'. Why is this? Presumably because a very firm belief that you will recover may lead you to neglect reasonable precautions. An over-confident influenza patient may get out of bed and do a full day's work as soon as his temperature goes down to normal, and the result is that his temperature goes up again. In the same kind of way, the over-confident undergraduate is so sure he will get a First Class that he neglects to study several of the books prescribed, and does not bother to go to any lectures in the last three weeks of term.

What shall we say about such examples? It might be argued that self-falsifying beliefs are just as interesting, from an epistemological point of view, as self-verifying ones. On the face of it, the existence of self-falsifying beliefs would be equally incompatible with our ordinary assumption that facts are independent of beliefs. What is puzzling is that believing a proposition *p* should have any effect at all upon the facts, one way or the other; *either* in the way of making *p* true *or* in the way of making *p* false. Our ordinary assumption is that believing a proposition has not even a tendency to make the proposition false (any more than a tendency to make it true) and neither reduces nor increases the probability of the proposition.

But perhaps we have not yet grasped the point of this objection about over-confidence. Perhaps it is this—if someone wishes to maintain that there are self-verifying beliefs, will he not have to admit that the same belief is self-verifying in some cases and self-falsifying in others? And this in turn may suggest that the whole conception of a belief which 'alters the facts' is a mistaken or confused one. If the same belief is followed in some cases by a situation which verifies it, and in others by a situation which falsifies it, surely the actual result, in either case, must be independent of the belief itself? Whether the patient recovers or not depends on his bodily state, and it makes no difference at all what his beliefs about it may be. Again, it might be said, your belief that you were going to get across the plank safely did not make it any more likely that you *would* get across safely (though in fact you did). For here is another man who holds the same belief about himself as you hold about yourself, and holds it equally firmly; and yet he does not in fact get across safely. He loses his balance when he is half way across and falls into the water.

Now if anyone were to maintain that believing a proposition is ever a sufficient condition for that proposition's being true, this objection would show, I think, that he was mistaken. But the suggestion we are discussing is not nearly so extravagant as that. The suggestion was only that in certain special cases believing a proposition *p* is a cause-factor or a part-cause which contributes to bringing about a state of affairs which makes the proposition true. At the most, it would be a necessary condition or *conditio sine qua non;* something whose absence would prevent *p* from being true. (For instance, there may be some things a person cannot do, *unless* he believes he can.)

But many other conditions must obviously be fulfilled as well. No matter what my beliefs are, I shall not succeed in getting across the river safely if the plank is struck by lightning when I am half way across, or if my companions who have crossed already (large, heavy men) have strained the timber to breaking-point. More important still, some of these other conditions which must be fulfilled are psychological ones. I may believe firmly that I am going to get across safely, but I shall not succeed unless I pay careful attention to what I am doing. Suppose a peregrine falcon flies past while I am on my way (I happen to be interested in rare birds) and I turn my head to have a better look at it. Then I shall almost certainly lose my balance and fall into the water.

This is just the kind of thing which the over-confident person is liable to do. He not only believes that he will be successful, but also believes, quite mistakenly, that this belief—the belief 'I am going to succeed'—is sufficient by itself to ensure that he will in fact succeed.

It is not quite true, therefore, that the same belief is self-verifying in some cases and self-falsifying in others. The over-confident man does, of course, believe that he will succeed; and the sensible man, who is neither over-confident nor under-confident, likewise believes that *he* will succeed. So far, we can say rather loosely that both of them hold 'the same' belief, in the sense that *A* believes that *A* will succeed and *B* believes that *B* will. But the over-confident man also holds another belief which the sensible man rejects. It is what philosophers call a 'second-order' belief: the belief, or perhaps the unconscious taking for granted, that a belief in one's own success is sufficient by itself to ensure that one will in fact succeed; which it certainly is not, though it may be a necessary condition for success (*a sine qua non*) in certain cases.

I would suggest that the disposition to hold such a second-order belief is what we mean by 'over-confidence'. At any rate, it is clear that the total belief-states of the over-confident man and the sensible man are not the same. Both believe that they are going to succeed in crossing the river, but the one man believes something which the other disbelieves—namely that believing one is going to succeed is sufficient by itself to ensure success.

We have now considered a number of examples which may help to illustrate the meaning of the term 'self-verifying belief'. But so far we have done nothing to solve the problem which was mentioned at the beginning. The mere suggestion that there might be self-verifying beliefs, still more the assertion that there are, does seem to conflict with our ordinary assumption that the real world is independent of our beliefs about it.

Let us try to imagine a world in which every proposition you believe is made true merely by your believing it, a world in which thinking always 'makes it so'. Would it be a world at all? Surely it would not, in any ordinary sense of the term 'world'. Or, if one prefers to put it so, it would be a purely subjective world. According to some speculative persons, the next world is of that sort. But surely this present world is not.

Now of course it has not been suggested that *all* our beliefs are self-verifying. Far from it. As we shall see presently, the class of self-verifying beliefs is quite a narrow one, even though we include in it cases where believing a proposition has no more than a tendency to make the proposition come true. But the problem still arises if there are any self-verifying beliefs at all, even in this rather wide sense of the term 'self-verifying'. If any beliefs at all have this character (and we can hardly avoid admitting that some do have it) it would seem, at least at first sight, that our ordinary notion of objectivity will have to be revised.

WHAT KINDS OF BELIEF ARE SELF-VERIFYING?

Before we attempt to solve this problem, it will be useful to consider just what this paradoxical class of beliefs consists of, and ask whether they have any distinctive feature in common. We notice at once that they are concerned with a very restricted subject matter.

In the first place, they are all beliefs about human beings, or at any rate about conscious beings. It might perhaps be unwise to say that only human beings can hold them. Perhaps non-human animals have some self-verifying beliefs, in so far as they can be said to have beliefs at all. Our cat at home is a very enterprising jumper. Perhaps he can only jump from the floor to the top of a cupboard because he believes he can (*potest quia posse videtur*). It is also logically possible that there are superhuman conscious beings who have beliefs, and that some of these beliefs are self-verifying. Indeed, if there are such conscious beings, we might perhaps expect that their self-verifying beliefs would be more numerous and more varied than our own.

Secondly, self-verifying beliefs always refer to the present or the future and never to the past: that is, they always refer to what is present or future at the time when the belief exists. The past cannot be altered, whatever our beliefs about it may be. On the other hand, it would be a mistake, though a tempting one, to suppose that self-verifying beliefs are concerned only with the future. When a man believes in this self-verifying way that he is able to do something, he has the ability now, though the exercise of it may be future.

Could we say, thirdly, that all self-verifying beliefs are beliefs which some conscious being holds *about himself*—that they are all 'self-regarding' beliefs? If we do say this, we shall have to include the believer's body as part of himself, in order to make room for such examples as 'he will get well if he believes he will get well'. If his belief alters the facts, or tends to alter them, in such a way that the proposition believed comes true, the facts in question are at least partly facts about the state of the believer's body. Indeed, the same applies, very often, to 'he can do it because he thinks he can'. The 'doing' is very often a psycho-physical process. Walking across the plank over the river is an activity which obviously contains bodily events as well as mental ones; and in the example quoted from Vergil the thing which the competitors could do 'because they thought they could' was winning a boat-race.

It is true that there are some cases, and important ones too, where the 'doing' is something purely mental, or as near to being so as any activity of an embodied conscious being can be. There is scope for what is called 'faith' in intellectual or imaginatively-creative activities. When we say that someone never succeeds in any of his undertakings because he has no belief in his own powers, the undertakings we have in mind may include constructing philosophical theories or composing sonatas. Again, one of the things we may succeed in doing if we believe we shall succeed, and fail in doing if this belief is lacking, is to alter our own emotional attitudes, for example to forgive someone towards whom we have hitherto felt resentful, or to cultivate the habit of seeing the other man's point of view.

Nevertheless, it is clear that in many of the cases where we say 'he can do it because he thinks he can' or 'he succeeded in doing it because he believed he would succeed', the doing *is* a psycho-physical activity. So if we wish to say that self-verifying beliefs are invariably beliefs which some person holds about himself, we shall certainly have to include his body as part of himself. (We need not, of course, suppose that his body is the whole of him.)

ARE ALL SELF-VERIFYING BELIEFS SELF-REGARDING?

But is it true that all self-verifying beliefs have this self-regarding character? It may seem so from the examples so far given. The question however, is a little more complicated than it looks. In the first example of all, *possunt quia posse videntur* could quite well be translated 'they can do it because other people think they can'; and so translated, the statement might still be true. Again, it might be true that the patient's chances of recovery are increased if other people (his doctor, for instance, or his family) believe he will recover; and conversely that his chances of recovery are decreased if these other persons do not believe he will recover, and still more if they believe that he will not. It might also be said that the man who has to walk across the plank over the river is more likely to succeed if his companions believe he will succeed, and more likely to fail if they believe he will fail.

On the other hand, it might be argued that this effect of other people's beliefs is secondary and indirect. Thus if the patient is told by his family or his friends or his doctor that they believe he is going to get better, it is quite likely that he himself will begin to believe so, even though previously he did not; and then what is self-verifying is not their belief about him, but his own belief about himself, which is caused or partly caused by their communication of their belief to him. Nor is it enough to say that they talk to him in this way 'just to encourage him' and leave it at that. For what *is* encouragement, or being encouraged? It consists at least partly in being induced to believe that one's prospects are better than one had previously believed them to be.

Indeed, it is not even necessary that these other people should tell the patient what their belief is. Their behaviour and demeanour, the emotions they express, the topics they discuss in his presence (for instance, plans for taking him with them on holiday in Denmark next summer)—all this may convey to him what their belief is, even if they do not actually tell him what it is. In the converse case, where they believe that he is *not* going to recover, they are very unlikely to tell him explicitly what their belief is. Nevertheless, from their behaviour and demeanour he may be able to 'gather' that they do believe this. And that might be just as effective in inducing him to hold the same belief about himself.

It is also conceivable that even though these beliefs which other people hold about him are not communicated to the patient explicitly, nor conveyed to him in the indirect ways which have been mentioned, they may still affect him telepathically. At any rate, it would be unwise to exclude this possibility. But then again the beliefs of other people would only affect the situation indirectly. The self-verifying belief would still be the one which the patient holds about himself, even though it is the telepathic influence of other people's beliefs which caused him to hold it.

But this kind of explanation (including the telepathic variant of it) does not cover all the facts. It can happen that *A*'s belief about *B* has a 'self-verifying' character even though *B* does not himself share that belief. For instance, John's Headmaster believes that John is capable of getting a scholarship at the University. John himself does not believe this, and still does not believe it in spite of all the Headmaster says to him. All the same, he is persuaded to sit for the scholarship examination, which he would never have thought of doing otherwise; and then, to his own intense surprise, he does get a scholarship. Here, of course, the Headmaster's belief is only verified because of the effect it has on John's own mind. But the effect it has is not at all to alter the boy's own belief about himself. When he was persuaded, reluctantly perhaps, to take the examination, he did not in the least believe that he was capable of getting a scholarship, as is shown by his intense surprise when he does get one. The Headmaster's belief verifies itself not by altering the boy's beliefs, but by altering his volitions and his actions.

This example seems to show that a self-verifying belief about a person need not necessarily be a 'self-regarding' belief, one which this person holds about himself, though very often it is.

Something similar might occur in several of the other examples we have considered, for instance the one about crossing the plank. Suppose that my companions all believe that I can cross safely. Some of them tell me so, others convey their belief to me by their gestures or their facial expressions. One slaps me kindly on the back, another smiles in an encouraging way from the other side and beckons to me to come over. I still do not believe myself that I can manage it. All the same, because they have conveyed to me that *they* believe it, I am induced to make the attempt; and then I find, to my own surprise, that I do in fact get across safely. Here again a person is able to do something, not because he believes he can (until he actually did it, he had no such belief) but because other people believe that he can; it is sufficient if these other people's beliefs, when they are conveyed to him, affect his volitions and his actions.

It is worth while to add that self-verifying beliefs do play a considerable part in personal relations between one person and another, as William James points out in his essay *The Will to Believe*.[1] Nor need these relations be very intimate or continuous. Perhaps my companions who help me to cross the plank by expressing or conveying to me their belief that I can do it, are people whom I do not know at all well. Perhaps I had never even met them until this morning, when we set out on our cross-country walk together. Perhaps the reluctant scholarship candidate had never even spoken to the Headmaster before (it may be a very large school) and just has one interview with him, lasting only twenty minutes. Indeed, the personal relations need not be of the 'face-to-face' kind at all. They may be conducted entirely by correspondence.

All that is required is that one person should express or convey to another some kind of 'faith' which he has in this other person. Because *A* believes that *B* is an honest man, and makes it clear to *B* that he does hold this belief, *B* is more likely to be honest in fact, or become so or remain so, than he would have been otherwise. It is not necessary that *A* should actually tell *B*, in speech or writing, what he believes. It is sufficient if his belief is conveyed to *B* in some indirect manner. (Indeed, this is likely, perhaps, to be more effective than direct 'telling'). For instance, they are talking about some plan of action which *B* is considering, and *A* discusses it on the assumption that *B* will ask for, and obtain, a day's leave of absence from his place of employment and will be able to earn the extra money he will need. By conducting the conversation on that assumption, he conveys to *B* his belief that *B* is going to behave honourably, without actually saying that he holds it.

Of course *A*'s faith may be falsified after all. Perhaps *B* just absents himself without permission and steals the money from the till in the shop the night before. But still, we ordinarily suppose that *A*'s faith makes it appreciably more likely that *B* will 'act up to' the belief which *A* has about him. The faith which one person has in another is an attitude which has a tendency, at least,

[1] *Selected Papers on Philosophy* (Everyman's Library), p. 118.

to justify itself, if he can somehow convey it to the other person.

Finally, to complete our survey of the kinds of belief which have a self-verifying character, we may notice that they do not have to be reflective beliefs, arrived at after a careful scrutiny of the evidence for and against the proposition believed. They may equally well be unreflective takings-for-granted. As we have seen, the man who believes he is going to get across safely does have to take reasonable precautions while he is on his way across. But he need not necessarily consider the evidence for and against the proposition 'I can do it' or 'I am going to get across safely'. It is quite possible that he *has* evidence for this proposition: for instance, he has often tried to do the same sort of thing before, and has been successful rather more often than not. But he need not consciously recall these facts about his past, or estimate what degree of probability they confer on the proposition which he now accepts and acts upon. He may well accept it without question, just take for granted that he will arrive safely on the other bank of the river: and this is enough to make it likely that he will in fact get across safely.

So far, then, our conclusions are these:—

1. Self-verifying beliefs are always about the present or the future, never about the past.

2. They are always beliefs about conscious beings.

3. They are often, but not always, self-regarding beliefs, beliefs which some person holds about himself (his body being counted as part of himself).

4. They need not be reflective beliefs. Often they are unreflective takings-for-granted.

We see now that this paradoxical self-verifying character is confined to quite a small class of beliefs, though quite an important one, since many of the beliefs contained in it have a direct relevance to human well-being. But however small the class of self-verifying beliefs may be, this does nothing to remove the paradox we are discussing. It still arises if any beliefs at all are self-verifying or have a self-verifying tendency. The idea that any proposition can be made true, or even likely, merely by being believed does seem to conflict with our ordinary assumptions about objectivity. Is there any way of solving this paradox? I shall now suggest that there is.

THE 'ACT-OBJECT' DISTINCTION

Let us begin by stating the proposed solution in an over-simplified form, more or less in the way an old-fashioned Realist philosopher of the 1920s would have put it, if he had happened to consider our problem.

It might be said, the word 'belief' is ambiguous: we must distinguish carefully between the *believing* and *what is believed.* Believing is a mental state or attitude. But what is believed is not a mental state or attitude at all; it is what logicians call a proposition, something which is either true or false.

Now it may be claimed that once we distinguish clearly between the believing and what is believed, the paradox which has been troubling us disappears. For surely there is nothing paradoxical in the suggestion that *believings* may 'alter the facts'? Mental states certainly do have effects. They cause changes in the person in whom they occur or exist, changes in his mind and often (perhaps always) in his body, and thereby they may indirectly cause changes in his physical environment. And since believings are mental states, they may perfectly well cause changes both in the mind and in the body of the believer. Indeed, it is perfectly obvious that believings do have effects, and often quite important ones too: whereas the suggestion that a *proposition* could cause changes is not so much false as nonsensical, though of course the uttering of it, or the writing of it down on paper, might very well do so.

Just what effects a believing might have is a purely empirical question; and there is no *a priori* reason why some believings should not cause changes of such a kind that the proposition believed becomes true, or more probable than it would have been otherwise. If we find empirical evidence (as we do) that some believings have effects of this kind, we may be a little surprised, since it is clear that most believings do not have them. But there is no monstrous paradox here. It is just one more illustration of the familiar fact that mental states have effects.

Thus, it would be argued, the statement that facts are independent of our beliefs is true in one sense of the word 'belief' but false in another. It is true that facts are always independent of the proposition believed; but they need not always be independent of the believing. Suppose the proposition is 'Timothy will succeed in walking across this plank'. It does not follow in the least that because there is this proposition, there will also be a state of affairs which makes it true, nor even that such a state of affairs is in the least degree probable. But suppose that someone, for instance, Timothy himself, *believes* this proposition; then his believing may quite well bring about a state of affairs which makes the proposition true, or at least more likely than it would have been otherwise. It may even be that in some cases believing a proposition p is a necessary condition for p's being true (p would not have been true, *unless* it had been believed).

DEFECTS IN THIS FORMULATION

There are two defects in this proposal for solving our problem. It is over-simplified in two different ways. First, it treats believings as if they were events or occurrences. It uses the term 'mental states' in an occurrent sense. Acquiring a belief is indeed a mental occurrence, and so is losing it. But having a belief (or 'holding it' as we say) is a disposition rather than an occurrence. So long as we have it, it is liable to manifest itself by occurrences of various kinds, both mental and psycho-physical. Instead of talking about 'believings' as if they are themselves events, we should talk about the events which are manifestations of a belief-disposition. One of them is the using of the proposition believed as a premiss in our practical deliberation, when we are considering what to do, and the giving of attention to the proposition and to the inferences which may be drawn from it. These *are* mental events or occurrences and they certainly have effects of one sort or another; but it is misleading to describe them as 'believings'.

The second defect, or over-simplification, is a rather strange view about propositions. They are spoken of as if they were *entities*, which are somehow 'there' and are quite independent of our thinking and speaking. You may have noticed the curious statement 'it does not follow that because *there is* such and such a proposition there will be a state of affairs which makes it true'.[1] But this difficulty can be avoided by reformulating the proposed solution in a slightly more complicated way.

Let us first translate the rather alarming statement 'There is the proposition *p*' into the harmless one 'The indicative sentence *s* makes sense', which is in turn equivalent to 'The indicative sentence *s* is either true or false' (or 'would be either true or false if someone were to assert it'). Let us suppose also that *s* is an empirical sentence, not an *a priori* one such as '$3 + 2 = 5$'. Then we proceed as follows: From the fact that the sentence *s* is *either* true *or* false, it does not in the least follow that *s* is true *rather than* false, nor of course that it is false *rather than* true. Nor does it in the least follow that the sentence is *likely* to be true rather than false, nor yet that it is likely to be false rather than true. What makes such an indicative sentence true or false is the state of the world, the actual state of affairs. (Human minds, and of course human bodies too, are part of the world.)

This is the cash-value of the statement that 'facts are independent of propositions'; and if the statement is translated in the way just suggested (as a statement about indicative sentences), it does not commit us to the view that propositions are subsistent entities. It merely amounts to saying that if an empirical indicative sentence *s* makes sense, nothing whatever follows from this as to the existence or non-existence of an actual state of affairs which the sentence would describe. And this principle *is* an essential part of our ordinary conception of 'objectivity'.

On the other hand, if some person understands and believes an indicative sentence *s*, this understanding of his and this belief which he holds will certainly have effects of one sort or another; and one of these effects, in suitable cases, might quite well be that a state of affairs comes into existence which makes the sentence true, or that the coming into existence of such a state of affairs becomes more probable than it would otherwise have been. Whether believing ever does have such effects is a question of empirical fact, and the answer to this empirical question seems to be 'Yes, in certain special cases'.

If so, there is after all no paradox in the notion of a self-

[1] P. 363, above.

verifying belief, provided we distinguish carefully between the believing and what is believed.

SELF-VERIFYING SENTENCES

There would however be a paradox in the notion of a self-verifying indicative sentence, a sentence which merely by making sense would thereby bring into existence the state of affairs described by it, or make that state of affairs more likely to exist.

Even magicians have not gone so far as to embrace such a paradox as this. They have only claimed that the *utterance* of certain sorts of sentence which make sense, or the *writing* of them (with suitable ceremonial precautions) tends to bring about a state of affairs such as the sentence would describe. They have not supposed that the mere fact that the sentence makes sense has any such consequences.

It is true that logicians, a very different class of persons, might claim that there are self-verifying sentences. An example would be 'This sentence contains five words'. There certainly is a sense in which it is self-verifying. This sentence is true just because it is the sentence that it is.

But there are two points to notice here. First, it is a very peculiar sentence, in that it is about itself. But the sentences with which we have been concerned in this discussion are not about themselves, though they may be, and often are, about the person who believes them or asserts them ('I am going to get across the plank safely' 'I shall be out of bed again a week from now'). Secondly, the sense in which 'This sentence contains five words' is self-verifying is not a *causal* sense. The sentence does not alter the facts in such a way as to make itself true. It does not alter anything. What makes it true (if the word 'make' is here appropriate) is just a fact about the sentence itself, the fact that there are indeed exactly five words in it. Although we can say it is true 'because of' the number of words it contains, this is not the causal sense of the word 'because'.

But when it is claimed that some propositons are made true, or tend to be made true, because they are believed, the word 'because' *is* being used in a causal sense. The contention is that believing does sometimes cause changes of such a sort that what is believed becomes true, or more likely to be true than it would otherwise have been. Provided we use the term 'self-verifying' in the causal sense which it has had throughout this discussion, it can be said, I think, that the notions of a self-verifying sentence —a sentence which merely by making sense altered the facts in such a way as to make itself true—would be an excessively paradoxical one, whereas the notion of a self-verifying belief-attitude would not.

OTHER PROPOSITIONAL ATTITUDES

Hitherto, we have been wholly concerned with self-verifying beliefs. But we may notice that it is not only belief which has this self-verifying tendency in suitable cases. Other propositional attitudes may have it too. Merely entertaining a proposition, barely thinking of it without either belief or disbelief, sometimes has a self-verifying tendency, especially when the entertaining is attentive and prolonged. Suppose the man confronted by the narrow plank across the river can be induced by others (or can induce himself) just to fix his attention on the proposition 'I am going to get across safely', the chances are that he will in fact get across safely. He need not necessarily believe the proposition. Indeed, we may have pretty good evidence afterwards that he did *not* believe it; we may observe that he is greatly surprised to find himself standing safely on the other side. It is sufficient if he entertains the proposition attentively ('fixes his mind on it') and excludes from his attention the contradictory of it 'I am not going to get across safely'.

Presumably this is what happens in what is called 'suggestion', including hypnotic suggestion, and we must remember that there is such a thing as self-suggestion and even auto-hypnosis. It is an empirical fact that suggestion, including self-suggestion, is sometimes an effective method of enabling people to do things which they could not otherwise have done. Nor need these 'doings' be merely physical ones. By means of self-suggestion, a man may be enabled to solve an intellectual problem which has hitherto baffled him, or the kind of stylistic problem which confronts nearly all writers from time to time, when we 'know roughly what we want to say but cannot see how to put it'. (You say to yourself before going to sleep 'To-morrow morning at 9.30 a.m. some appropriate words will come to me'; and more often than not they do.) In a similar way, suggestion, including self-suggestion, can enable one to alter one's emotional attitude to another person, for instance to change it from resentment to forgiveness: a result which one has been quite unable to bring about by a mere effort of will, or even by repeated and persevering efforts of will. It is worth while to mention another example, trivial though it is, because anyone can easily test it for himself. By merely entertaining the proposition 'My left forefinger is tingling' one can actually make it tingle (or at any rate some people can) provided one goes on entertaining the proposition attentively for half a minute or so.

In these examples (unlike the ones discussed earlier) we have been assuming that the proposition is entertained quite neutrally. One does not believe it or disbelieve it or doubt it or wonder about it. It is just bare or pure entertaining, just thinking of the proposition in an attentive manner and continuing to do so for some time.

Perhaps the word 'neutrally' may mislead. I have heard it objected that if we do entertain a proposition *p* in a completely neutral way, we are *ipso facto* entertaining its contradictory not-*p* at the same time.[1] The reply is that there are at least two kinds of neutrality. Our attitude may be neutral as between acceptance and rejection. We neither believe *p* nor disbelieve it. This is the sort of neutrality I have in mind. But our attitude may be neutral in another way also, in that we give equal attention to both *p* and not-*p*. In *this* respect the person I am discussing is not neutral. His whole attention is given to one of these two alternatives—and that is the one which 'comes true' or tends to come true.

But it would seem that self-verification can still occur when an attitude *other* than belief is added to this 'bare entertaining', an attitude of questioning or wondering, for instance. I not only entertain the proposition *p*; I wonder whether it is true, or ask myself how probable it is. Perhaps I also consider some of the logical relations which this proposition has to other propositions.

[1] I am much indebted to an American colleague for calling my attention to this difficulty, and greatly regret that I cannot recall his name.

I notice the consequences which follow from it, either with certainty or with probability. This is sometimes called 'supposing' (If *p*, then what?') and then I may find, disconcertingly, that the situation alters in such a way that the proposition *p* becomes true—especially if it is a proposition about myself or my own actions.

This may be illustrated by the unfortunate predicament of the beginner in bicycling, who sees an old lady crossing the street very, very slowly in front of him. He keeps on asking himself, 'Am I going to run into her? Am I going to run into her? What will happen if I do?' The result is that, sure enough, he does run into her. Here again, the important point is that his mind dwells upon the propositon, even though his attitude towards it is merely one of questioning and supposing, and not of belief.

DOUBT AND DISBELIEF

Not only so: the additional attitude we have, over and above the more entertaining may be an attitude of doubt, or even an attitude of disbelieving or rejection. Of course, we sometimes cease to entertain a proposition once we have rejected it. Having rejected it, we often dismiss it from our minds altogether and no longer think of it at all. After a careful look at the clouds and the weathercock, I reject the proposition 'It will clear up in half and hour' and decide to spend the whole afternoon in the library. And then I pay no more attention to this conceivable but (as I am persuaded) very improbable change in the weather.

But this 'dismissal' of a rejected proposition does not always happen. The proposition may be of intense interest to us, as the proposition 'I am never going to get better' is to a person who is seriously ill. He cannot dismiss this proposition from his mind. He is likely to entertain it attentively and repeatedly, even though he always entertains it disbelievingly, with an attitude of rejection. I would suggest that this makes the proposition appreciably more likely to be true. It alters the situation for the worse, or at least tends to prevent it from altering for the better. The same thing happens in wartime, if people repeatedly entertain the proposition 'We are going to be defeated', even though they always reject it.

In such examples as these, it almost looks as if *disbelieving* a proposition had a tendency to make the proposition true; and if one wishes a proposition *p* to be false, it is perhaps a good piece of psychological hygiene to give up disbelieving *p* and believe its contrary instead (not just its contradictory, not-*p*, but its contrary). Instead of disbelieving that he will remain an invalid for the rest of his life, the patient should believe that he is going to get well. Instead of disbelieving that your Country will lose the war, try to believe that it will win.[1]

It seems, then, that with propositions of the sort we have been discussing, it is the *entertaining* of a proposition (rather than the believing which sometimes accompanies it), which has a self-verifying tendency; and especially, prolonged and attentive entertaining. Likewise, perhaps, the most important point about faith is not so much that a man believes the propositions with regard to which he has faith, though he does of course believe them, but rather that his thoughts dwell upon these propositions, he meditates upon them, considers the consequences which follow from them, illustrates them by means of examples, real or imaginary. In short, he entertains them more frequently and more attentively than other men who do not share his faith, and questions of the form '*p*, so what?' are often on his mind.

If there is anything in these considerations, the problem we have been discussing was incorrectly formulated at the beginning. It should have been called the problem of self-verifying thoughts or entertainings; and 'Thinking makes it so' might have been a more appropriate title for this lecture than 'Self-verifying beliefs'.

'THINKING MAKES IT SO'

Let us now see what can be done to solve the problem which was stated at the beginning of this lecture. If there are self-verifying beliefs or self-verifying thoughts, are we compelled to alter our ordinary assumption that facts are independent of our beliefs, or more generally of our thoughts, entertainings of propositions

[1] I have discussed the puzzling concept of 'trying to believe' in an essay called *Belief and Will* (Aristotelian Soc. Supp. Vol. 1954, pp. 1–26, reprinted in *Philosophy of Mind.*, edited by Prof. S. N. Hampshire, pp. 91–116).

whether believed or not? Is there something wrong with our ordinary conception of 'objectivity'?

If we use the phrase 'Thinking makes it so' as a title for the class of phenomena we have been discussing, we notice at once that there are innumerable cases in which thinking does at least contribute to 'making it so', and yet we are not puzzled by this at all. There is a perfectly ordinary and familiar way in which a person's thoughts 'come true', namely whenever he succeeds in doing something which he intended to do. In any such action, the agent must have the thought of the state of affairs which he sets himself to bring about.

It is certainly *not* true, then, that facts are wholly independent of thoughts, and if our ordinary assumptions about objectivity imply that they are, there is something wrong with these assumptions. We have only to look at all these entities by which we are surrounded—chairs, tables, houses, tea-pots, motor-buses, clocks, gardens, streets. These objects came to be what they are, and where they are, because the human body, especially its central nervous system, its muscles and its limbs, is an apparatus whereby thoughts *can* 'come true'. And that is why the world around us, or at least the surface of this planet, is full of entities which the old Idealist philosophers might have called 'objectified thoughts'.

Again, we speak of 'hard facts'. But if all facts were equally hard, there would not be much point in this expression. Perhaps we only call them 'hard' when there is nothing whatever that we can do about them. But if so, there are at any rate degrees of 'hardness'. We can quite often do something to alter some state of affairs which displeases us or fails to satisfy us. And then some thought which we have is made to come true. We tend to forget that thinking—the entertaining of propositions—is a necessary constituent of doing, or at any rate of intentional doing. There are no doubt puzzles about doing. Indeed one of my own teachers, H. A. Prichard, was greatly puzzled by the question 'How is it possible to do anything?' But nobody supposes, nor should he suppose, that doing involves any *epistemological* puzzles about 'objectivity' or the relation of thoughts to facts.

INTERMEDIATE CAUSAL LINKS.[1]

When we say that facts are independent of our beliefs (or, more generally, independent of our thoughts) perhaps we mean that the entertaining of a proposition is never a *sufficient* condition for the existence of a state of affairs which makes it true. It may be a necessary condition, a *sine qua non*, and in any successful voluntary action it is; but pure and simple thinking never 'makes it so'. This is our ordinary assumption. So if we encounter cases where pure and simple thinking does appear to 'make it so, we are greatly puzzled.

To put it in another way: what would puzzle us very much would be a thought which *directly* caused its own verification, directly brought about a state of affairs whereby the thought 'comes true', without any intermediate causal links at all. This is very different indeed from anything that happens in ordinary voluntary action, where a long and complicated causal chain, with many intermediate links, intervenes between the entertaining of a proposition and the state of affairs which makes the proposition true (for instance the proposition 'I shall be home by half past twelve'). Even in a very simple action, such as voluntarily blowing one's nose, or writing one's name in the Visitors' Book, there are many intermediate links between the thought and the event which fulfils it or makes it 'come true'.

Now in the examples we have been discussing (unlike these familiar examples of ordinary voluntary action) it seems as if a thought does directly make itself come true, without any intervening causal links. It seems that pure and simple thinking does sometimes 'make it so'. But perhaps if we look more closely, we may be able to find at least some intermediate links between the thought and the event which verifies it or fulfils it. Or if 'find' is too strong a word to use, at least we may be able to form some more or less plausible hypothesis about the kind of intermediate links there might be.

Let us consider the Vergilian type of example (*possunt qua posse videntur*) from this point of view. Why is the thought 'that

[1] In this section, I am much indebted to some critical comments and suggestions made by Miss F. Anstey of the University of Reading.

I can do it' so important? Partly because it makes you free to try. But perhaps it is better to begin with the negative case (*non possunt quia non posse videntur*). This was illustrated by the example of the man who cannot walk across the plank because he thinks he cannot, and also by the golfers who were 'beaten because they expected it', if we take this to mean 'They could not win or draw because they thought they could not'. Such thoughts as 'I cannot do it', 'It is quite impossible that I should succeed', plainly have an *inhibiting* effect. They prevent one from even trying to do the thing in question. The converse thought 'I *can* do it' enlarges the field of choice for you. It makes you free to try. And if you do try with this thought in mind, there is at least a chance that you will succeed; whereas there is no chance of success at all if you do not even try. When the negative thought 'I cannot do it' verifies itself, it does so by preventing you from trying, and this is an intermediate link between the thought and the state of affairs which verifies it. And when the positive thought 'I can do it' verifies itself, the intermediate link is the trying which this thought makes possible.

THOUGHTS AND EMOTIONS

Another relevant point is that the entertaining of a proposition, especially a proposition about oneself, is liable to have emotional effects: not only when it is believed, but also when it just occupies one's attention. The thought 'I cannot possibly get across' is very likely to have such effects when one wishes to get across, and other people (who have crossed already) are impatiently awaiting one on the other side. In such a situation, one is likely to feel both frightened and ashamed; and fear and shame are incapacitating emotions. The same applies to the golfers who expect to be beaten in the golf match (assuming that they do not wish to be beaten).

It is a very familiar fact that emotions can have a profound effect upon a person's bodily state. Here, then, is another intermediate link, which helps us to understand how the entertaining of a proposition about oneself can bring about a state of affairs which makes the proposition true. The entertaining of the proposition arouses emotions, and these in turn have a disabling effect upon one's body, so that it really is impossible for one to do the thing which one thinks it impossible to do. And perhaps the 'positive' thought 'I can do it' or 'We can win some holes at any rate' makes itself come true, or tends to make itself come true, by *preventing* the person from having such upsetting and disabling emotions; it enables him to 'keep cool'. This perhaps is the way in which this positive thought makes one free to try, and to make full use of whatever capacities one has.

The same intermediate link—the emotional state which the entertaining of a proposition is liable to induce—is also relevant to the medical examples: the patient who gets better, at at least gets better more quickly, because he thinks 'I am going to get better', and the converse case where 'I am never going to get better' retards his recovery, or is a contributory factor in preventing it. Whichever of these thoughts he has, whether the positive thought or the negative one, it is likely to arouse quite strong emotions in him: and it is not very surprising that these in their turn should affect his bodily state. No doubt there are complications here (unconscious or subconscious wishes may be relevant as well). But at any rate there is no reason to suppose that 'pure and simple thinking' is sufficient by itself to bring about a change in his state of health without any intermediate causal links at all.

EFFECTS OF SELF-SUGGESTION

Finally, let us consider the writer who gets stuck in his work, and manages to solve his problem by making a suggestion to himself before he goes to sleep. Perhaps it will be said that the intermediate link here is a purely physiological one. When he got stuck in his work yesterday evening he was tired. At 9.30 this morning, after a good night's sleep, he is fresh again; so it is not very surprising that the problem which seemed so difficult yesterday is now solved quite easily.

No doubt this is a relevant point, but it can hardly be the complete explanation. If it were, there would be no difference between 'sleeping on' some problem and merely sleeping. This rather odd phrase 'sleeping on' implies that the problem was in your mind just before you went to sleep. (It is helpful to make a brief mental survey of the main points in it just before going to sleep). Something else was in your mind as well: the thought, one might say the 'quietly confident' thought, that the solution is going to occur to you at 9.30 tomorrow morning.

Moreover, anyone who has used this method must have noticed that when the solution does come, it very often comes 'ready made'. The word 'come' is important. It is not that one makes a fresh start with the process of groping or searching, and succeeds this time whereas one failed before. The answer 'just comes', almost as if it were being told to you by someone else. All you have to do is to seize upon it and write it down at once; before it fades out of your mind again. After that, you *will*, no doubt, have to grope and search once more in order to work out its implications; and this will no doubt be easier because you have had a good night's sleep.

Here it is more difficult to find the intermediate link between the thought 'the solution will come' and the event which verifies it. The Ancients get round this difficulty by personifying the 'missing link'. They called it 'the Muse' (or 'a Muse', for they supposed that there were nine of them). Sometimes they would begin a poem by invoking the Muse: a very proper procedure, so far as it goes, and it may well have been a psychologically effective one, but somewhat too speculative if interpreted literally.

We need not go quite as far as this. Instead, we can use the hypothesis of subconscious or unconscious mental activity. We can suppose that there are thought-processes which go on in us, even though we are not conscious of the processes themselves, but only of the results which they eventually produce. There is no *a priori* reason for thinking that a person *must* be consciously aware of every mental event which occurs in him; and there are, of course, other phenomena, not only in our intellectual lives but in our emotional and conative lives as well, which cannot easily be explained unless we are willing to suppose that mental events (important ones too) can occur in a person without his being aware of them.

We notice also—and there is some consolation in it—that yesterday's work was by no means wasted, even though it seemed to end in failure. It turns out to have been a necessary condition for this morning's success. Without these apparently unavailing efforts, there would have been no material, so to speak, for our subconscious or unconscious mental processes to work upon. The necessary material was provided by the memories, or memory-traces, which yesterday's efforts left behind them.

For our purposes, however, it is sufficient to point out that here too we can at any rate suggest an intermediate link between the thought and the event which verifies it or fulfils it. We do not have to suppose that the thought 'the solution will come to me to-morrow morning' is sufficient by itself to bring about the desired result, by a kind of miraculous action-at-a-distance in time.

Nevertheless, it is important to consider the fairly numerous and various types of case in which 'thinking it will be so' does indeed contribute to 'making it so'; and in some of them, this thinking does seem to be a necessary condition for the coming about of the event which 'makes it so', even though it is never a sufficient one.

Are there still some cases left over, where 'thinking makes it so' without any intermediate causal links at all? Perhaps there are, but for that very reason we describe them as 'paranormal' or 'supernormal'. What puzzles us about both telepathy and telekinesis is precisely the fact that we have not so far succeeded in finding any intermediate causal links in either case. It does not follow that we never shall. But hitherto we have not found any intermediate links between the agent's experience and the percipient's experience in telepathy. In telekinesis too, where a person's thoughts or wishes appear to cause movements in objects outside his body without any kind of physical contact, direct or indirect, we have not yet succeeded in finding any series of intermediate causal links between the thoughts or wishes on the one hand, and the physical movements on the other.

LECTURE 7

MORAL BELIEFS[1]

From time to time we have had occasion to mention the close relation between belief and action, and we have seen more than once that the epistemology of belief overlaps with moral philosophy, or rather perhaps with practical philosophy, the philosophy of conduct or intelligent behaviour, of which moral philosophy is a part. (It is not obvious that everything we do must be either right or wrong. And even if it were, we could still consider some actions from a purely prudential point of view, in so far as they are directed to the fulfilment of the agent's own wishes, whether long-term wishes or short-term ones. To put it in a Kantian way, hypothetical imperatives play a very considerable part in our conduct, as well as categorical ones.)

It is not very surprising that there should be this close connection between practical philosophy and the epistemology of belief. After all, intelligent action consists very largely in acting 'under the guidance of' or 'in the light of' one's beliefs.

But there is one very obvious question which we have not yet considered. What is the nature of moral beliefs themselves? Perhaps this question should be raised in a wider form: what is the nature of valuational beliefs in general, of which moral beliefs are a special case? Not all value concepts are moral ones. We use and understand value words of many different sorts, not only 'right' 'wrong' 'ought' 'virtue' 'vice', but also 'charming' 'disagreeable' 'interesting' 'fine' 'tragic' 'tedious', and many more. And any of these words may occur in sentences which appear, at least, to express beliefs. 'I am sure that *The Mysteries of Udolpho* is a very tedious book.' 'You have not read it, but I have; and I

[1] These two lectures on Moral Beliefs are a somewhat expanded version of the Burtwood Lectures delivered at Cambridge in 1965, under the auspices of Corpus Christi College, Cambridge. I should like to express my gratitude to the Master and Fellows of the College for inviting me to deliver these annual lectures in that year, and also for allowing me to use a revised version of two of the orally-delivered Gifford Lectures for this purpose.

think (or my opinion is) that it is quite interesting.' 'My opinion is that the view from the top of Skiddaw southwards is one of the finest in England.' Nevertheless, it would be generally agreed that moral concepts are the most important of all value-concepts; and in this discussion I shall confine myself almost entirely to moral beliefs.

The main question I wish to consider is just this: are there moral *beliefs* at all? It is perfectly obvious that there are moral sentences, and that these sentences are frequently used both in our public and overt discourse, and also in the private or inner discourse of each one of us, where words publicly spoken or written are replaced by verbal imagery of an auditory or visual or kinaesthetic kind. It is a mistake to suppose, as some philosophers seem to, that an intelligent being is always talking, if talking means 'talking to someone else', and that this is the only way in which intelligence, or intelligence at the conceptual level, could possibly manifest itself. This is one of the errors of a collectivistic and sociologically-minded age.

But though we all agree that there are moral sentences, and though we might all agree that there are moral judgements, meaning by this 'whatever moral sentences are used to express', there is profound disagreement about the analysis of moral judgements. For more than two centuries, ever since the Moral Sense theory was propounded by Hutcheson, a controversy has been going on about the analysis of moral judgements, and it is still unsettled. But at least it has become a little clearer what the issue is. It can be put quite simply in this way: does the distinction between 'true' and 'false' apply to moral judgements?

MORAL FACTS

Suppose that a person has risked his life in order to save the life of someone else, and you say 'his action was right'. Are you saying something which is either true or false? It *is* true or false that the action was done, that it was done at such and such a time and place, with such and such an intention. But is it true (or false either) that the action was right?

If we agree with you and say 'Yes, it was right', do we think that there is a properfy called 'rightness' which the action had, as it had the property of being done in Clapham yesterday afternoon and of occupying a period of $4\frac{1}{2}$ minutes? Suppose you gave a very detailed description of the action, a detailed description of everything the man did during those $4\frac{1}{2}$ minutes and also of everything that was going on in his mind. Would you add at the end 'There is another rather interesting fact which I have forgotten to mention. His action was right'? If a statement is true, there is a fact which makes it true, and if it is false there is a fact which makes it false.

It is a fact that the action was done in Clapham yesterday afternoon. This is what makes it true to say that it was done there at that time; and the same fact makes it false to say that it was done somewhere else or at another time, for example in Brighton or yesterday morning. Is it also a fact that the action was right? Are there *moral* facts? If we think that an utterance such as 'this action was right' is true or false, we must think that there are moral facts. If there are, such utterances as 'this action was right' express either knowledge or belief. In that case, there are moral beliefs and they are either correct or mistaken, as any other belief is.

Yet the notion of a 'moral fact' is rather a strange one. It is not easy to see what kind of a fact it could be, or in what sense it could be a fact at all. The view that rightness and wrongness are properties which actions have is likewise a strange one. It is still odder, perhaps, to say that *obligatoriness* is a property which some actions have, and that you are ascribing this property to an action (or rather, to a possible action?) when you tell me that I ought to do it.

It is not very surprising, then, that some philosophers have doubted whether the disjunction 'either true or false' applies to moral judgements at all. What is surprising is that the view that they are neither true nor false was only suggested fairly recently. Even Hutcheson and Hume were not wholly clear about it. They could be interpreted as maintaining that there *are* moral facts, but that they are facts about our own feelings. Hume says, for example, that a virtuous action is one which pleases us after a particular manner. He is certainly denying that there is a property called 'virtuousness' which the action itself has. Nevertheless, if someone who says it is virtuous is saying that it pleases him after a particular manner, surely he *is* saying something true or false about himself? Autobiographical remarks can be true or false. Indeed, he is perhaps saying something true or false about the action too, namely that it has the causal property of exciting a special sort of pleasant feeling in him when he witnesses or recalls or is told about this action. Hutcheson's Moral Sense theory could be interpreted in a similar 'autobiographical' way.

But such an interpretation of either writer would not, perhaps, be altogether fair. Perhaps what they wish to say is that when we make a moral judgement about some action, we are *expressing* our feelings about the action or our attitude towards it, and not stating that we have these feelings or this attitude. It is rather as if we took off our hat to the action or to the person who did it, or saluted him or congratulated him by saying 'Well done!' The most appropriate name for this feeling or this experienced attitude is 'approval', or 'disapproval' when the words we say are 'it was wrong' (this would be rather like shaking our fist at the man). This seems to me the most plausible version of the doctrine that moral judgements are neither true nor false. One may call it the Approval Analysis of moral judgements, or the Attitudinarian Analysis.

There is however another version of the doctrine that moral judgements are neither true nor false, and here it is held that they are analogous to imperatives. On this view, when I say to you 'This is the right thing to do' it is rather like saying 'Go on! Do it!' And if I say 'It was wrong to do that' this is rather like saying 'Don't do that sort of thing again'. I am not telling you *that* something is the case, as I should be if I were making a statement. It is more like telling you *to* do something, or not to do it.

But of course we cannot quite say that all moral judgements are commands. If we make the judgement 'Brutus ought not to have killed Caesar' or 'his killing of Caesar was wrong', it is too late now to tell him not to do it, or even to tell him not to do that sort of thing again. Moreover, if someone in Cambodia is now asking himself whether he shall pay his grocer's bill, we cannot very well tell him to pay it, though we can say that he will be acting rightly if he does pay it.

Nevertheless, it might be maintained that all these utterances *resemble* commands much more than they resemble statements, and that we might describe them as injunctions. When we say 'Brutus ought not to have killed Caesar' or 'it was wrong of him to do it' we might be saying something like this: "Let no one assassinate any of his political opponents, ever. But Brutus did assassinate one of his, when he killed Caesar.' And similarly: 'Let anyone who owes money to anyone else pay it. So if there is a man in Cambodia who owes money to his grocer, let him pay it.' (The word 'let' has the force of the Latin gerundive, *faciendum.*)

This version of the doctrine that moral judgements are neither true nor false may be called the Injunctive Analysis. There are several different varieties of it, and the one I chiefly have in mind is Professor R. M. Hare's in his well-known book *The Language of Morals.* But it must not be forgotten that the notion of an imperative plays a fundamental part in Kant's moral philosophy. Moreover, the theory that we mean by 'right actions' those actions which God commands, and by 'wrong actions' those which God forbids, is perhaps almost as old as Theistic religion itself. But though God's commands or prohibitions could not themselves be true or false, it *would* still be true or false that God has commanded us to do actions of one sort and has forbidden us to do actions of another sort. This theory, then, is irrelevant to our present discussion, though historically it may have helped to suggest the Injunctive Analysis of moral judgements by maintaining that moral judgements are at any rate closely related to commands.

THE APPROVAL ANALYSIS

In these two lectures we shall mostly be concerned with the Approval Analysis or Attitudinarian Analysis, as it may also be called. Your lecturer must confess that he has a prejudice in its favour, because it seems to accord with his own moral experience: if indeed he has any, for the writings of some moral philosophers make him suspect that he is not a moral being at all. But perhaps there are some others who feel a kind of spiritual affinity with the eighteenth century British Moralists of the so-called 'Sentimental' school; and it may be worth while to try to reformulate the approval analysis in the terminology of our own time, and to consider some implications of it which its original inventors did not sufficiently emphasize.

But before we turn to this task, there is one general remark to be made. It would be misleading to say that according to this type of moral philosophy the function of the word 'right' is *merely* to express an attitude of approval and the function of the word 'wrong' is *merely* to express an attitude of disapproval. For the word 'merely' suggests that it does not matter very much what a man approves of, and that the difference between approving and disapproving is not particularly important. It should not be supposed (though perhaps it sometimes has been) that according to theories of this type 'there is really no difference between right and wrong' and that those who hold them do not take the moral life seriously.

On the contrary, if it is the function of the word 'right' to express approval and of the word 'wrong' to express disapproval, they have a very important function indeed, and it still makes a very great difference to our lives and to our relations with our neighbours whether we say of an action 'it is right' or 'it is wrong'. Moreover, the difference which it makes is exactly as great as it is if moral judgements *are* true or false. On that view, there are moral facts, and a moral judgement is true if it corresponds with a moral fact and false if it does not. But even so, one might still fail to take such facts seriously. One might say 'Oh well, no doubt it *is* a fact that this action of mine was wrong. But what of it? Why make such a fuss about it? Why does it matter?'

Whether we take moral distinctions seriously is decided by considering how we live—in our inner lives as well as our overt behaviour—and not by considering which analysis of moral judgements we subscribe to.

'THERE OBVIOUSLY ARE MORAL BELIEFS'

But is it worth while to pay much attention to the doctrine that moral judgements are neither true nor false—either to the 'approval' version of it or to any other—if it entails (as it seems to) that there are no moral beliefs? Surely it is perfectly obvious that there *are* moral beliefs?

Still, we must not forget the distinction between belief 'that' and belief 'in'.[1] It is indeed obvious that there are moral beliefs-in. And these are what we are usually enquiring about when we ask what Mr. So-and-So's moral beliefs are. For example, he believes in telling the truth always, no matter what the circumstances are: or he believes in turning the other cheek, whatever the provocation. But when a man expresses a belief 'in' a type of action or a rule of conduct, he *is* expressing a valuational attitude. It need not be an attitude of moral approval. A man might believe in telling the truth always as being the most expedient policy, the one which pays best in the long run, despite some appearances to the contrary. But often a belief-in is, *inter alia*, an attitude of moral approval, and then a moral belief-in is at least a part of it. The same could be said of belief-in a person, for example the belief which most Englishmen had in Winston Churchill during the years 1940–45. This belief-in was amongst other things an attitude of moral approval, though it was also a trust in his intelligence, resourcefulness, energy and efficiency.

But is it not perfectly obvious that there are moral beliefs, and not just moral beliefs-in, but also moral beliefs-that? Surely it is true, for example, that moral judgements are made with different degrees of confidence? One may think that an action was wrong, without being sure that it was. One may be almost sure that it was wrong, but not absolutely sure; or again one may be absolutely sure, completely convinced, that it was wrong. To put it in another way, it clearly makes sense to ask the question 'was it wrong?' This question may be answered with different degrees of confidence, and we express these degrees of confidence in just the same way as the different degrees of confidence we may have when we believe that something is the case. Or again, we may be unable to answer the question; we may remain undecided between the two alternatives 'it was wrong' and 'there was nothing wrong in it', just as we are when we suspend judgement concerning the alternatives 'it rained in Glasgow last Sunday' and 'there was no rain in Glasgow last Sunday'. The same belief-like expressions are appropriate when we make moral judgements about a person (as opposed to an action). 'I think he is a kind person and an honest one too.' To this you may reply 'I am quite sure he is kind, and

[1] See Lecture 9, below.

I think he is honest too, though I am not absolutely sure about that'.

What are we to make of such utterances, if we accept the view that moral judgements are neither true nor false? There is an analogous case which we might perhaps find useful. I ask a friend where he is going to spend the Easter holiday this year, and he answers 'I think I shall go to Brighton, but I am not quite sure'.[1] Is he expressing an opinion? Is he making a true or false prediction about his whereabouts a month or so hence, though he makes it with something less than complete conviction? Is his utterance comparable with another which he makes 'I think the Easter week-end will be cold, as it often is'?

Now let us suppose that on Easter Monday I meet him in Yarmouth, and also that it is a fine warm day all over the country. I say to him 'So your forecast about your whereabouts was false after all. You were mistaken when you said you were going to be at Brighton; you made a mistake about the weather too.' But obviously when he said 'I think I shall go to Brighton, but I am not quite sure' he was not expressing an opinion at all (though he was, when he said he thought the Easter week-end would be cold). This is not because it is impossible to have opinions about one's own future actions. We do have them sometimes. I express such an opinion when I say 'I think I shall be sending this book to the publishers about three years from now'. This *is* just a moderately confident prediction or forecast about myself. It may quite well be false. I may easily be dead three years from now; and even though I am still alive at that time, it is perfectly possible that the book will not be ready for the publishers by then.

But the man who said 'I think I shall go to Brighton, but I am not quite sure' was not making a moderately confident prediction about his own future, nor was he saying anything true or false. He was expressing an intention, but a provisional and revisable one, and the words 'I think . . . but I am not quite sure' were a way of indicating its provisional and revisable character. Of course, he could also have used these words 'I think . . . but I am not quite sure' if he had been expressing an opinion. But that is because opinions too have a provisional and revisable character.

[1] In the United States, I am told, it is quite common for a person who is offered a choice between two cakes to say 'I *believe* I'll take this one'.

In a similar way, one might be expressing a provisional and revisable disapproval when one says 'I think it was wrong to do that, but I am not quite sure' and a provisional and revisable approval when one says 'I think it would be right to tell him, but I am not quite sure'. On the other hand, if you say you *are* quite sure it would be right to tell him—you have no doubt of it at all—we might hold that your attitude is one of firm and settled approval, and does not have the provisional and revisable character which mine has.

Such utterances as 'I am quite sure he is a kind man, and I think he is an honest man too, but I am not quite sure about that' might be elucidated in a similar way. One is here expressing two approval-attitudes about the same person (approving of him in two different respects). The first approval is firm and settled, the second is provisional and revisable. We are also able to give a meaning to the question 'was it right?' or 'is he a good man?', even if we do not think the answer to it is true or false. (The answer to the question 'Where are you going for the Easter holiday?' was not true or false either.) We can say that when one asks someone else, or oneself, 'was that action right?' or 'is he a good man?' the question expresses an undecided or indeterminate moral attitude.[1] One has not made up one's mind whether to approve or to disapprove; much as a man might ask another man, or himself 'Shall I go to Brighton?' when he has not made up his mind whether to go there or not.

There is one other point which should be mentioned now (I shall say more about it later).[2] Approvals and disapprovals have presuppositions, somewhat as beliefs-in have. As we shall see later, we approve or disapprove of an action, or a person, in respect of some characteristic which we believe it or him to have. This belief may be called the presupposition of our approving or disapproving attitude. This belief is a straightforward belief-that, about some matter of physical or psychological fact; and what is believed is true or false, in the straightforward sense in which it is true or false that it rained in Glasgow last Sunday. If the belief is mistaken, awkward questions arise about the approval or

[1] Cf. the question 'What am I to do?' which is an expression of indecision. The answer to it (usually) is an exhortation or a piece of advice, and neither of these is true or false.

[2] See pp. 398–9, below.

disapproval whose presupposition it is. But the point at present is that this belief, like any other belief about matters of fact, may be held with varying degrees of confidence.

If the belief is held with only a moderate degree of confidence and itself has a provisional and revisable character, the approving or disapproving attitude, whose presupposition it is, will also have a provisional and revisable character, at least if one is a reasonable person. If I think, but am not absolutely sure, that you intentionally caused great pain to another human being, I do disapprove of your action, but only in a provisional and revisable way. I say 'I think it was wrong, but I am not absolutely sure'; but I say so because I think, without being absolutely sure, that it *was* intentional, and *did* cause great pain. In this case, the disapproval is provisional and revisable because the factual belief which is its presupposition is provisional and revisable, an opinion and not a conviction.

Nevertheless, even though one is absolutely sure about the physical and psychological facts—even though one knows what they are in a fairly strict sense of the word 'know'—one's approving or disapproving attitude may still be provisional and revisable. This may easily happen when the action we are making a moral judgement about—whether past or proposed, our own action or another's—is one in which the agent is confronted with a conflict of duties. An obvious example is the action of telling a lie when the agent cannot otherwise keep a secret with which he has been entrusted. This action is wrong in one respect but right in another. This amounts to saying, on the theory we are discussing, that we approve of it in respect of one characteristic which it has, and disapprove of it in respect of another. The question is, whether to approve of it 'on the whole' or to disapprove of it 'on the whole'. Whichever of these two attitudes we eventually adopt, it is likely to be a provisional and revisable one, expressed by saying 'I think it is on the whole right but I am by no means sure' or 'I think it is on the whole wrong but I am by no means sure', even though in this case we are in no doubt at all about the physical or psychological facts.

So far, we conclude that although we do use and understand such expressions as 'I think it was wrong', 'I am sure it is right', this does not by itself settle the question whether there are moral beliefs in the belief-that sense. Let us now try another approach to that question.

'ETHICS WITHOUT PROPOSITIONS'

There is a well known paper by Professor W. H. F. Barnes called 'Ethics without propositions'.[1] Possibly the type of ethical theory he has in mind should rather be described as 'Ethics without assertions'. Indeed, he himself suggests so. It cannot be literally without propositions, since we have to entertain propositions e.g. 'an act of such and such a sort was done by So-and-So' in order to approve or disapprove. Sometimes we not only entertain the proposition but also believe it; sometimes we know it to be true. I may believe on good, though not conclusive, evidence that *A* told a lie to *B*, and disapprove of this action which I believe him to have done. Again, I may approve of some action which I actually witnessed yesterday and now clearly recall, or disapprove of one which I did a minute or two ago myself. Sometimes, however, we just entertain the proposition in a neutral way, without either belief or disbelief; we may approve or disapprove of a proposed action which has not yet been done and perhaps never will be. Indeed, if we disapprove, and express our disapproval, this may be sufficient to prevent its being done.

Could we say, then, that such an ethical theory is at any rate without *ethical* propositions, though certainly not without propositions concerning the 'natural' (non-ethical) characteristics of actions? Not quite. For surely the propositions which are the objects of our approvals and disapprovals may themselves contain ethical concepts, and frequently do? 'John has not done what he promised to do' is an obvious example. To make a promise to do something is to lay a moral obligation on oneself to do it. The concept of a promise, then, is very far from being an extra-moral or morally-neutral concept. What should we have to do to turn this proposition into a purely factual one, describing the situation in entirely non-ethical terms? The question is not easy to answer, but perhaps we could say something like this: 'John said to Tom the *words* "I promise to be back in half an hour", well under-

[1] *Aristotelian Society Supp. Vol.*, 1948, pp 1-39.

standing what he said: and then he went away; and more than half an hour has elapsed, and he has not come back although it was in his power to do so.'

Again '*A* has taken *B*'s watch' might appear to be a completely non-ethical proposition. But the little apostrophe *s* in the phrase '*B*'s watch' conveys the idea of property, and this again is certainly not an extra-moral or morally-neutral concept. If something is a man's property, he has a *right*, within limits, to use it as he pleases. What should we mean by saying that he has this right, if we accepted the Approval Analysis? We should be expressing approval of his having the power, within limits, to use the object in question as he pleases, and disapproval of any action by any other person which restricts, or deprives him of, this power. It follows, that in saying '*A* has taken *B*'s watch' we are already expressing disapproval of what *A* has done: unless we add 'with *B*'s permission', for one way in which *B* can do what he pleases with the watch is to lend it or give it to another person, and then he transfers his own power to use it as he pleases to someone else, either temporarily or permanently. What we shall have to say if we want to make a purely factual assertion is something like this. '*A* removed a certain watch from the place where it previously was, with the result that *B* involuntarily lost the power, which he had up to that time, of using it within limits as he pleased.' But would this be adequate, unless we also said 'and this power was one which we approved of his having'? For *B* might have had this power *de facto* for a long time, even though the watch was not his at all.

It is indeed exceedingly difficult to give an ethically-neutral analysis of the phrase '*B*'s watch'. Some additional clause is certainly needed. But perhaps it might be suggested that we need not necessarily be expressing approval of *B*'s power of using the watch, within limits, as he pleased. Might it be sufficient to say that such a power is in fact generally approved of? Conceivably we ourselves disapprove of what is called 'the institution of property' or take a neutral attitude about it, neither approving nor disapproving.

It is, of course, a matter of fact that approvals and disapprovals do exist, and it is an important fact too, which often has to be mentioned when one is trying to describe a social situation. A historian, for example, often has to mention the moral judgements which were made by the people he is describing, since much of their conduct would otherwise be unintelligible. But in so doing, he need not make any moral judgements himself. And certainly he need not himself approve of what they approved of (e.g. treating slaves as one pleases) or disapprove of what they disapproved of (e.g. refraining from taking vengeance for personal insults). What *is* necessary is that he should be capable of making moral judgements himself, and know from personal experience what it is like to approve of one type of conduct and disapprove of another. In short, the historian himself must be a moral being. Otherwise, he will not understand what he is talking about, and the moral judgements of the persons whom he is describing will be for him no more than curious noises which they made, inexplicably followed by wars, assassinations, rebellions and other catastrophic occurrences.

Perhaps, however, it is not very surprising that ethical words (those expressing approvals and disapprovals) should be so deeply rooted in our discourse that it is very difficult to get rid of them, and therefore very difficult to describe human actions in completely non-ethical terms. We do happen to be moral beings, after all. Or rather, we do not just happen to be. For if we were not, we should not be persons, though we might still be intelligent creatures with a human shape.

SOME LOGICAL PROPERTIES OF ATTITUDES

The examples we have been considering 'John has not done what he promised to do' and '*A* has taken *B*'s watch' could also be used to illustrate another point, and a more important one. They show that even if moral judgements are neither true nor false, they may still have logical properties. Even in 'Ethics without assertions' moral judgements may still have an analytic character, as they may in objectivist Ethics which holds that they *are* assertions. On either theory, it is wrong by definition to break a promise when it is in one's power to keep it; and on either theory it is wrong by definition to take someone else's property without his permission. No doubt, in both these examples, it might sometimes be the lesser of two wrongs. Taking someone else's property without his permission, or breaking a promise which we had made, might be the only way of saving a man's life in an emergency. Nevertheless, there is still *something* wrong in both these actions, even though it is 'on the whole' or 'on balance' right to do them in some exceptional circumstances. That there is something wrong in both of them is a matter of definition. It follows from the definition of the term 'property' in the one case, and of the term 'promise' in the other. This is still so, if we say that 'this is *X*'s property' just expresses our approval of his having the power, within limits, of using the object as he pleases and our disapproval of anyone who makes it impossible for him to use it thus; and likewise if we say that 'these words consitute a promise' just expresses our approval of the speaker's doing the action which the words describe (e.g. coming back half an hour from now) and our disapproval of his failure to do this action when it was in his power to do it.

But though a man who says 'it is wrong to break a promise' has expressed an *analytic* disapproval, as we may call it, he has nevertheless expressed something, and has conveyed something to his hearers. He has conveyed to us that he does have a moral attitude towards anyone who says 'I promise to do such and such an action' and then fails to do it, even though he still has the power to do it. Moreover, he has conveyed to us what that attitude is, and has shown us that he attaches the same meaning, or force, to the word 'promise' as we do.

It is possible, however, that an expression of approval might convey nothing. It might be completely empty or 'vacuous', and 'vacuity' too is an important logical property. Suppose I visit a strange country and wish to find out what the moral attitudes of the inhabitants are. I go to their wisest man and question him about it. He replies 'There are no moral disagreements here, as I am told there are in your part of the world. Here we are quite unanimous in our moral judgements. We all approve of right actions and of good men; and we all disapprove of wrong actions and of bad men.' Clearly he has told me nothing. He might as well have said 'All of us here approve of some actions and some men, and all of us disapprove of other actions and of other men'. The most I could learn from what he has said is that these people do have moral attitudes of some sort; and I was sure of this already.

It is worth while to notice that other sorts of 'non-assertive' utterances can be vacuous in a similar way. 'Do what you please' is a vacuous command. Though it has the verbal form of a command, there is nothing which it tells us to do, at any rate if we take it to mean *fac quod tibi placet*. (If we took it to mean 'Do what gives you pleasure' it could conceivably be disobeyed, and would therefore not be vacuous.) Again, suppose someone comes to me for advice and I say to him 'Just do what you think best'. My advice is empty, because it gives him no guidance at all about what he is to do. It is in fact a polite way of refusing to give him what he asked for.

Self-contradictoriness is another important logical property. If moral judgements are true or false it is analytically false, self-contradictory, to say 'there is nothing wrong in breaking a promise'. It cannot be analytically false to say this, if the attitudinarian moralists are right, because it cannot be false at all. Nevertheless, anyone who says it is still making an utterance which is in some sense self-stultifying or absurd. It is not open to us to reply 'Oh no, that cannot possibly be true'. The speaker never claimed that it was, if the approval analysis of moral judgements is correct. But it *is* open to us to reply 'Oh no, we cannot possibly agree with that', because there is an obvious impropriety in the way he has expressed himself. And the impropriety is a logical one. By saying 'there is nothing wrong in' he has expressed absence of disapproval; and then, by completing his sentence with the phrase 'the breaking of a promise' he has expressed disapproval, since we mean by 'a promise' a form of words such that we disapprove of the speaker's subsequent failure to do the action described in them, if it is still in his power at that time to do the action described.

LOGICAL PROPERTIES, CONTINUED: GENERALITY

Other logical properties come to light when we notice that it makes sense to ask *why* one approves (or disapproves) of such and such an action or of such and such a person. We approve of what John did, because he had promised to do it, and we approve of *any* action which is the keeping of a promise, or in so far as it is. I approve of you for giving a lift to a lame man and going ten miles out of your way to take him where he wanted to go, because I approve of *anyone* who takes some trouble to help anyone else who is in need of help. We disapprove of torturing suspected persons in order to get information from them, because it is cruel, and we disapprove of *any* cruel action even when it is done in order to achieve a result which in itself we approve of, such as the more efficient detection of criminals.

We see from these examples that there can be *general* approvals and disapprovals. We can and do approve not only of this person or this action, but of a *class* of actions or persons; and the same applies to disapproval.

It may be noted that many other human attitudes (and the verbal expressions of them) can have this same property of generality: for example, liking and disliking, admiring, being afraid of, even wishing. One may like cats: not just this cat or that one, but cats in general or cats as such. One may be afraid of Alsatian dogs, not just of the particular one which lives at the house round the corner, but of Alsatian dogs as such. These attitudes are relatively permanent ones. But even a very temporary one, such as wishing for a cup of tea now, may still have something general about it. Within quite wide limits any cup of tea will do. I am quite willing to drink this one in the Refreshment Room at the railway station, because it is at any rate *a* cup of tea.

Indeed, it may seem plausible to suggest that all the attitudes we have are in some respect or degree general. But this is not true of all the attitudes we can have towards other persons. There is one important exception, the attitude which may be called unconditional love. According to Christian ethics it is the best of all possible attitudes. So anyone who is discussing moral questions should say at least a few words about it, though I myself say them with fear and trembling.

It might be described as a non-general pro-attitude; and just for that reason, there is something paradoxical and mysterious about it, though it does exist, or at least approximations to it do. It differs from what one might call 'ordinary liking'. For in ordinary liking there is an answer to the question 'What is there about So and So that you like?' or 'in respect of what characteristic of his do you like him?' But here there is no answer. (You would still be 'for' this other person, no matter what he does and no matter what changes he undergoes, whether for the worse or for the better.) Or if there is an answer, it will have to be 'in respect of his *haecceitas*'. You are 'for him' just as being the individual that he is: just *this* person. And the notion of *haecceitas* is a very mysterious one indeed.[1]

But so far as one can see, nothing like this is true of approval and disapproval. Unconditional love is not itself a moral attitude. It is indeed the object of a moral attitude: it is something of which we approve very highly. But it is not itself a kind of approval. Indeed, it is quite compatible with disapproval. We may suppose that St Paul loved his Corinthian converts in this unconditional way, but he certainly disapproved of some of the things they did. Perhaps the most appropriate thing to say of unconditional love is that it transcends the sphere of morality altogether. For when we approve of some particular action, we do approve of it as being an instance of some *type* or *kind* of action; and when we approve of a particular person, we approve of him in respect of some characteristic or conjunction of characteristics which he has (usually dispositional ones); and these are *general* characteristics which other persons may have, such as courage or benevolence or trustworthiness. The same applies to disapproval. Approval and disapproval do have the logical property of generality, as many of our other attitudes have.

AN ANALOGUE OF DEDUCTIVE REASONING

We may now notice another logical property which approvals and disapprovals have. It is closely connected with this property of generality. Something analogous to *deductive reasoning* is possible in the sphere of approval and disapproval. Perhaps we may not wish to call it deductive reasoning, since expressions of approval of disapproval are neither true nor false. But at any rate we can speak of *logical derivation* here, and it is at any rate analogous to deductive reasoning of the syllogistic sort.

[1] Or perhaps the answer to 'what is there about him that you have a pro-attitude to?' is 'everything'. But this suggests the equally mysterious doctrine of 'individual essences', propounded by Leibniz.

That is what makes it possible to answer the question 'Why do you approve of this particular action?' or 'Why do you approve of this particular person?' (and also 'Why do you disapprove?'). We have seen already that such questions can often be asked and answered. We answer, first, by expressing approval of *all* actions of a certain kind or sort, and secondly by expressing our belief that this particular action was an instance of that kind or sort. We approve of *all* actions in which one person helps another person who is in difficulties,[1] and we believe that William did an action of this kind at 2.15 p.m. this afternoon, when he helped a blind man to cross the High Street. So we approve of the particular action which he did at 2.15 p.m. this afternoon. The same applies to our moral attitudes to a particular person. We disapprove of Archibald because he is unreliable; he hardly ever does what he has undertaken to do. We disapprove of all persons who seldom do what they have undertaken to do, and we believe that Archibald is a person of that sort.

This derivation-procedure is analogous to the syllogistic deduction 'All whales are mammals, and this creature is a whale; so this creature is a mammal'. The analogy is not, of course, complete. According to the theory we are considering, the major. premiss in our moral derivation-procedure is neither true nor false. It consists just in expressing an attitude to a type or sort of actions (or persons). The conclusion too is neither true nor false. Of the three distinguishable stages in our derivation-procedure—major premiss, minor premiss, and conclusion—it is only the minor premiss which is true or false. It *is* either true or false that William helped a blind man to cross the High Street at 2.15 p.m.; and it is either true or false that Archibald seldom does what he has undertaken to do.

Nevertheless, this derivation-procedure does resemble deductive reasoning in a very striking way, and it seems quite proper to apply the word 'logical' to it. In the example about helping the blind man, we are *committed* to approving of this particular action. And the commitment is a logical one. We cannot *consis-*

[1] If one burglar helps another burglar who has got into difficulties while climbing down a drain-pipe, do we approve of his action? Yes, in so far as it was an act of kindness or beneficence. But it had other characteristics as well. It was part of a burglarious joint-enterprise, which we disapprove of.

tently refuse to approve of this particualr action, if we approve of all actions in which one person helps another person who is in trouble, and believe that this particular action was an action of that kind.

The derivation-procedure which we have just considered depends on the relation between a type or sort on the one hand, and a particular instance of that type or sort on the other. This relation could also be described as the relation of class-membership. But there is another logical derivation-procedure which depends upon the relation of class-inclusion, i.e. the relation between a wider class and a narrower class included in it. This relation too enables us to express derivative or consequential approvals and disapprovals, and to answer the question 'Why do you approve (or disapprove)?'

For example, a celebrated Oxford philosopher, one of my own teachers, once expressed his strong disapproval of pictorial advertisements. When asked why he disapproved of them, he answered that such advertisements were ways of telling a lie without making a statement. The poster we see at the railway station advertising the seaside town of Snoring juxta Mare does not actually say 'the sun always shines there', but the picture conveys that impression and is intended to convey it.

We may analyse the philosopher's derivation-procedure as follows. In his major premiss he expresses disapproval of all voluntarily deceitful behaviour; in his minor premiss he expresses his belief that all displaying of pictorial advertisements is voluntarily deceitful behaviour; and in his conclusion he expresses his disapproval of all displaying of pictorial advertisements.

Of course, we may question his minor premiss, which expresses a straightforward 'belief that', and is either true or false. We may doubt whether such advertisements are intended to deceive, and also whether they do in fact deceive anyone. But we cannot object to the derivation-procedure which he used. It is a perfectly valid (logically-proper) way of explaining to us *why* he disapproved of all pictorial advertisements.

UNDERIVABLE APPROVALS AND DISAPPROVALS

It could fairly be said, I think, that in using either of these derivation-methods we are *justifying* our approvals and our disapprovals, whether of persons or of actions, as we justify our assertions and our denials by deductive arguments: and this, despite the radical difference there is between assertions and denials, which are true or false, and approvals or disapprovals, which are neither.

Finally, we may notice that in both cases alike the process of justification must stop somewhere; and this is another important logical feature which they have in common. If you ask me why I approve of charitable actions as such, I can only answer 'I just do approve of them, that's all. And surely you do too?' If it is said that this approval of mine is analytic, on the ground that the word 'charitable' already expresses approval, I have to reformulate my answer, but I still cannot justify it. 'I just do approve of anyone who loves his neighbour and tries to promote his neighbour's happiness or decrease his neighbour's misery. And surely you do too?' Suppose you disagree and say 'such people are silly and sentimental', thereby expressing disapproval; or perhaps you say 'people are welcome to behave in that way if they wish, of course, but there is nothing either good or bad about it' (expressing a neutral attitude, neither approval nor disapproval). Then there is nothing more that I can do to justify my own attitude. Nor would there be anything more I could do, if I were asked why I disapprove of causing pain to other sentient beings merely for the sake of one's own pleasure. Here again, I could only say 'I just do disapprove of it, that's all; and surely you do too?'

But of course the process of justifying an assertion or denial by deductive argument has to stop somewhere too. At some stage or other, we encounter indemonstrable premisses, as we encounter 'underivable' approvals or disapprovals. We certainly encounter such indemonstrable premisses if we hold an 'objectivist' view of ethics and maintain that moral judgements *are*, affter all, true or false. Suppose someone says that causing pain to other sentient beings merely for the sake of one's own pleasure is something which has an objective property of wrongness, regardless of anyone's approval or disapproval, and we ask him to justify what he has said. He can only reply 'I just *see* (or 'I just know intuitively') that it is so. And surely you can see it for yourself?' There still have to be what one might call 'ultimate' or 'underivable' moral judgements, whether we accept or reject the view that moral judgements are true or false.

IMPLICIT GENERALITY

Our conclusion so far is that 'ethics without propositions' (or 'without assertions' if we prefer) is certainly not ethics without logic. I have been speaking throughout about the approval analysis of moral judgements; but the same is true of the injunctive analysis. There is a 'logic of imperatives', as Professor R. M. Hare has shown. It would seem that there is a logic of approvals too; at any rate, we can say that approvals and disapprovals have logical properties. The one with which we have so far been most concerned is generality. We have seen that some approvals and disapprovals are general ones. Could it be said that *all* are? It could be said, at any rate, that all approvals and disapprovals have something general about them, even when what is approved of or disapproved of is a particular action or a particular person. They always have at least 'implicit' generality.

This is because we approve (or disapprove) of a particular entity *as having* such and such a characteristic, or *in respect of* some characteristic which it has, or *in that* it has some characteristic; and the same applies to disapproval. It is conceivable (and in many cases it is true) that other entities also have this same characteristic. I approve of your sending a cheque for £5 3s. 2d. to your bookseller. This is a particular action, done by a particular person, on a particular day. But I approve of it as being the payment of a debt. And this characteristic which it has is one which many other actions may have, actions done by other persons at other times and places. I approve of *A* as being a kind and friendly person and of *B* as being an honest one, and these are characteristics which other persons may have. I disapprove of myself as being afraid of Alsatian dogs, and afraid of many other things too which no man whom I approve would be afraid of. And this again is a characteristic which other persons may share.

This is the explanation of something which might otherwise puzzle us, the fact that we can both approve and disapprove of the same action, or person, at the same time. I approve of your action as being the payment of a debt; I disapprove of it in that it is a very belated payment, since you received the bill two and a half years ago. I approve of your making that remark to Robert just now, in that you were telling him the truth; I also disapprove of your making it, in respect of your unkind or discourteous way of putting it. We approve of King Henry VIII for his courage and his patriotism, but disapprove of him for his cruelty.

It would seem, then, that even in a particular approval or disapproval, where we approve (or disapprove) of just this action, or this person, there is something which might be called 'implicit generality'. In approving of this particular action in respect of the characteristic *C* which it has, we are implicitly approving of any other action which has the characteristic *C*.

APPROVALS 'PRESUPPOSE' BELIEFS ABOUT MATTERS OF FACT

We must notice, however, that the characteristic in respect of which we approve of something are not merely characteristics which it does in fact possess. We must know or believe that it does possess them. It may be a fact that hundreds of Eskimos are at this moment engaged in telling the truth to other Eskimos, but it is impossible for me to approve of what they are doing, since I am completely unaware of it. Even if I were on the spot and actually heard one Eskimo telling the truth to another, it would not be in my power either to approve or to disapprove of what he was doing, because I should not be able to understand what he was saying. To approve or to disapprove of something 'as having' the characterisitc *C*, one must either believe or know that it does have the characteristic *C*; and this is true whether the something is a person or an action. Moreover, in actual fact the entity in question need not have the characteristic *C* at all. It is enough that I *believe* that it has, whether on good evidence or not, whether correctly or incorrectly. And this belief, of course, is not itself a moral belief, nor is it a belief 'in'. It is a straightforward belief 'that' concerning some matter of physical or psychological fact.

If this belief is incorrect, it does not follow that the moral judgement I make is false. On the view we are discussing, it cannot be either false or true; what I am doing, when I make it, is just to approve, or to disapprove. Nevertheless, there is clearly some sense in which it is a mistake to approve, or disapprove, of *X*, if *X* does not really have the characteristic *C* in respect of which we approve or disapprove. It may be a very grave mistake too. It is no light matter to disapprove of a man for something which he did not do. Or if the word 'mistake' be thought too strong (on the ground that it suggests that there are 'moral facts' after all) at any rate we can say that such a disapproval is misguided or misplaced.

The same point could be put in another way by using the word 'presupposition' which I used earlier: although moral judgements cannot (on this view) be true or false, they nevertheless have 'presuppositions'[1] which *are* true or false. The same could be said of other 'non-assertive' attitudes, such as wishing and hoping, to which the distinction between truth and falsehood does not apply. If someone wishes to visit Utopia, or hopes to live there some day, it is a vain wish or a vain hope, because there is no such place. We are under a misapprehension if we cherish such a wish or such a hope; it has a false presupposition.[2]

Moreover, an approval or disapproval may be questionable, or doubtfully acceptable, because it has a questionable presupposition, even though it itself is neither true nor false. The fourth century saint, St Martin of Tours, cut his cloak in half and gave one half to a beggar. He was a serving Roman soldier at the time, wearing his armour. (At least, that is how he is commonly represented, and we will assume that the representation is correct.)

[1] See p. 384–5 above: I have borrowed this useful technical term from Professor P. F. Strawson, though he has not, I think, himself used it in this 'Ethico-logical' or 'Ethico-epistemological' context.

[2] Cf. 'They were afraid where no fear was'. They really were afraid, of course. To call it an 'imaginary fear' is therefore misleading. The fear actually existed and actually had effects. But it had a false presupposition. They believed, mistakenly, that the enemy were attacking them.

It was his military cloak which he cut—and then gave away half of it—and he cut it with his sword which was also part of his military equipment. We approve of his action highly, in that it was an act of Christian charity. But perhaps we also disapprove of it, in that he was bisecting what was not his to bisect, and giving away what was not his to give. The cloak, we say, was not his property, after all. It was part of his uniform, like a British soldier's greatcoat, and it was the Emperor's property, as the British soldier's greatcoat is the property of the Queen. St Martin has no right to do as he liked with it. The sword was not his property either, any more than the British soldier's bayonet is. He was not at liberty to use it just as he pleased, and certainly he was not at liberty to use it for cutting a piece of the Emperor's property in half.

But of course the disapproving part of our two-faced attitude is highly questionable, even though the approving part is not. The presupposition which our disapproval has—the belief that in the fourth century Roman Empire a Roman soldier's military uniform and equipment was the Emperor's property and not the soldier's own—is highly dubious; and it is even dubious whether the concept of 'a uniform' existed at that time at all.

In this lecture I have been trying to show that the difference between an 'attitudinarian' analysis of moral judgements and an 'objectivist' analysis, in which they are held to be true of false, is not quite so clear-cut as it looks. Whether we accept the one analysis or the other does not matter quite so much as we might suppose. Certainly approvals and disapprovals are neither true nor false. Nevertheless, they still have logical properties, as assertions and denials have. It looks as if the question whether there are moral beliefs[1] cannot be answered with a straightforward 'Yes' or 'No'.

In the next lecture, I shall begin by considering the logical concept of inconsistency, and shall try to shew that this too applies to approvals and disapprovals, as it does to assertions and denials. I shall then go on to say something about the relation between moral beliefs and feelings, and shall try to illustrate my remarks by asking you to imagine an intelligent being who has no feelings.

[1] Pp. 377 *et seq.*, above.

LECTURE 8

MORAL BELIEFS, CONTINUED: MORAL BELIEFS AND FEELINGS

INCONSISTENCY AND APPROVAL-DERIVATION

Something more must now be said about the important logical property of *inconsistency* and its relevance to the quasi-deductive derivation procedure which we have been discussing. (It has been suggested already that the judgement 'there is nothing wrong in breaking a promise' is something like a self-contradiction, even though we take it to be the expression of an attitude, and therefore neither true nor false.[1])

In a piece of deductive reasoning it is inconsistent to assert the premisses and deny the conclusion. If you do deny the conclusion, you have in effect denied one or other of the premisses which you yourself asserted. Does anything like this apply to the approval-derivation procedure which we have been considering?

Suppose that I have expressed approval of anyone who does a service to his neighbour; and I fully admit that William did do a service to a blind man by helping him to cross the street, but I do not approve of what William did. Of course, I am not thereby denying the approval I expressed of anyone who does a service to his neighbour. An attitude of approval, or the utterance expressing it, cannot be denied, as a statement can. But there is one thing we can do with both. Both a statement, which is true or false, and an expression of approval, which is neither, can be *withdrawn*. To put it vulgarly, we can 'back out of' either of them. (We can withdraw a command too, or an invitation, though these again are neither true nor false.) If I do not approve of William's action, I am withdrawing or 'backing out of' the general approval of all actions of that sort which I previously expressed. To put it in another way, I am *unsaying* what I previously said. And surely this is just what we mean by 'inconsistency'.

[1] Lecture 7, p. 390, above.

It must not, however, be supposed that it is always reprehensible (unreasonable) to unsay what one has just said. If it were, there could be no such thing as the empirical falsification of a universal assertion. 'All crows are black, and this is a crow. But good heavens! it is a grey one.' Here I am unsaying or withdrawing something I have just said, namely 'all crows are black'. But I do well to unsay it, because I have now discovered that it is false.

Can anything like this happen in the sphere of approvals and disapproval? I shall now suggest that it can. If I am right, here is another important way in which the 'logic' of approvals and disapprovals resembles the ordinary logic of assertions and denials.

AN ANALOGUE OF EMPIRICAL FALSIFICATION

'All crows are black' is inconsistent with 'this crow is grey'. A reasonable person cannot assert both. Which of them is he going to reject? If he is a reasonable person (not just an incorrigible theorizer) he is in no doubt about the answer. He rejects the universal proposition, however firmly he had believed it before. The experience of a particular matter of fact has the primacy over a generalization. If there is a clash between them, it is the generalization which must go.

A general approval or disapproval obviously cannot be falsified. If the attitudinarian analysis of moral judgements is correct, 'all actions of sort *A* are right' is not an assertion, and cannot be either true or false. If so, it cannot be falsified (i.e. shown to be false) either empirically or in any other way. Nevertheless, something analogous to empirical falsification can happen to it, as I shall now try to show.

Imagine you are an Englishman living at the beginning of the sixteenth century. From your earliest years, you have been brought up to approve of the burning of heretics. An ancestor of yours, greatly respected in the family, was a member of Parliament and voted for the statute *De haeretico comburendo* in the reign of King Henry IV, as doubtless many other good and pious men did. You share his attitude, without any reservations. But it so happens that you have lived all your life hitherto in a remote valley among the mountains of Cumberland, where no one is sophisticated enough to hold heretical opinions. So you have never yet had occasion to apply this general approval of yours to a particular instance, though you are perfectly sincere when you express your attitude by saying 'it is right to burn anyone who is a heretic'.

But then one day you leave your remote valley and go to London. And while you are there you actually witness the burning of a heretic. You are quite satisfied that he has had a fair trial; there is no doubt at all that he does hold highly heretical opinions. It might be expected that you would approve of this particular action which you see being done before your eyes. But not only do you fail to approve of it. You go farther. What you feel is the strongest disapproval, which could be expressed by saying 'what is being done here is utterly abominable'.

That settles the question, at least for you. In this clash between a general moral principle and a particular moral experience here and now, it is the principle that must go. It has not been falsified (as 'all crows are black' is by seeing a grey one) because, on the view we are considering, it cannot be either false or true. But it has been nullified or put out of court by the particular moral experience you have had. Something rather like an empirical test has been applied to this general approval of yours, and it has not stood up to the test. It has not been refuted, since it was not an assertion. But we could quite properly say that it has been rendered unacceptable. And you will admit that in some sense you were making a mistake when you accepted it.

What sort of mistake could it be? It was this. You did not fully 'realize' what it was that you yourself were approving of when you said 'it is right to burn anyone who is a heretic'. You did not know what such an action would be like if it were actually done. Something corresponding to Newman's distinction between notional and real assent[1] applies here. Your approval of this principle of action was notional rather than real, although it was perfectly sincere. Nor is this at all surprising. Much of our thinking, whether about conduct or other matters, is carried on by means of words; and very frequently we use words in an *uncashed* manner, without realizing at all fully what an actual situation would have to be like, if these words were to be a correct description of it.[2] To put it otherwise,

[1] *Grammar of Assent*, Ch. 4. See Series 2, Lecture 5, above.

[2] Cf. Series 1, Lecture 8, above, on the entertaining of propositions.

we use a verbalized concept without realizing fully what it would be like for this concept to have an actual instance.

Where approvals and disapprovals are concerned, the tendency to think of a type of action (or of person) in this 'uncashed' way is sometimes called 'lack of imagination'. And if the type of action is one in which the agent does something *to* another person, as it frequently is, we call this defect 'lack of sympathetic imagination'. This is a failure to realize what it would be like to be a person *to* whom an action of this type was done. The capacity for sympathetic imagination varies greatly from one man to another; and no doubt this is the explanation of much of the moral disagreement which exists in the world.

This 'notional' approving or disapproving of a type of action, or class of actions, is something like what happens when our approval (or disapproval) of a *particular* action has a false presupposition; that is, when we approve or disapprove of a particular action 'as having' such and such a characteristic, and it does not have that characteristic, though we believe that it has.[2] For example, we believe it was an example of truth-telling, because what the man said did in fact happen to be true; but he himself at the time thought it was false and intended to deceive his hearers. If we had known what he really was doing when he uttered these words, we should not have approved of what he did. We assumed that he told the truth intentionally. In a rather similar way, if you had known what kind of action heretic-burning actually is, you would not have approved of that kind of action. But this is not quite the same as saying that your approval had a mistaken presupposition. It was rather that you had an 'uncashed' *concept* of the type of action you were approving. Your failure was a lack of clarity, rather than a mistaken belief.

But it is more interesting to notice that this same 'notional' or 'uncashed' character may be found when our attitude is a neutral one, neither approving nor disapproving (the attitude which we express by saying 'this is not a moral question at all'). This neutral attitude too may be rendered unacceptable to us in the same way, by encountering an actual instance.

Let us consider an example in which the object of our attitude is a type of person, or a class of persons. Suppose that I have

[2] Cf. Series 2, Lecture 7, pp. 397–9, above.

heard from time to time that there are persons who forgive their enemies, but I have never met one of them, and I am told that they are not very numerous. Naturally I do not approve of them. How could one, when they are so silly? Still, being a fair-minded man, I do not disapprove of them either, since they do not do any harm to anyone except themselves. They are just eccentrics, or perhaps harmless lunatics.

But then, one day, I actually come across someone who has been very unkindly treated by another man, and forgives him for it. I get to know this person better, and find that he does this sort of thing repeatedly. Apparently he makes a habit of it, which is most extraordinary. And now I begin to change my attitude of moral neutrality. I find myself saying 'Well, really! he is a very nice person' (I am not compelled to use the officially-moral vocabulary) or 'he is really rather a splendid person, after all'. And then it occurs to me that I would not mind being that sort of person myself, if only I knew how to be; and if everyone were like him, the world would be a much better place than it is.

Here again, it is a case of 'cashing' our previously-uncashed symbols by experience of a particular instance, and the result of this is that our previous attitude of moral neutrality is rendered unacceptable. It is inconsistent with the attitude which we now have to this particular person. And here again it is the general attitude which must go, the attitude to a class or a type. What is decisive is 'how we feel' about this particular person who is a member of that class or an instance of that type. Here again we have something analogous to the empirical falsification of a general assertion. But here the parallel in the sphere of assertions would be a universal assertion which is both negative and disjunctive. Our previous morally neutral attitude could be expressed by saying 'No forgiveness of enemies is either good or bad'. A parallel to this would be 'no jaguar is either black or white', an assertion which is falsified when we find a black one in the forests of South America.

So much for the logical properties of approvals and disapprovals. It would seem that assertive and non-assertive theories of ethics do not differ quite so much as we might suppose, if expressions of attitude, which are neither true nor false, can nevertheless have logical properties and these logical properties are at least analogous to those which assertions have.

INTRA-PERSONAL AND INTER-PERSONAL INCONSISTENCY

So far, our conclusion is that even though moral judgements are neither true nor false, as the attitudinarian moralists maintain, they still have logical properties. One of the most important of these is inconsistency, and something more must be said about it. The inconsistency we have already discussed is the inconsistency of a person. If you approve of all who do services to their neighbours, and yet do not approve of what William did when he helped the blind man to cross the street, while fully admitting that he did it, then you are an inconsistent person, on this occasion at any rate.[1]

But inconsistency is of course a relational concept. Something is inconsistent with something else. What could a person be inconsistent with? He could be inconsistent with himself. That is one way of answering the question. But it needs some elucidation; 'himself', after all, is not exactly 'something else'. A clearer way of putting it is this: in such a case the two 'somethings', between which the relation of inconsistency holds, are *within* a single person; both of them are included in the same person's mental history. They are a saying of his and another saying of his which unsays the first. They need not necessarily be overt or publicly-uttered sayings. They might be wholly inward or private sayings, consisting of inner speech or verbal imagery, and perhaps they are more important when they are.

We can best describe this as intra-personal inconsistency. But not all inconsistency is of this intra-personal kind. The assertions 'all animals are carnivorous' and 'some animals eat only grass' are inconsistent with each other, no matter who makes them, whether publicly or privately, and no matter whether it is or is not the same person who makes both of them. Indeed, no one need actually make either of them. In this type of case, the relation of inconsistency holds primarily between 'assertibles', what we usually call propositions, and only derivatively between assertings of these assertibles.

It is the same when we speak of the inconsistency between two

[1] Lecture 7, pp. 393–4.

beliefs. They need not be beliefs held by the same person. Of course, they may be; and then the person who holds both at once is an inconsistent person. But if I believe that *p*, and you believe that not-*p*, it does not follow that either of us is an inconsistent person; and the difference which there is between us might still exist even if there were no inconsistent person in the world, although your belief is certainly inconsistent with mine. Here again, the relation of inconsistency holds primarily between the propositions believed, and only derivatively between the two believings or belief-attitudes; and this relation would still be there, even if neither of those propositions were believed by anyone.

Now if we are willing to hold that inconsistency can also exist in the sphere of approvals and disapprovals, are we to say that 'intra-personal' inconsistency is the only sort of inconsistency which can be found there? Or could an approval or disapproval of mine be inconsistent with an approval or disapproval of yours? And if it could, would this inconsistency-relation be a derivative or consequential one, as the inconsistency between two beliefs is a consequence of the inconsistency between the propositions believed?

A CHILD'S DILEMMA

These questions are somewhat puzzling. Let us consider a dilemma in which a child might find himself. 'Daddy disapproves of my staying in this afternoon, and Mummy disapproves of my going out. So what am I to do?' Is Daddy's disapproval inconsistent with Mummy's? We are inclined to say that it is. But this might be because both have a quasi-imperative character, as is shown by the child's question 'So what am I to do?' Of course, both are disapproval attitudes also. It is not true that their quasi-imperative character is the only character they have. But still both do have it. It is somewhat as if Daddy had said 'Don't stay in this afternoon' and Mummy had said 'Don't go out'. It is true that their quasi-imperative character is not sufficient by itself to make them inconsistent. If Daddy had disapproved of Tom's staying in and Mummy had disapproved of Matilda's going out, there would have been no inconsistency at all, however much imperative force these two disapprovals might have. But in the case we are considering both the quasi-imperatives are addressed to the same person;[1] and that does suffice to make them inconsistent with each other, since it is logically impossible for him to obey them both.

But now suppose that the child finds himself in a different dilemma some days later. 'Daddy approves of what I did yesterday and Mummy disapproves.' When the child reflects on this rather agonizing situation, the question he asks is not 'So what am I to do?' In this case, the object of these two parental attitudes is an action which has already been done. It is true that he may ask later 'So what am I to do next time?' For example, next time someone hits him over the head with a pillow, shall he hit back, as he did this time, or shall he turn the other cheek? Indeed, he is sure to ask this question at some stage of his reflections; for we assume that he is an intelligent child, and has already grasped, despite his tender years, that approval or disapproval of a particular action has an implicitly general character.[2]

But though he will, no doubt, ask himself later 'So what am I to do next time', his first question is likely to be a different and perhaps more important one, namely 'So what am I to think of myself?' Is he to approve of himself for having done this action, with Daddy, or is he to disapprove of himself, with Mummy? Or his question might be 'So what am I to feel about myself?' If he were to consult a philosopher about this latter formulation, he would probably be told that he cannot ask such a question, since feelings are not under one's voluntary control (he could only ask 'What *do* I feel?' and he must know the answer to that already). He might also be told that in any case approval is not at all like the warm feeling you have inside when you drink a cup of hot tea on a cold morning, nor is disapproval at all like having toothache. Nevertheless, he may quite well put his question to himself in that way, if there is unfortunately no philosopher at hand for him to consult. Whichever formulation he uses, he is asking whether he is to *agree* with Daddy's approval or with Mummy's disapproval, since apparently he cannot agree with both. It will probably not occur to

[1] Imperatives can also be inconsistent with each other when addressed to the same *group* of persons, as when 'Those behind cried "Forward!" and those in front cried "Back!" '.

[2] See Lecture 7, pp. 396–7.

him that a third alternative is always theoretically possible:[1] he might agree with neither, and take a neutral attitude, neither approving of himself nor disapproving. But as this is pretty obviously a moral issue (it can hardly be neither right nor wrong to hit another boy on the head) the possibility of taking a neutral attitude does not need to be considered.

This time the child's difficulty is not what it was in the previous example. The trouble is not that Daddy is in effect ordering him to do something which Mummy in effect orders him not to do, so that it is impossible to obey both. Neither of them is giving him orders at all, because the action approved of by the one and disapproved of by the other has already been done, and no question of obedience arises. The question is not which of his parents he is to obey, but which of them he is to agree with.

It seems clear enough that he cannot agree with both, in some sense of the word 'cannot'. But is this because Daddy's attitude is inconsistent with Mummy's? If they had been belief-attitudes it might have been. If Daddy believes that it will be fine by half past two, and Mummy believes that it will rain all the afternoon, these two beliefs *are* inconsistent with each other. But this is because the proposition believed by the one parent is inconsistent with the proposition believed by the other. The inconsistency between the two believing attitudes is derivative. Can anything similar be said about approving and disapproving attitudes? Could there be a similar derivative inconsistency between them, derived from (or defined in terms of) the inconsistency between their objects?

But how could this be so in the example we are considering, since Daddy's approval and Mummy's disapproval have the *same* object, an action which the child did yesterday? Still, we may notice that a similar difficulty could be raised about the inconsistency between a belief and a disbelief. If Daddy believes that it will be fine from 2.30 to 4.30, and Mummy disbelieves this same proposition, his belief and her disbelief are surely inconsistent with one another, since it is logically impossible that both should be correct. Nevertheless, though belief and disbelief are different attitudes, disbelieving the proposition 'it will be fine from 2.30 to 4.30' is

[1] It seems not to have occured to some adults either, and some of the unnecessary moral indignation by which the world is afflicted may be due to this cause.

logically equivalent to believing the proposition 'it will not be fine from 2.30 to 4.30'. Whatever inferences can be drawn by one who holds the disbelief that *p*, they are the same as those which can be drawn by one who holds the belief that not-*p*. Any evidence favourable (or adverse) to the disbelief that *p* is favourable (or adverse) to the belief that not-*p*, and in the same degree. If the disbelief that *p* is correct, the fact which makes it correct is also the fact which makes the belief that not-*p* correct; and if the disbelief that *p* is a mistaken one, the fact which makes it so is the fact which makes the belief that not-*p* a mistaken one. Let us see whether these considerations about belief and disbelief will help us. Perhaps they will, if we choose a suitable terminology.

'FOR' AND 'AGAINST'

Approval is sometimes called a pro-attitude, and disapproval an anti-attitude. Let us say, more simply, that when one approves of something one is *for* it, and when one disapproves of something one is *against* it. Daddy is *for* a certain action which the boy did yesterday, and Mummy is *against* that action. These two attitudes are certainly opposed to each other. As we have seen, we are strongly inclined to say that they are inconsistent with one another. But how are we to show that they are? Perhaps we might be able to show it, if we said that being against *A* is logically equivalent to being for not-*A* (as disbelieving that *p* is logically equivalent to believing that not-*p*). And surely this is true? If someone claimed to be against *A* but denied that he was for not-*A*, we should think that he did not understand the meanings of the words 'for' and 'against'.

For instance, if someone is 'against' enjoying the infliction of pain on others, this is equivalent to saying that he is 'for' *not* enjoying the infliction of pain on others, or 'for' the *absence* or non-existence of such enjoyment. But suppose that someone is 'against' a particular entity. Then we must say he is 'for' the non-existence of that entity. It may seem strange to suggest that if I am 'against' a particular person, I am 'for' the non-existence of that person. But strange and shocking though it is, surely that *is* what I am 'for', if I really am 'against' him *in toto*; in my eyes, it is just a 'bad thing' that he exists.[1] Fortunately we are not often 'against' a person (or even an animal) in this total way. Ordinarily, when we are 'against' a person, we are against his having some characteristic (usually a dispositional one, e.g. hard-heartedness or dishonesty) which we know or believe him to have; and this is equivalent to being 'for' his not having it.

In the example we are considering, what Mummy is 'against' is a particular action. Being 'against' *A* is logically equivalent to being 'for' the non-existence of *A*. Since being done is the way in which an action exists, being 'against' it is being 'against' its being done. And since in the case we are considering it is a past action, being 'against' it is being 'against' its *having* been done; and this in turn is equivalent to being 'for' its *not* having been done, though in fact it was.

This phraseology may seem a little complicated. But in fact Mummy might well express her attitude by saying 'Oh that he had not done it!' And Daddy might express his by saying 'How glad I am that he did do it!' (If he were a philosopher, he would add, with Hume, that he was glad 'after a particular manner'.)

Now the non-existence of *A is* inconsistent with the existence of *A*. It is a straightforward logical inconsistency. It is logically impossible that the same action should both have existed and not have existed at the same place and the same time, i.e. that it should both have been done and not have been done at that place at that time. In that case the inconsistency between the two attitudes of being 'for' the action *A* and being 'against it' is a derivative inconsistency, rather like the inconsistency between the belief that *p* and the disbelief that *p*. It is a consequence of the inconsistency between *A*'s having been done and *A*'s not having been done, since being *against* a past action *A* is logically equivalent to being *for* its not having been done.

But there is some difficulty in explaining what we should mean by 'it' or 'the action *A*'. If the action *A* has in fact been done, what could be meant by '*its* not having been done'? What could the 'it' be, which (we seem to be sayimg) might possibly have possessed

[1] This attitude would be the contrary of the attitude of unconditional love discussed above (pp. 392–3) and might be called 'unconditional hatred'. We may hope that it does not often exist, but it is at any rate logically possible that it might.

the property of not having been done? What a strange property for an action to possess! This is a familiar puzzle about the concept 'existence'; for being done is the way in which an action exists. But there is an equally familiar solution of it. Let us suppose that Tom hit one of his schoolfellows on the nose. Then when Mummy says 'Oh that Tom had not done it!' she means something like 'Oh that the *characteristic* of being a hitting of a schoolfellow on the nose had not been instantiated by what Tom was doing at that time!'

Alternatively we put it this way: 'Oh that the *description* "being a hitting of a schoolfellow on the nose" had not applied to (had not been true of) what Tom was doing at that time!' Daddy, on the other hand, is glad that this same description *did* apply to what Tom was doing at that time, or that this same characteristic *was* instantiated by what he was then doing. Daddy is 'for' the description's applying to the action (as in fact it did) or for the characteristic's being instantiated by it (as in fact it was); whereas Mummy is 'for' the description's *not* applying, though in fact it did, or 'for' the characteristic's *not* being instantiated, though in fact it was. Whichever way we put it, it is logically impossible that the same characteristic should both have been instantiated and not instantiated by what the boy was then doing, and it is logically impossible that the same description should both have applied and not have applied to what he was then doing.

If this is correct, it is not enough to say that the two parental attitudes are opposed to each other (still less is it enough to say that they are just different). They are inconsistent with each other, in much the same way as a belief and a disbelief can be; and their inconsistency is derived from, or definable in terms of, the inconsistency between their respective objects. What Daddy is 'for' is logically incompatible with what Mummy is 'for'. And that is why Tom cannot agree with both. It is not that it is just psychologically impossible for him to do so. It is psychologically possible, though it might not be very easy. He would have to get into a pretty confused state of mind first, but then he might manage it. When we say that he 'cannot' agree with both, we mean that he cannot do it without being (at least for the time) an inconsistent or illogical person; and his very puzzlement shows that this is what he is trying not to be.

It is worth while to add, before we take leave of this child and his troubles, that the second one ('What am I to feel about myself? Shall I agree with Daddy or with Mummy?') is something of a blessing in disguise. He learns an important lesson from it. He learns, or at least begins to learn, to judge for himself, and also to judge about himself, to make moral judgements about his own actions. He is learning to do his own approving and disapproving, instead of just being elated or dismayed when others approve or disapprove of him; and so he is on the way to becoming an autonomous and responsible moral being. Moreover, if he is a discerning child, he may discover that he *can* in a way agree with Daddy and with Mummy too. It may occur to him that Daddy approved of his action *as being* an act of self-defence, while Mummy disapproved of it *as being* a manifestation of rage. He has thereby discovered that the same action can (correctly) be described in two or more different ways, and that one might approve of it in respect of one of the characteristics it has, while disapproving of it in respect of another; and this is quite an important lesson too.

MORAL BELIEFS AND FEELINGS

We have seen that there are two versions of the doctrine that moral judgements are neither true nor false, the approval analysis or attitudinarian analysis on the one hand, and the injunctive analysis on the other. Something must now be said about the relations between the two.

It has been thought that the approval anlaysis has a serious defect, from which the injunctive analysis is free. One way of putting the point is this: it may seem that on the approval analysis a moral judgement does not *tell* us anything, whereas on the injunctive analysis it does. On both analyses alike, it is neither true nor false. But according to the injunctive analysis, it does tell us what to do in such and such circumstances; and is not this the most important thing we could possibly be told? 'That action was right' would mean, roughly, 'Go thou and do likewise', or more fully 'Let an action of this sort be done by anyone who is in circumstances like these'. In that case, we *are* being told what to do.

Before we consider this objection to the approval analysis, it is worth while to point out that although the distinction between 'true' and 'false' does not apply to expressions of approval or disapproval, there is another distinction which does. It is the distinction between sincerity and insincerity. It is perfectly possible to express approval of something (for example, by saying 'that action was right') when one does not in fact approve: much as one may bow to someone without actually feeling any respect for him, or smile at him when he comes into the room without feeling at all pleased to see him.

Moreover, expressions of attitude 'convey' one's attitude to other people, without actually telling them that one has it; and if one is insincere they 'misconvey' it (I am assuming that the hearer understands the language which the speaker uses). And now the distinction between true and false does come back into the picture. This conveying, or misconveying, consists in arousing a belief in the mind of the hearer. What is thus conveyed to you is true if my expression of attitude is sincere, and false if it is insincere. This belief of yours is not itself a moral belief, but a belief about a matter of fact. It is a belief, correct or not, about another person's moral attitude towards a certain action or class of actions, or towards a certain person or class of persons. What moral attitude a man has about something is a question of empirical fact, though not always an easy question to answer.

Let us now suppose that we go to a friend and ask him for advice about some moral problem. For instance, would it be right to reveal to the police something which was said to us in confidence, or to tell the judge and jury about it when we are being questioned in a court of law? Our friend replies 'It is always right to tell the truth'. Let us suppose also that this reply is a perfectly sincere expression of his attitude, so that we now know or have learned what his attitude is, at any rate in the everyday sense of the words 'know' or 'have learned'.

But was that all we wanted to know when we asked him whether it would be right to tell the truth in this particular case? We have learned that he has a feeling of approval towards invariable truth telling. Is that what we wanted to know? When we put our question to him, did we only want to find out about the state of his soul? Oh no, it would be said. We were asking him for guidance about what to do; and if this is what we are asking him for, it does not matter in the least what his feelings are, or even whether he has any. But according to the injunctive analysis he *has* given us what we asked for, when he says 'it is always right to tell the truth'. For according to that analysis, his answer amounts to saying 'Let everyone tell the truth always, no matter what the circumstances are'. So he *has* given us guidance about what to do.

DISCUSSION OF THIS OBJECTION

What shall we say about this criticism of the attitudinarian analysis? First, it is well to point out that one may approve of something or someone (in an occurrent and not merely dispositional sense of the word 'approve') without expressing ones' approval publicly to other people; and the same applies to disapproval. The moral judgements which a man makes privately 'in his own heart' are an important part of his moral life. They are especially important when they are moral judgements about his own actions, past or present, actual or proposed, or about his own character, that is, his own conative and emotional dispositions. A moral being is one who 'judges himself', approving or disapproving of himself. That is what having a conscience consists in. Why should we suppose that all his goods are in the shop-window and that there is nothing inside, or nothing that matters from a moral point of view? Of course, he may also go about the world telling other people what to do. But this is a less important function of a moral being.

So I would suggest that this criticism of the attitudinarian analysis arises partly from an excessive interest in publicity, a kind of Hellenic passion for the market-place, where everyone spends his day talking and being talked to. We are not always in what is called 'the hearer-speaker situation'; and I think we should be less than human if we were, though we should also be less than human if we were not in it pretty frequently. But even though we do confine ourselves for the moment to that situation, it is still not true that in learning 'how *X* feels' about some action, done or proposed, we have learned something entirely irrelevant to moral questions. If I admire and respect someone, it makes a great difference to me to learn 'how he feels' about some action I have done.

Suppose I find that he disapproves of what I did, and points out to me the characteristic in respect of which he disapproves of it. For example he says 'it was unkind to ask for the money back at that time, though the man had promised to repay it'. Somewhat dismayed by this, I go away and think it over. I reflect on the action again, its circumstances and its probable effects on others (not only on my debtor himself, but also perhaps on his indigent family). Then I may very well find that I disapprove of the action myself, and express this disapproval to myself, privately, by saying 'Yes, it *was* unkind, and I ought not to have done it'; and I resolve not to do that sort of thing again. The result may be similar if I learn how he feels about something I am proposing to do, but have not yet done. He expresses disapproval of it, and then (to my surprise, perhaps) I find myself feeling about it as he does. The result is that either I refrain from doing what I proposed, or, if I do it, I feel remorse afterwards.

MORAL INSIGHT

Moreover, we do well to pay some attention to the question 'how does So and So feel about it?' even when we do not particularly admire or respect him. Indeed, we may come to admire and respect him when we do learn how he feels. What is called moral insight may be found in the most unlikely quarters, in children for example; or in persons who are ignorant or ill-informed about most other matters. It may even be found sometimes in the persons called 'publicans and sinners'.

It is not of course easy to say what one means by 'moral insight', though we all agree that there is such a thing, and that some people have more of it than others. Perhaps it is best to reformulate the question and ask what one means by saying '*A* has *more* moral insight than I have'. On an attitudinarian theory one would mean something like this: When I learn how *A* feels about some action or person *X*, and in respect of what characteristic of *X* he feels so, I find myself feeling as he does, though previously I felt differently, or had no moral attitude about it at all. (Perhaps I had not even noticed that *X* did have the characteristic in question, for instance I had not noticed that *X* caused harm or inconvenience to others.) It is to be observed that this 'conversion-experience'—for that is what it is, on a small scale—not only alters our feelings at the moment, but also our dispositions. In future we shall tend to disapprove of *any* action which has the characteristics that *A* disapproves of in this one. (And similarly *mutatis mutandis*, if he expressed approval.) What makes this possible is the logical property of 'implicit generality' which all approvals and disapprovals have.[1]

It comes to this, then. On an attitudinarian theory, the statement 'there are persons who have more moral insight than I have' is equivalent to 'there are persons whose moral attitude to some action (or some person)[2] I tend to share, when I learn what their attitude is, and in respect of what characteristic of that action (or person) they have it, though I did not have that attitude previously.' On an objectivist moral theory, which holds that moral judgements *are* true or false, our statement 'there are persons who have more moral insight than I have' would mean something different, something like this: 'There are persons who intuitively apprehend moral facts which I cannot apprehend intuitively for myself, unless, and until, one of these persons draws my attention to them; but when he does, I can.' For example, now that you have pointed it out to me, I 'see for myself' that it was wrong to take vengeance on someone who had harmed me, though at the time I did not 'see' anything wrong in it at all.

But we must return to the attitudinarian analysis. To complete our reply to the criticism of it which we are discussing, there is something else we must notice. When we learn how someone feels about an action or a proposed action, we *are* in a way being told what to do. And when we notice how we ourselves feel about some action or proposed action, we are in a way telling ourselves what to do. It does not, of course, follow that we shall actually do it. But neither does this follow when the injunction is made perfectly explicit ('let everyone do *A* in circumstances *C*, and I am someone who is in circumstances *C*').

[1] Cf. Lecture 7, pp. 396–7.

[2] Some *other* person? Not necessarily. *A* might show more moral insight than I have in a moral judgement which he makes about himself—or of course about myself.

Approval, in other words, has in itself an action-guiding character. It is relevant to the settling of practical questions, and so is disapproval. Perhaps I may quote my namesake the eighteenth century British Moralist Richard Price. He was not himself an attitudinarian moral philosopher, but he made a striking remark which is true whatever analysis of moral judgements is correct. 'Excitement belongs to the very ideas of moral right and wrong.'[1] To put it in a more modern way, it is part of the meaning or force of the words 'right' and 'wrong' that we are *moved* to do the action to which the word 'right' is applied, and we are moved to abstain from doing the action to which the word 'wrong' is applied.

This practical or action-guiding character of approval and disapproval is ignored if we say that they are 'merely' feelings, or that expressions of approval or disapproval are 'merely' expressions of how the speaker feels. Approval *can* indeed be called a feeling; or rather an occurrent approval (as opposed to a dispositional one) can be called a feeling, and so can an occurrent disapproval. If any linguistic philosopher objects to calling it so, one may reply with the *ad hominem* argument that this is what we do call it; and it is very natural that we should, for approving and disapproving are *experiences* which we 'live through', as fearing and wishing are. But we have not said all there is to say about them when we call them feelings, though we have said something very important. They have an action-guiding character too.

Moreover, they still have it (we might say, they most noticeably have it) when the action approved of or disapproved of is one's own, or when the person approved of or disapproved is oneself. Each of us takes account of his own approvals and disapprovals, he admits or acknowledges their relevance, in deciding what he himself shall do. What makes someone a moral being is not the practical relevance he attributes to the approvals and disapprovals of others, but the practical relevance he attributes to his own; and especially to those of them which are approvals and disapprovals of his own actions, done or proposed, and to his own emotional and conative dispositions which manifest themselves in what he himself does. This is still true when he takes account of the approvals and disapprovals expressed by others who

[1] Selby-Bigge, *British Moralists* Vol. II, p. 180 (Section 707).

'have more moral insight than he has'. For these only become practically relevant for him when he 'makes them his own', by reflecting on them and accepting them for himself.

Let us try to imagine a person who goes about the world approving and disapproving of the actions and the characters of others, but it never occurs to him to approve or disapprove of his own. I suggest that he would not be a moral being, though he would no doubt resemble ordinary moral beings in some quite important ways. It is hard to say what he would be: perhaps what the Emperor Valerian was alleged (one hopes untruly) to be, when a proposal was made in the Senate to appoint him to the office of Censor some years before he became Emperor. We are told in the *Augustan History* that the proposal was carried with acclamation, and the Senators shouted 'Valerian has been a censor since his earliest boyhood', 'The whole life of Valerian has been a censorship'.[1]

A DIFFICULTY IN THE INJUNCTIVE ANALYSIS

Now according to the Injunctive Analysis, if I interpret it rightly, a moral being does have to make moral judgements *about* himself, and he also has to make these judgements *for* himself, at first hand, in an autonomous and responsible manner. There is no difficulty about the first of these requirements, but there is some difficulty about the second.

There is no difficulty about the first, because the injunctive moralists admit, and indeed insist, that what is enjoined in a moral judgement is a rule of action, such as 'let everyone always tell the truth'. By the very nature of such rules, anyone who accepts this rule is *ipso facto* committed to laying the injunction on himself —if he accepts the rule at all. The rule tells anyone what do do in such and such circumstances (namely those in which one is making a statement to another person); and I am someone, and let us suppose I am now in circumstances of the sort. So if I have accepted the rule, I am committed to judging, about myself, that it is right for me to tell the truth to this other person, and also committed to 'judging myself', in the sense of condemning myself, if I do not.

[1] *Historia Augusta*, Loeb edition, Vol. III, p. 8 (*Valeriani Duo*, ch. 5).

But there is a difficulty about the second requirement, that I must judge *for* myself in an autonomous and responsible way. It is not enough to realize that the rule applies to myself as well as to others. Of course it does. It is of the form 'let everyone do *A* in circumstances *C*'. And I am someone, and I am now in circumstances *C*. But if I go no farther than that, I have only noticed a logical truism. It is not even enough if I resolve to obey this rule whenever it applies to me, and carry out this resolution inflexibly for the rest of my days. Something more is required if it is to be for me a *moral* rule. I must accept the rule or consent to it. I must *approve* of the rule for myself.

But why should I accept it? I may know that a good many other people do accept it, and that if I fail to act in accordance with it, and only tell the truth when it suits me, they will disapprove of me. I much dislike being disapproved of. It is an unpleasant situation and makes social relations very difficult. I suspect also that other people will impose various pains and penalties on me, and I shall not like that either. So I resolve to follow this rule as a matter of expediency, and I act in accordance with it for the rest of my life. After all, honesty is the best policy in the long run, or at any rate the least disadvantageous one.

But if I accept the rule on that ground, it is not for me a moral rule at all, whatever it may be for others. If I am trying to look at the matter as a moral being, such prudential considerations are not relevant. There is only one consideration which is morally relevant when one is trying to decide whether to accept such and such a rule of conduct. It is this. Do I, myself, sincerely approve of this rule? In short, in a case like this what matters from a moral point of view, and the only thing that matters, is just what the critics of the attitudinarian analysis dismiss as irrelevant: namely 'how I feel' about the rule of conduct in question. When I consider this rule as carefully as I can, in a cool hour, do I myself feel approval of this rule or not? Unless I do feel approval of it, it is not for me a moral rule, even though I obey it more often than not, or even always. And the word 'feel' is important. It is not enough that I say the words 'I approve of it', even though I say them to myself privately, in inner speech. What I say to myself may still be said insincerely. Sincerity and insincerity are not merely matters of 'public relations'. When I accept a moral rule and say to myself 'Yes, I approve of it', this inner speech of mine must be an expression of the way I do myself feel about the rule.

What we feel about an action, done or proposed, especially when it is an action of our own, and what we feel about a rule of action, especially in cases where it is applicable to ourselves, is by no means a trivial matter. On the contrary, there is hardly anything which is more important. I shall not try to illustrate its importance by a kind of fable.

A FABLE: AN INTELLIGENT BEING WITHOUT FEELINGS

Let us imagine an intelligent being with no feelings. We will endow him with tactual sensations and sensations of temperature. He is able to feel a table with his hand, he can feel the warmth of a fire and the chilliness of an East wind. We will also endow him with organic sensations. He can feel (i.e. experience) headaches and toothaches, smarts and itches. He can feel hungry or thirsty, if we mean by this that he can experience certain sorts of bodily sensations in his mouth or his stomach. To this extent he does have feelings.

But he cannot feel either pleasure or displeasure. Consequently, there is a sense in which he knows what pain is, and another sense in which he does not. He knows what it is to experience toothache, but he does not know what it is to be displeased by this bodily sensation, or to dislike it. He can neither like nor dislike anything.

On the conative side, he does not differ much from the rest of us. He has wishes or wants, as we do. He has intentions and makes decisions. He carries out his decisions, sometimes successfully, sometimes not. But he does not feel satisfied when he succeeds, or dissatisfied when he fails. Nor does he feel satisfied when he gets something that he wants. The want just ceases for the time being, and that is all. And if he fails to get what he wants, he does not feel dissatisfied. He just finds that the want continues. He does not know what it is to be disappointed, though we can allow him to be surprised when one of his expectations is falsified.

His most striking peculiarity, however, is that he has no emotions at all. He never feels afraid of anything, though he can run away when he is in danger. He never feels angry with anyone, though he can hit someone or expel him forcibly from the room. He cannot feel dismayed or depressed or elated. He has no pity for anyone (nor of course for himself), though he is also incapable of rejoicing at the misfortunes of others. 'Sympathy' is a word he cannot understand, though he may be able to 'weep with them that weep' according to the Apostolic injunction, if he has sufficient control of his tear-ducts, and he could quite easily sigh with those who sigh, and groan with those who groan. He feels no liking for anyone or anything, and no disliking either. He is quite incapable of affection: he does not know what it is to have a warm feeling for another person, or to feel coldly towards him either. He cannot love anyone or anything, but also he cannot hate anyone or anything. He does not know what it is to feel remorse or repentance for something he has done. He cannot feel guilty about it, as he would if he were an ordinary human being. But he can resolve not to do that sort of thing again; and when he makes such resolutions, he may carry them out more successfully than the rest of us would.

HIS MORAL EDUCATION

What kind of a moral life would such a being have? Let us first consider his moral education. To give him every chance of growing up into a moral being, we will suppose that his parents and teachers are very good people (they do of course have feelings, like the rest of us). We will also suppose that he is an unusually intelligent and quick-witted child. He soon learns to understand commands, and it does not take him long to discover that a particular command can be implicitly general. When he is told to-day 'wipe your dirty shoes on the doormat before you come in' he understands that he is *always* to wipe them on the doormat before he comes in, whenever they are dirty. Throughout his childhood, he does what his parents and teachers tell him to do. Or rather, he always does it when it is logically possible to do it; for one command may contradict another, or it may be self-contradictory, for example when his uncle said to him 'Always tell the truth, but don't tell it when you are forbidden to'. It is true that he cannot very well be punished if by any chance he does something he is forbidden to do, or fails to do something he is told to do, since he is incapable of suffering. But he can be shown that he will not get what he wants unless he obeys, and will get it if he does obey, and he understands this very quickly. The lesson, however, is hardly needed, since he nearly always does what he is told.

To judge from his actions, he is indeed a model child. Later he becomes a model young man too, and not just by the behaviouristic criteria which we used when we concluded that he was a model child. Now that he is older, we must consider what is going on inside him, as well as his outward actions. By degrees, he has succeeded in 'interiorizing' these commands which his parents and teachers gave him. He has an 'inner voice' of his own now, which tells him to do the sorts of things which his parents and teachers formerly told him to do, and he always or nearly always obeys it. They find that they have no need now to tell him to do anything. They feel very pleased with him, and they say so. He cannot of course feel pleased with himself, because he cannot feel pleased with anything. When they tell him they feel pleased with him, he cannot understand what they are saying. Nor can he feel grateful to them for this tribute they have paid him, because he cannot feel grateful for anything. But he has often heard this unintelligible word 'pleased' before, and he knows just what to do when a remark of this kind is addressed to him. He has been brought up to say 'thank you' in such circumstances. What else could gratitude consist in, except a disposition to utter these performatory words (for surely saying 'thank you' *is* thanking)? So he says 'thank you', loud and clear, and then they feel still more pleased with him.

It would not be quite fair to say that his morality is just a morality of social conformity. It is true that he only does the things he has been told to do by others in his earlier years. But he does not in any way dislike doing them. Of course we cannot say that he likes doing them either; he neither likes nor dislikes anything. Still, he does them spontaneously, in the sense that no one else makes him do them. In doing them, he is obeying orders which he gives to himself, though in content those orders are the same as those which his parents and teachers gave him previously; or very nearly the same, because (being a very intelligent young man) he has tidied up one or two inconsistencies he noticed in them, and the orders which he gives himself constitute a perfectly consistent code of conduct.

But if we consider him as a moral being, we notice that there is something lacking in him. It might be misleading to call him heartless, because this might suggest that he is cruel or callous. It is true that he 'does not mind' if others suffer or even if he makes them suffer; and this is what we do say of heartless people. But the reason why he does not mind is that he does not know what suffering is. Ordinarily human beings who are called heartless do know what suffering is. It is not that they have no hearts. They have: but their hearts are not in the right place, as we say. The trouble with our imaginary being *is* just that he has no heart. It is not that it is 'in the wrong place'. It just is not there at all.[1]

Christian theologians would say that his chief deficiency is that he is entirely incapable of love (though of course incapable of hatred also) and that he is therefore something less than a person. They might even say that someone who hates his neighbours is in a better condition, since he is at least capable of loving them and it is at least conceivable that he might be 'converted'; whereas no such conversion is even conceivable in the case of our imaginary being. It is not possible that his present feelings towards his neighbours should be altered, because he *has* no present feelings towards them, or towards anything. It would be misleading to say even that he is indifferent towards them, because this would imply that he does (or at least could) like or dislike *something*, although he neither likes nor dislikes other human beings.

NO FEELINGS, NO APPROVAL OR DISAPPROVAL

But however important it is that our imaginary being is incapable of loving anyone, and although we may be inclined to agree that this does make him something less than a person, the defect which

[1] In one of Alexandre Dumas' novels about the reign of Henri III of France, two followers of the Duke of Anjou (the King's brother) are discussing the character of their lord, and one of them says of him *il est sans coeur*. But the Duke of Anjou, if Dumas is to be trusted, nearly always did what people *with* hearts would call wrong; our imaginary being nearly always does what people with hearts would call right.

concerns us now is a different one. It is this. He is incapable of approval and disapproval. He cannot either approve or disapprove of anyone or anything, and therefore he does not know the meaning of the words 'right' and 'wrong' as ordinary people use them. He is quite capable of obeying his 'inner voice', and there is no external compulsion which makes him obey. We have supposed that he does obey it much more often than not, and it might even be that he obeys it always. But what he cannot do, or even conceive the possibility of doing, is to obey it *because* he approves of what it says. Nor can he disapprove of the actions he sometimes thinks of doing which would be contrary to the dictates of his 'inner voice', nor yet of actions done by others which his inner voice would forbid him to do, if he were in the same circumstances, though he can refrain from doing such actions, and perhaps he nearly always does refrain from doing them.

Approval, and disapproval too, has an emotional element in it. It is something that one feels. That is why it used to be said, long ago, that morality is something which concerns the heart or (in Hume's words) is 'more properly felt than judged of'. Hume's remark is no doubt an overstatement. Nevertheless, there is no morality where there are no feelings. 'The heart' is an essential constitutent of a moral being, though certainly he needs a head as well, since he cannot be a moral being unless he has the capacity of thinking.

The 'inner voice' which our imaginary creature has is no substitute for a heart, though it does resemble a heart in being inward. This is because a person must *approve* of what his inner voice tells him to do, if its injunctions are to be for him moral injunctions. And ordinary moral beings like ourselves, if we have such an 'inner voice', may sometimes disapprove of its injunctions. For in their content they are the same as the injunctions which our parents and teachers taught us to obey in our childhood and youth, and some of these might quite conceivably be disapproved of, when we consider them in our mature years. For example, someone's inner voice might tell him 'Never treat a person with a black skin as an equal'. And then, some day, he might reflect on this injunction, and find that so far from approving of it, he disapproves of it; and then he might resolve to disobey this injunction in future, though he might well find such disobedience rather difficult, since it would be contrary to his habits and his upbringing.

But this possibility of revising his code of conduct is not open to the man 'with no heart' whom I have asked you to imagine. He cannot approve of any part of his code of conduct, nor disapprove of any part of it. He is 'rule-bound', as one might say. He cannot revise or abandon a rule which he has hitherto followed—unlike our other young man from Cumberland, who abandoned the rule 'It is always right to burn heretics' when confronted with a particular instance of its application.[1]

It follows that if there were a rational being with no feelings or no 'heart', his code of conduct would not be for him a *moral* code at all. In its contents it might conceivably be exactly the same as what ordinary people call 'the moral law', and it is even conceivable that our imaginary creature might always obey every single one of the injunctions which his code of conduct contains. What he cannot do is to obey them because he approves of them. Approval, and disapproval too, are experiences which he has never had, and is incapable of having.

It is impossible that he should be a moral being. The reason why he cannot be one is that he has no feelings, no 'heart'. He is not a moral being, however much the rest of us, who do have hearts, may approve of his outward actions.

Here ends my fable. We must now return from the world of imagination to the more thorny realm of philosophical analysis.

[1] Pp. 401–3, above.

LECTURE 9

BELIEF 'IN' AND BELIEF 'THAT'[1]

PART I

INTRODUCTION

Epistemologists have not usually had much to say about believing 'in', though ever since Plato's time they have been interested in believing 'that'. Students of religion, on the other hand, have been greatly concerned with belief 'in', and many of them, I think, would maintain that it is something quite different from belief 'that'. Surely belief 'in' is an attitude to a person, whether human or divine, while belief 'that' is just an attitude to a proposition? Could any difference be more obvious than this? And if we overlook it, shall we not be led into a quite mistaken analysis of religious belief, at any rate if it is religious belief of the theistic sort? On this view belief 'in' is not a propositional attitude at all.

On the face of it, this radical distinction between belief-in and belief-that[2] seems plausible to anyone who knows from the inside what religious experience of the theistic sort is like. But to many philosophers it seems to have hardly any plausibility. It seems obvious to them that belief-in is in one way or another reducible to belief-that. This reduction, they would say, is not really very difficult, certainly not difficult enough to be interesting; and that, presumably, is why epistemologists have seldom thought it necessary to discuss belief-in very seriously. Why make such a fuss about this distinction between 'in' and 'that', when it is little or nothing more than a difference of idiom?

I wish to suggest, however, that the distinction between belief-in and belief-that does at any rate deserve careful discussion. The

[1] This lecture, a rather radically revised version of one of the orally-delivered Gifford Lectures, was published in *Religious Studies* (Vol. 1, 1965–6) and is reproduced here by the Editor's kind permission.

[2] From now on, I shall sometimes write 'belief-in' and 'belief-that' with hyphens.

question whether belief-in is or is not reducible to belief-that is by no means trivial, nor is it at all an easy question to answer.

It is not trivial. Religious belief, whether we like it or not, is quite an important phenomenon. Those who have no religious belief themselves should still try to understand what kind of an attitude it is, and they cannot hope to understand it unless they pay some attention to what is said by those who do have it. Moreover, as we shall see presently, religious belief-in is by no means the only sort. Nearly everyone believes 'in' someone or something, whether he believes in God or not.

Nor is our question an easy one to decide. Quite a strong case can be made for each of the two views which have been mentioned, the 'irreducibility thesis' on the one hand, and the 'reducibility thesis' on the other. The decision between them is made more difficult (though also more interesting) because belief-in, or at least some instances of it, cuts across the boundary sometimes drawn between the cognitive side of human nature, concerned with what is true or false, and the evaluative side, concerned with what is good or evil. Either the boundary vanishes altogether, or we find ourselves on both sides of it at the same time.

There is also a preliminary enquiry, whose importance has not perhaps been fully appreciated by either party in this controversy. Neither perhaps has considered a large enough range of examples. The expression 'believe in' is used in a good many different contexts. For all we can tell beforehand, there might be several different sorts of belief-in, and the reducibility thesis might be correct for some of them, but incorrect or highly questionable for others. Let us begin, then, by considering 'the varieties of believing-in'; and it may be as well to consider some examples of *dis*believing-in too.

THE VARIETIES OF BELIEVING 'IN'

First we will consider a number of examples which seem *prima facie* to support the irreducibility thesis. Whatever merits this thesis may have, it is certainly an over-simplification to say that belief-in is always an attitude to a person, human or divine.[1]

[1] We need not here consider in what sense God may be described as 'personal'. It is sufficient for our purpose that in theistic religion personal pronouns are

Surely it is perfectly possible to believe in a non-human animal The blind man believes in his guide-dog. A medieval knight or a modern foxhunter might easily believe in his horse. A falconer might believe in this hawk and not believe, or believe less, in that one. And vegetable organisms, as well as animals, can be believed in. A keen gardener might believe in his chrysanthemums, but not in his strawberry plants.

Moreover, it is not only living things which can be believed in. One may believe in a machine. A motorist can believe in his car. Or, if he is more discriminating, he may believe in some parts of its mechanism but not in others, or not much. He may have great confidence in his brakes but less confidence in his battery.

It is even possible to believe in a non-living natural object. Let us consider a remark attributed to the seventeenth-century English statesman, Lord Halifax the Trimmer: 'The first article, in an Englishman's creed is "I believe in the sea".' It is true that for many centuries Englishmen did believe in the sea, though nowadays they would be better advised to believe in the air. Nor need the belief in the sea be confined to inhabitants of islands. It could well be said that the Vikings of the ninth and tenth centuries believed in it too.

Again, one may believe in an event, as opposed to a person or thing. In a war, or at least in its early stages, many people believe in the victory of their country. In some religious beliefs, it is an event which is believed in, and it may be either a past event or a future one. Examples are the Christian belief in the Incarnation, and the Second Coming of Christ.

In all these cases, one is believing in an entity of some sort, whether personal or non-personal, whether a substance or an event. But one may also believe in an institution. An entry in *Who's Who* many years ago concluded with the words 'believes in the British Empire'. At the time when they were written, those words were perfectly intelligible, though if someone were to write or utter them now we should be puzzled, because there is no longer a British Empire to be believed in, or disbelieved in either. Again, most people believe in their own university or

held to be applicable to the Supreme Being: and not only the pronoun 'he', but also (and more important) the pronouns 'thou' or 'you'.

college or school, and have less belief, or none, in other universities, colleges or schools.

But, further, one can believe not only in an individual entity, but in a class of entities. The falconer may believe in goshawks, in goshawks in general, as a species, and not merely in this particular goshawk of his own. (Indeed, he need not own one himself.) Many people nowadays believe almost to excess in penicillin—not just in this dose of penicillin or that, but in penicillin as such. There are also many who believe almost to excess in computers. In such cases, what is believed in is something very different from an individual person. It belongs to a different logical type: though it is true that the class believed in may happen to be a class of persons ('I believe in men who have worked their way up to the top, not in those who were born with a silver spoon in their mouths').

One may also believe in a class of institutions. Some people believe in private preparatory schools, though others disbelieve in them. In a letter to the London *Times* some years ago, the writer said 'I believe in railways'.[1] More recently a spokesman for a well-known motor company was reported to have said 'we do not believe in waiting-lists'. The emphasis was on 'we'. Here we have the converse point. Most motor manufacturers do still believe in waiting-lists. This company's lack of belief in them, or, more probably, disbelief in them, was rather unusual. (Perhaps a waiting-list is not exactly an institution. But it is something like one. It could at any rate be described as 'a social device'.) Again, there are still some people who do not believe in banks, and prefer to keep their money in a stocking or in a hole under the floor-boards. They do not just disbelieve in this particular bank or that. They disbelieve in banks as such. But most people believe in 'the banking system' pretty firmly.

But what is believed in may be even more 'abstract' than this. One may believe in a procedure or method or policy. Indeed, this is a very common type of belief-in. At one time many Englishmen used to believe in taking a cold bath every morning, and probably some still do. Some people believe in classical education. Many nowadays do not. Instead, they believe in an education which fits one for life in the modern world. Some people believe in abstaining from alcohol when they have to drive a car or pilot an

[1] Sir Egbert Cadbury, *The Times*, September 9, 1959.

aircraft immediately afterwards. Most of us only go to our dentist when we have toothache. But there are some who believe in going to him regularly once a year, whether they have toothache or not. An interesting example of *lack* of belief in a method or procedure (or perhaps of disbelief in it) could be noticed in a recent statement by the President of a well known educational body: 'Of course, we have never believed in measuring the effectiveness of what we do in terms of numbers alone.' There are many others who would say, more generally, that they have no belief in statistics. But there are some who seem almost to believe in nothing else.

Again, one may believe (or disbelieve) in equal pay for both sexes, in easier divorce, in the abolition of the House of Lords, in aid 'without strings' to under-developed countries, in settling all disputes by non-violent methods, and in all sorts of 'causes', good, bad or indifferent.

Indeed, it is not easy to set any limits at all to the types of 'objects' which may be believed in. (It will be obvious that many of the examples already given take us a very long way from belief in a person, either human or divine.) But since one must stop somewhere, I shall end my list with one more example, belief in a theory.

This is an instructive example, because at first sight belief in a theory might seem so obviously reducible to a set of beliefs *that*. What is a theory but a logically connected set of propositions? So when someone is said to believe in a theory, surely his attitude is just a rather complicated form of believing 'that'? He would believe *that* p, that q, that r, that p entails q, that r is highly probable in relation to q, etc. Now of course such beliefs-that are an essential part of belief-in a theory. But are they the whole of it? If this were a complete account of the believer's attitude, it would be more appropriate to say 'he accepts the theory' or 'he believes that it is correct' and not 'he believes *in* it'. Belief *in* a theory has some resemblance to belief in penicillin, or belief in an instrument such as the electron microscope. The theory, when you have understood it, gives you power: a power of satisfying intellectual curiosity, of finding things out which were previously unknown, of making verifiable predictions which could not otherwise be made, and of reducing an apparently disconnected mass of brute facts to some sort of intelligible order. When someone believes *in* a theory, it is this power-conferring aspect of it which he has in mind, and he esteems or values the theory accordingly. It is a fact about human nature that power of this kind is very highly esteemed by some people.

Moreover, a person may still believe in a theory though he is aware that it contains paradoxes which have not yet been resolved. In that case he cannot believe that it is entirely correct. But he may still esteem it highly, and believe in it as an intellectually powerful instrument. He may use it constantly in his own investigations and encourage others to do the same. He relies on the theory, we might even say he trusts it. But in the belief-that sense he does not altogether believe it. If I am not mistaken, this was the attitude which many scientists had to the Quantum Theory in the early days of its development.

Something rather similar applies to metaphysical theories too, or at least to metaphysical theories of the synoptic type, which attempt to provide us with a unified 'view of the world' or 'world-outlook'. Such theories, one may suggest, are believed *in* rather than just believed in the belief-in sense, and disbelieved *in* rather than just disbelieved. Indeed, it is doubtful whether words like 'true' or 'false', 'correct' or 'incorrect' are the appropriate ones to apply to them. 'Adequate', 'not wholly adequate', 'relatively satisfactory' are expressions which fit the case better. The adherents of a particular metaphysical world view, Schopenhauer's for instance, believe *in* it somewhat as a plumber believes in his bagful of tools or a housewife in her cookery-book. And like the plumber and the housewife, they may 'believe in it' with some reservations. What such a synoptic metaphysician offers us is a systematically ordered set of conceptual instruments, which will enable us (so he claims) to make sense of human experience, to unify apparently disconnected facts and reconcile apparently conflicting ones. To put it negatively, he claims to deliver us from the predicament of having to experience the world as 'just one thing after another': a predicament which some human beings dislike intensely, though others do not mind it.

REDUCIBLE 'BELIEFS IN'

We have now considered a number of examples of belief-in which suggest that it is quite a different attitude from belief-that. We have also seen how very various they are, although belief in a person (human or divine) may well be the most important type of belief-in. Still, despite these differences, they do all support the irreducibility thesis; or at least they seem *prima facie* to support it.

But it is not very difficult to find examples which point the other way. An obvious one is belief in fairies. Believing in fairies amounts to no more than believing that fairies exist. Again, if someone believes in the Loch Ness monster, he just believes that there is a very large aquatic creature which inhabits Loch Ness. We often hear people say they 'do not believe in the supernatural'. What they do not believe is *that* supernatural events occur or that supernatural beings exist.

The same applies sometimes even when one expresses belief in a person. If someone says he believes in King Arthur, he just expresses his belief *that* there was such a person, or at least a person who had some of the characteristics attributed to Arthur in the earlier versions of the Arthurian legend. For instance, he may believe that in the late fifth and early sixth centuries there was a Romano-British *dux bellorum* called something like Artorius, who commanded a troop of heavily armed cavalry and defeated the Saxons at Mons Badonicus about the year AD 500. This belief-in is very different indeed from the belief in Artorius which one of his own heavily armed cavalrymen ('knights') may have had. There is nothing in it of esteem or trust or loyalty. It is just a case of believing an existential proposition, believing that there was a person to whom a certain complex description applied. It is much the same when a classical scholar believes 'in' Homer. He believes *that* there was one poet and only one who wrote at least the greater part of the *Iliad* and the *Odyssey*, and that 'Homer' was his name.

Similarly, if someone disbelieves in Arthur or in Homer or in fairies, he just disbelieves an existential proposition. We may contrast this with the disbelief which British Tories had in Mr Gladstone. It was an attitude of disesteem or distrust. We notice, however, that they could not have this disbelief in him unless they believed *that* there was such a person. To disbelieve in him in one sense they had to believe in him in another. Nor could they disbelieve in his foreign policy unless they believed *that* he had one.

There does seem to be an attitude which might be called minimal or merely factual belief-in. One might be tempted to call it existential belief-in, since what is believed here is an existential proposition. That indeed is what it is, in the logician's sense of the word 'existential', so far as these examples are concerned.[1] But Existentialist philosophers have introduced a new and entirely different sense of the word 'existential'; and in *their* sense the word would apply to the kind of belief-in illustrated by our previous set of examples, where belief-in seems, on the face of it, to be irreducible to belief-that. It is perhaps one of their merits that they have paid more attention than most other philosophers to beliefs-in of this apparently 'irreducible' sort.

Be that as it may, there certainly is a minimal or merely factual sense of 'believe in'. This is a very common and familiar use of the expression 'believe in'; and 'believing in' in this sense certainly *is* reducible to 'belief that'. It is even possible that when a person says 'I believe in God' he is expressing no more than a minimal or factual belief 'in'. He may just believe *that* there is a God, or *that* God exists. When a religious person says it, he is almost certainly expressing something more; and this perhaps is the point of Pascal's distinction between *Dieu d'Abraham*, *Dieu d'Isaac*, *Dieu de Jacob* and *Le Dieu des philosophes et des savants*. It is perfectly possible to believe that God exists without being a religious person at all; and certainly the ordinary use of language allows us to speak of this 'belief that' as a 'belief in'.

Similarly, in 1492 when Columbus set sail, there may well have been geographers who could say, sincerely, that they too believed 'in' a westerly sea route from Europe to the Indies. Nevertheless, their belief-in differed very considerably from his. They just accepted an existential proposition, the proposition 'that there is' such a sea route. Columbus accepted it too. But he was prepared to risk his life on it. He 'put his trust in' this westerly sea route which he believed to exist, and they did not.

OTHER EXAMPLES OF 'REDUCIBLE' BELIEF-IN

There are also examples of a rather different kind where belief-in does seem to be reducible to belief-that. The proposition which

[1] We shall see presently that there are other example where the propositions believed belong to other logical types (p. 433–4).

the 'reduction' yields need not necessarily be an existential proposition. If I believe in the combustibility of nylon and the incombustibility of asbestos, I believe that nylon is combustible and asbestos is not. If I believe in the infrequency of lunar rainbows, I believe that lunar rainbows are infrequent. Again, if a philosopher says he believes in free will, the obvious rendering of this is 'he believes that all men (or all rational beings) have the power of free choice'. To say instead 'he believes that free will exists' or 'that there is such a thing as free will' is less explicit, and does not bring out the full force of the belief-in expression which we are trying to analyse.

Sometimes, no doubt, it does not matter very much whether the reduction takes an existential form or not. (One *can* say 'he believes that there is such a thing as the longevity of tortoises'.) But there are other cases where it does matter. For instance, someone says 'I have never quite believed in her blond hair'. If this is to be interpreted in a 'belief-that' sense, what exactly was the belief-that which the speaker could never quite hold? It certainly was not the belief that the blond hair existed. He never doubted its existence. But he did doubt whether it was the lady's own. He surmised that she wore a skilfully-made wig; or he surmised that though it was her own hair, its original colour had been very different. And now one or other of these surmises has turned out to be correct.

Finally, it is worth while to notice that the converse rendering of belief-that sentences into belief-in sentences is also possible, at least sometimes; and this gives some support to the doctrine mentioned earlier that the difference between the two is 'merely one of idiom'. Believing that all whales are mammals could equally be described as believing in the mammality of all whales. Believing that no Englishman plays ice hockey as well as some Canadians does not seem to differ from believing in the inferiority of all Englishman to some Canadians as ice-hockey players. Believing that the Sahara would be habitable if it were irrigated does not seem to differ from believing in [the habitability of the Sahara on condition of its being irrigated]. But here we have to insert brackets to avoid an ambiguity. 'If the Sahara were irrigated, then I should believe that it is habitable' and 'I believe that if the Sahara were irrigated, it would be habitable' are two different statements. We have to put in the brackets to show that our belief-in statement is the equivalent of the second, not of the first.

Sometimes the change-over from 'that' to 'in' is not easy to make with our existing terminological resources. The 'belief-in' rendering of a 'belief-that' sentence may be clumsy, long-winded, and inelegant: for example, 'I believe in his either coming this morning after breakfast or putting off his visit until lunch-time on the second Sunday of next month'. But certainly there are a good many cases where the difference between 'in' and 'that' can quite fairly be called a mere difference of idiom, and there are more of them than we might have supposed.

The relevance of this to our main question 'Is belief-in reducible to belief-that?' can now be seen. Equivalence is a symmetrical relation. If *A* is equivalent to *B*, it follows logically that *B* is equivalent to *A*. So if we are willing to use the syntactical expedients which have been illustrated, the number of 'belief-in' sentences which have 'belief-that' equivalents turns out to be much larger than we thought. Nor does it matter if some of these 'belief in' sentences have an exceedingly artificial air, so that no one would in practice be likely to utter them. They are intelligible, however complicated, long-winded and inelegant they may be.

TWO DIFFERENT SENSES OF 'BELIEF-IN'

It is only too obvious by now that the question 'Is belief-in reducible to belief-that?' is a complicated and difficult one. There is much to be said on both sides. We began by considering a number of examples which suggest rather strongly that no such reduction is possible. Instead, they suggest that belief-in is an attitude quite different from belief-that. We have now considered a number of other examples, which suggest equally strongly that belief-in *is* reducible to belief-that. What conclusion are we to draw when we consider both sets of examples together?

The obvious conclusion is this: there are two different senses of 'believe in'. On the one hand, there is an evaluative sense. This is illustrated by believing in one's doctor, or believing in railways, or believing in a procedure such as taking a cold bath every morning. Something like esteeming or trusting is an essential part of belief-in in this sense. (The other part of it would be conceiving or having in mind whatever it is that is esteemed or trusted.) As we have seen, the 'objects' of belief-in, in this sense, are enormously various. It is a mistake to suppose that its 'object' must always be a person. There is a corresponding sense of 'disbelief in', where our attitude is something like disesteem or distrust. This is quite commonly expressed by saying 'I do not believe in . . .', much as dislike is quite commonly expressed by saying 'I do not like. . .'. It is illustrated by 'we do not believe in waiting-lists', or by the disbelief in Mr Gladstone which most contemporary British Tories had. In this sense of 'believe in', believing-in does seem to be a quite different attitude from belief-that and irreducible to it. The same applies to the corresponding sense of 'disbelieve in'.

On the other hand, there is also a factual sense of 'believe in'. The most obvious examples of it are the belief in fairies or the belief in King Arthur. Belief-in, in this sense, certainly *is* reducible to belief-that. In these examples one believes an existential proposition. One believes *that* there is something to which such and such a description applies. But as we have seen, there are other examples of 'reducible' belief-in where the proposition believed is not an existential one. There is also a corresponding and equally reducible sense of 'disbelieve in'. If someone disbelieves in fairies, he just disbelieves that there are such creatures, or rejects the proposition that there are. And if he disbelieves (in this sense) in free will, he disbelieves or rejects the proposition that human beings have the power of making free choices.

Moreover, just because these two senses of 'belief in' are different, the attitude denoted by the one can be combined with the attitude denoted by the other. One may *both* believe that there is such and such a thing *and* have esteem for it or trust in it. The writer to *The Times* who believed in railways is an example. So is Lord Halifax's Englishman, who believed in the sea. Again, one may both believe that there is such a thing and have disesteem for it or distrust in it, like those who say 'we do not believe in waiting-lists'. Here disbelief-in, in the evaluative sense, is combined with belief-in, in the factual sense: and there is no inconsistency in this combination. In St James' Epistle a similar combination of attitudes is attributed to the devils who 'believe and tremble'. They believe that God exists, and we may suppose they believe it with full conviction too. At the same time they have an attitude of distrust towards him.

CONNECTIONS BETWEEN THE TWO SENSES

Let us assume that there are these two different senses of 'believe in', the evaluative sense and the factual sense. If there are, there is also a close connection between them, when the 'object' of evaluative belief-in is an *entity* of any kind. I cannot trust my doctor unless I at least believe that there is a person to whom the description 'being my doctor' applies. But the phrase 'at least' is important, as Professor Norman Malcolm has pointed out to me. A person who is believed in, in the evaluative sense, may be known to the believer by personal acquaintance. Malcolm's example is a wife who says of her husband 'I believe in Tom'. It would not be false to say of her 'she believes that there is such a person', but it would be saying too little. Similarly, if you believe in your doctor you probably know him by personal acquaintance (in some degree at any rate) though you do of course believe that he is your doctor, and probably hold other beliefs-that about him as well, for instance that he is about forty years old, and that he lives at No, 50A Tankerville Avenue. Again, the blind man who believes in his guide-dog knows the dog by acquaintance almost as one knows a human friend.

On the other hand, personal acquaintance is certainly not a necessary condition for evaluative belief-in. On the contrary, when one comes to be personally acquainted with a person whom one believes in, one's belief in him may decrease or even vanish altogether. (Fortunately this also applies to disbelief in a person, which quite often decreases or vanishes when one meets him.) To take an example of quite a different kind: the Managing Director may believe in waiting-lists so long as he has no personal experience of being put on a waiting-list himself; but at last this experience befalls him, when he is trying to get his mowing-machine repaired, and then his belief in waiting-lists is considerably shaken and may even be replaced by a disbelief in them.

The opposite 'conversion', from disbelief in a method or procedure to belief in it, may occur in a similar way. Many disbelieve in air travel so long as they have not actually tried it. But when they are compelled to try it, because there is no other way of getting to their destination in time, the result of this personal experience is that their disbelief in air travel vanishes and is replaced by a firm belief in it. These examples do, however, show that Professor Malcolm's point about acquaintance is relevant not only to belief in another person, but to other cases of evaluative belief-in as well.

IS FACTUAL BELIEF-IN A PRESUPPOSITION OF EVALUATIVE BELIEF-IN?

Shall we say, then, that anyone who believes in *X* in the evaluative sense must also believe in *X* in the factual sense—this at least, though he may know *X* by acquaintance too? This is an attractive suggestion. It offers us a neat and tidy way of formulating the relation between the two senses of 'belief in'; factual belief-in would just be a necessary condition for evaluative belief-in, or a presupposition of it. But unfortunately this is too neat and tidy to be true, if 'believing in *X* in the factual sense' is taken to mean 'believing that *X* exists', which is the natural way to take it. So interpreted, the formula proposed would fit some of the many varieties of evaluative belief-in, but not all of them.

For instance, does it fit belief in a procedure such as taking a cold bath every morning? At first we may be inclined to think it does. For surely anyone who holds this belief-in does also believe 'that there is' such a procedure? Some people still take a cold bath every morning and many people did so fifty years ago. Perhaps it will also be said that anyone who believes in taking a cold bath every morning must himself take one every morning (or most mornings); for if he did not, he could not be sincere when he claims to believe in doing so. In that case he not only believes but knows that there is such a procedure, and moreover he has acquired this knowledge-that by personal experience of instances of the procedure.

But these two arguments are inconclusive. A man might believe sincerely and very firmly in taking a cold bath every morning, even though he had been a bed-ridden invalid all his life and had never been able to take a bath at all. Or he might be a Bedouin who lives in the Mesopotamian desert and never has enough water to take a bath. It is conceivable too that neither of these persons has ever heard of anyone elso who took daily cold baths. Either of them might be an original thinker, who has managed to think of this curious procedure for himself; and having thought of it, he values it highly, without ever being able to put it into practice.

The same applies to belief in equal pay for both sexes. This is a policy which a man could believe in (and some presumably did) at a time when it had not been put into practice anywhere. Nor is it true that if such a man was sincere, he must have put it into practice himself, by paying his male butler and his female house-maid equally. He need not have had any employees himself; and if he had, they may all have been of the same sex.

In what sense, then, did he believe 'that there is such a thing as' paying the two sexes equally? Only in a pretty tenuous sense of 'there is'. It did not amount to much more than believing that the concept of paying the two sexes equally for the same work is not self-contradictory, or believing that the proposition 'the two sexes are paid equally for the same work', though false at that time, is not necessarily false.

Nevertheless, there was another and not quite so tenuous belief-that which he did have to hold, if he was sincere in believing in this policy. He had to believe that the policy was practicable, or in principle practicable, whatever obstacles might have to be overcome before it was put into practice. And if we like, we can describe this as a belief 'in its being practicable', and then we are using 'belief in' in its factual sense. Similarly any sincere believer in taking daily cold baths must believe that this procedure is in principle practicable, even if he can never practise it himself and has never heard of anyone else who did.

But what shall we say of belief in an 'ideal', such as the ideal of complete unselfishness? A man who believes in this ideal does have to believe that complete unselfishness is logically possible, not self-contradictory as some have alleged that it is. But does he have to believe that it is practicable? Surely a man may sincerely believe in an ideal while admitting that it is quite 'unrealizable'?

Indeed, it might be said that unrealisability is one of the distinguishing features of an ideal (as opposed, e.g. to a policy). Still, there *is* a belief-that concerning practicability or realizability which a sincere believer in an ideal has to hold. Whatever his ideal is, he has to believe that approximations to it are practicable, and approximations closer, or much closer, than those which exist at present. It may not be practicable for any human being, still less for most, to be completely unselfish in all his actions, utterances, thoughts, desires and feelings. But it is practicable for almost anyone to be a good deal more unselfish than he has been hitherto. At any rate a person must believe that it is, if he sincerely believes in the ideal of complete unselfishness. And if we like, we can formulate this belief-that in 'reducible' or merely factual belief-in terminology. Such a believer may be said to believe in its being empirically possible for these approximations to occur.

'BELIEF IN' AND 'CONFIDENCE IN'

It does seem to be true that factual belief-in is a necessary condition for evaluative belief-in, or a presupposition of it. But we must be careful to add that this factual belief-in may take many different forms, corresponding to the many different varieties of evaluative belief-in. It need not always take the form of believing an existential proposition, believing that *X* exists or that 'there is such a thing as *X*', when *X* is what is evaluatively believed in.

Nevertheless, the cases where it does take this form are of considerable importance. They make it very clear that we must distinguish between two different senses of 'believe in', and evaluative sense and a factual sense; otherwise we are led into absurd misunderstandings.

For instance, little Belinda says she does not believe in Santa Claus any more. The Christmas presents he brings her now are not nearly so nice as they used to be, and there are not so many of them either. Shall we say 'Naughty child! Little liar! You certainly do believe in him if you make these complaints about the way he has treated you'? Yet these comments would be justified if the factual sense of 'believe in' were the only one.

We may notice, however, that such misunderstandings do

not arise if we use the phrase 'confidence in' instead of 'belief in'. 'Confidence in' does not have these two difference senses, evaluative and factual; and the distinction between 'confidence in' and 'confidence that' is a pretty clear-cut one. If I say I have confidence in someone, it is pretty plain that I am expressing an evaluative attitude; and if I have lost confidence in him, because of something he has done or failed to do, what I have lost is pretty clearly an evaluative attitude. Of course, if I do lose confidence in him I must still retain my confidence *that* he exists. But no one is ever tempted to accuse me of inconsistency on that account.

Perhaps Belinda would have been wiser to say 'I have no confidence in Santa Claus now'. Or she might have said 'I have no faith in him now', or 'I don't trust him any longer'. Then we should have had no temptation to call her a naughty child or a little liar.

PART II

ANOTHER VERSION OF THE 'REDUCIBILITY' THESIS

So far it has been argued that there are two senses of 'believe in'. First there is a factual sense. Here belief-in is clearly reducible to belief-that. It is just the acceptance of a proposition; and the proposition accepted is often, though not always, an existential one. Secondly, there is an evaluative sense of 'believe in'. Here believing-in amounts to something like esteeming or trusting; and in this second sense, believing-in seems to be quite a different attitude from believing-that.

The conclusion one is inclined to draw is that the reducibility thesis ('belief-in is reducible to belief-that') is correct for one of the two senses of 'believe in' but incorrect for the other. Unfortunately the question cannot be settled quite so easily. Perhaps it has only been shown that the reduction has to take two different forms, one form for factual belief-in and another for evaluative belief-in.

A reductionist might quite well admit that there are these two different senses of 'believe in'. Yet he might still claim that evaluative belief-in can itself be reduced to belief-that, if we go the right way about it. All we have to do, he might say, is to introduce suitable value-concepts into the proposition believed. Once we have done this, the difference between factual and evaluative belief-in will turn out to be just a difference in the content of the proposition believed, a difference in the 'object' and not in the mental attitude of the believer; and believing *that* will turn out to be the only sort of believing, a conclusion very welcome to all sensible men.

In this revised version, the reducibility thesis is much more plausible; and whether correct or not, it draws our attention to certain important characteristics of evaluative belief-in which might easily be overlooked. But anyone who wishes to maintain it must indeed be careful to 'go the right way about it'. He must be careful to choose the appropriate value-concepts, if the proposed reduction is to be plausible. For instance, believing in one's doctor certainly cannot be reduced to believing that he is a morally good man. The value-concept which we must apply to him is not 'morally good' but 'good at . . .'. Nor will it suffice to believe that he is good at water-colour painting. Of course I may also believe this, and it may be true. But that kind of 'goodness at . . .' is irrelevant if I believe in him *as my doctor*. I must believe that he is good at curing diseases, or perhaps at curing the diseases to which I myself am particularly liable.

This brings out an important point about evaluative belief-in. When someone expresses a belief in another person, it is always appropriate to ask 'As what is he believed in by you?' or 'What is there about him, in respect of which you believe in him?' Again, if the falconer believes in goshawks, we may ask 'What is there about goshawks, in respect of which he believes in them?' Presumably he believes that hawks of this species are good at catching geese and other large birds in flight. It is true that the phrase 'good at' is only appropriate to persons and animals. It hardly makes sense to say that railways are 'good at' or 'bad at' anything. But other terms closely related to 'good at . . .' may be used, such as 'efficient', 'effective', good way of . . .'. The believer in railways believes that railways are an efficient or the most efficient way of transporting large numbers of persons and commodities over long distances by land. The believer in taking daily cold baths believes that this is an effective way of maintaining one's bodily health.

But we need to introduce another value-concept as well. Someone might believe very firmly that railways are a highly efficient way of transporting persons and commodities. But if he were very old-fashioned and eccentric, he might think that this was a reason for *not* believing in them. He might reject the view, held by nearly everyone else, that mobility is something good for its own sake. He might think it would be better if persons and commodities usually stayed where they are.

Again, we might believe that so-and-so is exceedingly good at extracting information from others by means of torture. But this would be a good reason for not believing *in* him, or *in* the policy of employing him in the service of the government or the police. We disapprove of that kind of efficiency, and the greater it is, the worse it is.

We see now what the other value-concept is, which has to be introduced into the proposition believed if this type of reductive analysis is to be plausible. It is colloquially expressed by the phrase 'good thing that . . .'. We do not believe it is a good thing that a man is good at extracting information by means of torture. But we do ordinarily believe it is a good thing that our doctor is good at curing diseases. Or the proposition which we believe (according to this analysis) could be formulated thus: 'My doctor is good at curing diseases, and a good thing too!' Similarly, the falconer believes it is a good thing that goshawks are good at catching large birds in flight. Some would not agree with him in believing that this is a good thing, even though they do agree that goshawks are good at doing it. Then they do not believe in goshawks, or only in the factual sense of believing that there is such a species of hawks.

Let us now consider Lord Halifax's Englishman who believed in the sea. If this belief-in is to be reduced to belief-that, in the way suggested, what is the proposition which the Englishman believed? It must have been a rather complex one, something like this: 'It is a good thing that my country, Great Britain, is completely surrounded by sea, since navies are a more efficient and less expensive means of defence than armies.' (Perhaps he also believed that navies are a more efficient and less expensive means of aggression and conquest.)

The same kind of analysis can be applied to the rather difficult example of 'believing in oneself'. Most commonly we use this phrase in a negative form. The trouble with Tom is that he does not believe in himself: he will never make a success of his life. What is this belief-in which he lacks? Certainly it is not just a factual belief-in. He does not lack the belief that he exists. He still does not lack it, even if he is a philosopher who accepts a very radical Humian or Buddhist theory of personal identity. According to the analysis we are considering, the proposition which he does not believe would be something like this: 'I am good at performing most of the tasks I undertake, and a good thing too!' A man who does believe such a proposition has a *general* belief in himself, as we might call it. But belief in oneself can be of a more limited or departmental kind. The question 'As what is so and so believed in by you?' is still relevant, even when 'so and so' is yourself. Thus an undergraduate might believe that he is good at understanding lectures, writing essays, and passing examinations, and that this is a good thing. Then he believes in himself as a student. But he need not believe that he is good at other activities in which he engages, such as football or mending punctures in the tyres of his bicycle.

It seems then that the proposed reduction of evaluative belief-in to belief-that must introduce *two* value-concepts into the proposition believed: not only 'good at . . .' ('efficient', 'effective'), but also 'good thing that . . .'. As we have seen, it need not be at all a good thing that someone should be 'good at his job' nor that something is an effective means or method of producing a certain result. And unless we do believe it is a good thing, we shall not believe *in* him or *in* it.

THE PROSPECTIVE CHARACTER OF BELIEF-IN

One merit of this analysis is to draw our attention to the relation between evaluative belief-in and time. If we just say 'I believe in Mr So-and-so' or 'in such and such a policy or procedure' no temporal predicate is attached to the object of our belief-in. But when we substitute a that-clause for the noun or name-phrase we must use a verb, and verbs have tenses.

We then notice an interesting feature of evaluative belief-in. In all the examples so far given it has a reference to the future, though not necessarily to the future only. It has a prospective character. This is not true of factual belief-in, which can be concerned entirely with the past. Belief in King Arthur is an example. On the other hand, if I believe in my doctor, I believe not only that it is and has been a good thing that he is good at curing my diseases, but that it will continue to be a good thing and that he will continue to be good at curing them.

But does evaluative belief-in always have a prospective character? Surely there can be an evaluative belief in a past event? For instance, Christians believe in the Incarnation. This is not only a belief that it happened, that there was such an event more than nineteen centuries ago. It is an evaluative belief-in as well as a factual one. According to the analysis we are considering, they do of course believe that it *was* a good thing that this event happened, that the results of it *have* been highly beneficial to the human race, and that there *was* no other effective means of producing them. But this is not all they believe. They believe that these results will continue to be beneficial and that there never will be any other effective means of producing them, at least so long as the present world-order continues. This is the sense in which they 'put their trust in' the Incarnation; and it is clear that their trust does have a prospective character. To put it another way, there is a connection between evaluative belief-in and hope.

Similarly one may believe in a person who is no longer alive, without having to believe that he is still alive in another world. A student of the Roman Empire may believe in Tacitus and disbelieve in Suetonius, or believe in him much less. (In the factual sense, of course, he believes equally in both of them. He believes that both of them existed and that both were Roman historians.) Is there anything prospective about this belief-in? There is. Some of the writings of both these historians still exist and can still be read. It could be said of each of them that 'being dead, he yet speaketh'. So the question 'Do we trust him?' or 'How much do we trust him?' still arises. And there is something prospective about this question. Beliefs about the future are relevant to it. For instance, I believe that archaeological evidence will continue to confirm most of what Tacitus says, but will not confirm so much of what Suetonius says. Moreover, I believe that if the lost parts of Tacitus' writings are discovered some day, they too will be confirmed by archaeological evidence. Trusting Tacitus, then, is not altogether different from trusting one's doctor; and in both cases (according to the analysis we are considering) our trust consists at least partly in a belief-that of a prospective kind.

Again, Englishmen have ceased to believe in the sea, though in Lord Halifax's time they did, and so did their successors until about a generation ago. Why is this? The sea is still there and still surrounds our country. But we can no longer rely on it to continue to 'deliver the goods' (security, power, etc.) which it did deliver formerly. It never will deliver them again unless there is a complete breakdown in our present technological civilization. If Englishmen still have a creed of this geo-political kind, the first article in it is certainly not 'I believe in the sea' but 'I believe in the air' or perhaps 'I believe in inter-continental ballistic missiles'. In that case, according to the analysis we are discussing, we believe not only that aircraft or ballistic missiles have been and still are efficient means of defence, but also that they will continue to be so for some years to come.

INTERESTED AND DISINTERESTED BELIEF-IN

This analysis suggests another question which we ought to consider. If I believe that it is a good thing that such and such a state of affairs exists, does the word 'good' just mean 'good for me', the believer? (Of course, what I believe to be a good thing for me may not in fact be a good thing for me at all. But this is not relevant. We are only concerned to elucidate what it is that I believe.) If 'good thing' does always have this sense, we shall have to say that evaluative belief-in is always an *interested* attitude, never a disinterested one.

This is a plausible suggestion, provided that we are willing to stretch the meaning of 'for me'. 'Good for *us*' would often be a more appropriate phrase. For instance, the doctor may be the family doctor or the doctor of all the inhabitants of the village in which I live. Then, if I believe in him, I am likely to believe that it is a good thing *for us* that *our* doctor is good at curing diseases. Still, in order to believe so, I must in some way 'identify myself' with a group (my family or the inhabitants of my village) as the use of the first person plural indicates. It is not enough that he is in fact the family doctor or the village doctor and that I believe him to be so. I must be in some way concerned about the health of the other members of my family or of my fellow-villagers. It must matter to me whether they are well or ill.

Again, I may believe in the Queen's doctor. Then I believe it is a good thing 'for us' that he holds this position and is very good at his job. And now 'us' has expanded so far that it includes the whole population of Great Britain or even of the entire British Commonwealth. It might even expand so far that it includes the whole of humanity. The believer in penicillin may well believe that it is a good thing for all mankind, for all of us everywhere, that this drug has been invented and is such an efficient means of saving lives and curing diseases. Nevertheless, it seems permissible to say that these beliefs-in are still interested ones, even though it is a matter of 'our' interest and not just the interest of 'me', the individual believer. There are collective interests as well as individual interests.

There is another question which has a bearing on this one. Indeed, it is perhaps another way of formulating the same question, if 'interested' has the wide sense just suggested. We may ask whether 'good' (in 'good thing that . . .') always has the sense of 'instrumentally good', 'good as a means'. Clearly this is the sense it has in many of the examples so far considered. It is not an intrinsically good thing that people should take daily cold baths. If anything, it is an intrinsically bad one, since it is often a painful experience to take them. But according to those who believe in this procedure, it is good as a means for maintaining one's health. Again, if someone believes in easier divorce, he certainly need not believe that it is a good thing for its own sake that married couples should be divorced more easily. But he does believe, rightly or wrongly, that if divorce were made easier, this would be an effective means of increasing human happiness or decreasing human misery.

BELIEF IN A FRIEND

But now let us consider belief in a friend; or rather, let us say belief in someone *as* a friend, since we might also believe in him 'as' something else, for example as a scholar or as a bee-keeper. The analysis of evaluative belief-in which we are discussing makes use of two value-concepts 'good thing that . . .' and 'good at . . .'. We find, however, that we have to take a new look at both of them when we consider belief in a friend.

If I believe in someone as a friend, I do believe that it is a good thing for me, advantageous to me, that he is my friend. I believe that he is disposed to be kind to me and to give me what help he can when I need it. So far, my belief in him is an interested one; I believe that my friendship with him is good as a means, a means to my own welfare or happiness, and that it will continue to be so. But is this all I believe? Clearly it is not. I also believe that my friendship with him, and his with me, is something good in itself, and will continue to be so. It is something which I value for its own sake. In this respect, then, my belief in him is disinterested. More than that, I value *him* for his own sake. According to the type of analysis we are discussing, this would amount to believing that it is just a good thing that he exists, and still would be even of I 'got nothing out of it'. In this respect again, my belief in a friend is disinterested.

Let us now turn to the other value-concept 'good at'. Does it make sense to say 'So and so is a friend of mine, but I do not believe in him at all'? Apparently it must, if 'good at . . .' is an essential part of the analysis of evaluative belief-in. For surely I might be quite convinced that he is 'no good at anything', a thoroughly inefficient person; and yet he might be my friend. It might be suggested that he *is* good at being friendly, and that this, after all, is a pretty important sort of 'goodness at . . .'. Very likely he is, but he need not be. I might be his only friend, the only person he gets on well with. Can it be said, then, that at any rate he is good at being friendly with me, though he is no good at being friendly with others?

But there is something odd about this use of 'good at . . .'. It is true that my doctor might be good at curing the particular diseases from which I personally suffer, and this might be the reason why I believe in him. It is true too that he need not be good at curing any other diseases. But he *would* have to be good at curing other people who suffer from the same ones. Similarly, my friend, if he is 'good at' being friendly with me, must also be good at being friendly with anyone else who resembles me in the relevant respects, whatever respects they are.

It comes to this: 'good at . . .', in the ordinary sense of the phrase, has a certain generality about it. It refers to a class of some kind. The class in question might in fact have only one member. I might happen to be the only person who has the characteristics required, e.g. the only indolent and red-haired person, educated at Manchester Grammar School, who has sailed twice round Cape Horn. But if 'good at' is the appropriate phrase, my friend would have to be good at being friendly with *anyone* who has this combination of characteristics, even though in fact there is no one else who happens to have them.

Perhaps we can now see what the trouble is. There is a sense in which every person is a unique individual. He is of course a member of many different classes. All the same, there is something unclassifiable about him. There is a sense in which he is 'just himself'. And this is what matters in inter-personal relations such as friendship. A friend likes me just as being myself, and I like him just as being himself. That is why it is inappropriate to say he is 'good at' being friendly with me, or that I am 'good at' being friendly with him.

Trusting is an essential factor in all evaluative belief-in. But it follows from what has been said that the trust we have in a friend is different from the trust we have in an expert who is 'good at' a particular job. The trust we have in an expert has a limited or departmental character. We trust him in so far as he is an engine-driver or an instructor in water-colour painting. But we need not trust him just as a human being. For all we can tell, he may be quite untrustworthy in some of his other activities. Trust in a friend, on the contrary, is non-departmental. We do trust him as a human being. Moreover, we trust him as the individual, unique human being that he is.

It seems then that the proposed analysis in terms of 'good thing that . . .' and 'good at . . .' does not apply very well to belief in a friend. The concept of 'good at . . .' is not relevant to this very important variety of evaluative belief-in. The concept of 'good thing that . . .' is indeed relevant to it. If we believe in a friend we do believe that it is and will continue to be 'a good thing' that he exists and is the individual person that he is. But we believe it is a good thing not only as a means, but also for its own sake. Belief in a friend cannot be just an interested belief-in. This is a logical impossibility. If our belief in another person were wholly interested, it would be improper to describe him as our friend.

To make matters more difficult, the expert on whose skill or efficiency we rely, for instance our doctor or teacher, may become our friend as well; and then we believe in him and trust him in two ways at once. Friendship may creep in, unawares, into many of the relations between one person and another. Something like it may also creep in when there is a relation between a person and an animal, for instance between the blind man and his guide-dog, or the falconer and his goshawk. And there is a faint analogue of it when someone gives a proper name to a machine on which he relies (he may call his motor-car 'Jane'). After all, the capacity for love, in all its many degrees and forms, is quite an important part of human nature. Philosophical analysts have to put up with it, even though it makes their work more complicated.

THE MERITS AND DEFECTS OF THIS REDUCTION

We have now considered two different proposals for reducing belief 'in' to belief 'that'. Both are useful. We learn something from each of them when we try to apply it to the many different sorts of examples in which the expression 'belief in' is used.

From the first we learn that there are two senses of 'belief in'; on the one hand, a factual sense where 'belief in' *is* reducible to 'belief that', and often though not always consists in believing an existential proposition; on the other hand, an evaluative sense, where 'believing in' is equivalent to something like esteeming or trusting.

What do we learn from the second and much more plausible proposal? The aim of it is to show that even though there is an evaluative sense of 'belief in', this too can be reduced to 'belief that' if suitable value-concepts ('good thing . . .' and 'good at . . .' or 'efficient' or 'effective') are introduced into the proposition believed.

This second type of analysis is instructive and illuminating. It brings out the prospective character of evaluative belief-in, an important one which we might not otherwise have noticed. It also helps to make clear just what the content of a particular belief-in is. When someone or something is believed in, it is always appropriate to ask '*as being what* is he (or it) believed in?' The answer often is 'as being good at such an activity' or 'as being a good (efficient) way of achieving such and such a result'. Moreover, the person believing does have to value the activity which he thinks *A* is 'good at' or the state of affairs which he thinks *B* is an efficient means of achieving; and this is the point of the phrase 'good thing that . . .'. There are many beliefs-in whose content cannot be fully explicated unless thsee two concepts 'good thing that . . .' and 'good at . . .' (or 'efficient') are brought in somewhere. Finally, once they *are* brought in, we see that there are two types of evaluative belief-in, interested and disinterested, and also that some evaluative beliefs-in are both at once, when 'good' in 'good thing that . . .' includes both 'good as a means' and 'good for its own sake'. This again is an important point, which we might not have noticed otherwise.

But there are defects in this analysis too, however helpful and instructive it is. We shall do well to make all the use of it we can, but it will not take us all the way. As we have seen, it does not fit one very important type of example, belief in a friend. Here the concept 'good at . . .' plays no part, although 'good thing that . . .' does. Our friend's efficiency, or lack of it, is irrelevant to our belief in him, if we do believe in him *as* a friend.

But further, the proposed reduction does not completely fit any of the examples to which we have tried to apply it. In all of them, it leaves something out. At an earlier stage of the discussion it was suggested that 'esteeming or trusting' is an essential feature of evaluative belief-in. We now see, I think, that *both* esteeming *and* trusting are essential features of it. This reductive proposal does provide fairly well for the esteeming, by means of the concepts 'good thing that . . .' and 'good at . . .' (or efficient'). But does it provide for the trusting? Can this be done by insisting on the prospective character of evaluative belief-in?

Suppose I believe not only that my doctor has been and is good at curing my diseases, but also that he will continue to be so; and not only that it is and has been a good thing that he is good at this, but also that it will continue to be a good thing. But what if I do believe these two propositions as firmly as you please? Believing them may be a necessary condition for trusting him, but it is not the same as trusting him. Trusting is not a merely cognitive attitude.

To put the same point in another way, the proposed reduction leaves out the 'warmth' which is a characteristic feature of evaluative belief-in. Evaluative belief-in is a 'pro-attitude'. One is 'for' the person, thing, policy, etc. in whom or in which one believes. There is something more than assenting or being disposed to assent to a proposition, no matter what concepts the proposition contains. That much-neglected aspect of human nature which used to be called 'the heart' enters into evaluative belief-in. Trusting is an affective attitude. We might even say that it is in some degree an affectionate one.

The beliefs-that, to which this reductive analysis draws our attention, are indeed an essential part of our belief-in attitude. When we trust someone or something, these beliefs-that are the ones we must mention in order to answer the question 'in respect of what do you trust him (or it)?'. And this question is a perfectly proper one, and does require an answer. But when it has been answered, we still have not explained what trusting is, or what it is like to trust or 'put one's faith in' someone or something. Perhaps we can only know what it is like by actually being in the mental attitude which the word 'trusting' denotes. But fortunately there are few persons, if any, who have never trusted anyone or anything; and if it is disagreeable to be compelled to talk about 'the heart', the fact remains that most of us have one, as well as a head.

APPLICATION TO BELIEF IN GOD

The most important of all the varieties of evaluative belief-in is belief in God. It is also the most difficult to discuss, if only because so many of us nowadays do not know what it is like to have it. Still, one may ask whether any light is thrown on it by the conclusions we have reached, even though most of the examples discussed have been of a non-religious kind.

Belief in God (in the evaluative sense) clearly does have the 'warmth' or 'heart-felt' character which we have noticed in other evaluative beliefs-in. It is certainly a pro-attitude, and both esteeming and trusting enter into it. But does the distinction between 'interested' and 'disinterested' belief-in apply to it, and does it have a prospective character, as non-religious belief-in has?

It looks as if evaluative belief in God were both interested and disinterested at the same time, interested in some respects and disinterested in others. If the phrase 'good thing that . . .' may be used here, then surely it is a good thing for the believer himself (and for all of us) that God is loving, compassionate and merciful, that he answers prayers, that he gives his grace to us, that he is a refuge to us in times of trouble. Nothing could be more advantageous to us than the existence of God, if he is what theists believe him to be. The prospectiveness is there too. We believe not only that all this is and has been 'a very good thing' for each of us individually and all of us collectively, but also that it will continue to be so. God has been 'good to us' and we trust him to be good to us always, come what may, and even at times when he seems not to be ('Though he slay me, yet will I trust in him').

But if we were to stop at that, our belief in God would be an interested belief-in. His existence would only be good as a means, however important and even indispensable that 'means' might be; and if we loved him, our love (so far) would only be a kind of 'cupboard love'. From this point of view he is regarded just as 'the giver of gifts'. We value his gifts; we are sure that we could not get on without him. But so far, we do not value *him* for his own sake.

But as soon as we start thanking God for his gifts, being grateful for them with a gratitude which is not just 'a lively sense of favours to come', our belief in him ceases to be wholly interested. We are beginning to value him for his own sake, and to believe that it is a good thing, intrinsically good, that he exists and is what he is; and not just 'a good thing', but the fundamental 'good thing' without which there would be no others.

At this stage, the nearest analogue in inter-human relationships would be belief in a friend, where there is a similar combination of interested and disinterested believing-in. It is perhaps significant that some theistic mystics have referred to God as 'The

Friend'. But as the definite article indicates, they did not think of him as just one friend among others. Friendship of the ordinary kind is a relation between equals, and in this important respect the analogy breaks down.

After all, if once we make the distinction between interested and disinterested belief-in, it is almost obvious that belief in God is normally a combination of both. It might be perfectly sincere if it were wholly of the interested sort, but we should be inclined to think that there was something incomplete about it. Even so, it would still be quite different from the belief-that of Pascal's *philosophes et savants* who believe in God only in the factual sense. Even a wholly interested belief in God is still evaluative and not merely factual. It cannot be reduced to the mere acceptance of an existential proposition.

LECTURE 10

RELIGIOUS BELIEF AND EMPIRICIST PHILOSOPHY

In matters of religion the most common attitude nowadays is probably an agnostic one. An agnostic (literally a 'don't know' man) is a person who holds that there is a third alternative between Theism and Atheism. A theist asserts the existence of God; an atheist denies it. An agnostic does neither. He suspends judgement on the ground that we do not have sufficient evidence to decide the question, and so far as he can tell there is no likelihood that we ever shall have. At any rate, this is the classical version of Agnosticism, the one T. H. Huxley had in mind when he invented the term.

But in the past thirty or forty years a new and more radical version of Agnosticism has been propounded. Until then, all three parties in this controversy—theists, atheists and agnostics—had shared a common assumption. All three assumed that statements about God (or about other supernatural entities) were at any rate meaningful. It was agreed by all three that the statement 'God exists' is in fact either true or false, whatever difficulties there might be in discovering which it is, and even if these difficulties were insuperable.

This is the assumption which is now denied. Instead, it is suggested by contemporary Agnostics that statements about God are empty or devoid of meaning, indeed are not genuine statements at all. They do not tell us anything. They are not even false. ('It is at least false' is nowadays something of a compliment.) When someone says 'God loves us' one cannot even suspend judgement about this utterance, as the old Agnostics wished to do, because there is no intelligible proposition to suspend judgement about.

This modern doctrine does have one important point in common with the old Agnosticism. It is neutral as between Theism and Atheism, or believers and disbelievers. But instead of suspending judgement, it says that both sides are talking nonsense, on the ground that the very question they are disputing about is a meaningless question.

Yet if we consider the effects which this view has on the mind of the educated public, we see that they are very different from those which the classical Agnosticism had, and to a religious person much more disturbing. In the old days, men used to have 'religious doubts'. But if they can be persuaded that there is nothing to doubt about—it is all just a muddle—they will lose interest in religion altogether, and will no longer *even* have doubts about it.

And this, of course, is what the Atheists always wanted. Their aim was to get rid of God out of the universe. What better way could there be of achieving this, than a demonstration that sentences about God are devoid of meaning? If this can be shown, the very thought of God will be dismissed from the minds of all sensible men, and they will not even ask the question whether it is reasonable to believe that he exists. Although it would be quite wrong to call this modern doctrine a form of Atheism, it is really doing the Atheist's job for him, and doing it more effectively than he did.

STATEMENTS OR RECOMMENDATIONS?

Faced with this awkward situation, a theist might perhaps think it advisable to 'agree with his adversary quickly', according to the Gospel injunction, or at least to agree with him on one important point. Might a theist admit that his religious utterances are neither true nor false, but deny that they are meaningless?

For obviously it is a mistake to suppose every meaningful utterance must be either true or false. Commands, such as 'Shut the door!' are neither true nor false, but they are perfectly meaningful. We can understand this sentence perfectly well, but we cannot either assert it or deny it. What we *can* do is to obey it or disobey it.

Similarly, recommendations, such as the recommendation to take a cold bath every morning, or to say the Lord's Prayer twice a day, are perfectly meaningful, though they are neither true nor false and cannot be either asserted or denied. What we *can* do is to adopt the procedure recommended, or refrain from adopting it.

Now suppose we tried to conceive of Theism as a system of recommendations. Could we then evade the objections of the Agnostics, both old and new? For both sorts of Agnostic assume that the Theist is at any rate claiming to make assertions. And if that is not, after all, what he is claiming to do, both sorts of Agnostic criticism will lose their relevance. So let us try to conceive of Theism as a set of recommendations. The advantage of this way of looking at it is that, although recommendations are not true or false, there is a sense in which they are empirically testable. We can try out the procedure recommended to us, and discover whether it does or does not produce the effects it is designed to produce. If the doctor recommends us to do breathing exercises twice a day in order to avoid catching influenza in the winter, we can try it and see whether it works. This applies to intellectual procedures as well as practical ones. Geographers recommend us to conceive of the earth's surface as divided up by lines of latitude and longitude. They claim that this will enable us to grasp the relations between one place and another more easily. We try it, and find that it does have the desired result.

What then are the recommendations which a Theist makes? He makes a number of different ones, and claims that there are close connections between them. First he recommends a certain way of 'seeing' or 'viewing' the world, the adoption of a certain sort of 'world-outlook'. This is his metaphysical recommendation. The function of a metaphysician, as has already been suggested,[1] is to provide a synoptic world-outlook, or as we also say, a 'standpoint' or 'point of view', which will render the facts of experience comprehensible. A Theist recommends us to 'see' or 'view' the world as the creation of a Supreme Being who is infinite in power, wisdom and goodness and loves every single one of the persons he has created. Most Theists, though not all, have also recommended a special way of seeing or viewing what we may call the 'human scene'. They recommend us to see it as a kind of preparatory school designed for the education of immortal personal beings, by means of which we can, if we choose, make ourselves fit for eternal bliss in another and better world after death.

[1] See Lecture 9 above (*Belief 'in' and belief 'that'*), p. 431.

The claim is that if we do 'see' or 'view' the facts of experience in the way recommended, they will become more comprehensible and also more endurable. For this way of seeing them or viewing them is also a way of 'taking' them, a way of adjusting ourselves to them emotionally as well as a way of comprehending them intellectually. Indeed, many if not all of the various world-outlooks or *Weltanschvungen* which metaphysicians have recommended have this double purpose, to offer us both a way of 'seeing' the facts and a way of 'taking' them or adjusting ourselves to them; and this is one of the reasons for suspecting that the works of the great metaphysicians will always be read, however much their critics insist that they are nonsensical.

Secondly, Theists recommend a particular way of life, what Professor R. B. Braithwaite calls an 'agapistic' way of life. They recommend each of us to try to love his neighbour as himself, and to love him, moreover, in the unconditional manner described above.[1] This recommendation is at once moral and prudential. The Theist recommends this way of life to us because he himself approves of it, and approves of it more than any other type of conduct; and in expressing this approval of it, he claims that we shall approve of it too if we try to live in that way ourselves, or if we seriously consider how we feel about other people who try to live in that way. But he also recommends it on the ground that no other mode of life is in the long run satisfying to human beings, or to any beings who are persons; in that respect, his recommendation is a prudential one.

This twofold recommendation about conduct is closely connected with his metaphysical recommendation. For Theists claim that we shall not find it possible to love our neighbours in the recommended way, unless we also 'see' them or 'view' them (and ourselves too) as beings whom God himself loves in the same unconditional manner; if we do not view them in this way, we shall find some of them so repellent that the most we can manage is just to tolerate them, and perhaps even this will be beyond our power.

We shall see later that Theists make another recommendation too. But for the present let us consider those we have already mentioned. Let us begin with their recommendation about con-

[1] See Series II, Lecture 7, *Moral Beliefs*, pp. 391–2.

duct. Is it empirically testable? In so far as it is an expression of moral approval, the only way of testing it is to consider whether we ourselves approve of the 'agapistic' way of life when we seriously consider other persons who live it or seriously try to live it ourselves. Do we ourselves share the Theist's moral attitude when we are confronted with particular instances of the type of conduct he approves of? It is essential that we should consider particular instances. The approval he has expressed is a general one, approval of a *type* of conduct, and it is only too easy to accept it—or reject it—in an 'uncashed' manner, without realizing what an actual instance of this type of conduct would be like, if we met with it in another person or if we performed it ourselves.[1] Alternatively, the approval which the Theist has expressed can be regarded as approval of a type of person, a wholly charitable person. And here again we must consider particular instances—particular persons who are instances of that type or approximate to being so—if we are to be clear what this general approval really amounts to, and to agree with it (or disagree with it) understanding fully what we are doing. It would obviously be too much to say that this approval of a charitable way of life is universally accepted—accepted, that is, by all who have seriously considered it, in the light of particular instances. But it would not be too much to say that it is very widely accepted.

The prudential recommendation, moreover, is capable of a straightforward empirical test. It is either true or false that the way of life recommended satisfies us in the long run more than any other. And there is some empirical evidence, though not conclusive evidence, that this empirical claim is true, even if we take 'the long run' to be no longer than the duration of our present earthly life. It seems, then, that the Theist's recommendations about conduct, both his moral recommendation and his prudential one, receive a considerable amount of empirical support: the first from our moral experiences, the second from what we observe in ourselves and others about the effects of various types of conduct upon the agent's long term happiness.

[1] Cf. Lecture 7, *Moral Beliefs, continued* pp. 402–4.

IMMANENT AND TRANSCENDENT WORLD-OUTLOOKS

So far the Theist has done fairly well in the examination to which we are subjecting him. We might even say that he has satisfied his empirically-minded examiners in this first part of his examination. But his prospects of even a Pass Degree become much less promising when they question him about his metaphysical recommendations.

Here, as we have seen, he is recommending a particular sort of world-outlook. Here again, his recommendation is not true or false (no recommendation could be). But still, it is open to a test. If we adopt it, will it in fact do what he claims it will? Will it render the facts of experience comprehensible? Unfortunately it has two suspicious features which may make us inclined to answer 'No'.

The first is the nature of the outlook itself. Unlike some other world-outlooks, the Theistic world-outlook is not a purely immanent one, as some forms of Pantheism, for example, are. Like the exponents of other world-outlooks, the Theist is recommending a conceptual scheme, which is to be used for making the facts of experience comprehensible. But he is doing more, whether he likes it or not. He is making assertions. He does not merely propose that we make use of the *concept* of a creative and loving Supreme Being. He asserts that this concept has an instance, that there actually *is* a Supreme Being who created the world, that he actually *is* infinite in power, wisdom and goodness, and moreover that he actually *does* love every single person whom he has created. To put it in another way: in the Theistic world outlook, the idea of such a Supreme Being is not just a conceptual device, an 'auxiliary concept' to be used for facilitating certain intellectual operations.

Let us contrast it with the concept of a set of lines of latitude and longitude, which geographers invite us to use in order to render the spatial relations of various parts of the earth's surface more comprehensible. A geographer never dreams of claiming that these lines (or the grid-like structure which they form) are actually existing entities, or that they do actually embrace the earth's surface like a network of wire. They are merely conceptual devices, and when a geographer recommends us to conceive of them he is not asserting that there are any additional entities in the world, over and above those which we actually observe. But this is just what the Theist does assert. He asserts that there *is* an additional entity, over and above those which we learn about by means of sense-perception, memory, and scientific and historical investigation. He is not merely proposing that we use a certain concept or set of concepts for rendering the universally admitted facts comprehensible. He asserts that there is another fact over and above these universally admitted ones, namely the fact that there is a God—a loving God—who created the world. He claims, moreover, that this is the fact upon which all the universally admitted ones depend, and that it alone renders tham comprehensible. This is the sense in which his world-outlook is not a purely immanent one.

Most Theists also assert that every human being is immortal, and that there is another world (or worlds) in which human beings continue to exist, as persons, after death. Here again they claim to be asserting facts. There might be philosophers who merely recommend us to think of ourselves and other human beings 'as if' we were immortal, and then add 'of course it does not really make any difference whether you actually are immortal or not'. That is *not* what most Theists have said. Most of them have asserted that all of us are as a matter of fact immortal, whether we like it or not (as many of us, perhaps, do not) and that this fact does make a great deal of difference, since if it were not a fact the 'human scene', as we observe it in this present life, would not be comprehensible. Here again, they are asserting that the universally admitted facts are not the only facts there are; and at this point too the Theistic world-outlook breaks through the boundaries within which a purely immanent world-outlook is confined.

IMMORTALITY

We naturally wish to ask whether there could conceivably be any empirical evidence for these 'transcendent' assertions which appear to be integral parts of the world-outlook which the Theist recommends. As we have seen, he makes two different sorts of transcendent assertions: first those concerning God and his attributes (including his relations to ourselves) and secondly those concerning human immortality. The examiners will obviously want to question him about both. But as the assertions about immortality have a more limited scope, because the persons referred to in them are finite beings, let us begin with these. Humane examiners begin with the easier questions, and go on to the more difficult ones later.

If 'immortality' means quite literally 'endless personal existence', it is difficult to see how there could be empirical evidence for the proposition that every human being is an immortal person, or indeed for the proposition that even one human being is. At most, there could only be empirical evidence that the personal existence of some human beings had not ended yet, although they had been dead for some thousands of years. If they had managed to exist as long as this, it might be difficult to find any conclusive reason for thinking that they would not go on existing *ad indefinitum*, though we could not have any conclusive evidence for thinking that they would.

But being an immortal person does at any rate entail continuing to exist, as a person, for some period of time after bodily death. Personal immortality entails what is called personal survival. Might there be empirical evidence that a person does survive in this sense? Let us consider the proposition 'The person *A* has survived the death of his physical organism'. It is clear that *if* this proposition be true, there is one person, namely *A* himself, who has conclusive evidence of its truth. If he finds himself having experiences after he has died, and can remember experiences which he had before he died and recognize them to have been experiences of his own, he has conclusively verified the proposition 'I have survived'. No amount of philosophical argument purporting to show that the conception of survival is nonsensical could have the slightest weight against this first-hand empirical evidence. If *A* had been familiar with any such argument and still remembered it, he would simply conclude that there must have been something wrong with it—either some false premiss, or some logical fallacy. He might of course find that he had rather a different sort of body from the one he had before. But this would not worry him, provided he found that his new body fulfilled the same functions as his previous body had, that of being the centre of his perceptual world and of being responsive, more or less, to his will. Similarly the prediction 'I shall survive death' is conclusively verifiable by me if it be true. All I have to do is to wait until I am dead; and then, if the prediction be true, I shall be able to know that it is true.

But as philosophers have pointed out, the proposition 'I have survived death' is not capable of being conclusively falsified, if it be in fact true. The same applies to the prediction 'I shall survive death'. The reason for this curious asymmetry is fairly obvious. It might in fact be false that I shall survive. But if I do not, I shall not have any experience whatever after I am dead, and shall not then be able to have empirical evidence for or against anything; so I shall be in no position to learn by expreience that the proposition 'I shall survive death' has turned out to be false, because I shall no longer be an experient at all. And it is difficult to see how any other person could have conclusive empirical evidence of its falsity either. It comes to this, then: if all of us now living as physically embodied human beings are in fact going to survive death (as most Theists say we are) each of us will be able to see for himself that he has survived it, when the time comes. But if none of us do in fact survive, none of us will ever be able to see for himself that this Theistic assertion was false, though it might in fact *be* false all the same.

I have been speaking here of conclusive empirical verification and falsification. There might however be empirical *evidence*, evidence less than conclusive, either for or against the assertion that all human personalities continue to exist after death. There is in fact empirical evidence against it, the evidence provided by the biological sciences for the causal dependence of consciousness upon physiological processes. There is also some empirical evidence *for* survival, or at any rate for the proposition that some human personalities continue to exist for some time after their physical organisms are dead. The evidence comes from psychical research, the empirical investigation of 'paranormal' phenomena, and it cannot be ignored, however difficult some of it is to interpret.[1] Your lecturer's personal opinion is that this evidence is

[1] Cf. C.D. Broad: *Lectures on Psychical Research,* Chs. 10–15 and Epilogue.

strong enough to justify the following piece of advice: 'Do not be absolutely sure that you will *not* continue to exist, as a person, after the death of your physical organism; there is a chance that you may, and this chance (or risk if you prefer to regard it in that way)[1] is not so negligibly small that a prudent person can afford to ignore it altogether.'

But however strong the adverse evidence was, it would have no strength at all against personal experience of one's own survival. And however strong the favourable evidence was, it would still receive confirmation from personal experience of one's own survival: and if it could still receive confirmation, this would be enough to show that it could not have been maximally strong already.

So much for the Theist's assertions about human immortality. We can say this for him, at any rate: the assertion that human personality continues to exist at least for some time after death is one to which empirical evidence is relevant, and if it be true, each of us will be able to verify it conclusively so far as his own survival is concerned, though none of us will be able to falsify it conclusively if it be false. For our present purposes, it is unnecessary to discuss the Theist's assertions about the 'other world' (or worlds). It would not be very difficult to make some empirical sense of them, if human personalities do continue to exist and to have experiences after death. It would be sufficient if these experiences were interrelated in some systematic manner. It would not matter much if the 'other world', or worlds, had the purely phenomenalistic character which some philosophers have attributed to this one. Again, it might be that one or another of the Idealistic philosophies was true of the other world, though false of this one. Nor need we assume that the entities of which the other world is composed, whatever entities they might be, would obey laws at all like the laws of physics; and their spatial and temporal properties might well be different from those with which we are now familiar. Religious people themselves sometimes say that the other world is 'spiritual' rather than material; this seems to be a way of saying

[1] We describe it as 'a risk' if we regard the continuance of personal existence after death as an evil rather than a good. It seems likely that quite a large number of persons have a wish, conscious or unconscious, *not* to survive bodily death. Some of those who disbelieve in survival may be 'wishful thinkers', just as some who believe in it are.

that the causal laws which prevail there are quite different from those which prevail in the familiar physical world.[1]

It seems that the Theist has done fairly well in this part of his examination too. His assertions about human immortality are indeed disbelieved by many, and doubted by many more. Many find them too good to be true, and some too bad to be true. But at any rate we can make some sort of empirical sense of them, since personal immortality does entail personal survival, and the proposition that human personality continues to exist after death is one to which empirical evidence is relevant. In other words, it *is* believable or disbelievable, and does not just have to be dismissed as empty or meaningless.

TRANSCENDENT ASSERTIONS ABOUT GOD

But now at last he has to face the most difficult part of his ordeal. We must now question him about the most obviously transcendent of his transcendent assertions, the ones concerning God Himself. Perhaps it is necessary to insist again that a Theist does not merely recommend us to view the world 'as if' there were a God who created it and loves each of the persons whom He has created. This 'as-iffish' world outlook, which might be called a Para-Theistic one, has of course been recommended by Kant, for example. But it is not the outlook of a Theist. He asserts that God does actually exist, and even that he exists in a sense in which nothing else does. *Qui est*, 'He who is', is one of the descriptions which Theists have given of him. A Theist is quite unequivocally asserting a transcendent existential proposition, and the assertion of it is an essential part of the outlook which he recommends.

But how can any empirical evidence be relevant to such a proposition? And if it is not, how can we even understand the recommendation which is made to us, that we should try to 'see' or 'view' the world as the creation of such a Being? Surely we do not know what it is that we are recommended to do, since we cannot even conceive what it would be like for the Theist's existential assertion to be true?

[1] If anyone is interested in speculations on this subject, he may be referred to an article by the author on 'Survival and the Idea of "Another World"', in the *Proceedings of the Society for Psychical Research*, Vol. 50, 1953.

This difficulty has been stated in a very striking way by Professor A. G. N. Flew, He argues that no conceivable empirical fact, nor combination of empirical facts, could *falsify* the Theist's assertions about God and his relations to the world (including his relations to ourselves). It is interesting to notice that Theists themselves have sometimes come near to admitting this. *Deus noster est deus absconditus*, it has been said. 'Our God is a hidden god.' There is even a hymn in which we read these two very remarkable lines: 'He hides himself in wondrous wise, As if there were no God.' This strange and fascinating phrase *Deus absconditus* appears to imply that however much empirical evidence there is to suggest that he does not exist, he does exist all the same; in other words, it seems to be claimed that no amount of adverse empirical evidence could conceivably falsify the basic Theistic propositions —just the point which Flew himself has made. But if no empirical evidence could conceivably falsify these propositions, surely they are completely empty? If it makes no difference to anything whether God exists or not, if everything in the world might be just what it is whether he exists or not, then surely we are saying nothing when we assert that he does exist? And with regard to the empirical facts which touch us most closely, the facts of human life, what meaning can there be in asserting that there is a God who created the world and loves every single one of us, if no amount of human misery, however great, would have the least tendency to falsify these assertions? It seems to make no diference at all whether they are false or true; and when someone asserts them, it seems that he has told us absolutely nothing.

The same criticism may be put in another way. The trouble with the Theist, it might be said, is that he has an answer to everything. Whatever difficulty you raise, he can always explain it away. These sufferings and disasters are chastisements for our sins, or trials of our faith; they are part of the educational process which is designed to fit us to be citizens of the Kingdom of Heaven hereafter. Again, if someone does not receive what he earnestly prayed for, it was for his good that he should not receive it. He may think that his prayer was not answered; but his failure to receive what he asked for is itself the answer. At the worst, the Theist can always say 'Of course, God's purposes are inscrutable'. Up to a point, it is obviously an advantage to have an answer to objections. But one can have too much of a good thing. If you have an answer to every conceivable objection, if you can still maintain your thesis no matter what the facts may be, then surely there are only two possibilities open: either you were not asserting anything at all, or else you were asserting an analytical proposition such as '$2 + 3 = 5$' or 'from if *p*, then *q*, it follows that if not *q*, then not *p*'. (These proposition *are* true whatever the facts may be). But an existential proposition cannot be analytic. Surely we must conclude, then, that when you say 'There is a God' you are not asserting anything at all?

It would follow from this criticism that even the modest-seeming 'Para-theistic' recommendation to view the world *as if* it were the creation of a benevolent Supreme Being is equally empty, because the if-clause would itself be empty. For (it would be said) if the world were *not* the creation of a benevolent Supreme Being, everything would be as it is now; and everything would be as it is now, if the world *were* the creation of a benevolent Supreme Being. When a hypothesis is completely empty (as it is alleged this one is) a person is not making *any* recommendation to us when he says 'I invite you to view the world as if this hypothesis were true'. There is nothing which he recommends us to do.

THEISM REDUCIBLE TO RECOMMENDATIONS ABOUT CONDUCT?

We may of course suspect that this criticism proves too much. If it were correct, all adherents of Theistic religion (and of a good many other religions too) must have been in a state of mental confusion which is almost incredible. Yet it is not easy to think of any answer which would satisfy our empirically-minded examiners.

But first, before we consider whether any answer is possible, let us consider what the effect of this kind of criticism would be. Its effect would be to reduce Theism to a set of recommendations about conduct. As we have seen, the Theist does make such recommendations, and they are certainly not devoid of content.[1] 'Love your neighbour as yourself' is very far from being an empty recommendation. If we take it as a moral

[1] Pp. 458–9, above

imperative, it is obvious that we can too easily disobey it. (The possibility of disobeying is here the analogue of the possibility of falsification.) 'Love your neighbour as yourself' is not at all like the command of the schoolmaster who said 'Stand up, or else do not stand up; I *will* be obeyed!' Nor does it at all resemble the equally vacuous command 'Do as you please'.

As we have seen, 'Love your neighbour as yourself' can also be taken as a prudential maxim. We are then being advised to live in this 'agapistic' manner, on the ground that no other way of life is in the long run satisfactory to a human being. Interpreted in this way, what we are being told is again very far from being empty, since we can only too easily fail to act in the way advised. Moreover, as we have seen, there can be empirical evidence for or against the assertion that no other kind of life is in the long run satisfying. So this assertion is by no means empty either. It is not a metaphysical assertion, but a psychological one. Moreover, such evidence as we have seems to support it quite strongly, though not conclusively. At any rate, it seems to be true that no person can in the long run be happy unless he loves at least some other persons in the unconditional manner recommended.[1]

These recommendations about conduct are certainly an essential part of the Theistic outlook. Indeed, all the higher religions, whether Theistic or not, do make recommendations about conduct. The recommendations are not quite the same in all the different religious outlooks (a Buddhist, for example, recommends compassion, whereas a Theist recommends unconditional love). But there is a very considerable resemblance between them. And if we are to judge them by their fruits, it would appear that all the higher religions, and most of the varieties (orthodox or heterodox) which we find within each of them, are capable of producing very admirable types of human character, if their respective recommendations about conduct are followed.

Nevertheless, there is no higher religion, with the possible

[1] It may be objected that we cannot be *recommended* to love anyone (still less to love anyone in the unconditional manner which Theists have in mind) on the ground that it is not in our power to put ourselves into an emotional attitude by a mere act of will. Nevertheless, it is in our power to cultivate an emotional attitude, or to make efforts to acquire it by degrees. If we cannot be commanded to love our neighbours, we can at any rate be commanded to cultivate a loving attitude towards them.

exception of Confucianism, which is wholly reducible to a sort of recommendations about conduct. All the others make metaphysical assertions as well; and to say they make them 'as well' is to say too little, since the recommendations about conduct are intimately related to the metaphysical assertions. The Theist's recommendations that we should love our neighbours is not independent of his metaphysical assertion that there is a God who created all of us and loves each of us; and the Buddhist's recommendation of compassion is not independent of his metaphysical assertion that all beings who have desires are bound to suffer, and will continue to suffer in a series of incarnations which cannot end unless or until desires are wholly extinguished.

PROFESSOR J. H. HICK ON THEOLOGY AND VERIFICATION

Let us now consider whether a Theist can make any reply to the objection that his metaphysical assertions are empty, on the ground that no conceivable empirical evidence could falsify them. In an article on 'Theology and Verification'[1] Professor J. H. Hick has argued that though the Theistic assertions concerning God are neither verifiable nor falsifiable by anything which might happen in this world, they are capable of being verified or falsified by happenings in the next; consequently, they *are* after all either true or false, though in this present life we cannot find out which they are. If after death we found ourselves living in a community having the characteristics which God's Kingdom is described as having, we should have empirical evidence of God's existence and of his love towards us. The evidence would be stronger still, if we then had experiences describable as 'having personal relations with' such a Being. We must notice, however, that this empirical evidence would only be available to a limited class of persons, namely those traditionally described as 'the Blessed in Heaven'. What would our position be if we were less fortunate, or less deserving, and found ourselves after death in a community very unlike God's Kingdom, and more like what is traditionally described as 'the Kingdom of Darkness'? Might we then be tempted to change out previous opinion that the Theistic assertions about

[1] *Theology To-day*, Vol. XVII, No. 1, April 1960.

God were completely devoid of content, and to say instead that they were false?

If we were consistent, we should have to resist this temptation. Did we not maintain in our earthly lives that no conceivable state of affairs, however dreary or unpleasant, could have any tendency to falsify the Theist's assertions about God? In short, we should not become Atheists as a result of our after-death experiences—or at least we should not be logically entitled to, if we were consistent. We should be obliged to remain Agnostics as we were before; not Agnostics of the old-fashioned sort, who admit that the Theist's statements about God are either true or false, and then claim that we have no means of deciding between these two alternatives, but Agnostics of the Post-Positivist sort, who hold that the Theist's statements are empty, because not even in principle falsifiable. There would be nothing in our after-death experiences, however dismal or unpleasant or terrifying, to compel us to change our views: we had provided for the situation beforehand by saying that no conceivable experiences could falsify these statements or count as evidence against them. *A fortiori* there would be nothing to compel us to change our views, if we found ourselves after death in a world containing roughly the same mixture of goods and evils as there is in our present life on earth.

There is only one point on which we should have to change our opinion in the situation supposed. We should have to admit that we *had* survived death, distressing as this admission might be. But though most Theists do assert that we survive death, and indeed that we are immortal, and though it might even be that the existence of a loving God *entails* the survival of the human personalities he has created (as some Theists have maintained) the converse entailment certainly does not hold. *If* it be a fact that human personality survives death, that fact would be compatible with all the metaphysical world-outlooks except epiphenomenalist materialism; and so far as I can see, if it were true that all persons, once they have come into existence, continue to exist for ever, this too would be compatible with all the metaphysical world-outlooks, with the same exception.

It seems that, on Hick's view, statements about God would resemble statements about survival in being verifiable but not falsifiable. It is true that there would still be an important difference between the two. The statement that I shall survive death will be conclusively verified by me if I do find myself surviving, and the statement that I shall not survive cannot be conclusively falsified by myself or by anyone else, though it might in fact *be* false. But on Hick's view, statements about God could not, I think, be *conclusively* verified by anyone, or at any rate by any human person, though if he were one of 'the blessed in Heaven', he could obtain evidence strongly supporting them. On the other hand, no one in the less favoured parts of the next world could conceivably have any evidence against these statements about God. He could only have evidence of the same general sort as we have now; and as we have seen, this evidence can always be explained away.[1] If the existence of evils in this present world is not to be allowed to count as evidence against Theism, neither is the existence of evils in some other world, even though greater in degree. It seems, then, that if Professor Hick is right there could be strong though not conclusive empirical evidence for the existence of God, as also for his goodness, in the life after death, but neither then nor now could there be conclusive evidence against it.

But if this is a correct interpretation of Hick's argument, he is making an important assumption which needs to be explicitly stated. For brevity, let us use the traditional word 'Heaven' for the after-death state in which a person can have experiences which will provide him with empirical evidence for the existence of God. (We need not think of Heaven as a place, but rather as a state of consciousness in which experiences of certain sorts occur.) On the traditional view, which Hick, I think, accepts, no one can be in Heaven at all unless he has acquired a suitable sort of character. The latent assumption which needs to be made explicit is this: that a person's character, the conative and emotional dispositions he has acquired, affects his *cognitive* powers and enables him to be aware of facts he could not otherwise be aware of. On the view under discussion, they are empirical facts (though other-wordly ones) since they provide him with empirical evidence for an existential proposition. To put it in another way, the assumption is that a person who has acquired certain conative and emotional dispositions is able to have experiences disclosing facts to him which others are not able to discern. On the traditional view, these

[1] See pp. 465–7 above.

conative and emotional dispositions are in part moral ones. Moral goodness, and a pretty high degree of moral goodness, is supposed to be a necessary condition for the discernment of the facts in question. Whether it is supposed to be a sufficient one, is a question which we shall consider presently; but at any rate it is supposed to be a *conditio sine qua non.*

The assumption which has just been stated is a very disturbing one. The consequence of it is that there are facts about the world (and very important facts too) which are not accessible to all normal observers. You do not have to be a conscientious promise-keeper in order to observe that Saturn has rings; you have only to look through a telescope. You do not have to be kind to children in order to discover what happened in the reign of King Richard I; you have only to read the documents. But it would seem that you *do* have to be as charitable as the Good Samaritan was, in order to discern the facts which are empirical evidence for the existence of God; though even then, if Hick is right, you will not be able to discern them till after you are dead.

Disturbing though it is, this assumption, or something like it, might nevertheless be true. Or, to put it the other way round, the postulate of unrestricted public verifiability might be false. It might be that in some spheres (though not in the sphere of ordinary sense-perception) the cognitive powers which a person has do depend in some way on the kind of person that he is. But is this a paradox? On the contrary, it is almost a platitude in one important sphere at least, the relation of a person with other persons.

If we are ourselves very selfish or unkind, there will be facts about the conduct and the emotional attitudes of other persons which we shall not be able to notice. Or if we do notice them at a purely behaviouristic level (observable bodily movements and utterances, observable emotional symptoms such as weeping or smiling) are we not extremely likely to misinterpret them? We do not conceive it possible that when a person helped someone else who was in trouble, he did it out of plain straightforward compassion, or just because he is kind and charitable and wishes for his neighbour's good. Human beings, we say to ourselves, just are not like that. He must have done it because he wanted gratitude or admiration, or because he thought that the man he helped would be a useful ally later, or just because he was brought up to behave like that, and has never grown up sufficiently to ask himself what point there could possibly be in such behaviour. And so we move in the world of personal relations like blind men, unable to grasp what is going on around us. Here our moral defects do restrict our cognitive powers. Indeed, they might do so in our historical studies too, you do not need kindness to learn what happened in the reign of King Richard I. But you may need some in order to understand it. You may also need to have some idea of what it feels like to be devotedly loyal to someone who is set in authority over you.

If we consider other sorts of emotional dispositions, not moral ones but somewhat allied to them, we might find that they played some part even in the natural sciences, and especially in the work of men of scientific genius. Were not some of these men moved by sheer admiration for the cosmic spectacle, and even by a kind of disinterested love for it? Without this emotional attitude, would they have made the discoveries which they did make?[1]

It now appears that when a Theist (or indeed an advocate of some other religious world outlook) recommends us to cultivate certain moral virtues, he does so for three reasons and not only for the two we have mentioned already—because he approves of these virtues for their own sake, and because he thinks we cannot in the long run be happy unless we acquire them. The third reason is that unless we acquire certain moral virtues, especially charity, he thinks we shall not be capable of having certain sorts of *cognitive* experiences—experiences which we must have if we are to test for ourselves the adequacy of the world-outlook he is recommending, or even if we are to understand clearly what that world-outlook is. 'He that doeth the Will shall know of the doctrine'—if we take this to mean that one does not know of the doctrine unless one does the will.

DEVOTIONAL PRACTICES AND LATENT SPIRITUAL CAPACITIES

But though the acquisition of certain moral virtues is held to be a necessary condition for having these experiences, which will

[1] This attitude is excellently expressed by the scientific poet Lucretius, and is perhaps also the one which Spinoza described as *amor intellectualis Dei*. (Spinoza's God was *Deus sive natura*.)

provide evidence for the existence of God, it is not usually thought to be a sufficient one. In all the religious outlooks certain other practices are recommended which have no direct connection with the acquisition of moral virtues. We may call then 'devotional practices' (prayer is the most obvious example), and they may be either public and outward, or private and inward. It seems to be thought that the private and inward ones are those which matter most, and that if they are lacking the public and outward ones will have but little efficacy. The practices recommended vary greatly from one religion to another, and even within the same religion between one sect or denomination and another. The practice of them is what makes the difference between merely accepting a religious creed and being a religious person. The habitual practice of them is what 'piety' consists in.

What is the point of these practices, and why are they recommended, in one form or another, by exponents of all the religious world-outlooks? And why is special importance attached to the private and inward ones? The assumption underlying these recommendations seems to be an assumption about human capacities. It is similar to the assumption mentioned already, in connection with recommendations about moral conduct, that what a person is capable of being aware of depends in some degree upon the kind of person he is. The assumption is that every human being has certain capacities—let us call them spiritual capacities for lack of a better name—which remain latent and unactualized in most of us, unless and until steps are taken to develop them. On this view, most of us nowadays are in a state of spiritual immaturity, however adult we may be in other respects. In spite of our scientific and technological achievements (or partly because of them?) it might be that the majority of civilized Western men in these days are *more* immature spiritually than their predecessors in the Middle Ages. They have the spiritual capacities which every human being has, but have taken little trouble to develop them.

What we call 'a spiritual person' (a repulsive phrase, but it is hard to find another) is not, of course, just a person who knows things which others do not. Nevertheless, according to the assumption we are discussing, he *is* a person who has experiences which unspiritual persons do not have; and though these experiences are not purely and simply cognitive, it is held that they provide him with evidence for certain important propositions, evidence which unspiritual persons are not able to obtain. On the Theistic view, it is evidence concerning the existence and attributes of God, and especially for the proposition that God loves us. Furthermore, it would be claimed that a spiritual person's experiences provide him with a better understanding of the Theistic world-outlook itself: he understands, better than the rest of us, what is *meant* by saying that there is a God who created the universe, and that he loves each one of us, including those of us who deny that he exists, or think it nonsensical to say He does.

One result of this (it would be said) is that a spiritual person feels himself to be 'more at home' in the universe than unspiritual persons do. He has a certain serenity and inward peace which others cannot help envying and even admiring. They cannot see that he is in the least entitled to have it, in a world so full of troubles as this world is. Yet it seems a little unplausible to suppose that this serene attitude is just the product of a state of mental confusion. Indeed, the existence of such persons is in practice the most persuasive argument in favour of a religious world-outlook, and probably always has been. When we meet such a person, we can hardly help wishing that we ourselves could be like him, and we cannot help wondering whether there may not be something to be said for the world-outlook which he accepts, however strange or even absurd that outlook may seem to us to be. The inward peace mentioned just now is not exactly a moral characteristic. But no one has it unless he has a considerable degree of moral virtue too, and somehow or other the moral virtues themselves assume a different quality in a person of this kind. We not only approve of them, as we approve of them in anyone else, but also feel attracted by them. Hume distinguishes somewhere between the 'awful' and the 'amiable' virtues. A person of the kind we are describing may possess both. He may, for example, be capable of heroic self-sacrifice. But somehow, in him, the awful virtues are amiable too. Theistic moralists would say that this is because he has charity or love of his neighbours for their own sake, that all the other virtues he may display are consequences of this, and that charity cannot but be amiable in all its manifestations.

TWO KINDS OF 'LATENCY'

It has been suggested already that the religious or devotional practices recommended by the Theist are intended to develop the latent spiritual capacities which he assumes to be present in all of us. There are, however, two different ways of conceiving of this 'latency'. On one view, these capacities are latent in the sense that they are unactualized, as a child of two years old might have a latent capacity for Higher Mathematics. But a rather different view has been suggested by Professor John Baillie, in which 'latent' would be equivalent to 'subconscious'.[1] If I interpret him correctly, he holds that every normal human being has an actual (not merely potential) awareness of God, but that in very many of us this awareness exists only 'at the bottom of our hearts' and not 'at the top of our minds'; indeed, 'at the top of our minds' we may doubt or even deny what we are aware of all the time at the bottom of our hearts. It seems possible that in some human beings this awareness of God would be unconscious rather than just subconscious. It might be 'repressed'—to use the terminology of the Depth-psychologists—so that it is inaccessible to the person's consciousness, unless and until steps are taken to remove the repressing forces.

On this view, the purpose of the devotional practices would be to raise our awareness of God into clear consciousness, to bring it out from the bottom of our hearts into the top of our minds: or perhaps, rather, to remove the inhibitions or barriers or blockages which have hitherto kept it out of consciousness. (According to Christian teachings, there is such a blockage in all of us; it is called 'Original Sin'.)

It might be suggested that there are also subconscious, or unconscious, *emotional* relations with God. If there is an awareness of God, at any rate 'at the bottom of our hearts', there might also be at the bottom of our hearts a need or wish to love Him. Such a need or wish, however little we are aware of it, however firmly we reject it when by any chance we are half-conscious of it, might conceivably be present all the time in every normal human

[1] *Our Knowledge of God*, Ch 2 (Oxford University Press, 4th impression, 1946).

being. It might indeed be claimed by religious people that no one can be wholly happy, unless this need or wish is satisfied in some degree.[1]

Whichever way we put it, whether we speak of unactualized capacities or of subconsciously-actual mental states, we are claiming that this 'something in us' which makes us spiritual beings has to be conceived as both cognitive and emotional at the same time. Or is it perhaps so close, as it were, to the centre of our personalities that it belongs to a level at which the distinction between cognition and emotion, awareness and love, no longer applies?

The two views I have been stating about the spiritual nature of human beings—the one which speaks in terms of unactualized capacities, and the other in terms of actual but subconscious (or unconscious) psychological states—are not, after all, so different as they look. On either view, a conscious awareness of God and a conscious love of him are actually present only in a minority of human beings. Yet on either view the potentiality for such conscious awareness and love is something which all of us possess, and the aim of the devotional practices is to actualize this potentiality. To put it in another way, the aim of them is so to change a person's inner life that he becomes consciously aware of God, consciously accepts God's love for him, and consciously loves God in return.

According to Theistic religion, the capacity for such a conscious relationship with God is the special prerogative of *persons*. For love of this conscious kind cannot be compelled. It has to be given freely. If we are 'of more value than many sparrows', the reason is, perhaps, that we are capable of loving God as conscious, responsible and autonomous beings. It is in our power to refuse to love Him, even though we have a subconscious need or wish to love Him: and even though we become conscious of this need or wish, we can still refuse to satisfy it. The choice is ours.

MEDITATION

If these are the reasons a Theist might give for recommending the use of devotional practices, we have now to ask what kind of

[1] Cf. St Augustine *Cor nostrum inquietum est donec requiescat in Te.*

practices they are, and what state of mind we are supposed to be in when we practice them. One of the most important of them in the practice of meditating or ruminating on certain narratives which we have heard or read, or which have been conveyed to us in other ways, for example by means of pictures or statuary. In Christian Theism they are chiefly narratives in the Gospels, both those which are presented as records of historical fact, and those presented as parables. Or they may be narratives from the lives of saintly persons, or more or less imaginative representations of God's ways of dealing with men, such as we find in the Psalms and the Old Testament prophets. The important point is not that we should believe these narratives, or how firmly we believe them if we do. What is recommended is that we should think of them, assiduously and attentively, 'think over' them and ruminate upon them. It is the *entertaining* of these propositions, repeatedly and attentively, which matters at this stage, not the assent to them. If we are able to 'cash' them with mental imagery, so much the better. Here again Newman's distinction between notional and real assent is relevant. The distinction applies to entertaining too, as indeed he himself insists. (His term for entertaining is 'the apprehension of propositions'.) The propositions, or, rather, sets of propositions, which we are asked to entertain must be entertained in a 'real' and not a merely 'notional' manner. We have to try to 'realize' or 'bring home to ourselves' what it would be like if these propositions were true, or if these paintings or statues represented an actual state of affairs.

We may also believe these propositions, or some of them, but the important thing is that we should be *interested* in them, interested enough to try to 'realize fully' what their content is and to let our thoughts dwell on them. If we believe them without being interested in them, and without any tendency at all to ruminate over them or meditate upon them, we cannot expect that this will have much effect in developing our spiritual capacities. What we think about, privately and inwardly, and think about often, is much more important from this point of view than what we believe, and much more likely to alter our personalities. Belief can come later. This is one reason why the fashionable phrase 'total commitment' is so misleading. It suggests that everyone must start his spiritual life by being totally convinced of something, presumably without much evidence (if any) and without any clear conception of what it is that he is convinced of. A man might believe every clause of the Athanasian Creed with total and unshakable conviction without being a spiritual person at all.

PROFESSOR R. B. BRAITHWAITE ON 'STORIES'

What has just been said may remind you of the important function assigned to 'stories' in Professor R. B. Braithwaite's Eddington Lecture *An Empiricist's View of the Nature of Religious Belief*.[1] He too insists that the stories need not be believed, though of course they may be, and that what matters is that we should meditate upon them, no matter whether we believe them or not. But his conception of what these stories, or rather our meditations upon them, are to do for us is different from the one most Theists would accept. He thinks that their function is just to make us capable of following an 'agapistic' way of life. Most Theists would no doubt agree that this is part of their function. But Braithwaite does not seem to take into account the effect which such meditations might have in developing a person's latent spiritual capacities; or rather, he makes no distinction between spiritual capacities and moral ones. He does not consider the possibility that there might be latent capacities in all of us, which, when developed, might enable us to obtain *evidence* relevant to the truth or falsity of the basic Theist assertions concerning the existence of God and God's relations to ourselves. The Theistic world-outlook, as he conceives it, is a wholly immanent world-outlook, just a way of 'seeing' the facts of human life. According to his interpretation, we are to 'see' them as opportunities of serving our neighbours and of cultivating a loving attitude towards them; and the basic Theistic assertions concerning God are themselves 'stories', which if duly meditated upon will enable us to 'see' the facts of human life in this agapistic way, and to act and feel accordingly. On his view, it does not matter whether these stories are true or false, any more than it matters whether the events described in the parable of the Good Samaritan did actually happen. He does not discuss the Theistic

[1] Cambridge University Press.

assertions about human immortality, but presumably he would take the same view about these.

But surely no Theist would admit that his assertions about the being and attributes of God, are mere 'stories' in this sense; and certainly he would not admit it about the two assertions on which he lays most emphasis, namely, the assertion that there is a God who created the world, and the assertion that He loves every single one of the persons He has created. A Theist would say that it matters very much whether these assertions are true or false, indeed that nothing matters more; and he claims that they are in fact true.

His reply to the objection that there can be no evidence for them, since no possible conjunction of empirical facts could falsify them, is this: he claims that it *is* possible to obtain evidence for them, and that it is empirical evidence (though not of course perceptual evidence), because it comes from certain experiences. He says that there are experiences of 'drawing near to God', of entering into an 'I-thou' relation with Him and even (as Newman puts it) of 'holding converse with Him'.[1] But the Theist also says that this evidence is not accessible to every normal human being, as the evidence for the existence of Saturn's rings is. It is accessible only to those human beings whose spiritual capacities have been in some degree developed; and although he thinks that every human being does possess these capacities, he also thinks that in many they remain latent and unexercised. 'Seek and ye shall find' is the traditional way of putting this.

It seems to me that Theists are here making an empirical claim which can be empirically tested. It is something like the claim made by a man who recommends a system of physical excercises to us, or a system of memory training. The test is: try it, and see for yourself what effects it has. Perhaps you may have to try it for a long time, and a good deal of effort may be needed; the same might be true of a system of physical exercises, which is recommended to us on the ground that it will improve our health or strengthen our muscles. But the question is quite straightforwardly this: Does it work? And that question is an empirical one. According to some Christian thinkers, Professor Hick, for example, we shall have to wait till after we are dead to get the complete answer to the question 'Does it work'? Even so, we might perhaps have some experi-

[1] *Grammar of Assent* (Longmans, 1947), p. 89.

ences even in this life which would encourage us to think that it does.

It might be, of course, that one sort of religious or devotional practice suits one person and a rather different sort suits another person. That might be one reason why there are different religions in the world; and even within Theistic religion, many different sorts of religious or devotional practices are recommended (for example, those recommended by Mohammedan Sufis differ from those recommended by Christians, and even within the Christian variety of Theism those recommended by Catholics differ considerably from those recommended by Presbyterians). Which sort of religious or devotional practices suits a particular person best might depend to a considerable extent on his personal idiosyncracies, or—to look at it in another way—on the particular sort of 'hindrances' or repressions or fixations which keep *his* spiritual faculties in a state of latency and prevent them from being exercised. As has been suggested already, we can quite well conceive of religious or devotional practices as methods designed to remove or weaken inhibiting factors, which might very well vary somewhat from one person to another.[1] But the claim is that every person does have spiritual capacities; that every person has the power to arouse them from their state of latency, or free them from the inhibitions which prevent them from being exercised, by using religious or devotional practices of one sort or another; and that when these faculties are exercised, we can have experiences which will provide us with evidence for the basic Theistic assertions concerning God and His relations to ourselves.

SEEKING AND BELIEVING

If someone decides to set about testing this empirically testable claim, he does not have to believe any theological propositions at all in the initial stage of his investigation; still less does he have to believe them with complete and unshakable conviction, for which he has at that stage no evidence. All he has to believe is, first, that the use of certain religious or devotional practices is in fact recommended by certain persons, and secondly, that those who recom-

[1] p. 476, above.

mend the use of these practices do themselves claim that they are effective methods of developing the latent spiritual capacities of human beings. These two propositions are not very difficult to believe.

Nor does he have to begin by trusting everyone or anything; certainly not by trusting God Himself, since at the beginning he is quite uncertain whether there is any such Being, or even perhaps whether it makes sense to say there is. He may of course trust the persons who recommend these methods to him, in the sense that he trusts them to be speaking sincerely, and is sure that they do genuinely believe in the methods they recommend. All the same, it is not at all necessary that he should begin by trusting the methods themselves. It is true that no one would think it worth while to try them out, if he was quite certain beforehand that they could not possibly work. But he does not have to be certain beforehand that they will. He only has to think that they are worth trying. It seems to be supposed by some that we cannot act resolutely unless we are absolutely convinced beforehand that we are going to succeed. But if any supposition is obviously false, surely this one is. And it is just as false when the actions in question are inward and private ones (directing our thoughts in a certain manner attentively and repeatedly) as it is when they are outward and public ones.

THE THEISTIC HYPOTHESIS

But though we do not have to begin by believing any Theological propositions at all, we do have to attend to and consider what may be called the basic propositions of Theistic religion: that there is a God who created the world, and that he loves each one of us. The second proposition is, of course, a very astonishing one indeed, and it would be asking too much of any reasonable man to demand that he should accept it without enquiry, and an insult to his intelligence to demand that he should begin by believing it with total and unshakable conviction. Still, it is required of us that we should consider both these Theistic propositions seriously, the second as well as the first, though it is not required that we should begin by believing either of them. We have to 'take them seriously', in the sense of being interested in them, interested enough to expend a certain amount of time and energy in trying out the procedures recommended to us. In short, we do have to begin by paying serious attention to what is called the Theistic hypothesis, though we do not have to begin by accepting it. The Theistic hypothesis, however, is a more complicated one than it used to be. We can no longer formulate it as the hypothesis that the basic propositions of Theistic religion are true, since some philosophers have doubted whether they are genuine propositions at all, that is, whether the sentences purporting to express them have any meaning; and if they have none, they are not even false. The Theistic hypothesis must therefore be reformulated in a two-stage manner. It is the hypothesis that the sentences 'There is a God who created the world' and 'He loves each one of the persons whom he has created' do express genuine propositions, i.e. that each of them is *either* true *or* false; and the further hypothesis that both these propositions are true.

There is another reason why we have to be interested in this two-stage hypothesis and pay serious attention to it. The two basic propositions of Theism play an essential part in the procedures whose efficacy we are trying to test, as indeed is implied by describing these procedures as religious or devotional practices. One of these practices is prayer. We obviously have to entertain the proposition that there is a God, and also the proposition that He is benevolently disposed towards us, in order to pray in the way Theists recommend, and moreover we have to take both these propositions seriously.

Perhaps it will be objected that we have to do more; that after all we have to *believe* them, and cannot possibly pray unless we do. Might it not be an empirical fact, however unfortunate and regrettable, that we have to begin by believing the basic Theistic propositions without any evidence, if we are to obtain any evidence for those propositions later? Some theologians seem to think that this is indeed an empirical fact, and not even a regrettable one. That is the source of what may be called the 'taking the plunge' conception of religion; and it seems to be thought that it is in our power to take this plunge just by an act of will. But if we do consider a proposition carefully (as these religious teachers admit we must) is it even possible to believe that proposition without having any evidence for it at all? Of course, if we do not consider a proposition *p* carefully, and do not even ask ourselves whether there is evidence for it or not, we may get into the state which Cook Wilson calls 'being under an impression that *p*'.[1] But this unreasonable or non-reasonable state of mind is just the one which could *not* be induced by an act of will. It comes about through not willing, though failing to exercise what we called the freedom of assent,[2] which is also a freedom to suspend judgement.

What one *can* do, by conscious and wide-awake act of free choice, is to take a proposition as a hypothesis. This is the state of mind sometimes called 'supposing'. We do, I think, have to take it as a hypothesis that there is a God, and that he is benevolently disposed towards us, if we are to pray in the way a Theist recommends. But taking a proposition or a set of propositions as a hypothesis is not believing, and still less is it believing with total and unshakable conviction.

THE AGNOSTIC'S PRAYER

We have all heard of the Agnostic's prayer 'O God, if there be a God, save my soul, if I have a soul', and much derision has no doubt been poured on it. But it is a perfectly sensible prayer for an Agnostic to offer, and unless he begins by praying in some such way, one cannot see how he is ever to begin praying at all, nor how he is ever to be converted from Agnosticism to Theism. One must start somewhere, and how else is an intellectually-honest man to start? He need not insert his if-clause into the prayer itself (nor *mutatis mutandis* into the praises or expressions of thankfulness which are also recommended religious practices). But before he starts to offer his prayer he does have to do some supposing. He says to himself 'Let me suppose for the moment that there is a God and that he is benevolently disposed towards me', and later he will find that he is able to get himself into this 'supposing' frame of mind whenever he wishes, without needing to formulate it in words. After all, he is making what might be called a devotional experiment, and how else is he to do it?

It is something like what an actor does when he throws himself

[1] See Series I, Lecture 9, pp. 208–16.
[2] See Series I, Lecture 10.

into his part. For the time being, he tries to behave and speak, and feel too, as if he were the Prince of Denmark. But he does not have to believe that he *is* the Prince of Denmark, still less to be unshake ably convinced that he is. Similarly, our agnostic has to try to 'take the role' of a pious person addressing his Heavenly Father, though he does it privately, in his own heart, and not on the public stage as the actor does. It could be called an imaginative exercise, an attempt to 'put himself in the shoes of' a type of person whose habitual thoughts and feelings are very different from his own. What he has been told is that if he goes on doing this for a long time, he will himself become a different kind of person, and will begin to have experiences of a sort which he has never had before. This is the empirical proposition which he is trying to test.

It must, of course, be admitted that there is something belief-*like* in the attitude which he takes. As we have seen already,[1] there can be attitudes which resemble belief in some respects but differ from it in others. The attitude of the person we are discussing does resemble that of religious believers in several ways. He takes certain propositions about God seriously, as they also do, though he only takes them seriously as hypotheses. Because he takes them so, he acts 'in the light of' these propositions, as religious believers also do. The actions in question, both in him and in religious believers, are primarily inward and private ones. His private thoughts are directed to the same topics as theirs are, and the words which he inwardly utters (e.g. the words of the Lord's Prayer) are often the same as those which they inwardly utter. The production of mental imagery is another important sort of inward activity; and like the production of inward words, it is to some degree under our voluntary control, though to a lesser degree. Here again, what goes on in his mind may resemble what goes on in the minds of religious believers. He may image or picture to himself some event described in the Gospels, the adoration of the Magi, for example, and they may do the same. He may try to imagine what it would have felt like to be an actual witness of this event, and so may they. But though these episodes in his inner life may quite closely resemble episodes in theirs, they come about in a different way. He is taking a hypothesis seriously as a subject for investigation, and is making experiments (psychological experi-

[1] Series II, Lecture 4, on Half-Belief.

ments on himself) in the hope that he may eventually obtain evidence relevant to the truth or falsity of that hypothesis. But this is not what they are doing. What he takes as a hypothesis, they believe; and some of them believe it with full conviction. His attitude, though belief-like, is not believing. We might call it assiduous supposing.

SEEKING AND BELIEVING 'IN'

So far we have been asking how far his attitude resembles believing *that*. Does it also resemble believing *in*? We have seen earlier[1] that belief-in may be directed to many different sorts of objects. One may for example believe in a method or a procedure (e.g. in taking a cold bath every morning, or in classical education). The man we are considering is *using* a method or procedure. He uses it very much as a man would who believed in it. Nevertheless he does not at present believe in it, nor of course does he disbelieve in it either. He is taking it seriously and trying it out, in order to see whether it works. What he does believe in is the empirical principle 'Try it and see for yourself'.

But when we are discussing the philosophy of religion, the sort of belief-in which most concerns us is belief in God. In a religious person's belief in God, the most obvious feature is our attitude of trusting. But how can one trust someone unless one believes (or knows) that there *is* such a person and that he has certain characteristics, benevolence for example, or veracity? Our agnostic does not believe that there is a God, or that He is benevolently disposed to human beings, though he does not disbelieve these propositions either. He is just interested in them and takes them seriously as a hypothesis worthy of investigation. So when he tries out the religious or devotional practices which are recommended to him, he is not in a position to trust God, as religious people themselves do when they carry out these practices. What he *can* do is to try to imagine what it would be like to trust Him. Difficult though this may sound, it is not impossible that he should succeed. Let us again consider the actor who is playing the part of Hamlet. For the time being he tries, as we say, to 'identify himself' with Hamlet. In so

[1] Series II, Lecture 9, above, pp. 429–30.

doing, he has to try to imagine what it would feel like to trust his faithful friend Horatio. He need not believe that Horatio exists or ever did exist. The emotional pro-attitude which is an essential part of belief *in* a person does presuppose the belief (or knowledge) that the person exists and has certain characteristics, trustworthiness for example. Yet an attitude somewhat like it may be imaginatively assumed, if one takes it as a hypothesis that such a person exists and has these characteristics. Supposing that *p*, without believing it, may have some of the consequences which believing *p* would have.

It may be that religious thinkers of the 'Taking the plunge' persuasion have been misled by the belief-like features which we do find in the attitude of the empirically-minded enquirer we are discussing, and have concluded that because it is belief-like in certain ways it must actually be an attitude of belief, and even that it must be an attitude of complete conviction. But if our long and devious investigation of the epistemology of belief has shown anything, surely it has shown that belief is a complex attitude which manifests itself in many different ways. This is one of the lessons which the dispositional analysis of belief has to teach us. As has been remarked already, we should expect that there would be cases where some of these manifestations are present and others lacking, belief-like attitudes which are not quite attitudes of believing.

CONCLUSION

In this final lecture I have been trying to sketch an 'Empiricist view of religion' which differs considerably from Professor Braithwaite's, one which does not part company so decisively with traditional conceptions of Theism. I have suggested that the Theistic world-outlook lays itself open at one crucial point to an empirical test. This is because an assertion about human nature is an essential part of it. The assertion is that every human being has spiritual capacities, latent in most persons and partially developed in some; and moreover that when and if these capacities are developed, or freed from the inhibitions which keep them in a latent state, experiences will be forthcoming which will support the basic Theistic propositions themselves, the propositions concerning the being and attributes of God and God's relations to us upon which the Theistic way of 'viewing the world' depends. This assertion about human nature and its latent spiritual capacities can be empirically tested. Moreover, Theists themselves recommend a procedure for testing it. The procedure is difficult to carry out; but though difficult, it is not in principle impracticable. It is open to anyone to try it and see for himself whether it does produce the effects it is alleged to produce. 'Try it and see for yourself' is one way of formulating the empiricist principle.

INDEX